In *ort*

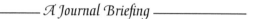

A Journal Briefing

Whitewater
Volume IV

Including Monica, China, the Starr Report

From the Editorial Pages of
The Wall Street Journal.

Edited by Robert L. Bartley
with Micah Morrison & Melanie Kirkpatrick
and the Editorial Page staff

DOWJONES

The Wall Street Journal.
Dow Jones & Company, Inc.
200 Liberty Street
New York, N.Y. 10281

Introduction

On September 9, 1998, Independent Counsel Kenneth Starr delivered a report to Congress containing, in the words of his mandate, "substantial and credible information" that "may constitute grounds for impeachment." His staff worked on the report all hours through Labor Day weekend, traditionally the invisible starting line of election campaigns. When it arrived the following Wednesday, the midterm Congressional elections were only eight weeks away.

As the report arrived, President Clinton's political support was already melting. The turning point came with his petulant August 17 speech, when he addressed the nation for less than five minutes to confess that he and Monica Lewinsky, a White House intern, had indeed had sexual relations--an allegation he had strenuously denied for seven months. Mr. Clinton spoke to the nation after Mr. Starr's prosecutors had deposed him for four hours at the White House, before the grand jury by closed-circuit television. When tapes of his deposition were released, they showed him under probing examination; in going before the nation that evening he still displayed obvious anger. The confrontation was a huge win for the Starr team, perhaps a decisive one.

The core of Mr. Starr's report concerned the President's effort to conceal the affair. It charged that the President had committed perjury in his deposition in the Paula Jones sexual harassment case, and again before Mr. Starr's grand jury. It charged that he had obstructed justice and tampered with witnesses in reaching an understanding with Ms. Lewinsky to conceal the affair, in trying to arrange a job in New York, and in coaching Betty Currie, his secretary, before her testimony. Finally, it charged that he had abused his powers as President by a number of otherwise legal acts including making privilege claims courts quickly dismissed. While some commentators thought the latter a reach, Congress quite plausibly might decide to impeach for illicit use of otherwise legal Presidential powers--using his sweeping pardon power to free accomplices in crime, for example.

Except to news spinners in and around the White House, the report involved much more than sexual misconduct. Indeed, all the offenses could be grouped under one heading, "abuse of power." This has also been the unifying theme of what now becomes four volumes reprinting editorials and articles from our coverage at The Wall Street Journal. Clear presidential guilt in the Lewinsky episode cast further doubt on the already strained excuses and evasions chronicled in "A Journal Briefing: Whitewater," Volumes I, II and III. From Arkansas to Washington, from Whitewater to Lewinsky, the ultimate issue was Presidential character and the mode of governance it creates.

As Mr. Starr readied his report to Congress, he also reconvened his grand jury in Washington, signaling that his investigation wasn't over. In the middle of 1998, indeed, he finally took formal leave from his law firm, an act suggesting further action ahead. He had already convicted 14 criminals, including Clinton crony and former Associate Attorney General Webster Hubbell, as well as Governor Jim Guy Tucker of Arkansas. And as the Nixon Watergate scandal showed, if the President was subject to impeachment for obstruction of justice, it would be reasonable to suppose that he had co-conspirators subject to indictment.

The introduction to the Starr report, indeed, offered a number of pregnant phrases. It said the Lewinsky job search attracted the attention of Mr. Starr's prosecutors because it resembled the Hubbell job search, and that they were investigating whether "Mr. Hubbell concealed information about certain core Arkansas matters, namely, the much publicized Castle Grande real estate project and related legal work done by the Rose Law Firm, including the First Lady." The report also pointed out that when the Attorney General and special three-judge court gave a go-ahead to investigate the Lewinsky matter, Mr. Starr was already investigating other matters:

"Evidence was being gathered and evaluated on, among other things, events related to the Rose Law Firm's representation of Madison Guaranty Savings & Loan Association; events related to the firings in the White House Travel Office; and events related to the use of FBI files. Since the current phase of the investigation began, additional events arising from the Lewinsky matter have also come under scrutiny, including possible perjury and obstruction of justice related to former White House volunteer Kathleen Willey, and the possible misuse of the personnel records of Pentagon employee Linda Tripp."

The report said that it was sending the Lewinsky material because it met the impeachment threshold, and "information of this type belongs in the hands of Congress as soon as the Independent Counsel determines that the information is reliable and substantially complete." The report added, "All phases of the investigation are now nearing completion." Mr. Starr had earlier promised to abide by Justice Department guidelines, which restrain politically tinged indictments during election campaigns. His report said, "This Office will soon make final decisions about what steps to take, if any, with respect to the other information it has gathered. Those decisions will be made at the earliest practical time, consistent with our statutory and ethical obligations."

In short, batches of hailstones were still blowing in the thunderheads, and could come raining down at any moment. Also, Judge Susan Webber Wright had muttered something about "contempt" for the President's testimony in her court. Judge Wright's dismissal of the Paula Jones case was on appeal to the Eighth Circuit, and the Lewinsky admissions made Mrs. Jones's basic account not only plausible but compelling. Mr. Starr was also appealing the dismissal of the tax charges he'd brought against Mr. Hubbell; District Judge James Robertson had ruled the three appellate judges erred in giving Mr. Starr jurisdiction over these crimes. And Susan McDougal was on trial again in Santa Monica on charges of bilking conductor Zubin Mehta and his wife in a credit-card scam. The judge repeatedly rebuked Mrs. McDougal for not taking the proceedings seriously.

And as Labor Day pressures built, Attorney General Janet Reno finally opened a formal 90-day preliminary inquiry pointing toward an independent counsel concerning 1996 campaign violations. Indeed, she opened three different inquiries--naming first campaign major-domo Harold Ickes, then Vice President Gore, and as the Starr report impended, the President himself.

With the Starr report landing in this atmosphere, the best the President's defenders could do was to urge that the nation "get it all over with" through a Presidential plea bargain. The notion was that having confessed the sexual liaison, he would now confess perjury, dropping the absurd semantic defense his lawyers had concocted for him. In turn, he would be censured but remain in office. What this would do about the circulating hailstones remained unexplained.

Bill Clinton had indeed repeatedly managed to bounce back from the mat before, as these volumes have also recounted. He'd come from behind in 1992 to win the Presidency. His low in March of 1994--marked by the resignations of Mr. Hubbell and White House Counsel Bernard Nussbaum, as well as revelation of Hillary Clinton's implausible $100,000 profit in cattle futures back in 1978--may have been expensive for Democrats, who that year lost the House of Representatives for the first time in 42 years. But in 1996, Mr. Clinton bounced back to win more than 49% of the vote. When the Lewinsky revelations first exploded in January of 1998, prominent television commentators speculated on how quickly he would be out of office. But he bounced back again, with a counterattack in which Clinton adviser James Carville declared "war" on Mr. Starr, while Mrs. Clinton espied a "vast right-wing conspiracy." The "Comeback Kid" remained in the White House.

Yet the Labor Day 1998 low seemed different. In particular, the President's own political party was starting to desert. Retiring Congressman Paul McHale of Pennsylvania was the first to call for the President's resignation; his reward was an accusation, attributed by Clinton-friendly broadcaster Geraldo Rivera to a "source very close to President Clinton," that he hadn't been truthful about the medals he'd won in the Marine Corps. The next evening Mr. Rivera felt compelled to issue an apology. The Congressman concluded, "You can't call for the President's resignation without the White House retaliating." Yet others followed his lead.

The Thursday before Labor Day, Senator Joseph Lieberman of Connecticut took the floor to declare the obvious: "The President apparently had extramarital relations with an employee half his age and did so in the workplace, in the vicinity of the Oval Office. Such behavior is not just inappropriate. It is immoral. And it is harmful, for it sends a message of what is acceptable behavior." The sentiment was quickly repeated by another Democrat, Bob Kerrey of Nebraska, who'd won a Congressional Medal of Honor as a Navy Seal in Vietnam and who'd declared in a 1995 interview, "Clinton's an unusually good liar, unusually good." And also by New York's Daniel Patrick Moynihan, who by the Sunday talk shows was remarking, "What we have before us, and we ought to get on with it, is an impeachment procedure."

As the President's team tried to rebut the Starr report, Democratic leaders in both the Senate and House choked on the semantic perjury defense--that the President's under-oath testimony relied on definitions of sexual relations that did not include receiving oral sex. "There is a basic understanding of the standard of truthfulness that the President has failed to meet," Senate Minority Leader Tom Daschle declared. House Democratic leader Richard Gephardt said the matter would rise or fall not on "fine distinctions of legal argument but straight talk and the truth."

This was dramatic, for until Labor Day the Democrats had been a Tammy Wynette party, standing by their man. Their theme had been that all accusations against him could be dismissed as "partisanship." Through long hours, indeed years, of Congressional hearings they stood ready to make excuses for the President and impede investigation of his activities.

"I will not permit Republican political operatives to set the agenda of the House Banking Committee," Chairman Henry Gonzalez declared in refusing a 1993 investigation of the Whitewater/Madison Guaranty affairs that later led to the conviction of the McDougals and Governor Tucker. Subsequently the Republicans took control of Congress and House Banking Chairman Jim Leach seized on such pregnant issues as whether the Clintons properly paid taxes on Whitewater, since they reported no income from the 1992 assumption of their share of its debt by Mr. McDougal. But in the end Chairman Leach, a moderate and civilized man, was unable to make himself heard over Clinton defenders such as Reps. Gonzalez and Barney Frank.

And so it went through a series of Congressional investigations, led by Republicans of varied disposition and pedigree. In the House

Governmental Affairs Committee, Henry Waxman managed to upstage both a courtly Chairman, William Clinger, and a combative one, Dan Burton. The feisty Alfonse D'Amato gradually lost his spunk against the droning Paul Sarbanes. For all his experience at Watergate and prosecutorial and acting experience, Senator Fred Thompson was foiled by Senator John Glenn, who won his ambition to repeat his youthful exploits in the space program with a NASA announcement that he would be launched into orbit in a test of effects on the elderly.

Above all, Attorney General Janet Reno, against the urging of FBI head Louis Freeh and her own appointed special investigator Charles La Bella, found increasingly implausible reasons to avoid appointing yet another independent counsel on the Clinton-Gore 1996 campaign fundraising. Even her capitulation to 90-day inquiries at Labor Day had the effect of kicking the ultimate decision on an independent investigation beyond the mid-term elections, though it left a dark cloud over the President, the Vice President and Democratic chances to keep the White House in the year 2000.

By Labor Day, Senator Moynihan was declaring a "crisis of the regime." The crisis arose because, contrary to the assertions of the President's defenders and the easy assumption of the electorate, character matters after all. Given the Arkansas background, the ever-mounting indications compiled in these volumes and the lessons of human experience, this was a Presidency altogether too likely to come to grief, at some time or another, in some way or another. The institutions of government--the electoral process, the competition of parties intended to police abuse--had failed to avert it. But other institutions, principally the judiciary and Mr. Starr, the subject of so much abuse, had not let it be buried. Congress and the electoral process must now deal with it in 1998 and through the year 2000.

Among the institutions that failed in adequately discharging its watchdog role was the press. It can scarcely be said that the Clinton Presidency enjoyed a fawning press; from time to time the press would wax hot over the President's failings. But from the first Whitewater report by Jeff Gerth of the New York Times in 1992, what has been lacking has been follow-through. The Clinton campaign mastered the art of "spin" and carried these skills into the White House, and gradually the press became content to report merely the spin. Only a small band of reporters, themselves often under attack from the White House, roamed Arkansas and probed relentlessly into the underlying reality. The press in general--until the uniformly negative assessment of the President's August 17 speech-- never stitched together the recurrent scandals with the theme that in the end character is destiny.

Around Labor Day, the press was joining the Democrats in reassessment. Mortimer Zuckerman asked in his U.S. News & World Report: "How, we must ask, could someone be so reckless as to stake his public reputation and effectiveness as a national leader on the discretion of a young woman who was looking for a Washington adventure, a woman who would hold on to a dress as a souvenir of a sexual relationship? What appalling judgment to get involved with such a woman in the first place--and then expect her to keep quiet about it."

Al Neuharth, founder of USA Today, wrote an even more contrite column: "He now is a self-confessed liar and philanderer. He long has been a double-talking double-dealer. Shame on him. But shame on many of you, and on me, too." He recounted his support of the Clinton candidacy, and concluded, "I apologize for failing to use my podium these past years to point out the President's serious shortcomings. Bill Clinton is brilliant. But he's full of baffle and B.S. He's unfit to sit in the Oval Office."

These four volumes, if I may say so, testify that we at The Wall Street Journal owe no such apologies. Over the six years of articles they represent, our commentary has had many critics. We have been glad to endure this in return for equally effusive praise from others. Controversy is our business. But we would like to say that, as hard as it is for the critics to believe, we have not been "out to get" the President, the Democrats or the state of Arkansas (where the jury pool has been magnificent). Our motives have not been personal or partisan. And while we do express a viewpoint, our distress has not been all that ideological; while Mrs. Clinton's health care plan and the like were not our cup of tea, in the end Bill Clinton won re-election on a program of restraining government, by ratifying the Reagan revolution.

In our own minds, our overriding motives have been journalistic, helping our readers comprehend their lives and times. We wrote, published and collected these articles not as a vendetta but as a statement of news judgment. From the first our conviction was that the Clinton character would prove to be the big story of his Presidency. We were wrong in believing the electorate would understand this in 1996; yet even in his victory the campaign funding scandal exploded. The more we learned and the more we wrote, the more we were convinced that at some point a dam had to burst and the character story would explode in one way or another. We are proud not that we've contributed to the President's troubles, but that our news judgment has been vindicated.

No, we did not predict that the President would run afoul of Oval Office sex with a 21-year-old intern. Or that little Paula Jones would succeed where the Republican Party had failed, bringing him to account in a legal deposition. Or that another wronged woman, Linda Tripp, would feel the need to protect herself by recording conversations that led to uncovering his lies. Or that tin-eared Kenneth Starr would get the silken President to blow his cool before a national audience. Or that within a period of three weeks the President would morph from invincible to impeachable.

No, we did not predict Labor Day of 1998. But anyone who followed the articles in these volumes could not be in the least surprised.

ROBERT L. BARTLEY
Editor
The Wall Street Journal
September 16, 1998

TABLE OF CONTENTS

The Thompson
Hearings

As President Clinton settled into his second term, three independent counsels blessed by his own Justice Department were still investigating the Administration. But in the closing weeks of the 1996 presidential race, the campaign finance issue had exploded into public
debate. In an October 8 front-page Journal story, reporters Glenn
Simpson and Jill Abramson detailed the funneling of cash to the
Clinton campaign from various entities linked to Indonesian billionaire Mochtar Riady's Lippo Group.

Other newspapers quickly added new details about cash from Asia
and Clinton operatives. John Huang, a former Lippo employee sta-
tioned at the Democratic National Committee as a senior fund-raiser, was hastily shifted out of his post. The New York Times revealed
a critical Oval Office meeting on September 13, 1995. At the meeting,
a group including the President, Mr. Huang, Lippo Group scion
James Riady, influential Arkansas businessman Joseph Giroir and
deputy White House counsel Bruce Lindsey had decided that Mr.
Huang would be transferred from his Commerce Department job to
one of the top fund-raising posts at the DNC. The revelations seemed
to point to Mr. Clinton's involvement in a conspiracy to shred the
campaign finance laws.

After the election, Attorney General Janet Reno brushed aside
Congressional requests for an Independent Counsel, declaring the
Justice Department would handle the probe. Republicans controlling
both houses of Congress thought they'd finally found the right man

to head an investigation in Senator Fred Thompson of Tennessee, a former Watergate Committee counsel and movie actor with an air of careful gravity. A serious investigation loomed in the summer of 1997, where this fourth volume of the Wall Street Journal's collected editorial page coverage begins. Senator Thompson opened the hearings on a dramatic note, saying his committee had found evidence of a plan by "high-level Chinese government officials" to "subvert our election process."

But the committee quickly became bogged down in fierce political warfare led by the ranking minority member, Senator John Glenn of Ohio. Although Senator Thompson's charges of Chinese influence would later prove to be largely true, efforts by the Republican majority to explore the allegations were met with sharp attacks by the Democratic minority, a sophisticated White House "spin machine," and resistance from the Department of Justice. As summer turned to fall, the Thompson Committee struggled on, sifting through the activities of a remarkable cast of characters—an enigmatic Macau businessman with a suitcase full of cash, Indonesian moguls, Buddhist monks, Arapaho Indians, Arkansas hustlers, White House operatives, CIA assets.

Despite mounting evidence of White House links to illegal funding activities, Ms. Reno continued to resist calls for an independent counsel. Criticism of the Attorney General and a seemingly rudderless Justice Department investigation intensified.

Mr. Clinton also faced trouble from two Arkansans—Paula Jones, who was pressing a sexual-harassment suit, and his old Whitewater Development Co. partner, Jim McDougal, who was cooperating with Mr. Starr following his conviction on multiple bank fraud counts. In the face of such an array of problems, "it's an apt time to discuss precisely what needs to be investigated, and why," the Journal wrote. "The large issue is abuse of power. Indeed, this concern unifies all of the Clinton scandals from John Huang to Jim McDougal to Paula Jones. We entrust Presidents and Governors and other high officials with formidable powers over the law, our pocketbooks and our national security. Our system relies on them using those powers responsibly, not wantonly."

Editorial Feature

Campaign Probe: Dems Bet Public Doesn't Care

Even overly patient Fred Thompson gets fed up once in a while. "Senator Levin, do you have anything on *this* campaign?" the GOP chairman of the Senate's campaign-finance hearings quipped.

He was talking to Carl Levin, the Michigan Democrat and Ben-Franklin-with-a-combover look-alike who was, for the fifth or sixth but certainly not the last time, trotting out alleged Republican excesses not from 1996, but from 1992. Mr. Levin plowed ahead anyway, and before this is over he'll probably turn the selling of

Potomac Watch

By Paul A. Gigot

the Lincoln Bedroom into a probe of Honest Abe himself. Lincoln was, after all, a Republican.

After three days of hearings, their tenor is clear: Chairman Thompson, a former prosecutor and actor, is playing the detail man, striving to ferret out facts, make connections, build a case. The Democrats are responding by saying everybody does it, blaming a "system" they're now desperate to "reform," if only Republicans would let them. In the Short Attention Span Theater that is modern American politics, Mr. Thompson has the tougher role.

He won't get any help from John Glenn, the committee's ranking Democrat, who shows zero interest in discovering if U.S. foreign policy was up for sale in 1996. He devoted most of his opening 35 minutes Tuesday to Haley Barbour, the former Republican Party chairman, who deserves his day in the dock for raising foreign money. But a visitor from Mars might have thought that Mr. Barbour, and not President Clinton, was the commander-in-chief with power to determine, or auction off, U.S. foreign policy.

Mr. Glenn also doesn't mind that Wang Jun, a Chinese businessman and arms dealer, made it into the White House for coffee. His deeply probing response was to claim that Mr. Wang had hosted a dinner, in Beijing, for George Bush and former National Security Adviser Brent Scowcroft. Never mind that the dinner took place in April 1996, years after either man held any power. Mr. Glenn entered politics as a hero but seems determined to leave it as James Carville.

New Jersey freshman Bob Torricelli was even more inventive, implying a racist GOP motive by analogizing these hearings to the 1950-51 Kefauver probe into "Italian-Americans." Mr. Torricelli claimed to have seen these on a "flickering television screen"—which is a tribute to his memory, not to mention his cynicism, since the Kefauver hearings ended five days after he was born. They concerned the Mafia.

John Glenn Jr.

This Democratic argument is ingenious in its use of political cynicism. By declaring the exercise merely partisan, Democrats play to an already cynical public, which is more likely to ignore the details. If everyone in politics is to blame, then no one in particular is, certainly not the president. And if the hearings are merely about campaign finance reform, then congressional oversight of the executive is beside the point.

Whether this line succeeds depends on whether Mr. Thompson can retain the interest of the press corps, which already is acting bored. TV offers only token coverage. On Day II, outside the hearing room, White House spinner Lanny Davis was chortling that the Republican story was "too complex" to draw an audience, while Democrats had a simple, powerful theme.

What's lost in this spin contest is that Mr. Thompson is accumulating some intriguing facts. His first witness, Richard Sullivan, was a tremulous former Democratic National Committee fund-raiser who described the pressure to hire John Huang, the mysterious fund-raiser who now wants congressional immunity.

Mark Middleton, a former White House aide from Arkansas, put in a word. So did Joe Giroir, the old Rose Law Firm hand and U.S. operative for Indonesia's Lippo Group, which has big interests in China. Former White House enforcer Harold Ickes also recommended Mr. Huang, who had to take a pay cut for the job and who had little previous fund-raising experience. Finally, Mr. Clinton himself suggested the hire, though, as usual, he now says he can't recall why or to whom. Why this full-court press for an obscure Commerce official?

GOP Sen. Don Nickles also disclosed a memo, turned over by the White House just days ago, that showed a White House willing to sell "Invitations to participate in official delegation trips abroad." The "contact" was listed as then-White House aide Alexis Herman, now secretary of labor. This is the same Ms. Herman who claimed during her confirmation hearings that she played no role in organizing Commerce Department trade missions.

Since when is it partisan to ask what was really going on in government? And what's the point of writing new campaign rules before Congress tells us how and why the old ones could be broken with such impunity?

One senator who understands this is Joseph Lieberman, the only Democrat who's behaving as if he'd like to know what happened in 1996. Debating immunity for John Huang, the Connecticut senator said he was skeptical. While he's all for reform to curb fund-raising excesses, he said, "Another way is to punish people who did wrong by sending them to jail or fining them substantially."

Accountability. What a novel idea.

REVIEW & OUTLOOK

The Lippo Connection

This week the Thompson campaign finance hearings will discuss in public the connection between the world of the Lippo Group and the world of Bill Clinton. It's about time.

At the moment, John Huang is the most famous former employee of Indonesia's Lippo Group. Others who have worked for Lippo include onetime Associate Attorney General Webster Hubbell and Joseph Giroir, former managing partner of Little Rock's Rose Law Firm, which in turn employed the young Hillary Clinton. Bill Clinton's associations with Lippo go back at least to the early 1980s. Now it is 1997, and this long association has arrived on the doorstep of a Congressional committee investigating politics and money.

John Huang

We are also prepared, of course, to see this week's hearings brushed off as irrelevant or boring, as were last week's hearings. It had slipped our notice that Congressional oversight is now mainly supposed to serve as bread and circuses for the local sophisticates. But if they're having a hard time staying awake, maybe they should give the summer interns a chance to find the relevance.

In fact, the first week of hearings advanced understanding of some troubling, "previously known" episodes. Former Democratic National Committee finance director Richard Sullivan put Arkansas operatives

Joseph Giroir and Mark Middleton in the middle of an effort, sanctioned by President Clinton, to move Mr. Huang to the DNC. This included a Giroir meeting on September 13, 1995, with the President.

Other participants in the September 13 meeting were Mr. Huang, Mr. Clinton's loyal aide Bruce Lindsey and James Riady, a top official of Lippo Group. Mr. Huang left Lippo in 1994, after being given a $700,000 bonus, and went to work for Ron Brown's Commerce Department. After the September 1995 White House meeting, Mr. Huang left Commerce for the DNC. The question is, with what orders? At the moment, we're supposed to believe that poor John Huang made all these terrible and embarrassing decisions all by himself.

The important thing about the Riadys in particular is not that they are members of Indonesia's admirably successful ethnic Chinese minority, but unlike all the rest, they are honorary Arkansans. James Riady's relationship with Bill Clinton and Mr. Giroir, the former

James Riady

Rose partner, goes back to the early 1980s, when Lippo bought $16 million worth of stock in Worthen Bank of Arkansas, in partnership with financier Jackson Stephens. Family patriarch Mochtar Riady installed young James in Little Rock as a director.

The purchase of Worthen Bank back in 1984 began a period of intense collaboration between Stephens Inc., long a kingmaker in Arkansas politics, and the Riadys, including the purchase of Hong Kong Chinese Bank. In March of 1996 an official for Stephens Inc. told us that all business affairs between the Arkansas investment giant and Lippo ended in the late 1980s.

But a relationship remained between the Riadys and President Clinton. Lippo's Hong Kong boardroom is decorated with a portrait of Mochtar Riady with Bill and Hillary Clinton. Mr. Giroir—again, cited by the former DNC finance chairman last week as urging that former Lippo hand John Huang start raising campaign money—is currently in business with the Riadys through his Arkansas International Development Corp.

In the final days of the 1996 Presidential campaign, alleged money-laundering became an issue with reports that the Federal Deposit Insurance Corp. had in 1994 issued a rare cease-and-desist order against Lippo Bank in the U.S. to ensure the "timely, accurate and complete reporting, to law enforcement and supervisory authorities, of known or suspected criminal activity." The order was lifted in 1996, and in a letter published on October 28, Lippo Bank President James Per Lee protested our "money-laundering" characterization, calling the FDIC's action "a routine compliance examination." But in March of this year, the FDIC issued another order against Lippo, requiring it to increase capital, shore up assets and improve oversight.

Out of all this extraordinary history emerged John Huang, whose resume just happens to read Lippo/Commerce/DNC. Irrelevant? Boring? Only if you're content to allow what you "already know" become the gold standard for American political behavior into the next century.

REVIEW & OUTLOOK

Troubled Justice

"I do not have any confidence anymore in the Justice Department's ability to carry out a credible investigation," an exasperated Senator Fred Thompson declared last week. Shortly after that, the Senate Governmental Affairs Committee, in a rare bipartisan display, voted 15 to 1 to reject objections from Justice and grant immunity to four Buddhist nuns. New Jersey Democrat Robert Torricelli said Justice had "complicated the work of this committee."

Janet Reno

Now in the past few days, the Thompson committee has begun to examine the fantastic career of Bill Clinton's Little Rock friend, Charlie Trie. An FBI agent described how Mr. Trie funneled huge amounts of money from an enigmatic entrepreneur in Macau named Ng Lap Seng to Democratic coffers. Yesterday came tales of Mr. Trie trying to haul sacks of checks to the Clinton defense fund. Mr. Trie is somewhere in China, asserting that no one will find him.

And we are asked to believe that Janet Reno's Justice Department will get to the bottom of the whole campaign finance story. We no longer believe that.

Let it be noted that early on we supported the idea of letting the department's Public Integrity Section, rather than a new Independent Counsel, investigate what is, in truth, a Clinton campaign finance scandal. One of our core concerns in the Clinton saga has been directed at the damage done to the institutions of government. Accordingly, we thought there was an argument for letting Public Integrity prove it could conduct a credible investigation, free of all the usual Clintonesque stonewalling and double-talk. This, however, would have required real leadership and support from the Attorney General. The available evidence suggests otherwise.

The Buddhist nuns at the center of the immunity dispute are four minor figures who apparently acted as conduits for money laundered into a fund-raiser at a California temple hosted by the Vice President, a "covered person" under the independent counsel statute. Yet Justice resisted the immunity request, as if somehow it might actually bring charges against the nuns. This preposterous stance tipped the whole committee's vote against the department.

Earlier, Justice intruded itself into the "Chinese conspiracy" flap. Senator Thompson had characterized an FBI briefing as evidence of a "Chinese plot to subvert our election process." Democrats on the committee protested, which is fine, but then Assistant Attorney General Andrew Fois, a Clinton appointee, shot off a letter to Senator Thompson stating his conclusions were "not necessarily those of the law enforcement or intelligence communities." But Mr. Fois apparently neglected to check with the appropriate agencies. After a second FBI briefing, committee Democrats quietly shifted support to their Republican chairman.

Meanwhile, the department's criminal investigation of Representative Dan Burton for allegedly shaking down a lobbyist is in fast-forward, with subpoenas flying and agents dispatched to far-flung locales. Mr. Burton, of course, heads the campaign finance probe in the House.

*   *   *

Fairly or not, the Meese Justice Department of the early Reagan years endures as a metaphor for politicization. Well, if that's the benchmark, where along any such spectrum should we place the Clinton-Reno Justice Department?

Yes, Ms. Reno has a reputation for personal probity. But during her tenure, the White House has shown little respect for any of the formerly accepted norms of independence accorded Justice, and Ms. Reno has appeared all too willing to play along at key junctures. Consider the record:

Two weeks into her tenure, Ms. Reno took the unprecedented step of firing every U.S. Attorney in the land, calling it a "joint decision" with the White House. Investigations across the country, including a probe of the Clintons' financial dealings with a failed S&L named Madison Guaranty, were disrupted.

The White House then positioned Webster Hubbell—a crook, it turned out—at her right hand as Associate Attorney General. After the Foster suicide, Ms. Reno didn't object when the White House thwarted access to Justice investigators seeking to examine his office. In a call to White House Counsel Bernard Nussbaum, Deputy Attorney General Philip Heymann asked, "Bernie, are you hiding something?" Mr. Heymann resigned soon after, in our view taking with him whatever hope for independence existed at Justice.

In 1994, two independent counsels, Kenneth Starr and Donald Smaltz, were named to investigate the Clintons and their associates. Both have faced Justice Department interference in their probes. Mr. Smaltz's investigation had been "significantly curtailed by the Justice Department," Legal Times reported in March 1995, just when he was zeroing in on Arkansas poultry powerhouse Don Tyson. Justice filed an amicus brief with the Supreme Court supporting the White House's position that lawyers who met with Hillary Clinton should not have to turn over Whitewater-related notes to Mr. Starr's office, as instructed to by the Eighth Circuit Court of Appeals. In a rebuke, the High Court let the Eighth Circuit order stand.

The record of the Travel Office affair shows that White House aides abused the authority of the FBI, an arm of Justice. Justice's Public Integrity Section then brought a trumped-up embezzlement case against Travel Office head Billy Dale. A jury tossed it out in two hours.

The department's criminal division hasn't had a permanent head for almost two years. The acting head is the father of a lawyer for John Huang and so must routinely recuse himself; the probe is being handled by an assistant to the acting head. Ms. Reno's new deputy, Eric Holder, a self-proclaimed political protégé of the late Commerce Secretary Ron Brown, says Justice lawyers advised him there was no need for him to recuse himself from the department's now-internal probe of Commerce under Mr. Brown. Mr. Brown and his Commerce Department, of course, are at one of the key intersections of the campaign finance scandal.

To put it bluntly, if all this had happened across five years when the President was Ronald Reagan and the Attorney General was Ed Meese, and if we were in the midst of Congressional hearings such as those on display this week in Senator Thompson's committee room, claims of independence such as those being made by Janet Reno would have been run out of town by the political establishment. Ms. Reno's claims are not credible because this Administration's behavior across five years has made them incredible. As of now, Justice under Janet Reno is getting an unprecedented, unearned free pass.

Review & Outlook

Bankruptcy of Justice

Senator Fred Thompson's campaign finance hearings resume today, and promise to regale scandal aficionados with campaign contributions from impoverished Buddhist nuns, the scalping of Arapaho Indians and Al Gore's $50,000 telephone calls from his Vice Presidential office. With the television networks now carpet-bombing the death

Fred Thompson

of Princess Di, it will be instructive to learn if they find time to plumb the character and veracity of the present and prospective leaders of the world's superpower.

Much was missed the last time around, with full coverage only from Fox News and delayed tapes on C-Span. After broadcasting the opening statements, CNN said it would "consider additional live coverage of the proceedings as news warrants"—which turned out to be only Haley Barbour's appearance to explain a few Republican miscues. Somehow we think there was news in, say, FBI agent Jerry Campane's testimony, excerpted alongside, about Charlie Trie of Little Rock relaying a million dollars from a mysterious Mr. Wu of Macau, and presumably taking instructions from Mark Middleton of Arkansas and the White House. Mr. Middleton hides behind the Fifth Amendment to avoid giving his version of events.

With this kind of help from network news judgments, Bill Clinton has been amazingly successful at dodging the fusillade of bullets headed his way since the original Whitewater disclosures. Consider the events merely since the last set of Thompson hearings adjourned for the August recess:

• Vice President Gore, demonstrating just how much he has learned, took advantage of the holiday weekend to float another revision to his story about those fund-raising calls from his office. Defending the solicitations in March, Mr. Gore said he had only placed a "few" calls. Later that number went up to around 50; last week, it climbed to 86. On Tuesday the White House summoned reporters and asked them to believe Mr. Gore didn't know anything was strange about contributions from Buddhist monks, though the spinners refuse to attach their names to the stories.

• Independent Counsel Donald Smaltz indicted Michael Espy, Mr. Clinton's first Secretary of Agriculture, on 39 counts charging he had accepted more than $35,000 in favors, mostly from companies regulated by the Agriculture Department. The unfortunate Mr. Espy may not know enough to trigger hushing, since the White House has not bestirred itself to fund his legal bills the way it did when similar misfortune struck Webster Hubbell.

• Michael Brown, the son of late Commerce Secretary Ron Brown, pleaded guilty to a misdemeanor charge of illegally funneling $4,000 from the Oklahoma company Dynamic Energy Resources to the Senate campaign of Edward Kennedy. That is to say, it appears the Justice Department allowed him to cop a plea, since Dynamic Energy and its owners, Nora and Gene Lum, have been linked to allegations of broader wrongdoing involving, among others, John Huang and presidential counselor Mack McLarty.

• Independent Counsel Kenneth Starr scored two victories. In Little Rock, co-defendant William Marks pleaded guilty to one felony count of conspiracy to defraud and agreed to cooperate with Mr. Starr's prosecution of former Arkansas Governor Jim Guy Tucker, a critical potential witness in the investigation of the Clintons. In Washington, the U.S. Court of Appeals for the District of Columbia, overturning a lower court ruling, said that the independent counsel could have a look at notes taken by Vincent Foster's lawyer in the Travelgate affair.

Taken in isolation, the various incidents might be dismissed. We're not particularly interested in how many phone solicitations Al

Gore can get on the head of a pin without benefit of a controlling legal authority. But a common theme does emerge: the misuse of high office. Misuse in small ways—in Mr. Gore's case making solicitations from government offices despite a rather quaint law most in Washington respect, or in Mr. Espy's case making a habit of taking entertainment from those you regulate.

Also, inevitably, misuse in large ways. Above all, in subverting the process of justice. This is what Mr. Starr's investigation is ultimately about: whether the Clinton Administration tried to close down investigation of earlier misdeeds in Whitewater. The theme continues in the campaign contributions chapter. Indeed, the bankruptcy of justice comes to a head in Attorney General Janet Reno's refusal to name an independent counsel on the campaign finance issue.

Al Gore

Whatever one thinks of the independent counsel law, clearly its specifications have been met. Yet Ms. Reno, her mysterious "career prosecutor" advisers and now presumably Deputy Attorney General Eric Holder continue to deny the obvious: That what is involved here is not a series of isolated incidents, but a pattern of illegal conduct, and that what needs to be investigated is whether that pattern was directed from the Oval Office.

Editorial Feature

Neglected Testimony

Excerpts from the testimony of Jerome Campane, special agent of the Federal Bureau of Investigation, before Sen. Fred Thompson's (R., Tenn.) committee investigating illicit campaign contributions. Mr. Campane served with the FBI for 22 years, the last six of them as head of a squad of Washington agents investigating white-collar crime, government corruption and money laundering. He testified July 29 on the investigation of contributions through onetime Little Rock restaurant owner Charlie Trie to the Democratic National Committee and President Clinton's legal defense fund.

Special Agent Jerry Campane: . . . I would like to take this opportunity to summarize what we have learned about Mr. Trie to date. . . . I caution that our investigation is still ongoing and that some of the most significant associates of Mr. Trie—most notably Mr. Ng Lap Seng [subsequently referred to by his Mandarin Chinese name, Mr. Wu]—have not as yet agreed to talk to us. . . .

Trie and his sister sold Fu Lin [their Little Rock restaurant] around 1990, and Trie then focused exclusively on cultivating various Asian business opportunities. Trie formalized his new Asian trading efforts in October of 1992 by incorporating a company he called Daihatsu International Trading Corp. Trie pursued trading opportunities involving products as varied as safe deposit boxes and chickens, but few, if any, of these ventures ever developed into successful business deals. Trie also sought to profit by facilitating the establishment of business deals between businessmen and political figures from Little Rock and China. . . . In early 1994, Trie submitted a bid to buy and refurbish the dilapidated Camelot Hotel in downtown Little Rock. A review of Little Rock's city records and interviews . . . reveals that Trie enlisted outside investors, including Mr. Wu, a Macau real estate tycoon and casino owner. . . .

A review of Federal Election Commission records revealed that in May and June of 1994, Trie and his wife wrote three checks to the DNC for a total of $100,000. Also in June of 1994, Daihatsu records reveal that Trie purchased tickets [for] seating at two tables at a DNC presidential dinner and fund-raiser at the Mayflower Hotel [in Washington]. Mr. Wu and a number of China and Taiwanese businessmen and their spouses attended the event as Trie's guests.

Charlie Trie

For the year 1994, Trie contributed a total of $127,500 to the DNC. In 1995, Trie contributed another $50,000, and in 1996, he contributed $29,500. . . . White House WAVE records [entry logs] indicate that Trie visited the White House at least 23 times from the period 1993 through 1996. . . . Trie left the United States earlier this year and is now reported to be living outside Beijing, in China.

Now, Mr. Chairman, let me turn to the question of what the records show and what we believe the sources to have been for Mr. Trie's contributions. . . . First, it does not appear that Daihatsu was a profitable international trading venture. . . . Nevertheless, despite the lack of any evidence of business activity, bank records for all personal and business accounts maintained by Trie indicate that from 1994 to 1996 Trie received a steady stream of funds by wire transfer from foreign sources, the bulk of which was wired from accounts maintained by Mr. Wu or companies that he controls.

Trie's bank records from mid-1994 through the end of 1996 revealed periodic wire transfers, from Mr. Wu to accounts associated with Trie or one of his businesses, totaling over $900,000. . . . Our investigation found that Mr. Wu wired money from several different foreign sources into three bank accounts maintained by or accessible to Mr. Trie. Trie then shuffled the money among six domestic accounts, four of which ultimately served as the source of a contribution to the DNC. . . .

Sen. Susan Collins (R., Maine): You mentioned that beyond tracing wire transfers as they come into the United States that you have not at this point been able to determine the ultimate source of the funds. And that means that you have determined that nearly a million dollars was wired to Mr. Trie by Mr. Wu or his affiliated companies, but you do not know whether this was Mr. Wu's own money or whether he himself was serving as a conduit for others.

Mr. Campane: That is correct, Senator. We attempted to interview Mr. Wu when our investigators traveled to Asia. He would refuse to submit to an interview for us.

Sen. Collins: Do you know, Mr. Campane, how Charlie Trie and John Huang are connected?

Mr. Campane: Well, it is clear that they both lived in Little Rock in the late 1970s or early 1980s when Mr. Huang was working in the Worthen Bank in Little Rock. . . . When the first lady was honored at an event in Little Rock, and Mr. James Riady flew in from Jakarta, people remembered this because they were impressed by it, to attend this ceremony honoring the first lady, and they saw James Riady and Charlie Trie talking to each other in a context where they knew each other very well and seemed to be friends. . . .

Sen. Collins: Another name that seems to come up quite frequently, including in your testimony this morning, is Mark Middleton. Did you attempt to interview Mark Middleton about his relationship with Charlie Trie?

Mr. Campane: We did not attempt to interview Mark Middleton. It is my understanding that he has indicated that he would assert the Fifth Amendment if any questions were put to him. . . .

Senate Democratic Counsel Alan I. Baron: In the course of your investigation into Mr. Trie and his relationship with Mr. Wu, did you find any evidence that money from the Chinese government was involved in any of the transfers to Mr. Trie that you have described?

Mr. Campane: I am unable to say whether any of the funds that appeared to originate with Mr. Wu may have come from an earlier originating source. . . .

In light of the fact that most of [Trie's] business ventures appeared to be failed, we do have some sense of his expenses, and they were quite extraordinary. . . . Extraordinary in the sense that he spent an awful lot of money for what appeared to be absolutely nothing in return, except for these nine $100,000 transfers from Mr. Wu. .

.. And in addition to that, there are substantial withdrawals throughout all of the accounts that he has access to for cash. It is not unusual for Charlie Trie to write a check for $50,000 in cash, $20,000 in cash.

To give you a further example . . . when Mr. Wu came to Little Rock to view the Camelot Hotel and make a final determination as to whether he, in fact, wanted to be the financial backer for Mr. Trie's proposal, there was a meeting in a hotel room, and an eyewitness told us that Charlie Trie turned to Mr. Wu and said, I need some money for expenses, and Mr. Wu opened a suitcase, which was described as full of cash, and handed Charlie Trie approximately $20,000 in cash. That story was told to us to illustrate the point . . . that Charlie Trie never appeared to be spending his own money. He

---

If Mr. Wu was continuing to put well in excess of a million dollars into a series of American companies, none of which was earning any money, the question arises, what was he after?

---

was always spending money given to him from Mr. Wu or from other foreign sources.

Sen. Arlen Specter (R., Pa.): Mr. Campane, did your investigation deal with Mr. Trie's appointment to the President's Commission on Pacific Trade? . . . And was it necessary for the president to sign a special executive order to create a position for Mr. Trie on that Commission on Pacific Trade?

Mr. Campane: Yes, Senator. It's my understanding that the commission as it was originally composed was already full, and in order to add additional positions, an executive order was necessary.

Sen. Joseph Lieberman (D., Conn.): OK. Let me ask . . . about the 23 visits to the White House. . . . Do we have any evidence that on any of those visits Mr. Trie was asking for something for either one of his businesses or one of the people who was abroad who was forwarding him money?

Mr. Campane: We have no evidence of any conversations he may have had with anyone at the White House, but there is some evidence that a Chinese-American woman that he employed . . . wrote a letter for him to deliver to the president at a time when the People's Republic of China were holding military exercises in the Straits of Taiwan. . . . Charlie Trie wrote that letter to the president expressing his concern, and I think primarily because Charlie Trie was worried that if the relationships between Taiwan and Beijing continued to deteriorate, it would cost him money. That is, his business opportunities of being a big international export-importer with China would suffer dramatically. . . .

Sen. Lieberman: Mr. Campane, in your work on Charlie Trie, did you investigate the activities he had with regard to the PLET, the President's Legal Expense Trust?

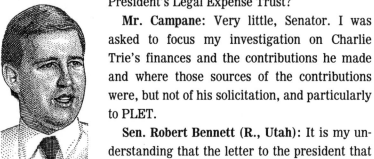

Mr. Campane: Very little, Senator. I was asked to focus my investigation on Charlie Trie's finances and the contributions he made and where those sources of the contributions were, but not of his solicitation, and particularly to PLET.

Sen. Robert Bennett (R., Utah): It is my understanding that the letter to the president that you have described arrived at the White House within hours of the $460,000 to the presidential legal defense fund. Do you have any confirmation of that?

Mark Middleton

Mr. Campane: I have—I cannot confirm that at this time, Senator. I would have to check the records.

Sen. Bennett: OK. Well, I come back to the fundamental question that I raised at the beginning, to which we do not have a firm answer, but we might make a few suggestions. If Mr. Wu was continuing to put well in excess of a million dollars into a series of American companies, none of which was earning any money, the question arises, what was he after, what would he get that he would consider to be an adequate return on that investment? The answer is clearly nothing financial. So we must look elsewhere to see what he was trying to get a return from.

Sen. Daniel Akaka (D., Hawaii): You said that [two former Trie employees] stated their belief that Trie lacked the background or ability to be a national fund-raiser for the DNC . . . and that possibly Mark Middleton from the White House may have directed Trie's efforts. What proof is there of this suggestion?

Mr. Campane: The only—I wouldn't characterize it as proof. We have the interview of Jody Webb, who said that Charlie Trie was constantly on the telephone with Mark Middleton at the White House; that Mark Middleton appeared to be the most significant former Little Rock friend or person he knew that had moved to work in the White House that he was in the most contact with; that they were friends; that Charlie Trie was also a friend of Mark Middleton's brother; that he used his brother, Larry Middleton, who worked at Stephens Inc., to help him with the delegations of Chinese businessmen and politicians he brought to Little Rock. Larry Middleton would come over and help him put on seminars and business demonstrations.

Chairman Thompson: . . . You have laid out the fact that Mr. Trie came to Washington, started a consulting business, became involved with Mr. Wu. Obviously, Mr. Wu is the source of many of these funds. You do not know if Mr. Wu got the funds from someone else, is that correct?

Mr. Campane: That is correct. I do not know that.

Chairman Thompson: Apparently, Mr. Wu would not need many funds from other sources. He is apparently a very wealthy individual. Is that correct?

Mr. Campane: That is correct.

Chairman Thompson: All right. . . . There is no indication, I guess I should say, that Mr. Trie had any impact on White House policy, is that correct?

Mr. Campane: That is correct.

Chairman Thompson: But he did submit a letter, apparently hand-delivered personally to the president, with regard to the Taiwan-mainland China situation.

Mr. Campane: That is correct.

REVIEW & OUTLOOK

Tossing Gore

On the eve of new hearings by the Thompson committee, Attorney General Janet Reno felt forced to relax her hard-line stance against an independent counsel in the campaign contributions scandal, starting a review of phone calls by Vice President Al Gore. Conceivably Ms. Reno is edging toward facing the real issue, which is not the Vice President but the President. More likely this is another stall, reflecting a Martha's Vineyard decision by Bill Clinton to divert the pursuing wolves once again by throwing another child from the sled. Sorry, Al.

Al Gore

The Justice Department pre-hearing statement promised to review whether "allegations that the vice president illegally solicited campaign contributions on federal property should warrant a preliminary investigation under the independent counsel act." But the central issue is not whether Mr. Gore's phone calls broke some quaint statute. Nor whether he was sentient at the Hsi Lai Temple fund-raiser. Nor whether there is some metaphysical distinction, as in the latest collapsed excuse by Ms. Reno and her mysterious "career prosecutors," between "hard money" and "soft money." Nor whether Democratic National Chairman Don Fowler knew he was talking to the CIA when he talked to the CIA on behalf of Roger Tamraz, a rogue Mr. Fowler had already been warned shouldn't have White House access.

The issue that needs to be investigated is whether all of these various fund-raising outrages are the result of a conspiracy set in motion by the President of the United States. As detailed July 7 by our Micah Morrison, Mr. Clinton unleashed John Huang at a meeting on September 13, 1995, approving his transfer from the Commerce Department to work as a fund-raiser at the Democratic National Committee. Also at this significant meeting were three members of Mr. Clinton's inner circle: senior aide Bruce Lindsey, Arkansas wheeler-dealer Joseph Giroir and Indonesian financier James Riady. White House accounts of the meeting are full of stonewalls and half-truths. If Mr. Clinton agreed then to raise money by means he recognized as illegal, he would be party to a criminal conspiracy. This is what we need an independent counsel to investigate.

Under the Independent Counsel Statute, the Attorney General's 30-day review is followed by a "preliminary investigation" of up to 90 days, after which Ms. Reno could petition a special judicial panel for a counsel if there are "reasonable grounds." The Attorney General plays a large role in defining the independent counsel's prosecutorial jurisdiction. Whether Justice can somehow maintain a bright line between Al Gore and Bill Clinton here is open to much doubt. What both men appear to share is John Huang and his enterprises.

Thanks to Senator Fred Thompson's hearings, we know Mr. Huang was the key mover in the Hsi Lai Temple event, just one example of the deeds carried out on Mr. Clinton's behalf. The temple scam began around March 15, 1996, when Mr. Huang and fund-raiser Maria Hsia escorted the temple head, Venerable Master Hsing Yun, to a 10-minute meeting with Mr. Gore. Mr. Huang followed up with an April 11 memo discussing a "fund raising lunch." Meanwhile, a National Security Council aide had warned Mr. Gore's deputy chief of staff to take "great caution" with the event, presumably because of Chinese sensitivities to Vice Presidential utterances before the Taiwan-based organization. When the fund-raiser came up $55,000 short of its goal, the Buddhist nuns testified last week, Mr. Huang initiated what clearly appears to be the laundering of 11 checks for $5,000 each through temple adherents.

Meanwhile, even as more dots get connected, elements of the media have undertaken to exonerate China. "No smoking gun" to show a Chinese connection has become not a "shred of evidence," according to David Rosenbaum of the New York Times. John Judis in the September 22 New Republic called Mr. Thompson's inquiry into a China connection "a disastrous blunder."

But mounds of pretty compelling circumstantial evidence now exist that China connections played a role. Presidential money pal Charlie Trie has fled to Beijing. His patron, Macau-based Ng Lap Seng, has been linked by the FBI to some $900,000 in funds wired to Mr. Trie from abroad; Mr. Ng has significant business interests in China and is a member of one of its rubber-stamp provincial advisory boards.

The Riadys' Lippo Group, former employers of John Huang and longtime allies of the Clintons, have extensive interests in China, with a piece of that pie in the hands of Arkansas's Joseph Giroir. While Mr. Giroir was attempting to broker business deals for Lippo in China and the U.S., his Arkansas associate, former White House aide Mark Middleton, was in Taipei, allegedly shaking down public officials for campaign donations as tensions with China mounted and the Seventh Fleet steamed for the Taiwan Strait. Of course, everybody has now been lawyered up, issued denials and fled to the Fifth Amendment.

Whatever Al Gore's legal exposure in this affair, he shouldn't be left to take the fall for someone else. We don't for a minute believe all this stuff was born in the office of the Vice President. Janet Reno shouldn't be allowed to pursue an independent counsel investigation that ignores the possibility of a conspiracy directed out of the Oval Office.

Review & Outlook

Abuse of Power

In the campaign-contributions scandal the Justice Department has now broached the possibility of an independent counsel for the President, not merely the Vice President. So it's an apt time to discuss precisely what needs to be investigated, and why.

On their face, the Justice inquiries revolve around phone solicitations from government property. Legal literalists naturally want "a crime," seizing on some specific statute that may have been broken. But pettifoggery can be a distraction; the phone calls are important chiefly as a way Justice can back out of the corner it painted itself into on the larger issues.

"Soft money" is a second distraction. Here the argument is about some artificial line drawn in the pretense you can limit political campaigns without limiting free speech. Since the laws try to limit "hard money" spent directly on a campaign, naturally a gray market springs up in "soft money" arguably spent exercising free speech. And naturally, everyone does it. McCain-Feingold and similar "reforms" simply play at moving the artificial line this way or that. The solution to soft money is to make the hard money contributions legal, with prompt and thorough disclosure.

* * *

The large issue is abuse of power. Indeed, this concern unifies all of the Clinton scandals from John Huang to Jim McDougal to Paula Jones. We entrust Presidents and Governors and other high officials with formidable powers over the law, our pocketbooks and our national security. Our system relies on them using those powers responsibly, not wantonly.

Bismarck had a point that we may not always want to know how laws and sausages are made. Yet a President is not a king, subject to no higher law. Presidential abuse of power quickly runs afoul of the law, not only in trivial ways such as phone calls, but in the larger ways codified in less clear-cut but more serious crimes called conspiracy and obstruction of justice. This is what, using the tools that events have given us, we need an independent counsel to investigate.

Bill Clinton

These more serious matters are what Kenneth Starr and before him Robert Fiske have been investigating for nearly four years now. The issue has not been so much what happened with the Whitewater real estate as whether the powers of the Presidency were mobilized to cover up a crime committed back in Arkansas—and later whether the powers of the White House were mobilized against Travel Office employees, and finally whether the same powers were traduced in the collection of FBI files. Mr. Starr may have been slow in making this case, but he faces a code of *omerta*. Webster Hubbell will not reveal his secrets despite his plea bargain, Susan McDougal is willing to stay in prison rather than testify, Jim Guy Tucker is still fighting, and of course, Vincent Foster Jr. is dead.

This is the context in which the campaign contributions episode arises. We know that illegal foreign contributions were accepted and belatedly returned. We know that resources such as White House coffees and the Lincoln Bedroom were mobilized. We know that the Vice President not only made technically illegal calls, but also appeared at a solicitation that led to money laundered through Buddhist nuns. We know that Mr. Huang's efforts were set in motion at a meeting with the President, top aide Bruce Lindsey, James Riady of Indonesia and Joe Giroir of Little Rock on September 13, 1995.

We do not know whether minds met on that date in an illegal conspiracy. We do not know whether the prospect of contributions led to Commerce Department favors for specific industrial projects, such as the Entergy Corp. construction in China or oil deals in Azerbaijan. We do not know whether there was a bidding war between Taiwan and China over U.S. aircraft carriers during the missile firings in the straits, or whether perhaps the Arkansans were shaking down both sides. We do not know how the Justice Department came to prosecute Billy Dale of the Travel Office, or why the IRS now comes to audit Paula Jones. These are the kinds of things—the possible abuse of White House power and authority—that we need an independent counsel to investigate.

The code of *omerta*, by the way, has drawn tightly around the contributions issue. Charlie Trie has vanished into China. Thai lobbyist Pauline Kanchanalak has departed for Bangkok. Trie moneyman Ng Lap Seng sits silent in Macau. John Huang takes the Fifth—or as we now so delicately put it, requests immunity—when asked to testify before Congressional committees. Arkansan Mark Middleton, the former White House aide so busy in Taipei, also takes the Fifth, though his lawyer tells us he'll cooperate with the Justice probe. California businessman Johnny Chung simply doesn't bother to respond to Congressional subpoenas.

* * *

As to *why* we want any of these matters investigated, we should ask ourselves how we want our government to behave in the future. At this point in history Bill Clinton cannot be re-elected and almost as certainly could never be impeached. He remains a charming rogue you mistrust but cannot help but like, and in three years he will be gone. But if he leaves without some measure of at least historical accountability, he will have established a raft of damaging precedents for all future Presidents and indeed all future politicians.

We need to have these issues investigated first because citizens should know how their government operates. But also because we want future politicians to understand that they hold power as a trust, that consequences will ensue if they use it merely to pursue their appetites. Because, that is, we do not want Presidents to behave like kings.

Labor Emerges,
Indonesia Collapses

The campaign finance scandal continued to cascade through the fall of 1997. In September, Attorney General Reno replaced the head of the faltering Justice Department probe with a new career prosecutor, Charles La Bella. In a New York federal court, three leaders of the Teamsters labor union pleaded guilty to conspiracy in a broad scheme to illegally channel union funds to Teamster President Ron Carey's re-election effort, the Clinton-Gore campaign, the Democratic National Committee and others. In October, the White House belatedly turned over to Justice and Congress a series of videotapes—covered by subpoenas issued months earlier—of the President hosting fundraising events at the White House.

For a second time, Ms. Reno rejected an independent counsel in the campaign finance affair, turning down a request from House Judiciary Committee Chairman Henry Hyde. Yet simultaneously she opened a preliminary inquiry under the Independent Counsel Statute into the narrow question of whether the President and Vice President made improper telephone funding solicitations from the White House. The Reno letter to Rep. Hyde rejecting a special prosecutor was "in effect a defense brief exonerating the President," the Journal wrote. "Having determined in her opinion that a great many angels can dance in the Lincoln Bedroom without breaking the laws, she shocked the Beltway with her letter absolving the White House of most of its sins. This evades the main point of abuse of power."

Meanwhile, declining economic conditions in parts of Asia were adding new factors to Mr. Clinton's Beltway woes. Indonesia was in a tailspin by October, with its currency losing 35% of its value over eight weeks. With the Clinton Administration seeking a $3.5 billion International Monetary Fund bailout package, the Journal noted that Indonesia happened to be "the home of some billionaires responsible for a certain tumult in the American political system." It might be appropriate, for example, for the Lippo Group's James Riady to return to the United States and answer questions about the Oval Office meeting with the President that launched the career of controversial fund-raiser John Huang. Mr. Riady, while apparently leaving Indonesia along with other wealthy citizens of Chinese extraction, did not show up on U.S. shores.

Wall Street Journal contributing editor Mark Helprin caused some tumult of his own on October 10 with a powerful and widely debated polemic calling for the President's impeachment. Terming Mr. Clinton "the most corrupt, fraudulent and dishonest president we have ever known," Mr. Helprin wrote that as Governor of Arkansas he "was at the heart of criminal financial dealings and bribery involving his wife and various felons who were his close associates. Upon his elevation to office, he worked hard to suppress and obfuscate the details of what he had done, while continuing the same pattern as both he and the same and a new set of dishonest associates hid, withheld and destroyed records, purloined FBI files, used the IRS to intimidate opponents, plotted to cage government business, met with drug dealers, arms traders and mobsters, raised illegal campaign money, sold influence and shook down the Chinese."

REVIEW & OUTLOOK

Other People's Money

So it now emerges after the UPS strike that three members of Teamsters President Ron Carey's re-election team have pleaded guilty to moving around a lot of campaign money in ways that added up to fraud. We have been noting for years in such contexts that money is fungible, but perhaps never more so than when it isn't yours. In this instance, it appears that large balls of money were tossed around by various political playmakers at the Teamsters, the AFL-CIO and the Democratic Party.

In light of these developments, it struck us as a good time to draw attention again to the *Beck* decision. This is the 1988 Supreme Court decision that said union members are entitled to stop union leaders from using other people's money, namely their dues, for politics with which they disagree. At the moment, Oklahoma is serving as a case history in how difficult it is to regain control of your own money in union politics.

Ron Carey

The minimum wage increased to $5.15 an hour recently and posters announcing that went up in workplaces all over America. But in Oklahoma the poster also informed union workers that they had a right to a refund of any portion of their dues not used for contract negotiations and administration.

State Labor Commissioner Brenda Reneau says the poster is needed because most workers aren't aware of their rights under the *Beck* decision. In an opinion written by liberal icon William Brennan, the Court held that the Communication Workers of America must refund most of the dues paid by Harry Beck, one of its members. It found that 79% of the money taken from Mr. Beck went for programs unrelated to collective bargaining, namely politics. The court ruled that Mr. Beck shouldn't have to support political candidates and causes he found abhorrent.

In 1992, after much delay, the Bush Labor Department issued final rules requiring unions to provide a better accounting of where worker dues were spent and employers to post notice of worker "refund" rights under *Beck*. Both orders were rescinded by President Clinton within two weeks of his assuming office. Since then the Clinton Administration has acted as if *Beck* was the product of an extraterrestrial court rather than the law of the land.

The Oklahoma poster was designed to respond to numerous questions Ms. Reneau's office received from workers asking about their rights. Even so, her simple act of sending out 25,000 posters to employers has drawn fire.

A state assistant attorney general, prompted by a question from a pro-union state senator, issued an "informal" opinion within one day saying that employers aren't required to post the notice. But the author made clear this instant opinion was only his own, and Attorney General Drew Edmondson said that at first blush he thought Ms. Reneau had the authority to send out the posters. Ms. Reneau says there is precedent for minimum wage notices to contain other information, pointing to federal posters that have highlighted child labor laws.

Ms. Reneau is no stranger to controversy, having defeated a longtime incumbent in 1994 on a platform of representing all workers. Her office uncovered a massive pattern of inaccurate reporting of wage data under the Davis-Bacon Act, which requires federal construction projects to pay "prevailing" or union wages. Her findings led to the conviction last July of a union official on charges he deliberately filed false pay and employment statistics to boost Davis-Bacon wage rates in Oklahoma.

We hope in the weeks ahead, as the political system tries to draw the right lessons from what is emerging from the campaign-finance horrors, that some thought is given to enforcing *Beck*. *Beck* is about not requiring any citizen, even union members, from providing cash to underwrite someone else's slovenly, never-accounted-for political projects.

Editorial Feature

Price Controls on Democracy

By Pete du Pont

Hard cases, it is said, make bad law. The hard cases of Clinton campaign cash corruption are pushing Congress toward very bad law—the McCain-Feingold bill, which would, in effect, impose price controls on political involvement.

The First Continental Congress understood well the consequences of legislated prices, which had been imposed during the Revolutionary War. In June 1778 it concluded that "limitations on the prices of commodities are not only ineffectual for the purposes proposed, but likewise productive of very evil consequences to the great detriment of the public service and grievous oppression of individuals."

But the failure of price controls reaches back to the beginning of government. As Robert L. Scheuttinger and Eamonn F. Butler document in "Forty Centuries of Wage and Price Controls," in 2150 B.C., the Kingdom of Babylon adopted the Code of Hammurabi. Among its provisions were wage and price controls. For example, the code said the price to hire a 60-ton boat shall be "a sixth part of a shekel of silver per diem," and the pay of a carpenter "four grains of silver per diem."

'Boundless Avarice'

Twenty-five centuries later, in A.D. 284, the Roman Emperor Diocletian, complaining of "raging and boundless avarice," decreed that "maximum [prices] be fixed" for all goods and services.

Hoarding, riots, a black market and a failed economy soon followed. Four years later Diocletian abdicated his throne.

Sixteen centuries after that, nations ranging from Lenin's U.S.S.R. to Hitler's Germany to Richard Nixon and Jimmy Carter's America imposed wage and price controls. All failed to achieve their purpose and caused more problems than they solved.

So it makes perfect sense in the world of Washington to insist that they be imposed again. This time Sens. John McCain (R., Ariz.) and Russ Feingold (D., Wis.), aided and abetted by Common Cause, the New York Times and President Clinton, want to impose price controls on political speech and campaigns. Their legislative proposal contains a wide variety of price controls: on campaigns (an overall spending limit), on private broadcasters (advertising rates), on government (postal rates) and on out-of-state contributors to a candidate (the proportion of contributions they may give is restricted).

The legislation is a mind-numbing example of government by the numbers. The overall spending limit for Senate races "shall not exceed the lesser of $5,500,000, or the greater of $950,000 or $400,000 plus 30 cents multiplied by the voting age population not in excess of 4,000,000 and 25 cents multiplied by the voting age population in excess of 4,000,000." Oh, that is unless the candidate runs in a state that has no more than one VHF TV transmitter licensed for operation, in which case 80 cents is substituted for 30, and 70 for 25.

In addition the bill proposes free television time for candidates. Each candidate would be entitled to a total of 30 minutes, to be used Monday through Friday between 6 and 10 p.m., in minimum bites of 30 seconds and a maximum of five minutes; but no more than 15 minutes on any one station. Breathtaking in its complexity, McCain-Feingold calls to mind a statement attributed to Soviet official Vladimir Kabaidze in 1936: "We cannot tolerate the proliferation of this paperwork any longer. We must kill the people producing it."

Other reformers offer alternative schemes of government control. Max Frankel, writing in the New York Times Magazine, is for "chasing political commercials off the air and giving ballot-worthy candidates enough free air time to present themselves to the voters." Two think-tankers, Thomas Mann of the Brookings Institution and Norman Ornstein of the American Enterprise Institute, want to eliminate political party "soft money" and narrow the definition of how much an individual or organization can spend advocating or opposing a public policy issue. And House and Senate Minority Leaders Richard Gephardt (D., Mo.) and Tom Daschle (D., S.D.) want to amend the Constitution, weakening the First Amendment to permit campaign price controls.

All of these ideas are bad economics, bad politics and, as 40 centuries of experience have proved, very bad public policy.

In addition to the First Amendment problem—the Supreme Court ruled unanimously in *Buckley v. Valeo* that political contributions are protected speech—there are enormous fairness issues. Mr. Frankel's formulation hints at them: giving "ballot-worthy candidates" free air time. So who is "ballot-worthy?" Strom Thurmond and the Dixiecrats in 1948? Eugene McCarthy's challenge to Lyndon Johnson in 1968? Harry Browne or Ralph Nader, last year's Libertarian and Green candidates for president? What impartial arbiter would decide who may or may not run for election in America?

Another affront to liberty is the McCain-Feingold proposal to limit a candidate's out-of-state contributions to 40% of all contributions. Under such a provision, non-Louisianans who don't want to see David Duke elected to the Senate might be unable to contribute to his opponent.

Limiting issue advocacy is another clear and present danger to American democracy. McCain-Feingold would permit the federal government to regulate campaign speech that contains "express advocacy" intended to affect an election. But advocacy of issues is what elections are about. There should be more of it, not less.

Any state or local party activity, from voter registration to kaffeeklatsches, that "might affect the outcome of a federal election" would also be covered by national campaign controls, effectively federalizing local elections. All this is Big Brother writ large, a bit of Leninism superimposed on modern America.

Finally comes the question of political action committees. Let's be clear, we are not talking of legalizing illegal acts—foreign contributions to political campaigns, solicitations from government offices or making contributions in the name of another. We are considering whether people of similar beliefs—union members or right-to-life advocates—may contribute to a common organization to increase their political impact.

McCain-Feingold purports to outlaw them all. But under the independent expenditure sections of the bill, a union, for example, could advertise and advocate anything it likes. If it spends $35 million, as the AFL-CIO did in last year's congressional elections, opposing candidates would be allowed to spend a like amount in addition to their legislated spending limit. Which is a loophole big enough to drive a Lippo through.

So what is the answer to the dilemma of money and politics in this season of discontent? Disclosure—full, accurate, daily disclosure.

Congress should defeat McCain-Feingold and repeal the arcane existing campaign spending rules (which encourage, for example, presidential campaign staffers to sleep across the river in Vermont to avoid their motel bills counting against New Hampshire spending limits) and take a pledge against price controls.

Then let the sunlight in. The quagmire we are in is the result of the post-Watergate campaign reforms. Is it likely that a new set of government regulations will be any better than the old set?

Electronic Reporting

Instead of superregulating an already overregulated activity, require every campaign contribution, hard or soft, direct or indirect, to be reported to the Federal Election Commission electronically the day it arrives. If President Clinton's campaign wants to take $50,000 from John Huang, it can. If the Democratic National Committee wants to accept $300,000 checks from federal employee unions, or the Republican National Committee from Phillip Morris or Archer-Daniels-Midland, that's OK, too. But it will be reported in the morning paper. And the people will decide if it is wrong when they vote.

What do you suppose the voters would have decided if what we now know of Al Gore's solicitations from the White House, the Chinese connections and the cost of nights in the Lincoln bedroom had been reported nightly on the evening news in the last two weeks before the election? A well-informed electorate will safeguard American campaigns far better than any appointed group of the best and brightest Washington regulators.

Mr. du Pont is the editor of IntellectualCapital.com, where this article first appeared. He is a former Republican governor of Delaware.

Review & Outlook

In Defense of Teamsters

"The fact that my motivation was misguided idealism can in no way excuse my decisions."

Thus did Democratic political consultant Michael Ansara plead guilty this month to committing fraud to steal last year's Teamster election. With that one potent phrase, "misguided idealism," Mr. Ansara has broken the code not just on this Teamster fiasco but also on the entire campaign finance scandal of 1996. Let us explain.

As we read the court record so far, this Teamster scandal is a long way from the cement overshoes and offers you can't refuse of union lore. What the guilty pleas and public documents expose is a win-at-any-cost desperation that consumed many American liberals after the GOP took Congress in 1994. With their entire legacy at risk, they would do whatever it took to win, as President Clinton once memorably promised. In the end, liberal activists are the ones who corrupted the Teamsters, not vice versa.

Keep in mind that Ron Carey, the "reform" Teamster president, had brought the politically independent union back safely into the liberal Democratic fold in the early 1990s. The union that had once endorsed Ronald Reagan became part of the rebellion that brought John Sweeney and Richard Trumka to power at the AFL-CIO in 1995.

Mr. Carey dispatched union operatives to defeat the suddenly Republican Congress. In the 1995-96 Oregon Senate race, the Teamsters ran a high-profile "independent" ad campaign that helped elect liberal Ron Wyden by a nose. The union was also a leader of the

'96 Project, a union effort to defeat GOP House freshmen. In a rare example that made the light of day, political stunts aimed at then Rep. Jim Longley of Portland, Me., were traced by a local reporter to an operative working out of the local Teamster office. Mr. Longley lost his seat last year.

So when Mr. Carey was challenged for re-election by the son of Jimmy Hoffa, much more was at stake than just another cushy union job. A valuable ally of both the Democrats and New Labor was threatened. That's when Mr. Ansara and his friends entered the campaign to betray taxpayers who were spending $23 million of federal funds to supervise the Teamster vote.

Ron Carey

None of them are lifelong Teamsters, to say the least. Mr. Ansara is a Democratic consultant whose "idealism" was formed as a member of the hard-left Students for a Democratic Society in the 1960s. Mr. Carey's campaign manager, Jere Nash, had his virtue formed in another crucible of good intentions, the liberal lobby Common Cause. "I have worked for good government my entire life," Mr. Nash said in court, while pleading guilty to fraud and making false statements. "I have successfully resisted ends-justify-the-means thinking before this campaign."

What the Nash-Ansara crowd brought to the Carey campaign was a network of liberal donors and contacts who could rescue Mr. Carey from the Teamster rank-and-file. One such was Citizen Action, a Nader-style group formed in the early 1970s as—get this—a "consumer watchdog." It is one of those Beltway outfits that is constantly denouncing everyone else's morality. Yet according to prosecutor's documents, Citizen Action figured prominently in the Ansara-Nash fraud. (A third Democratic consultant, Martin Davis, has also pleaded guilty.)

"Ansara met with a wealthy individual who during 1996 was engaged in fund-raising for Citizen Action. The wealthy individual agreed to solicit contributions for the Carey campaign from others, in exchange for IBT [Teamster] contributions, in a multiplied amount, to organizations chosen by the wealthy individual or donors solicited by him, which included Citizen Action," says paragraph 36 of the U.S. attorney's "information" in the Teamster case. Most people will recognize this as money laundering.

Paragraph 37 adds, "Citizen Action helped the wealthy individual obtain donors for the Carey campaign by refunding monies to various persons, including the wealthy individual, which persons then used the refunds to contribute to the Carey campaign."

A Citizen Action statement insists that "no officer or employee" of the group "knowingly participated in this scheme." But all told, according to court records, the Teamsters gave Citizen Action some $475,000 in 1996, perhaps a dozen times more than it had ever given before. The AFL-CIO chipped in some $1.5 million more, a Citizen Action spokesman tells us.

This cash, in turn, was used by Citizen Action to finance a $7 million political campaign against Republican candidates. In the New Jersey Senate race alone, Citizen Action spent $317,000 on a vicious radio campaign against Republican Dick Zimmer. The radio ads echoed the campaign themes of victorious Bob Torricelli and allowed the Democrat to save his money for later in the campaign. In short, the Teamster scandal had real-world political consequences, tainting Mr. Torricelli's victory at a minimum.

If the U.S. attorney documents are any guide, this Teamster saga deserves a much longer run. The court filings drop tantalizing evidence about the involvement by other liberals, including Democratic Party officials, Clinton-Gore campaign officials and "the Secretary-Treasurer of the AFL," who happens to be Richard Trumka, who for the record denies any wrongdoing. Other groups cited in the prosecutor filings include the National Council of Senior Citizens and Project Vote, a get-out-the-vote exercise promoted by former White House political aide Harold Ickes.

Wherever the criminal probe ends up, all of this ought to tell us something about the political sincerity of those promoting campaign-finance "reform." Put it this way: Mr. Carey, Citizen Action, the AFL-CIO and Bob Torricelli all claim to be for it. We'll stop laughing when they apologize for giving the Teamsters a bad name.

REVIEW & OUTLOOK

Asides

Equal Justice

Attorney General Janet Reno has now decreed there is no reason to wonder whether President Clinton had anything to do with the Lippo Group, Charlie Trie and the rest of the pattern of irregularity and illegality that marked his re-election campaign. This does not mean that the federal government is giving up on campaign finance laws.

On the same day, federal prosecutors in Boston charged former Smith Barney executive Robert B. Maloney with laundering $39,000 of his own money into his brother's congressional campaign. If convicted Mr. Maloney faces a year in prison and fines totaling $1.7 million.

REVIEW & OUTLOOK

Reality Check

Washington's pundits spent the weekend struggling to come to grips with the Promise Keepers and their "agenda," which looked pretty straightforward to us. Indeed, maybe the rest of the country should start worrying that the nation's capital is now operating under some weird alternative reality.

Just 24 hours before the release of videotapes of Bill Clinton hosting campaign contributors at the White House, Attorney General Janet Reno released a formal letter that was in effect a defense brief exonerating the President. Having determined in her opinion that a great many angels can dance in the Lincoln Bedroom without breaking the laws, she shocked the Beltway with her letter absolving the White House of most of its sins. This evades the main point of abuse of power.

While we return to this below, we should stop to note that on their face Ms. Reno's arguments are not totally unreasonable. After all, the *current* campaign finance laws are an edifice of rules so complicated that an entire agency cannot keep track of them, let alone enforce them. And the Beltway response? Pass more of the same, in the form of the McCain-Feingold reform bill.

Our next stop on the Beltway reality tour brings us to today's vote in the Senate on the Lott-Nickles Paycheck Protection Act. This proposal essentially would give Congress's imprimatur to the Supreme Court's *Beck* decision, which freed union members from having their dues used for politics they find disagreeable. The Clinton

Administration, and Ms. Reno's Justice Department, refuse to enforce the Court's decision. In Beltway speak, the amendment to enforce the Constitution is a "poison pill" to kill McCain-Feingold.

Once again, a reality check is in order. Especially so since McCain-Feingold itself has at its center restrictions on political advertising and bans on currently unregulated campaign contributions very much like those the Supreme Court has found unconstitutional in a series of major decisions. Justice Brennan's language in *Buckley v. Valeo* is hard not to get:

The "First Amendment denies government the power to determine that spending to promote one's political views is . . . excessive. In the free society ordained by our Constitution, it is not the government but the people . . . who must retain control over the quantity and range of debate . . . in a political campaign." This, it seems to us, is as clear as public policy ever gets.

We have written recently here that campaign-finance reform has taken on the air of an ersatz religion in Washington. Certainly we don't gainsay its proponents' dedication to their cause, but we are growing increasingly concerned that this obsession to the exclusion of all else is blinding the city to recognizing the more serious implications of the Clinton scandals.

The Reno letter to Rep. Henry Hyde shows just how susceptible this obsession is to being endlessly diverted. Her letter sets out to demolish every tree in sight, without ever noticing the forest. And armies of reporters are deployed to "prove" that some subsection of the campaign finance law was absolutely, positively violated. All the while, what should be the real issue of this Presidency escapes notice or comment specifically, that this Administration's abuse of the powers of high office has no precedent in modern times. None.

Janet Reno's Hyde letter is of a piece. We now have this long document that asks the nation to believe that it should take the word of her department's "career prosecutors" that most everything they've heard about the Clinton camp and its world of money is just journalism. In other words, trust us.

We wonder if the Attorney General would entertain a few journalist's questions: Did her career prosecutors depose under oath the following men: Bruce Lindsey, Joseph Giroir, John Huang and James Riady? Officially, Justice refuses to say, asserting its investigation is ongoing.

These four men met with the President at the White House on Sept. 13, 1995. What needs to be investigated is whether they agreed that the following year's campaign required them to amass an enormous fund quickly, and illegally if necessary—which is to say whether they launched a criminal conspiracy. We know that after that meeting, Mr. Huang was dispatched to the Democratic National Committee and the questionable funds began to flow, not least from monies under the control of Mr. Riady, an Indonesian whose contributions were illegal.

According to Friday's Washington Post, Ms. Reno's prosecutors haven't even permitted FBI agents assigned to the probe to ask about this potential conspiracy. Reporters Susan Schmidt and Robert Suro wrote that FBI officials believe Justice "prevented them from focusing on or even interviewing senior administration and Democratic National Committee officials."

If that is true, it constitutes abuse of power. Just as Filegate was about the abuse of the powers of the FBI and Secret Service. Just as the White House's repeated subpoena delays, "miraculous" document discoveries and suddenly discovered TV tapes are an abuse of the most minimal good-faith relationship that allows legal proceedings to function at all.

Against five years of such abuse, ably documented by the Washington press corps, the Clinton White House is totally and unequivocally supportive of McCain-Feingold. What more do you need to know?

Editorial Feature

The Reno Brain Trust

By MICAH MORRISON

Attorney General Janet Reno's landmark letter to House Judiciary Committee Chairman Henry Hyde on Friday certainly is lawyerly enough.

Take the central point, Chairman Hyde's concern over White House dealings with Johnny Chung, Charlie Trie, the Lippo Companies and others: On the one hand, Ms. Reno wrote, it is not a crime to sell "mere access to the President or the White House," so no amount of evidence of this would trigger an investigation. On the other hand:

Yes, it would be a crime to promise official action in soliciting contributions. And yes, there are reports that "certain Government actions favorable to a contributor followed or preceded a contribution." And let us skip lightly over the illegal sources of the contributions, or a conspiracy to break the campaign laws themselves. Before authorizing any independent investigation, Ms. Reno wants overt evidence of a connection between contributions and policy—Oval Office tapes, perhaps, or the spontaneous confession of participants.

'We're Aware of No Evidence'

And by this standard, there is no reason to investigate—"at this time we are aware of no specific and credible evidence—indeed, we're aware of no evidence whatsoever—indicating that the President may have demanded, sought, received or accepted, or agreed to receive or accept any of these donations or contributions in quid pro quo exchange for official action, or participated in any criminal conspiracy to do so," Ms. Reno wrote.

In short, no smoking gun, no independent counsel. This is not the only possible legal view. Other philosophers might look at, say, the intent of the statute.

In her letter Ms. Reno said again that she would continue to rely on the career officials of the Justice Department. Yet recently she had to remove Laura Ingersoll, who headed the campaign finance investigation, replacing her with Charles La Bella, who made a lot of waves but lost the big case with his prosecution of Imelda Marcos and Adnan Kashoggi. So it seems pertinent enough to inquire where Ms. Reno is getting her advice on the independent counsel law.

Janet Reno

The veil covering this question was lifted last June, when Ms. Reno presented the John Marshall Awards, the department's internal Oscars. In the category for providing legal advice, the citation reads "Presented to Jo Ann Farrington in recognition of her involvement with nearly every Independent Counsel matter coming before the Department of Justice. Due to the sensitivity of these issues, and the public necessity that the actions of public officials be appropriately scrutinized, Ms. Farrington has played an essential role in providing timely, accurate, and objective advice concerning the Independent Counsel Act and its requirements. Her unparalleled diligence and expertise have assured thoughtful and effective analysis of Independent Counsel requests."

Ms. Farrington is indeed a career bureaucrat, a deputy chief of the Public Integrity Section, the department's cops for public officials. Ms. Farrington joined Justice in 1980, during the Carter administration, and was named to her present post in 1992, under President Bush. Little is known about her legal or political views, and Justice declines to make her available for an interview or even to release her photograph. Justice spokesman Bert Brandenburg bristles at any suggestion that career prosecutors might be tailoring their decisions to fit their political beliefs or suggestions from the White House, saying the Public Integrity Section is staffed by "dedicated public servants who are strictly nonpartisan."

Lacking any more evidence, it might be worth noting that before joining Justice, Ms. Farrington clerked for Judge Patricia Wald, known as the most vociferously liberal member of the D.C. Circuit Court of Appeals. It is also true that her husband, Whayne Dillehay, got his start as editor of Ralph Nader's journal Critical Mass Energy. He is currently executive director of the International Center for Journalism. Between journalistic enterprises he served as a spokesman for Reps. Edward Markey (D., Mass.) and Charles Schumer (D., N.Y.).

At the time of Ms. Farrington's Marshall Award, Justice was invoking a distinction between "hard" money directly benefiting presidential candidates and "soft" money for party-building purposes to deny an independent counsel appointment. Phone calls from government facilities for soft money, the reasoning went, were not illegal, therefore no independent counsel. But in September, when the Washington Post reported that money raised by Mr. Gore went into "hard" accounts, the distinction evaporated.

Other career prosecutors advising Ms. Reno on independent counsel matters are Lee Radek, chief of the Public Integrity Section; Craig Donsanto, director of the election crimes branch; and Deputy Assistant Attorney General Mark Richard, supervisor of the campaign finance probe. Mr. Radek, the Public Integrity chief, made his views on the independent counsel statute known in a July interview with the New York Times Magazine. He called it an "insult. It's a clear enunciation by the legislative branch that we cannot be trusted on certain species of cases."

In the only public court test so far, the Farrington-Radek reading of the independent counsel statute was slapped down by the Special Division of the U.S. Court of Appeals, which administers the law. In February 1996, the two signed a motion opposing Donald Smaltz, the independent counsel investigating former Agriculture Secretary Mike Espy, who had gone directly to the court seeking to broaden his probe. They argued that the Special Division could not approve this request without the "concurrence" of Justice, and that the matter was "not related" to Mr. Smaltz's jurisdiction. The brief claimed that Mr. Smaltz was seeking to "vastly expand" his assignment, and in a footnote hinted at a "significant potential for abuse of power."

The Special Division struck down Justice on both counts. In an April 1996 ruling, it noted that the "plain language" of the independent counsel statute "in no way suggests that the concurrence of the

Attorney General is required before the court can refer a related matter." A month later, with the unsealing of Mr. Smaltz's indictment of two Mississippi farmers accused of fraudulently obtaining more than $700,000 in crop subsidies, the "related matter" was revealed to be central to Mr. Smaltz's probe—an alleged intervention by Mr. Espy's chief of staff, Ronald Blackley, to rig the subsidy bid. The Mississippi farmers pleaded guilty. Mr. Blackley was indicted in April on three charges of making false statements related to $20,000 he received from his Mississippi associates.

Mr. Smaltz took the extraordinary step of directly appealing to the Special Division because he'd already had unhappy experiences with Justice's interpretation of the statute. His September 1994 mandate was to probe allegations that Secretary Espy had accepted illegal gratuities from agribusiness, including Arkansas poultry giant Tyson

Don Smaltz

Foods. Mr. Smaltz's investigation quickly led him to Arkansas. By early 1995, Tyson and White House officials were mounting an aggressive campaign against him. White House Counsel Lloyd Cutler publicly criticized Mr. Smaltz and suggested that Ms. Reno fire him. A Tyson spokesman traveled to Capitol Hill to complain, and Rep. Jay Dickey (R., Ark.) placed calls to Justice to seek ways to limit the probe.

In the midst of this, news reports indicate, Mr. Smaltz sought specific permission from the attorney general to probe deeper into Tyson's dealings with government officials, but Ms. Reno shot him down. Legal Times reported in March 1995 that Mr. Smaltz's inquiry had been "significantly curtailed by the Justice Department." The ruling, Legal Times noted, was good news for the president, "since Smaltz was reportedly edging closer to Clinton's own relationship with Tyson Foods, a major force in Arkansas business and politics."

According to two former Justice Department officials, in July 1995 Mr. Smaltz was called on the carpet at Main Justice in a showdown over the Tyson probe. In a meeting attended by Ms. Reno, Deputy Attorney General Jamie Gorelick, Public Integrity's Ms. Farrington and other senior officials, Mr. Smaltz was ordered to stop investigating Tyson.

Mr. Smaltz's office declined repeated requests for an interview.

Mr. Brandenburg, the Justice spokesman, says that "independent counsels frequently consult with the Justice Department over questions of jurisdiction. The attorney general requested, and the Special Division approved, an investigation into acceptance of gifts by Mr. Espy from organizations or individuals with business pending before the Department of Agriculture, including Tyson Foods." Chairman Hyde, who will begin oversight hearings next week into Justice and independent counsels, might want to hear Mr. Smaltz's account of these episodes.

In any event, Mr. Smaltz did manage to press on. In September, he indicted Tyson Foods lobbyist Jack Williams on criminal charges of providing favors to Mr. Espy and lying to investigators about it. Earlier this year, Mr. Williams was convicted on the false-statement charges, but the case was overturned after the judge learned that one of the investigators had perjured himself in an unrelated matter.

William Clinger

The traditionally elite Public Integrity Section also had a brush with former Rep. William Clinger (R., Pa.), when Mr. Clinger was chairman of the House Government Reform and Oversight Committee. When conducting an inquiry into the White House Travel Office firings in 1995, Chairman Clinger found himself dealing with Michael Sussman, a former aide to Hillary Clinton's health care task force. A photograph of Mrs. Clinton was prominently displayed in Mr. Sussman's office, a former Justice official says. He had been tasked from the Criminal Division to Public Integrity to process the committee's requests for Justice Department documents.

Mr. Clinger complained to Michael Shaheen, the respected long-time head of Justice's internal watchdogs, the Office of Professional Responsibility. The chairman asked whether the appointment was appropriate, in light of Mr. Sussman's "obvious involvement in sensitive issues at the White House during the period leading up to and subsequent to the firing of Travel Office employees as well as his inter-relationship with Harry Thomason's activities at the White House." Justice's Mr. Brandenburg says that Mr. Sussman "had no decision-making authority" at Public Integrity, "and as soon as his role was questioned, he was removed."

Separately, Mr. Clinger's letter to Mr. Shaheen also asked about Justice's unsuccessful prosecution of former Travel Office head Billy Dale, and in particular the leak of a plea negotiation letter to prosecutors from Mr. Dale's lawyer. After the jury acquitted Mr. Dale on all counts, the letter was made public by sometime presidential lawyer Robert Bennett, who represented Mr. Thomason, a Clinton crony, in the Travel Office affair.

A full review of White House meddling into Justice's sensitive prosecutorial powers would likely have to go back to the first days of the Clinton administration. In their 1996 book "Main Justice," reporters Jim McGee and Brian Duffy reveal that Justice, and particularly the Criminal Division, was targeted for an early shake-up by incoming White House Counsel Bernard Nussbaum. In a confidential report to the president cited by Messrs. McGee and Duffy, Mr. Nussbaum set out plans for a sweeping overhaul of a Justice Department in "crisis" and a "badly tarnished" Criminal Division.

Another Clinton Operative

One result was the appointment of Associate Attorney General Webster Hubbell, who later pleaded guilty to fraud. Another was the unprecedented firing of all sitting U.S. Attorneys. Mr. Nussbaum himself resigned after meddling in the early stages of the Whitewater inquiry. "Main Justice" does not say what Mr. Nussbaum had in mind for the Public Integrity Section and the independent counsel statute.

Today, another Clinton operative, Beth Nolan, awaits confirmation as chief of Ms. Reno's Office of Legal Counsel, where she has worked for more than a year. Prior to that Ms. Nolan worked in the White House counsel's office, where her tasks included Whitewater damage control. According to a "task list" compiled by one of the White House scandal managers, Jane Sherburne, among Ms. Nolan's tasks was monitoring Mr. Smaltz's "charter" and "scope of inquiry."

Next Wednesday, Ms. Reno is scheduled to appear before Mr. Hyde's committee to discuss the campaign finance probe. She must also decide by then whether to move to a preliminary review of Mr. Clinton under the independent counsel statute. But behind the increasingly convoluted rulings emanating from Ms. Reno's office is a broader question. To wit, what have five years of scandal done to the once-hallowed Public Integrity Section, and to the Justice

Department more generally? Under President Clinton and Attorney General Reno, the most powerful law-enforcement agency in the world seems adrift, and even dangerous.

Mr. Morrison is a Journal editorial writer.

REVIEW & OUTLOOK

A Riady Bailout

With the Indonesian rupiah having lost 35% of its value since the middle of August, negotiations are starting for a new bailout by the International Monetary Fund. At the same time, the Clinton Treasury is asking U.S. taxpayers to ante up $3.5 billion for a big new bailout fund called the New Arrangements on Borrowing.

Ironically, Treasury Secretary Robert Rubin mused lately that bailouts like the one in Mexico mean that international investors are not punished for their mistakes. The biggest outrage in the Mexican case, as we've said ourselves, is that the first money went to bail out purchasers of dollar-linked *tesobonos,* who were paid in full, including the enormous interest-rate premiums that had risk written all over them. Now of course the scene has shifted to Southeast Asia, and we have to ask once more, who will get the IMF money?

As we've made clear, we think that devaluing a currency invariably causes more problems than it cures; the less costly alternative would be sharply tightening monetary policy and forcing the economy to adjust. But the sale of wayward banks to foreign investors, who presumably will be allowed to evaluate loan portfolios, is a courageous step. Certainly it contrasts with devising ways to protect the jobs of bank managers and the net worth of shareholders— always a tempting approach because managers and shareholders will be important members of the local elite.

Now comes Indonesia, the home of some billionaires who've been responsible for a certain tumult in the American political system. Of course, the Lippo Group owned by the Riady family is not the only big Indonesian conglomerate, or even the most powerful one. Still, Indonesian businesses clearly have been into big forex speculation—in the form of dollar-denominated loans they are now trying to cover.

It's never hard, indeed, to see an IMF loan as a way to finance capital flight by local moguls. One way to make matters clear is to draw the extreme view. To wit, the money flows this way: from the U.S. taxpayers to the IMF to the Riadys to Bill Clinton's campaign.

James Riady

As it happens, U.S. Congressional Committees would like to chat up certain citizens of Indonesia. James Riady could tell us whether the word "illegal" was mentioned in the Oval Office on September 13, 1995, when he was there with President Clinton, Bruce Lindsey, Joe Giroir and John Huang, and Mr. Huang was dispatched to raise funds. For that matter, Indonesian gardener Arief Wiriadinata could explain what he meant when he was taped at a Presidential coffee saying, "James Riady sent me." The Rev. Michel Camdessus of the IMF says Indonesia's "fundamentals are basically sound," so presumably he's not thinking of conditionality including extradition.

Now, it might not be entirely fair to pick on all of Indonesia for the transgressions of its Arkansas outpost. Indeed, cynicism about an Indonesian bailout is one of the things that happens when the President of the United States suffers a trust gap.

On the other hand, the Indonesian case merely underlines a lot of serious questions about the whole international bailout game. Senator Lauch Faircloth blocked an appropriation for the New Arrangements on Borrowing, and has introduced legislation to stop it permanently. He notes that the U.S. would not have enough voting power to veto loans from the $23 billion honey pot, and that in any event its mere existence is a "moral hazard." These points are certainly worth stopping to think about. Indeed, they even seem to worry Mr. Rubin.

REVIEW & OUTLOOK

Who Is Janet Reno?

So maybe Janet Reno will dispatch someone to interview the President of the United States about fund-raising charges, all the while averring that there is no need to appoint an independent counsel. That is to say, the President's minions will question him to see whether there's any reason he should be questioned by someone independent.

At least this seems to be the latest deal being cooked up by the legal eagles of Justice and the White House, with billing and cooing from the President and the Attorney General in respective press conferences. Extension of Ms. Reno's inquiry until Dec. 2 is intended as a bow to get her past hearings today before Congressman Henry Hyde's Judiciary Committee. What will bear watching is the committee's Democrats, a menagerie with Barney Frank on point.

Ms. Reno's position gets more preposterous by the hour. After all, the whole idea of an independent investigation is independence. The intent of the present Independent Counsel Act is that when accusations involve the President and other high officials, their own appointees should not be the investigators. Before the statute, Justice Department practice—in Watergate and Teapot Dome, for example—was to appoint a special prosecutor to operate independently of the Attorney General and other Presidential appointees. The President could always fire a special prosecutor, but at a high political price, as President Nixon discovered when he dispatched Archibald Cox.

Which system works best remains a question for another day; the statute is the tool history and events have given us to deal with corruption in high places. At present, it is being construed as a shield by Mr. Clinton and Ms. Reno; the career officials appointed to cook up rationalizations peer into its entrails and find reason not to do, or at least to delay, what the occasion so clearly demands.

If a controversy has reached the point where it's necessary to question the President, it has long since passed the point where an independent counsel is required. After getting "mad" about the delay in releasing videotapes of White House coffee solicitations, Ms. Reno hauled a member of the White House Counsel's office before a grand jury. If White House lawyers are being taken to a grand jury, surely it should be done not by Justice but by an authority with some measure of independence.

Janet Reno

In defending her position, Ms. Reno has been at once defensive and self-righteous. Yet in fact throughout her tenure, the press, the Congress and the public have treated her with extraordinary deference, due to her gender, her demeanor and her sufferings with Parkinson's Disease. Ed Meese would have been run out of town way back over Waco.

Consider her record as Attorney General. Appointed to the job after the misfortunes of Zoë Baird and Kimba Wood, she arrived to find Webster Hubbell already ensconced as "White House liaison." In our first "Who Is Webster Hubbell?" editorial, he had already come to our attention for helping to engineer the reversal of a Justice Department position in a corruption case, leading to the resignation of a U.S. attorney. Even before confirmation, Ms. Reno quickly endorsed the new position.

About her first act as Attorney General was the unprecedented dismissal of all 93 sitting U.S. Attorneys, a sweeping step toward politicization of the Justice Department. This led to the speedy replacement of prosecutors in Washington and Little Rock, the jurisdictions where Independent Counsel Kenneth Starr now operates. Ms. Reno also resisted appointment of an Independent Counsel in the Whitewater affair, only to reverse her position when the President made a political decision to the contrary.

Today Mr. Hubbell is a convicted felon, and Ms. Reno's Justice Department a shambles, with many top positions unfilled. The head of the Criminal Division, in particular, has been on "acting" status for two years; and the acting head had to recuse himself from the campaign finance inquiry because his lawyer son was hired to represent some of the potential defendants.

Meanwhile, a Federal Court is taking a new look at one of Ms. Reno's proudest accomplishments as a district attorney back home in Florida. As our Dorothy Rabinowitz reported yesterday, a three-judge panel of the 11th Circuit Court has accepted jurisdiction in the case of Grant Snowden, a former policeman Ms. Reno convicted of child abuse in 1986, on the basis of the kind of hysterical evidence then fashionable but now discredited. Indeed, when a first jury acquitted Mr. Snowden, Ms. Reno set out to get him with a whole new set of charges. She came to White House attention, and her present high office, as a champion of children.

Ms. Reno's record as Attorney General is far from one of independence; it is a record of pliability. Which of course is why Bill Clinton, a shrewd judge of character, chose her in the first place.

REVIEW & OUTLOOK

What's Become of Labor?

The strange saga of the Teamsters and their president Ron Carey continues to roll alongside the larger campaign finance story like a loud tin can rolling through the street. Democrats no doubt wish someone would stomp on it. Instead Rep. Peter Hoekstra has been holding useful hearings this week into the invalidated 1996 Teamsters election. One watches the proceedings and comes away with the impression of a U.S. labor movement and its leadership simply drifting leftward and away from the mainstream of the country's life, even as its own members settle in the center.

Ron Carey

Indeed, with the Teamsters story the issue of labor's politics has taken genuinely bizarre turns involving no less than Barbara Zack Quindel, the federal election monitor for the union's elections, who resigned last month.

Just before that, Ms. Quindel suddenly had to recuse herself from deciding whether Mr. Carey should be allowed to run in a new Teamsters election next year after it was learned that Mr. Carey personally overruled another Teamster official and approved a $5,000 Teamsters donation to a left-wing political group called the New Party. Both Ms. Quindel and her husband, Roger Quindel, are active in the New Party.

In addition, it turns out that Mr. Quindel and other New Party members are currently serving on the board of the Wisconsin affiliate of Citizen Action. This in turn is the left-wing lobbying group that has been shown in court to have funneled illegal contributions to the Carey campaign after the Teamsters gave Citizen Action $475,000.

The New Party is the brainchild of Joel Rogers, a University of Wisconsin professor who now serves as national party chair. A believer that "property rights are unequally distributed under capitalism," he has joined with unions to promote super-minimum wage initiatives in various cities. The New Party's national organizer was a longtime activist in the radical Teamsters for a Democratic Union, and many party members are active Teamster supporters of Mr. Carey.

The increasing role of the 1960s Left in the affairs of U.S. labor unions is an interesting but for some reason underreported story. Journalist Dan McGroarty, however, has reported in these pages that the New Party is one of several left-wing groups to achieve a position of influence in unions since John Sweeney's election as AFL-CIO president in 1995 led to moving out the more moderate, anti-Communist leadership of Lane Kirkland.

John Sweeney

Mr. Sweeney has formed alliances with a range of left-wing groups—from Acorn, which agitates for tenant rights, to the Democratic Socialists of America, of which Mr. Sweeney is a member. The DSA advertises itself as the largest "openly socialist presence in American communities and politics." This month its leaders were embarrassed when it was widely reported that Kurt Stand of the International Hotel and Allied Workers Union and a member of DSA's governing Political Committee had been an active spy for the East German secret police for 20 years.

The Forward newspaper has reported that four former SDS members are involved to varying degrees in the Teamsters scandal, most notably Michael Ansara, who pleaded guilty last month to committing fraud in last year's Teamster election. The other former SDSers are Ira Arlook, the executive director of Citizen Action; Heather Booth, a founder of Citizen Action who now works as the Democratic National Committee's liaison to labor; and Paul Booth, an official at the American Federation of State, County and Municipal Employees who is said to have played a key role in steering support to the Carey campaign.

Free association is a deservedly hallowed right in this country, and the John Sweeneys and Ron Careys of the world can flog whichever politics they choose to. What we've been asking here lately, though, is what justifies all their special dispensations from rules everyone else must abide? They are largely protected from class action lawsuits by aggrieved union members and don't have to give a thought to antitrust laws.

Most relevant to our subject today, the Supreme Court did rule in *Beck* that members couldn't be forced to have dues money spent on politics with which they disagreed. Bill Clinton won't enforce this law. If labor's new leadership wants to do politics and do deals with the 1960s New Left, maybe that's also something their members ought to be able to express an opinion about.

Editorial Feature

Impeach

By Mark Helprin

Here we stand in a clearing of the most difficult century of human history, wanting our deserved rest, and standing with us may be the most corrupt, fraudulent and dishonest president we ever have known.

At the very least the president, before he became president, was at the heart of criminal financial dealings and bribery involving his wife and various felons who were his close associates. Upon his elevation to office, he worked hard to suppress and obfuscate the details of what he had done, while continuing in the same pattern as both he and the same and a new set of dishonest associates hid, withheld and destroyed records, purloined FBI files, used the IRS to intimidate opponents, plotted to cage government business, met with drug dealers, arms traders and mobsters, raised illegal campaign money, sold influence and shook down the Chinese.

If we tolerate crime and corruption in the belief that they are but a small challenge to our great stores of virtue and probity, when next we look those great stores will be gone. Although it has its own price in damage and pain, holding the president to account would mean that future presidents would be, if not uncorrupt, less corrupt. Anyone aspiring to the presidency, from senators and governors to young state legislators and attorneys general, would have great incentive to stay on the straight and narrow.

The consequences of letting it all pass would expand through generations to come, altering the fundamental equations of government and the relations of the governed and the governing. It would legitimate the most disturbing myths and prove the most cynical accusations. If it is left to stand it will shift power insufferably toward a class of manipulators and cheats. We have moved in that direction before, but have always pulled back. Now we are in danger of not pulling back.

Perhaps most frightening to the politicians in whose hands rests the ability to remove him is the president's popularity. But the machinery of impeachment is structured in a constitutionally miraculous fashion to burn away the many layers of deliberate confusion laid on by the arrogant hand of power. It can, in clarifying the facts and stating bluntly the truth, transform the protective angels of presidential popularity into devils of the most relentless pursuit. Those

Bill Clinton

who are reluctant to hold the president to account because he enjoys a 65% approval rating seem not to understand that he enjoys a 65% approval rating because they are reluctant to hold him to account.

The president's supporters who willfully sleepwalk through the stream of charges against him feel that an attack on him is an attack on their beliefs. They are mistaken. If he is removed from office, a president and vice president of the same political party and persuasion will remain. The near-impeachment and subsequent resignation of Richard Nixon did not, except for the strange interlude of Jimmy Carter, compromise a 24-year GOP presidential sweep. Besides, in so promiscuously adopting his opponents' positions, this president of muddy waters has removed a great deal of meaning from political battle and made opposition to him no longer a matter of politics or policy but mainly a matter of decency.

As for his allies in Congress, they float on the wind like birds and will fly with the president only as long as he travels in buoyant air. Do not imagine that after counting the bodies thrown from the presidential sled the likes of Ron Dellums or Sen. Bob "Miracle Baby" Torricelli would stand by their captain even through a light drizzle.

The president shifts blame. The sad faces that have been paraded before the camera before they quit or go to prison are the faces of people taking a rap, voluntarily or otherwise. But a president is responsible for what his minions do, especially when he directs them.

He shifts arguments. His adventures in fund raising become his passion for campaign reform and then are transformed into indignation that his political rivals have prevented him from leading the American people into the cathedral of virtuous politics. He manages this because he may actually believe it.

He and his apologists shift focus. They are astounded at the temerity of critics who compare him to Richard Nixon, and they love to make their contempt and astonishment clear. But there is an answer for them, which is that it is indeed possible to compare the two, and that in the daily exercise of comparison Mr. Nixon is animated in a ghostly walk toward Mount Rushmore. At least he had shame. At least he resigned. At least Republicans, broken-hearted though they may have been, finally stopped defending him.

This president shifts out of the way, like a bullfighter. Of his many capes the vice president and Mrs. Clinton are the most waved in the wind. The president's wife is, of course, inextricably tied to the mass of escalating lies, but no matter what her crimes, sins or pretensions, she holds no office, and is therefore unremovable from office. She is a distraction, a diversion no less than the moon-faced underlings about to take a rap.

The vice president is even more so, having by virtue of his office and his character great distractive potential. But though one of the distinct pleasures of modern political life, indeed of life in general, is to observe him as he simultaneously wounds and baffles himself, to bring the great cannon of a Senate trial to bear upon him would be like using an elephant gun to shoot an apple pip.

The person in question here, as from the beginning, is not Al Gore. It is not Janet Reno. It is not Webster Hubbell, or Craig Livingstone, or Dan Lasater. And it is not Hillary Clinton. It is no one of these or anyone else but the president of the United States himself, in all his power and despite all his power.

Each time a new infraction is unearthed, the president sits back, crosses his arms, and trumpets through his surrogates, "Where's the proof, the notarized film footage of me doing wrong? Don't you know? You can't catch me, I'm the gingerbread man." He defines the rules of the game and controls the initiative, which is another way of saying that what we have here is a bunch of lawyers throwing out a lot of smoke and chaff. But the time has come to cut through that smoke and chaff with a resolute move that will leave all the maneuvering and obstruction in its wake.

President Nixon did not himself break into the Watergate. Nor were any direct orders uncovered implicating him. But a nation led by a worrying press made the appropriate connections even without judicial proof, and the president was driven from office. A quarter of a century ago, however, America had a general expectation of law and propriety, a press in implacable opposition, and a president who knew the difference between right and wrong even if he did not always observe it.

Though these are now remarkable mainly for their absence, one thing is the same: The key congressional processes are controlled by the nonpresidential party. Because the press is languid and the public largely indifferent, responsibility falls on Congress. If justice is to prevail someone in Congress will have to step out in front and take some fire. Otherwise, nothing moves. A quarter of a century ago, the Democrats acted with anger for having lost the presidency and surety for having won Congress. Now the Republicans act with timidity for having lost the presidency and lack of certainty for having won Congress. They seem to be ignorant of Nelson's Trafalgar memorandum: "No captain can do very wrong if he places his ship alongside that of an enemy." That is, to fight.

Why is Congress so pale in tooth and claw? Along with a great deal else in American life, much of what goes on in Washington is treated as a game. Only the clever get to rise, and they are proud of doing what it takes to win, whatever that may be. To paraphrase Maynard Keynes, when people like this are alone in a room, there is nobody there. But the difference between life and a game is that whereas the logic of a game demands doing what will succeed, the logic of life demands doing what is right. This may at times be an indiscretion, but indiscretions rightly motivated are the way history moves. Half of statesmanship is taking the somewhat blind step that carries no assurance of success but which has about it all the qualities of what is just.

The Republican Party and its intellectuals have been searching hard for theme and direction. Futurism, the Contract With America, national greatness, capital gains: These have fallen flat not only because they are bereft of urgency but because they are as well an evasion of duty. Politically, there can be only one visceral theme, one battle, one task. If the party embraces it, the party will solidify. If it rejects it, it will drift.

The task is to address the question of President William Jefferson Clinton's fitness for office in light of the many crimes, petty and otherwise, that surround, imbue and color his tenure. The president must be made subject to the law.

When that moment arrives it will signify the rejection of flattery, the rejection of intimidation, the rejection of lies, the rejection of manipulation, the rejection of disingenuous pretense, and a revulsion for the sordid crimes and infractions the president has brought to his office. It will come, if it does, in one word. One word that will lift the fog to show a field of battle clearly laid down. One word that will break the spell. One word that will clarify and cleanse. One word that will confound the dishonest. One word that will do justice. One word. Impeach.

Mr. Helprin, a novelist and Journal contributing editor, is a senior fellow at the Hudson Institute.

Elected With Stolen Money

Toward the end of 1997, the idea was taking hold that the money quickly but illegally raised for the Clinton-Gore campaign was instrumental in the early advertising on which the 1996 victory had been built. Disgraced campaign architect Dick Morris bragged about his advertising blitz, though financing it was not his department. "We now know why Mr. Clinton was willing to risk breaking campaign laws in order to raise and spend so much money," wrote Wall Street Journal columnist Paul Gigot. "He was paying for an unprecedented barrage of early TV attack ads that doomed Mr. Dole even before a single vote was cast."

Much of this information was disclosed in Senator Fred Thompson's Governmental Affairs Committee hearings, though they limped to a close at the end of October. Evidence of Senator Thompson's charges about Chinese government money had yet to emerge, and he complained of the many witnesses who had fled the country, refused to testify under the Fifth Amendment, or defied committee subpoenas. An ill-advised December 31 deadline had also hampered the Thompson probe from the outset, encouraging witnesses to stonewall and run the clock out. Still, the hearings had produced much valuable information.

Despite the obstacles, Senator Thompson had focused on a number of areas, including leads from China and Macau. The committee also explored the involvement of Interior Secretary Bruce Babbitt in a scheme involving deputy White House chief of staff Harold Ickes and big Democratic Party contributors seeking to head off the establishment of a rival casino in Hudson, Wis. Mr. Ickes testified before the Senate panel about his wide-ranging activities on behalf of the Clinton campaign, including its ties to Laborers International Union head Arthur Coia—a major Democratic contributor indentified by the FBI as a "criminal associate" of known mob figures—and to the troubled International Brotherhood of Teamsters. As more information emerged about the Teamster connection, the Justice Department in September 1998 opened a preliminary inquiry under the Independent Counsel Statute into possible perjury by Mr. Ickes during his Senate testimony.

The Thompson Committee was done. But the issues of a "China connection" and a special prosecutor for the campaign finance affair were far from over. Nor were Secretary Babbitt's troubles behind him. On November 13, 1997, the Attorney General opened a preliminary inquiry into whether an independent counsel should investigate Mr. Babbitt's handling of the Indian casino license.

Editorial Feature

A Stolen Election

Some of us owe Bob Dole an apology. Here we've been holding the Kansan responsible for losing to President Clinton. But we now know the election was lost even before Mr. Dole had entered the first Republican primary.

Potomac Watch

By Paul A. Gigot

This is what the Senate and media probes have taught us about fund raising in the 1996 campaign. We now know why Mr. Clinton was willing to risk breaking campaign laws in order to raise and spend so much money. He was paying for an unprecedented barrage of early TV attack ads that doomed Mr. Dole even before a single vote was cast.

Don't take my word for this. The proof comes from Mr. Clinton himself as revealed by the latest batch of videotapes. "The fact that we've been able to finance this long-running constant

Bob Dole

television campaign," he told well-heeled donors at a May 21, 1996, White House lunch, "has been central to the position I now enjoy in the polls." To the extent those ads were financed with illegal money, Mr. Clinton stole the election.

Mr. Clinton's words confirm the case already laid out by his own campaign Rasputin, Dick Morris, both in his candid book and in his

Senate deposition. "In my opinion, the key to Clinton's victory was his early television advertising," writes Mr. Morris in "Behind the Oval Office." "There has never been anything even remotely like it in the history of presidential elections."

Mr. Morris's Blitzkrieg

That's for sure. Mr. Morris describes a blitzkrieg that began in July of 1995, ran mainly in swing-voter states where Mr. Clinton was unpopular, and showed every TV viewer from "150 to 180 airings" or "about one every three days for a year and a half."

None of this came cheap, which is where the lawbreaking comes in. Keep in mind that in return for accepting taxpayer campaign funds, Mr. Clinton promised to limit his campaign spending before the 1996 political conventions to about $37 million. But this wasn't nearly enough to pay for what Mr. Morris had in mind.

Which is why they conjured up the now-famous soft-money loophole. Mr. Morris has told the Senate he paid for the first batch of TV spots, on crime in July 1995, with $2.4 million in "hard money" that everyone agrees was legal. But hard money is subject to strict limits that make it difficult to raise.

Dick Morris

"Soft money" is supposed to go only for political parties and can be raised in more or less unlimited amounts. Mr. Clinton's insight—and his lawbreaking—was that he could use soft money to finance TV spots that were technically paid for by the Democratic National Committee but in fact were masterminded by, and run on behalf of, himself.

Such coordination is illegal, but Mr. Morris describes Mr. Clinton's role on page 144 of his book: "Every line of every ad came under his informed, critical, and often meddlesome gaze. Every ad was *his* ad." (Mr. Morris's emphasis.)

Many readers will remember those ads, even Republicans who've tried to forget them. They were often grainy black and white jobs, linking Bob Dole to Newt Gingrich. They echoed the themes of the Clinton campaign—that "DoleGingrich" was slashing Medicare and ruining education. And they just happened to be produced by the same consultants who wrote the hard-money Clinton campaign ads.

Former White House politico Harold Ickes has told the Senate that Democrats spent between $40 million and $55 million on these pro-Clinton soft-money spots. As much as $1.5 million a week was spent in the fall of 1995 during the decisive battle of the budget.

A Morris memo to Mr. Clinton on Feb. 22, 1996, shows how, week after week, the DNC spots dwarfed spending for official campaign spots by two and three to one. "If Dole is nominated, we need no additional CG [Clinton-Gore] money before May 28," the same memo says, "since we can attack Dole with DNC money."

This voracious demand for cash helps explain why Mr. Clinton was personally eager to place John Huang at the DNC. It explains why he was willing to demean his office by appearing, as revealed in the latest videotapes, next to Charlie Trie, Johnny Chung and James Riady—all of whom have fled this country rather than explain themselves to the Senate. These are the folks who were raising soft money, much of it we now know by dubious means.

We also know that the DNC has returned some $3.1 million raised by these and other upstanding fellows. But as they say on Wall Street, Mr. Clinton still got the benefit of the "float." He received interest on the ill-gotten cash but only had to repay it after he'd won. And in political terms he got to spend it early, when it was most helpful. More than one businessman has gone to jail for misappropriating "float" like this.

As for the legality of misusing soft money, listen to Mr. Clinton's own ideological friends. Common Cause has called use of the soft-money loophole a "massive illegal" scheme. The president's own former deputy attorney general, Philip Heymann, has assailed the Justice Department as "flatly wrong in saying that there is no evidence of massive violations" of the law.

These liberals assuage their Democratic loyalties by blaming Republicans too. And Republicans eventually did exploit the soft-money loophole. But they were third-rate perpetrators, copycat burglars. The GOP's soft-money campaign only began in earnest in April, after Mr. Dole had exhausted his own public campaign funds during the primaries. All told the GOP spent less than half of what Democrats spent through the soft-money backdoor.

But the Clinton-Morris ad onslaught had already beaten Bob Dole by January. All throughout the government shutdown debate, Mr. Clinton's soft-money ads thundered across the country without reply, linking Mr. Dole indelibly to the unpopular Mr. Gingrich.

Such impressions are hard to shake. As Mr. Morris now puts it, "Negatives which run so deep and have hardened for so long cannot be uprooted by normal political means." In swing states like Wisconsin and Michigan where the ads ran, Mr. Clinton led by more than he did in core Democratic states like Rhode Island and New York.

As Democrats and liberal columnists kept telling us at the time, the polls barely changed throughout 1996. While Mr. Dole sometimes led Mr. Clinton in the summer of 1995, Mr. Morris reports that the president emerged in January with a 47%-38% lead. With the exception of his August convention "bounce," which quickly reversed, Mr. Dole got no closer until Election Day, when he lost, 49%-41%.

Sly as a Ward Boss

I don't believe the ad campaign is the only reason Mr. Dole lost. He also had to overcome a strong economy, a feckless campaign and his own age and Senate tenure. But if you believe that TV ads are decisive in politics—and Mr. Clinton says on tape he believes it—the president stole his re-election as slyly as any Chicago ward boss ever did. In this age of media politics, breaking campaign-finance laws to run tens of millions of dollars in TV spots is the moral and practical equivalent of stuffing ballot boxes.

In America, we don't rerun presidential elections. But how an election is won should affect the respect with which a president is held and is surely part of his legacy. The enduring legacy of Mr. Clinton's re-election is that you can cheat and win. And if you're going to cheat, do it first, and do it enough, so you are certain to win. If all hell breaks loose later, you then control the Justice Department, and you can even claim to favor "campaign finance reform."

This is a legacy of cynicism that will echo through our politics for years.

Letters to the Editor

Can Election 'Theft' Be Proven?

In response to Paul A. Gigot's Oct. 17 Potomac Watch column "A Stolen Election": Stealing an election is a very serious charge. Will it stand up?

There was one provably stolen presidential election, that of 1876, in which several Southern states sent in two sets of electoral votes, one favoring the Republican, Rutherford B. Hayes, and the other favoring the Democrat, Samuel J. Tilden. Congress created a commission to rule on the legality of the votes. That commission wound up having eight Republicans and seven Democrats, and in every disputed case, the commission ruled on strict party lines in favor of Hayes, who had in fact lost the popular vote to Tilden. Although there is no evidence that Hayes was in on the fraud, he was ever after known as "Old 8 to 7."

And, of course, there is 1960. It is an article of faith that John F. Kennedy "stole" the election from Richard Nixon. Columnist Cal Thomas wrote that the late Chicago Mayor Richard J. Daley stole the election by using the names of dead people for extra votes in Chicago, as well as with fraudulent vote-counting. Rush Limbaugh guffawed that "if 4,000 votes in Chicago had gone the other way, Richard Nixon would have been elected." Never mind that had the 27 electoral votes of Illinois gone to Nixon, JFK still would have won.

Mr. Gigot seems to be saying that the Clinton-Gore campaign "stole" the 1996 election through the use of television ads paid for with illegally obtained funds. They did this through the magic of "soft" money, which has essentially no legal limits. By the same logic, it could be alleged that the GOP "stole" Hillary's health-care with the "Harry and Louise" ads, and that George Bush "stole" the 1988 election with the noxious "Willie Horton" ad.

Of course, we know that those huge corporate contributions to the GOP were strictly legal and aboveboard, and the donors expected no quid pro quo from President Dole. Sure. Right.

NORTON N. BLACK
Tucson, Ariz.

* * *

My compliments to Paul Gigot for focusing on the real issues behind what can only be described as one of the most despicable presidential elections in recent memory. The fact that President Clinton used the Democratic National Committee as a conduit to finance his re-election bid is the "credible evidence" Attorney General Janet Reno insists is required to warrant the appointment of an independent counsel.

The media and political pundits' reports on the investigations into the fund-raising scandals have been illuminating but have not yet yielded the "smoking gun" which would prompt Ms. Reno to act. The smoking gun is simply Dick Morris's book and the admission by White House counsel Lanny Davis that President Clinton managed the DNC's $44 million ad campaign. Mr. Davis's admission is startling because he admits that the president actively took part in a conspiracy to subvert existing campaign finance laws.

I urge Janet Reno to stop her stonewalling and appoint an independent counsel. If a solid investigation (unlike Ms. Reno's) should lead to impeachment proceedings, then that is the price Mr. Clinton must pay for breaking the law.

JAMES J. SIMMONS
Syracuse, N.Y.

* * *

Mr. Gigot's column comes as no real surprise. This is the way Bill Clinton has operated all his campaigns. He worked the same illegal side of the street in all his Arkansas races. The sad fact is the major media knew that Bill Clinton had no compunction about using whatever means were necessary to assure his election in 1992 -- not only did they choose to ignore most of it, but they became Mr. Clinton's biggest booster club. There was ample opportunity between 1993 and the 1996 election for all the big media to expose this hypocrite. But mostly they simply followed the Clinton line. An occasional swerve off that line just for show and before you know it, back on track behind the Clinton White House "big lie" campaign.

DONALD MALONEY

Port Chester, N.Y.

* * *

I agree with Mr. Gigot, but the larger question is what are we going to do about it? How about blitzing the American people with TV and radio ads condemning Clinton policies and his outrageous attitude toward the American people. Most Americans seem to accept what they see and hear in the media as the truth. Instead of trying to be nice guys, Republicans need to stand up for what is right, regardless of how it affects their re-election chances. They should show some guts and lead this country.

JACK BAILE

Atlanta

* * *

Dear Mr. Gigot, please try to get over the fact that Mr. Clinton won the election. You could just put one of those, "Don't blame me, I voted for Dole or Bush" bumper stickers on your car. Or you could just resign yourself to listening to Rush 'round the clock. But please, for the sake of your readers . . . get over it.

CHIP VENTERS

Wilmington, N.C.

* * *

Mr. Gigot strings together excerpts from Dick Morris's self-promotional book, a comment or two from a videotape, and selections from Senate hearings, waves his journalistic wand, and absolves the American people of the obligation to respect the lawful election of the president of the republic. He asks us to believe that Mr. Dole lost the election (presumably "his" if Mr. Clinton "stole" it), because of a few well-timed and well-aimed television ads. Gee, if victory required merely showing pictures of Mr. Dole standing next to Newt Gingrich, the Democrats missed their chance to win Congress by showing all the other Republicans standing next to Mr. Gingrich. How bizarre, the same ads didn't stop Mr. Gingrich from being re-elected.

Mr. Gigot's fantasy is, of course, that there is nothing genuinely unpopular about the Republicans. They would win every election if only they could dominate the airwaves as effectively as they have since . . . since President Nixon used fund-raising, dirty tricks and divisive anti-liberal campaigns. It's the height of arrogance to suggest that Bill Clinton's re-election will launch a legacy of cynicism. Mr. Gigot apparently has grown disenchanted with a political system that doesn't send all the money to Republicans.

ANDREW LOHMEIER

Arlington, Mass.

Editorial Feature

Do Independent Counsel Probes Take Too Long?

"Independent counsel matters take too long" is a criticism that's pregnant with condemnation but short on specifics. Too long compared to what? The only other institution that has a similar mission for comparison is the Justice Department.

Rule of Law

By Donald Smaltz

I believe the independent counsel's investigators and prosecutors do not take any longer or are any less efficient than their Justice Department counterparts. All things considered, you may find they are actually more efficient and take less time. I say "all things considered" because I want to discuss some impediments to independent counsel investigations not encountered by their Justice Department counterparts.

In my experience, from the inception of the investigation to the indictment, a "generic" white-collar case runs from 12 to 48 months, with the norm about 3½ years. Is it inappropriate to expect an independent counsel to complete the investigation phases more quickly than the Justice Department does?

From the get-go, the newly appointed independent counsel encounters some real impediments to even starting his investigation. Consider that, upon assuming office, a newly appointed U.S. attorney steps into a fully functional Justice Department office, complete with security-cleared staff, agents and assistant U.S.

attorneys possessing a base of institutional knowledge. Conversely, the independent counsel starts from ground zero—no telephone, no office, no staff, no lawyers, no agents, no computers, no fax.

It generally takes three to 12 months before the independent counsel's organization is adequately equipped and staffed to function efficiently. So when do you start the clock on the independent counsel—when he is appointed or when his office is up and running?

A second set of impediments not encountered by Justice Department prosecutors are the unintended consequences of the attorney general's "preliminary investigation." The attorney general may consider only the specificity of the alleged criminal conduct and the credibility of the source of that information. This is a very low threshold indeed, which Congress has set, tilting the process in the direction of appointment of an independent counsel. Moreover, in making the determination, the attorney general is limited to questioning witnesses who voluntarily agree to interviews and reviewing documents voluntarily produced.

The attorney general does not have any of the basic prosecutorial tools so necessary for thorough investigation because she is statutorily forbidden "to convene Grand Juries, plea bargain, grant immunity, or issue subpoenas." How in the world can you ever get to the bottom of things if you can't use compulsory process?

The attorney general's investigation does, however, walk all over the supposed crime scene, leaving indelible footprints. Those prints portend a variety of mischief for the independent counsel. First, this alerts the subjects of the investigation where the investigation is coming from and whom it's heading toward. Second, this alert causes them and others to "lawyer up," with the inevitable exchange of information among lawyers and their clients. Third comes the lawyer's public espousal of his strategy—often complete with a public relations adviser.

Thus, while few white-collar criminal cases take on a public persona at the investigative stage, it is the exceptional independent counsel investigation that does not become a media curio, transforming the independent counsel into an instant political figure. The media no longer reports the matter as a government investigation but rather as a political event.

Other factors contributing to the length of independent counsel investigations are false statements. The career prosecutors and agents in my office are uniformly of the belief that there is more lying, perjury and obstructive behavior in the investigative stage of independent counsel cases than in ordinary white-collar cases. One explanation might be that in independent counsel investigations the witnesses are often people whose entire existence revolves around the swirl of politics. Whatever the reason, the lie translates to more delay, more false trails, more investigative effort, and more time.

Another factor contributing to the delay of independent counsel investigations absent from most Justice Department prosecutions is that persons resisting independent counsel investigation see the question of the independent counsel's jurisdiction as a productive avenue for delaying tactics.

Justice Department investigations are rarely resisted on jurisdictional bases at the grand jury level, while independent counsel investigations are frequently challenged. That means documents are not produced until the challenge is resolved. Where the ruling lengthens into weeks or months the ability to conduct an orderly and deliberate examination is destroyed. Without the documents, witness interviews are delayed. Given the volume of motions filed in the investigatory phase of an independent counsel's activities, it is not surprising that there are delays in the courts.

Once an indictment is returned, there is little the government attorney can do, whether one with the Justice Department or an independent counsel. The prosecutor is captive to the court's calendar. Yet it is only in independent counsel matters that responsibility for delay is laid at the feet of the independent counsel. His Justice Department counterpart is seldom tagged with such responsibility.

Delays in trial exact another toll from the independent counsel that the Justice Department doesn't pay. Since the office of the independent counsel is a temporary one, its personnel are by definition temporary also. Everyone has plans to return somewhere—sooner rather than later.

One example: We have a case indicted on Oct. 18 of last year. After many delays, the trial date is now set for Oct. 28 of this year. Because of the trial delays, I had to recast the trial team on three different occasions. If the case delays another month, I may have to do it a fourth time because two different U.S. attorneys who consented to the detailing of their assistants to this office want them back.

When considering whether independent counsel matters really

take too long, reflect on these additional tasks not encountered by the Justice Department before you automatically respond that independent counsel investigations take too long.

Mr. Smaltz is the independent counsel appointed on Sept. 12, 1994, to investigate former Agriculture Secretary Mike Espy. This is excerpted from a speech he gave in Washington last week.

Editorial Feature

The Chippewa Connection

By JOHN H. FUND

In the past few days, the White House and Sen. Fred Thompson's investigating committee have been tussling over documents concerning a proposed Chippewa Indian casino in Hudson, Wis. The Interior Department quashed the casino in 1995, overruling for the first time a decision by its regional office at the behest of rival casino tribes who were also big Democratic Party contributors. And documents from resulting lawsuits in Wisconsin show direct presidential involvement in something very close to a quid pro quo sale of government policy.

So the Chippewa casino, seemingly a trivial issue, has suddenly become a highly sensitive one. Until yesterday, the White House seemed determined to claim executive privilege on 10 documents relating to the casino decision, including memos written by President Clinton and his former deputy chief of staff, Harold Ickes. The subpoenaed memos were discovered some two months ago but were not turned over to Sen. Thompson (R., Tenn.) because, the White House claims, they are "subject to a claim of privilege." As a result, the Thompson committee was not able to question Mr. Ickes and other witnesses about these memos' contents last month.

Bitterly Opposed

Interior Secretary Bruce Babbitt, whose office denied the casino license, sent an Oct. 10 letter to Sen. Thompson in effect retracting his previous denial that he told an old friend and lobbyist that Mr. Ickes had ordered a quick decision against the Chippewa casino. Barbara

Crabb, chief judge of the U.S. District Court for western Wisconsin and a Carter appointee, has reviewed summaries of the memos the White House had been withholding and ruled that "there is considerable evidence that suggests that improper political pressure may have influenced agency decision-making."

The controversy over the casino license began in 1993, when three Wisconsin Chippewa tribes proposed a casino at a greyhound racing park in Hudson, Wis., near the Minnesota border. The project was bitterly opposed by seven other tribes with existing casinos, who feared they would lose business. In November 1994 the Minneapolis office of the Bureau of Indian Affairs recommended that the land be placed in

Bruce Babbitt

federal trust, a necessary move before any license could be granted. The opposing tribes swung into action.

The Wisconsin State Journal has reported that they hired Patrick O'Connor, a former Democratic National Committee treasurer, to try to kill the project. On April 24, 1995, while President Clinton was in Minneapolis, Mr. O'Connor participated in a meeting with him and White House counsel Bruce Lindsey. Asked in a deposition last April whether he discussed the Hudson casino and dog-racing track with the president, Mr. O'Connor related, "When he got to me, I said, 'Mr. President, the Indian tribes that I represent are concerned about a possible casino going in near Hudson, Wisconsin. . . .' At that juncture, he said 'Bruce.' And Bruce came over." President Clinton then told Mr. Lindsey to "talk to O'Connor here about his concerns about tribes that he represents," Mr. O'Connor testified. Shortly after the meeting, Mr. O'Connor said Mr. Ickes tried to call him on the matter, but they never connected.

Four days after his talk with President Clinton, Mr. O'Connor arranged a meeting between five tribal chairmen and DNC Chairman Donald Fowler, on April 28, 1995. At that meeting, Lewis Taylor of the St. Croix tribe has said in a deposition, a "generic donation" to Democrats was discussed: "I told Mr. Fowler that, you know, that we've got a number of heavy-duty issues that we needed help on and our friends are the Democrats and therefore I think we should donate to assist in some of these causes." According to Tom Krajewski, a tribal lobbyist, Mr. Fowler "listened. He took notes. He asked questions. He got the message: 'It's politics and the Democrats are against it and the people for it are Republicans.' "

Mr. Fowler acknowledges that he contacted the Interior Department and Mr. Ickes on behalf of the tribes. But he has said in Senate testimony that "whatever they contributed or didn't contribute had nothing to do with my actions in that regard."

On May 8, Mr. O'Connor wrote a memo to Mr. Ickes at the White House in which he said that President Clinton, Mr. Lindsey and Mr. Fowler had all been briefed by opponents of the Hudson casino. On May 25, depositions filed in federal court show, Mr. Ickes' office called the Interior Department about the casino. (Mr. Ickes says he can't recall such a call.) The tribal lobbyists also attempted to, as one lobbying memo put it, "increase pressure" through Vice President Al Gore's office.

Harold Ickes

All this activity seems to have paid off. On June 6, an aide to Mr. Ickes was told by Heather Sibbison, a special assistant to Secretary Babbitt, that it was "95% certain the application would be turned down." On June 29, a letter rejecting the casino was prepared for Ada Deer, the head of the Bureau of Indian Affairs, but she declined to sign it.

Instead, she suddenly decided to recuse herself because she had contributed to the Wisconsin state senate campaign of a former Chippewa tribal leader. Opponents had feared that Ms. Deer, an Indian from Wisconsin, would be sympathetic to a proposal from Wisconsin tribes. Judge Crabb has questioned whether "Deer may have wanted to back out once she understood that higher level officials in the department wanted plaintiffs' application rejected for political purposes."

In any event, the casino application was formally rejected on July 14, 1995, the day Secretary Babbitt told his old friend, Paul Eckstein, that Mr. Ickes had ordered him to make the decision. Mr. Eckstein, who has known Mr. Babbitt since they were Harvard Law School classmates, was in the secretary's office that day in a last-ditch appeal to save the license. He has told Senate investigators that he asked his friend why Democratic donations by tribes opposed to the casino should be relevant in any decision. Mr. Babbitt replied that "these tribes" had contributed "on the order of half a million dollars, something like that." (In fact, campaign disclosure reports show that the Wisconsin and Minnesota tribes that opposed the casino contributed at least $300,000 to national and state Democratic Party organs in 1995 and 1996, almost all of it after the casino was rejected.)

Last year, Secretary Babbitt adamantly denied to the Senate making those statements. But after Mr. Eckstein gave a sworn deposition, Mr. Babbitt wrote Sen. Thompson on Oct. 10, "I do believe that Mr. Eckstein's recollection that I said something to the effect that Mr. Ickes wanted a decision is correct. Mr. Eckstein was extremely persistent in our meeting, and I used this phrase simply as a means of terminating the discussion and getting him out the door." (Mr. Eckstein insists that Mr. Babbitt mentioned Mr. Ickes at the beginning not the end of the conversation.)

Tribal Politics and Cash

This is not the first time the Clinton administration has been accused of mixing tribal policies and campaign cash. Cheyenne-Arapaho tribal leaders in Oklahoma seeking return of tribal lands say Nathan Landow, a longtime Al Gore fund-raiser, persuaded them to donate $107,000 to the Democratic National Committee, after which they got into a White House lunch with President Clinton. The DNC gave the money back this spring after it was reported that it came from the destitute tribe's welfare fund, and the lands haven't been returned. Also, a flood of campaign contributions from native Chamorrans on Guam last year coincided with a shift in Clinton administration policy toward more autonomy for the U.S. island.

"As witnessed in the fight to stop the Hudson dog track proposal, the office of the president can and will work on our behalf when asked to do so," Larry Kitto and Patrick O'Connor, lobbyists for the St. Croix and Oneida tribes, wrote their clients in a September 1995 solicitation for campaign funds for the Clinton-Gore team. Since then, the administration has cozied up even more to Indian gambling interests. This month, President Clinton nominated a replacement for Ada Deer as head of the Bureau of Indian Affairs; his nominee is Kevin Gover, a former Clinton fund-raiser and current lobbyist for Indian gambling interests.

Mr. Fund is a member of the Journal editorial board.

Letters to the Editor

Ickes Statement on Casino Issue

In his Oct. 22 editorial-page piece "The Chippewa Connection," John H. Fund states: "Mr. Ickes' office called the Interior Department about the casino. (Mr. Ickes says he can't recall such a call.)" This is not what Mr. Ickes said. In fact, Mr. Ickes testified in an Oct. 8 public hearing before the Senate Governmental Affairs Committee that he had Jennifer O'Connor of his staff check with the Interior Department on the status of the casino matter.

Additionally, in the transcript of Mr. Ickes' deposition to the Senate Committee on Governmental Affairs of Sept. 22, 1997, Mr. Ickes stated several times under oath that his office had contacted the Department of Interior to determine the status of the matter. For example, on page 36 of his deposition, Mr. Ickes stated: "My recollection is that she [Jennifer O'Connor, who worked directly for Mr. Ickes] made an inquiry at the Department of Interior to find out what the status was, and my recollection is that she told me that . . . it was somewhere in the maw of Interior, a decision was being made in connection with this." And on page 39 of his transcript, Mr. Ickes states: "she [Ms. O'Connor] checked, 'here is the status of it Harold', and my recollection is that was the end of it." Accordingly, Mr. Fund's article, and his implication that Mr. Ickes is obfuscating on this matter, are wrong.

AMY SABRIN
Attorney for Harold Ickes

Washington

REVIEW & OUTLOOK

Coia's Connections

If perceptions are important in Washington, the Clinton Administration looks pretty bad right now in its apparent past coddling of unions operating on the edge of the law. On top of the growing Teamster scandal, in which taxpayers paid $23 million for an invalid election, now comes word that a union monitor is about to file charges against Arthur Coia involving ties to organized crime. He is a longtime ally of President Clinton and current president of the Laborers union, which represents 700,000 construction workers.

This problem has been festering for years. In November 1994, the Justice Department filed a civil racketeering complaint against the Laborers, charging that Mr. Coia was "associated with and controlled and influenced by organized crime." The same year the FBI wrote the White House Counsel's Office warning that Mr. Coia was a "criminal associate" of known mobsters. Nonetheless, then deputy chief of staff Harold Ickes, who as a private attorney had represented the Laborers, allowed First Lady Hillary Clinton to address the union's February 1995 convention in Miami. He stipulated only that she should avoid private conversation with Mr. Coia.

A week after Mrs. Clinton's speech, Justice and the Laborers reached an unprecedented agreement. A few officials left, but Mr. Coia was allowed to remain as president and was put in charge of the task of cleaning up the union. The Reader's Digest has reported the agreement baffled many law enforcement officials. In a court hearing on the agreement, U.S. District Judge Emmet G. Sullivan asked,

"Here's a man, the president of the union, who's accused of being associated with organized crime. Why wasn't Coia removed?"

The Justice Department reserved the right to take over the union if Mr. Coia's self-cleaning job failed, and indeed that is exactly what these charges suggest. Federal officials say the union's in-house prosecutor will seek to oust Mr. Coia on charges that he associated with mobsters and allowed them to run parts of his union. The question all this raises is: Did the cozy ties between Mr. Coia and his union and Mr. Clinton and the Democratic Party have anything to do with his kid-glove treatment before the 1996 election?

Arthur Coia

Those ties were extensive. Last year Rep. Bill McCollum's hearings on the Coia matter documented 127 different contacts between Mr. Coia and President Clinton, including warm personal letters and the exchange of expensive golf clubs as presents. His union bought $157,000 in tickets to Mr. Clinton's second inaugural, and Mr. Coia sits on the board of the "Back to Business" committee that defends the Clintons on Whitewater. The Laborers union gave $2.6 million to Democrats in the last election.

Mr. Coia also was not bashful about using his influence to seek federal grant dollars. He personally lobbied President Clinton for grant money at a fall 1994 Oval Office meeting, and Mr. Clinton told the union president that Mr. Ickes would be his intermediary on such matters. In fiscal years 1995 and 1996, the Laborers union received more than $29 million in federal grants, mostly to administer worker training and education.

The White House insists it has done nothing wrong, and points to the latest action against Mr. Coia as proof that "the system works." But it didn't work three years ago, when the Justice Department originally insisted on Mr. Coia's removal but then oddly backed down. The whole matter cries out for a far more complete explanation of what happened here than the Clinton Administration so far has been willing to offer. No such explanation is ever likely to be given, which suggests that yet again either Congress or the press will have to dig it out instead.

Review & Outlook

Clinton's Charlie Horse

No question about it, the president of the United States and the president of China have a lot to talk about: trade, regional security, Hong Kong, Taiwan, Asian currencies, Tibet, Japan, Russia, human rights. These are the affairs of state, the very thing we elect presidents to do for all the rest of us. So when the president of the United States sits down to discuss such heavy matters with the Chinese leader, you probably don't want his mind filled with, say, the whereabouts of Charlie Trie.

But of course this is precisely what we have—a president so prone to living his life on the edge, in this instance the edge of the campaign finance laws, that a lowlife like Charlie Trie will loom as a large, unavoidable presence in any room the two men occupy for their discussions.

Charlie Trie is the remarkable fellow who rose from a modest restaurateur in Little Rock, Ark., to become one of President Clinton's most active and successful campaign fund-raisers across Asia. When Congress subpoenaed Mr. Trie to discuss these matters with him, he fled to China. His whereabouts is unknown, at least to those who would like to talk with him.

We have to assume, however, that Mr. Trie's whereabouts is not unknown to the Chinese authorities. We may further assume that the Chinese have, shall we say, "deposed" Mr. Trie on these matters. And that in turn they have briefed President Jiang Zemin about what Charlie Trie knows.

Which means of course that Bill Clinton knows that if the smiling fellow seated across from him really wanted to hurt him, he would send Charlie Trie back to the United States to talk.

We would say that the president of China has the president of the United States in check, if not mate.

In a perfect world, some time would be found in President Jiang's schedule to let him talk with Special FBI Agent Jerry Campane. Mr. Campane, recall, briefed the Thompson committee on what he'd learned about Charlie Trie's fund-raising efforts on Mr. Clinton's behalf. About Mr. Trie's alliance with a Mr. Wu reportedly of the Macau underworld; about directing hundreds of thousands of dollars from foreign accounts at the Bank of China to the DNC. About the Chinese and Taiwanese businessmen who as his guests attended presidential fund-raisers in Washington; about a total of $900,000 in wire transfers from Mr. Wu to accounts associated with Mr. Trie; about his visit to a White House coffee with a Chinese arms dealer in tow.

Charlie Trie

Needless to say, none of this publicly disclosed information about Charlie Trie will ever be mentioned on Wednesday. But everyone in these summit talks will understand it. One could not help but be struck, for example, how late last week the Chinese embassy was putting out that they would not welcome any talk from the U.S. president about human rights or alleged interference with U.S. elections. Going so public with such proscriptions would normally be regarded as nearly mind-boggling diplomatic arrogance. But not with the Trie card pocketed by the Chinese.

This is the price we are paying for having as president a man who has reduced all of public life to a calculation of personal political advantage. Conservative philosophers have traditionally warned of the dangers of hyper-politicization, and this presidency has become a case history of that warning sprung to life.

Even domestic affairs carry the instinctive taint of this politicization. The Reno Justice Department, for example, has just commenced antitrust actions against Microsoft. So suspicious minds might be forgiven for noticing the existence of a group in Silicon Valley called "Gore-Tech," whose executives periodically interface with the vice president. A leader of the Gore-Tech group is John

Doerr, a local venture capitalist. Mr. Doerr is also understood to be the unofficial leader of the faction of Silicon Valley that is anti-Microsoft. A Silicon Valley fund-raiser this September for Mr. Clinton netted $700,000.

Now, people all over Silicon Valley swear vehemently that this Clinton-Gore networking and the glittering fund-raising dinners is wholly independent from any Justice Department action against their common enemy at Microsoft.

We're willing to believe this, we guess. But we don't believe Charlie Trie or John Huang were innocents. We don't believe that Ron Brown's junkets around Asia with U.S. execs in tow were innocent, nonpartisan trade missions. We don't believe ex-bouncer Craig Livingstone's acquisition of hundreds of FBI files was just a mistake. And on and on and on.

The presidency of Bill Clinton, if nothing else, has been an exercise in compromise. The compromises have been made to further himself. And not least of the things by now compromised are his credibility and his character. This has real effects in the real world. The fact that he is unable to talk to the president of China in an uncompromised position, as would most any other American president imaginable, is a dangerous problem of his own making, and one that he has been permitted to get away with.

REVIEW & OUTLOOK

White House Allies

The Clinton Administration needed to really knock heads with organized labor if it was going to win fast-track trade approval. But in light of this White House's relationship with the troubled Laborers and Teamsters unions, we have to wonder. How could a White House get so close to these two unions, then expect people to somehow take it seriously on fast track?

Last week, a federal overseer formally charged Arthur Coia, president of the 700,000-member Laborers International Union, with accepting kickbacks and having "knowingly permitted organized crime members to influence the affairs" of his union. Mr. Coia will remain as union president pending the resolution of the charges.

None of this comes as a surprise to federal law enforcement officials. Three years ago, the Clinton Justice Department prepared a 212-page complaint that demanded action to "rid the union of domination and influence by members and associates of organized crime." It detailed how Mr. Coia and his associates "employed actual and threatened force, violence and fear of physical and economic injury to create a climate of intimidation and fear." It charged that union leaders had conspired with mobsters to loot the union of its health and welfare funds. It specifically declared that Mr. Coia had "associated with, and been controlled and influenced by, organized crime figures."

But even then the White House and Mr. Coia enjoyed a warm relationship. Mr. Coia has described Deputy Chief of Staff Harold Ickes as his intermediary at the White House; Mr. Ickes had represented the

Laborers as a private attorney. Congressional investigators have documented 127 different contacts between Mr. Coia and President Clinton, including personal letters and the exchange of expensive golf clubs as presents. Mr. Coia enjoyed a security clearance through his appointment on a Presidential commission. In January 1995, Democratic National Committee Finance Chairman Terry McAuliffe wrote a memo to the White House identifying Mr. Coia as one of the party's "top 10 supporters."

The next month, First Lady Hillary Clinton traveled to Florida to address the annual convention of Mr. Coia's union. A week later, the Justice Department and the Laborers reached an unprecedented consent decree. Federal officials dropped their demand that Mr. Coia be removed, and indeed he was placed in charge of purging the union of mob influence under federal oversight. Now, three years later, Robert Luskin, the federal oversight officer, has decided that the mob ties he

Arthur Coia

details that Mr. Coia had between 1986 and 1993, when he served as secretary-general of the union, now require his removal as president.

This three-year delay in acting against Mr. Coia had interesting political effects. The DNC was able to count on Mr. Coia's continued financial generosity, including $627,000 in soft money that helped finance the Dick Morris ads supporting President Clinton that are now viewed as having played such a big role in the 1996 Democratic victory. Post-election, the Laborers followed up by buying $157,000 in tickets to Mr. Clinton's second inaugural and also lent the Clinton inaugural committee an additional $100,000.

During the same time that Mr. Coia was left in charge of the Laborers, the Justice Department supervised a $23 million taxpayer-financed election for the Teamsters Union, which had been under federal supervision since 1989. Now Ron Carey's victory has been invalidated, and former federal judge Kenneth Conboy, now the union's overseer, will soon decide if Mr. Carey will be disqualified from running in a new election.

The Clinton Administration's track record on downplaying evidence of union corruption cries out for a full and complete explanation. That this White House would manage to lose a free trade fight with organized labor is somehow not too surprising.

REVIEW & OUTLOOK

Freeing Freeh

I want to make sure that no stone is left unturned, and Director Freeh and I will jointly approve any investigations close-out before it is closed out.

As I stated then, the fact that we don't trigger a preliminary investigation under the act, does not mean we are not investigating a matter. We are fully prepared to trigger the Independent Counsel Act and pursue any evidence that a covered person committed a crime, if any should arise in the course of our investigation.

We continue to investigate every transaction brought to our attention. We will not close the matter again, I reiterate, unless Director Freeh and I sign off on it.

— Attorney General Janet Reno, to the House Judiciary Committee, Oct. 15, 1997.

This promise comes due December 2, the deadline on the formal "preliminary investigation" into whether Ms. Reno must appoint an independent counsel to investigate fundraising by President Clinton and Vice President Gore. Separately, an inquiry is under way on fundraising by former Energy Secretary Hazel O'Leary and yesterday Ms. Reno found it within herself to sign off on a preliminary inquiry into Interior Secretary Bruce Babbitt's handling of the Indian casino license. The independent counsel law provides that if any doubt remains at the end of a preliminary investigation, the counsel should be appointed to resolve it. The case can be closed only if the Attorney General "determines that there are no reasonable grounds to believe that further investigation is warranted."

With regard to the President and Vice President, it is impossible to believe that FBI Director Louis Freeh would concur in any such decision. It is an open secret in Washington that he believes the appointment is long overdue. In an October 3 Washington Post article, Susan Schmidt and Robert Suro cataloged ongoing complaints from FBI investigators that Justice guidelines actively prevented them from gathering evidence against "covered persons" under the Independent Counsel Act. Those who've been in joint briefings on

Louis Freeh

Capitol Hill say that as the Attorney General explains her reasons for refusing an appointment, the director sits with his teeth clenched until jaw muscles start to twitch.

The Justice campaign-finance investigation is at best a curious legal exercise. In her testimony to Henry Hyde's Judiciary Committee, Ms. Reno was at pains to describe its extent: a staff of 120, hundreds of interviews, millions of pages of documents. She repeatedly refused to discuss details on the grounds of grand jury secrecy. To complaints about failing to procure the White House tapes, she pointed out that an active grand jury investigation was under way, and the law "does not allow me to discuss grand jury subpoenas and their enforcement."

Trouble is, the independent counsel law specifies, "In conducting preliminary investigations under this chapter, the Attorney General shall have no authority to convene grand juries, plea bargain, grant immunity, or issue subpoenas." The thought is that if a subpoena needs to be issued, an independent counsel needs to be appointed. Presumably the grand jury's mandate, and its interest in White House tapes, runs only to non-covered persons. But Ms. Reno did not explain this to the committee.

Ms. Reno and her advisers have been creative in coming up with arguments against appointing an independent counsel. They have tried to narrow the question away from a pattern of conspiracy and into trivial events -- as Representative Bob Barr put it, examining the taillight of the 37th car in a 50-car pileup. So come December 2, it is not impossible that she will determine that there are no reasonable grounds for future investigation.

But Director Freeh will no longer have to clench his teeth. Under the law, the independent counsel decision is clearly Ms. Reno's call, and he's had no standing to object. Her promise to the committee is of course not legally binding; she still has the authority to overrule him, as President Nixon had the authority to fire Watergate special prosecutor Archibald Cox. But with the testimony invoking his name Mr. Freeh is free; he will have every reason to go public. Indeed, he will have no choice, since Congress and the press will immediately ask him whether he concurs.

Ms. Reno, in short, seems to have painted herself into a corner. Come December 2, she will have two choices: Go ahead with an independent counsel, or face a confrontation with the FBI. Who knows which Janet Reno might herself choose? But her boss at the White House will have to calculate where his political interests lie, choosing between the slow torture of another independent counsel, or a possible firestorm with the one law enforcement figure in his Administration who retains an aura of integrity.

Review & Outlook

Asides

Carey's Accomplices?

Former federal judge Kenneth Conboy did more than throw Ron Carey off the ballot for re-election as Teamster president yesterday. He also named several other parties who were involved in the scheme to illegally divert union money into Mr. Carey's campaign. Judge Conboy said Service Employees President Andy Stern, the AFL-CIO and officials of the American Federation of State, County and Municipal Employees were allegedly involved. Most intriguing was Mr. Conboy's finding that Mr. Carey personally phoned Clinton-Gore finance director Terry McAuliffe to thank him for raising what Mr. Conboy calls improper campaign funds. The independent counsel statute that Attorney General Janet Reno refuses to trigger includes officials of national presidential campaign committees among its covered parties. The Teamsters scandal could have far-reaching implications if it leads to a full-blown investigation of union contributions in the 1996 elections.

REVIEW & OUTLOOK

The Trouble With the Unions

It's time for a close, hard look at the role U.S. labor unions now play in politics. Yes, we all agree the system benefits from the widest political participation, but the issue here is whether the unions' current political role is doing more to tarnish and wreck the system than improve it.

Ron Carey, president of the 1.4 million-member Teamsters union, has been barred from seeking re-election after a federal election officer found he had illegally diverted $1 million in union funds into his campaign. Also this month another federal monitor called for the removal of Arthur Coia as president of the 700,000-member Laborers union over charges he had ties to organized crime. Most every institution engaged in politics is subject to some sort of checks and balances. The unions' position, however is very much unbalanced.

U.S. labor law was largely crafted in the New Deal 1930s and was based not on common law, but on a notion that competing power blocs such as big business and labor would dominate society and had to be "managed" by regulators. This helps explain why unions enjoy an exemption from class-action suits and in most states they can require the payment of union dues or fees to hold certain jobs. Such deviations from the legal norm have given unions a state-sanctioned coercive power that wouldn't be tolerated in any other area of American life.

Unions collect billions of dollars every year in mandatory dues and fees from members, and much of it is spent on politics. In 1988 the

Supreme Court's *Beck* decision by liberal icon William Brennan held that union members are entitled to stop union leaders from using other people's money, namely their dues, for politics with which they disagree. But the Clinton Administration rescinded regulations enforcing *Beck*, and it is effectively impossible for the one-third or more of union members who routinely vote Republican to reduce the money that unions spend on politics—more than 95% of which goes to Democrats.

In 1996, the union leadership felt threatened by the GOP takeover of Congress and plowed an additional $35 million into attack ads that all but claimed Republicans would throw their grandmothers out of trains. Because much of this money was taken from union dues in violation of *Beck*, unions probably represented the largest single improper infusion of money into the now infamous 1996 campaign. Yet coercive union dues money in politics remains the one issue that campaign finance reformers won't discuss.

They should, because the union's ability to channel other people's money into maintaining political clout tempts the weak and attracts outright crooks. Look at the individuals caught in the web of Teamsters/DNC scandals for proof of that.

Efforts to maintain this status quo by the union leadership can also veer into violence and intimidation. During the August Teamsters strike against United Parcel Service, Rod Carter, a former University of Miami linebacker who drove a truck for UPS, decided to work through the strike to support his family. His decision was mentioned one day on the local TV news. A few hours later, his wife received a threatening phone call at home from a man who said his name was Benny. The next day six Teamsters jumped Mr. Carter with an ice pick, wounding him.

The Dade County State Attorney's office has charged three Teamsters, including a Benigno Rojas, with attempted second-degree murder. Their trial is set for December 8. Two of the defendants have already pleaded guilty and are listed as possible state's witnesses. David Weinstein, an assistant state's attorney, confirms that phone records from the case show a call was placed to Mr. Carter's house from the home of Teamster Local 769 President Anthony Cannestro the same night Mrs. Carter heard from "Benny." Mr. Carter is contemplating a civil suit against the union.

Given that the President refuses to vigorously enforce a Supreme

Court decision or laws against union excesses, citizens in California and other states are acting. Last week, the signatures of 800,000 Californians were filed to place a "paycheck protection" initiative on the June 1998 ballot. It would require employers and unions to seek written permission from workers before any part of their dues or salary could be used in political campaigns. A similar law passed in Washington state in 1992 with 72% support; since then the number of teachers who contribute to their union's PAC has declined to 8,000 from 48,000.

Given such results, unions are vowing to spend $20 million to $30 million to defeat the California initiative. They have already called companies and told them that if they support "paycheck protection" they can expect retaliatory anti-business initiatives.

To his credit, GOP Governor Pete Wilson has put the issue on his front burner. He urges a strong fight to end "this shameful political shakedown that blatantly violates the rights of workers." Republicans back in Washington have so far displayed a simpering timidity toward taking on their political opponents. Whatever their relationship with Bill Clinton, we don't see how they can justify not joining the battle against these destructive, coercive union practices.

LEISURE & ARTS

An Impeachment Scenario

By Martin Anderson

It should be said straight out that "The Impeachment of William Jefferson Clinton" (Regnery, 275 pages, $24.95) is not for the politically fainthearted. It is about thinking the unthinkable—and making it seem plausible. The authors are "Anonymous" (whoever that may be) and R. Emmett Tyrrell, the editor of The American Spectator. Through his magazine, Mr. Tyrrell has courageously investigated the scandals surrounding the Clinton administration during the past five years.

Today, if you were to bring up the idea of impeaching the president in polite society, you 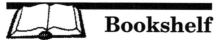 **Bookshelf** would be met with arched eyebrows, condescension, derision or contempt—or all of the above. Mr. Tyrrell and his co-author say: . . . hold on, wait a minute—look at the record, the whole sorry, sickening list of charges and allegations leveled against our 42nd president.

Look at the abuse of presidential power in the Travelgate affair, the illegal possession of 900 confidential FBI files of former White House staff members, the use of taxpayer money to build a political data base in the White House containing hundreds of thousands of names, the use of the IRS to intimidate political opponents, the obstruction of justice in the investigation of the death of White

House adviser Vincent Foster, the Whitewater affair and campaign finance corruption in 1996.

The charges come so fast and furious that even political pros and media pundits cannot keep up with them. Trying to get a taste of the Clinton scandals is like trying to drink water from a wide-open fire hydrant.

Mr. Tyrrell's book, which is part fact and part fiction, reminds us that there is more at stake here than mere media sensationalism or partisan bickering. It gathers together the key facts of a growing number of abuses of power—a constitutional matter. It pulls material from news reports, congressional hearings and subpoenaed documents. Then it moves forward to 1998 and shifts into a fictional mode, deftly creating possible political actions and media commentary, weaving a plausible and disturbing case for impeachment. As the book proceeds into this political hell it lets the reader decide at each step of the journey whether or not it is reasonable to continue. It's easy to take the whole trip.

Many people seem to believe that to impeach a president is to convict him. Mr. Tyrrell and "Anonymous" take care to point out that this is not the case. An impeachment is like an indictment; it just says there is enough evidence of wrongdoing, hard or circumstantial, to have a trial. The essential question the authors pose is whether there is sufficient evidence to support impeachment proceedings in the House against President Clinton.

Now, for most Americans, even to ask such a question about a president is preposterous and repellent. That's a healthy reaction, even when there are grounds for taking the question seriously. And perhaps we can, in fact, set to one side the charges that our president lies, or that he may have bent the law in raising campaign funds. But we have a harder time ignoring the possibility that he may have used the powers of his office to hurt or intimidate his fellow citizens.

Is the evidence compelling? The book says, "You decide." What is engaging about "The Impeachment of William Jefferson Clinton" is the use of mystery and fantasy to draw the reader into examining the disturbing political question of impeachment. And there are reasons not to dismiss this "nonfiction novel" out of hand.

Take the case of the FBI files. It is still a mystery how the confidential files of 900 men and women who worked in the White

House for Presidents Reagan and Bush, and who are now private citizens, found their way into file cabinets located in the Clinton White House. I have worked in the White House for two presidents. I know the FBI. I know what kind of damaging material is contained in the files of sensitive background investigations of White House staff members. And I know (as who does not?) that those files cannot walk by themselves from FBI headquarters to the White House.

Why should we be concerned about wandering FBI files? Because there is at least one good reason for operatives to go to the trouble of acquiring hundreds of confidential files of their political opponents -- and that is political blackmail.

Is the possession of 900 secret FBI files by the White House sufficient grounds for charging "high crimes and misdemeanors"? Are there other alleged Clinton abuses -- concerning the use of the FBI in Travelgate, Whitewater perjury, the soliciting of hush money for Web Hubbell or the rifling of Vince Foster's office -- that fit impeachment categories even more stringently?

To answer those questions would be to give the plot away.

Mr. Anderson is a senior fellow at the Hoover Institution of Stanford University.

Thwarting Justice

Throughout the winter of 1997, pressure mounted on Attorney General Reno to name a special prosecutor in the campaign finance matter. A December deadline loomed on whether to close out a Justice Department preliminary investigation into the narrow question of fund-raising phone calls by the President and Vice President, or proceed to the next stage, a request to a special three-judge panel of the U.S. Court of Appeals for an independent counsel.

One of the worst-kept secrets in Washington at the time was FBI Director Louis Freeh's opinion that a counsel should be named. In October testimony before the House Judiciary Committee, Ms. Reno had declared that "Director Freeh and I will jointly approve any investigations close-out before it is closed out." Nevertheless, on December 2, she rejected the appointment of a counsel, prompting a barrage of criticism.

In other developments, Independent Counsel Kenneth Starr closed his investigation of the death of deputy White House counsel Vincent Foster with a comprehensive report detailing his clinical depression and suicide. In the probe of former Agriculture Secretary Mike Espy, a federal jury in Washington convicted Mr. Espy's chief of staff, Ronald Blackley, of lying to conceal payments he received from associates doing business with the Agriculture Department. The Journal closely followed the investigation by Independent Counsel Donald Smaltz, paying particular attention to his running battles with the Justice Department. The significance of the Blackley conviction, the Journal wrote, rested in the fact that Mr. Smaltz "had to fight a battle of nearly two years with the Department of Justice merely to bring Mr. Blackley to trial."

The catalog of problems at the Department of Justice was growing longer.

REVIEW & OUTLOOK

Freeing Freeh—II

The weekend news coverage has been full of speculation that Attorney General Janet Reno is about to let the President and Vice President off the hook on the political contributions scandal. Leaks say her aides have recommended against appointing an independent counsel, and that the White House is breathing easier.

We search this coverage in vain for any mention of FBI Director Louis Freeh, and the extraordinary promise that Ms. Reno made to Rep. Henry Hyde's Judiciary Committee October 15. So we guess we should repeat some of the points in "Freeing Freeh" in these columns November 14. The Attorney General twice said she would not close any investigation "unless Director Freeh and I sign off on it."

A formal "preliminary investigation" is under way on whether Ms. Reno should appoint an independent counsel for the President and Vice President. The law specifies she must go ahead with the appointment unless she is able to "determine that there are no reasonable grounds to believe that further investigation is warranted." That would sure sound to us like closing down an investigation, and the world would certainly be entitled to ask if Director Freeh has signed off.

The excuse factory at Ms. Reno's Public Integrity section has focused on particular phone calls, oblivious to illegal actions directed by a conspiracy to do *anything* necessary to fund Dick Morris's grandiose re-election plans. As Rep. Bob Barr put it during Ms. Reno's testimony, this is like finding a defective taillight in the 37th car in a 50-car pileup. Never mind that the President himself depicts a conflict of interest in telling reporters, "I have gone out of my way to have no conversation with her—about this or, frankly, anything else, which I'm not sure is so good."

The import of the Reno promise is that the public will learn whether the Director shares Public Integrity's narrow view. The assumption on Capitol Hill is that he emphatically rejects it, but has deferred to the Attorney General. With her October 15 promise, a rejection of an independent counsel would give him an obligation to go public. Indeed, it would open the way for Chairman Hyde's committee to inquire whether his agents have been obstructed in determining whether the campaign finance investigation leads to those covered under the Independent Counsel Act.

Louis Freeh

"You can't ask someone whether a covered person committed a crime," is the way one Justice Department lawyer described the procedure to Susan Schmidt and Robert Suro of the Washington Post. Their October 3 article described how the FBI wanted to proceed directly to the President and Vice President, but that on this issue the Justice Department task force "studiously avoided seeking out new information."

The approach has apparently become more vigorous under the new task force head, Charles La Bella. But the independent counsel law is still being ignored. Justice brags about finally questioning the President and Vice President, but this only proves that the time for an independent counsel is already past.

Perhaps this week Ms. Reno will be able to see the whole pileup, not the taillight on the 37th car. If not, she will be doing the law a disservice, and herself as well. And she will certainly be putting Mr. Freeh on the spot.

Editorial Feature

In Re: Vincent Foster

By MICAH MORRISON

Back in 1994, with the release of Special Counsel Robert Fiske's report on the death of Deputy White House Counsel Vincent Foster, The Wall Street Journal stated an explicit position: "Barring some unimaginable new disclosure, we find no reason to doubt that the former White House counsel committed suicide in Fort Marcy Park."

Clinical depression was from the first the simple, Occam's razor explanation for the spectacular death in July 1993. But the initial reports from Mr. Foster's associates denied evidence of depression and instead painted a picture of a person both steeled and stalwart. We—speaking here for not only myself but the other editorial page writers and editors who contributed to Clinton coverage—learned in conversations with psychiatrists over the year that close associates of a suicide, in subconscious self-defense, typically start by denying any symptoms of depression. But also that further investigation nearly always reveals troubling incidents or a family history of the disease. The Fiske report finally provided this essential key, though its conclusions were somewhat clouded by the sweeping denial that Whitewater had anything to do with Mr. Foster's mood—instead dwelling on our own editorial series, "Who Is Vincent Foster?" and "Who Is Webster Hubbell?"

New Disclosures

Now Independent Counsel Kenneth Starr has compiled the results of a much more comprehensive investigation, a 114-page "Report on the Death of Vincent W. Foster Jr.," released in October by the Special Division of the U.S. Court of Appeals for the District of Columbia. "An evident clinical depression," was the diagnosis of Alan Berman, executive director of the American Association of Suicidology and one of the many experts Mr. Starr brought in to assist with the probe. "There are signs of an intense and profound anguish, harsh self-evaluation, shame, and chronic fear." Mr. Foster's "last 96 hours show clear signs of crisis and uncharacteristic vulnerability," Dr. Berman writes. In poignant new disclosures,

Vincent Foster

Mr. Starr reports that Mr. Foster cried while talking to his wife on the Friday before his death, and in a letter to a friend wrote that "pressure, financial sacrifice, and family disruption are the price of public service at this level. As they say, 'The wind blows hardest at the top of the mountain.' "

The wind was blowing hard at Mr. Foster from many directions. Though there was no "single, obvious triggering event" to explain the suicide, Mr. Starr writes that Mr. Foster seemed particularly plagued by the Travel Office affair. Other matters troubling him included litigation surrounding Hillary Clinton's Health Care Task Force and media criticism, led by our editorials. But also issues related to the Clintons' personal finances, their tax returns and the "1992 sale of their interest in Whitewater." (Working on the Clinton tax returns, Mr. Foster noted that Whitewater was a "can of worms"; one big problem may have been failure to report a $32,000 gift from Jim McDougal in assuming Whitewater's debts.)

In counterpoint to Mr. Starr comes "The Strange Death of Vincent Foster" (The Free Press, 316 pages, $25), by Christopher Ruddy, skeptic-in-chief of the official explanation. And also "The Secret Life of Bill Clinton" (Regnery, 460 pages, $24.95), by Ambrose Evans-Pritchard. And it happens that this week Clinton intimate and former Associate Attorney General Webster Hubbell publishes his portrait of Mr. Foster's decline and other Washington travails in "Friends in High Places" (William Morrow, 334 pages, price: 100,000 riadys—just kidding).

Mr. Starr's report convincingly answers the questions Mr. Ruddy has raised over the years and repeats in his book. Yes, the testimony of family members and forensic evidence indicates that Mr. Foster did own the gun by which he died. No, there wasn't a second "neck wound," or four forensic pathologists or one of the six autopsy attendants would have noticed it. Yes, microscopic examination shows there was "soil-like" debris on Mr. Foster's shoes. No, Craig Livingstone and William Kennedy did not arrive to identify Mr. Foster's body until more than an hour after initially overlooked car keys were discovered in his pocket. Yes, carpet fibers on Mr. Foster's clothing mostly matched those in his home and car.

Most of the other allegations, including the recollections of much-touted witness Patrick Knowlton, represent the confusions inevitable in any large investigation of a dramatic event. The alternative would be a coverup embracing President Clinton, Mr. Fiske, Mr. Starr, two congressional investigations and by now a cast of thousands. Get real.

Mr. Starr's refutation has unleashed a torrent of criticism of Mr. Ruddy, especially from conservative magazines anxious to divorce themselves from allegations of conspiracy-mongering. Having declared our own view back in 1994, we'll still decline to join the current orgy of Ruddy-bashing. Yes, he and a few allies are obsessive in refusing to accept the answers Mr. Starr now provides. But that does not mean his questions never should have been asked.

Consider the circumstances: A high official and friend of the president died of a gunshot wound in an isolated park. The head of the FBI had been summarily fired the preceding weekend. The investigation fell into the clumsy hands of the U.S. Park Service police. Except for a few Polaroids, the crime-scene photos didn't turn out. There were no autopsy X-rays, though the paperwork for them incorrectly indicated they had been taken. White House personnel raided Mr. Foster's office the night of his death, and later obstructed a search by official investigators. New accounts of files and notebooks missing from the Foster office kept surfacing. New witnesses kept popping out of the woodwork, often as a result of such conspiracy theorists as G. Gordon Liddy. With most of the mainstream press not asking the obvious questions, should anyone who does be dismissed as ipso facto a nut?

Webster Hubbell's new book, though obviously self-serving, adds some interesting inside details to the story of Vincent Foster's decline. He writes that Mr. Foster was upset that the White House staff refused to provide the Journal with his photograph. When we ran an editorial featuring a silhouette with a question mark over Mr. Foster's name, Mr. Hubbell says he "later wondered if the question mark felt too close for comfort." He agrees that Mr. Foster was particularly worried about the handling of the Travel Office firings, and also the prospect of facing congressional hearings. Most interesting of all is the role of Hillary Clinton, too busy to listen to her old colleague, snapping " 'Fix it, Vince!' " over the legal problems of the Health Care Task Force. "It hurt him deeply," Mr. Hubbell writes. "The stress was getting to us all."

Insistent Questioning

The personal tragedy of Mr. Foster's death was compounded more than anything else by the massive failure of the initial investigation. That failure has been belatedly but persuasively corrected by Mr. Starr's painstaking efforts; instead of arguing with the Starr report, Christopher Ruddy and the like should take it as a tribute to their insistent questioning. Congress, for its part, could help prevent future debacles by amending the federal assassination statute to give the FBI automatic jurisdiction over apparent suicides of senior officials.

This will not, however, be the last we hear of the strange fate of Vincent Foster. Like Banquo's ghost, his reproachful presence hovers over the Whitewater land deal, the Rose Law Firm billing records, the midnight raid on his White House files and the Travel Office affair. Mr. Starr's current report dryly notes that "those investigations have not concluded." The question is how well those matters will sustain the sort of intense scrutiny Mr. Starr brought to the events in Fort Marcy Park.

Mr. Morrison is a Journal editorial page writer.

REVIEW & OUTLOOK

An Independent Prosecution

The spinmeisters around the Attorney General have been floating for a week the suggestion that today's scheduled puff of smoke from Main Justice will signal no independent counsel investigation into the financial compulsions of the 1996 Clinton-Gore campaign. Any such decision may not go down easily, on several fronts. There was tough talk Sunday from Senator Orrin Hatch about hearings into the impending Reno decision. Even more to the point, yesterday brought a conviction in an independent counsel case that this Justice Department actively opposed.

A federal jury in Washington convicted Ronald Blackley, chief of staff to then-Agriculture Secretary Mike Espy, on three counts of lying to conceal $22,000 he received from associates with business before the agency. The significance of this lies in the fact that Independent Counsel Donald Smaltz had to fight a battle of nearly two years with the Department of Justice merely to bring Mr. Blackley to trial.

In February 1996, the two top officials in Justice's Public Integrity Section, chief Lee Radek and senior independent counsel adviser Jo Ann Farrington, signed a motion before the Special Division of judges of the U.S. Court of Appeals opposing Mr. Smaltz's request for an expansion into Mr. Blackley's activities. Mr. Smaltz had taken the unusual step of going directly to the Special Division of federal judges after Ms. Reno blocked his earlier request for an expanded inquiry into Arkansas poultry giant Tyson Foods.

In the Tyson case, as reported by our Micah Morrison in October, Mr. Smaltz was called on the carpet by Ms. Reno and other top officials and ordered to stop investigating. In the Blackley case, top Justice officials argued before the Special Division that allegations of corrupt activities by Mr. Espy's chief of staff were "not related" to Mr. Smaltz's jurisdiction and that independent counsels could only expand their investigations if Justice said it was all right.

The Special Division ruled against Justice on both counts, saying the matter was indeed related and that the "plain language" of the independent counsel statute "in no way suggests that the concurrence of the Attorney General is required before the court can refer a related matter."

This ruling may be seen as of a piece with other signs of increasing unease on the federal bench with Executive Branch conduct—most famously, last June's Supreme Court rebuffs to the Clintons in the Paula Jones case and Mrs. Clinton's failed bid for governmental attorney-client privilege. And in this instance, when Mr. Blackley—duly indicted—moved to dismiss his case on the grounds that Justice had opposed the jurisdictional expansion, Judge Royce Lamberth offered a stinging rebuke. "In this court's view," Judge Lamberth wrote in a November opinion denying Mr. Blackley's motion, "adherence to an Executive Branch policy that directs a prosecutor to not pursue indictments against Executive Branch employees for their criminal ethical violations is in direct contravention with the task with which an independent counsel is charged."

Whatever one feels about the Independent Counsel Act, it is the law of the land. The burden lies with the Justice Department to make clear its adherence to the law's demands. In a post-conviction statement yesterday, Mr. Smaltz said the Department of Justice's "opposition significantly delayed our investigation and prosecutions."

Review & Outlook

The Reno Decision

Before the dust thrown up by Janet Reno's decision yesterday clouds everything, we'd like to make one point as clearly as possible. The Attorney General and indeed her President have every legal right to decide against the appointment of an independent counsel. But if this country's system is to function at all, there is every reason why that decision should have *political* consequences.

For example, Ms. Reno's decision in October in testimony before Rep. Henry Hyde's Judiciary Committee to involve the Director of

Janet Reno

the FBI in these matters was a *political* calculation. Ms. Reno pledged that "Director Freeh and I will jointly approve any investigations close-out before it is closed out." A moment later, she repeated her promise: "We will not close the matter again, I reiterate, unless Director Freeh and I sign off on it." The die is cast, and this Administration will have to live with what results, like it or not.

White House behavior yesterday suggested they don't at all like Louis Freeh's known preference for letting an independent counsel get to the bottom of the fund-raising incidents. Pressed after giving a non-answer yesterday to whether the White House still had confidence in Mr. Freeh, the White House's Mike McCurry simply snapped: "It is about as good as I am going to do for you."

That's actually a pretty good summary of the Administration's attitude toward Congressional subpoenas or federal judicial orders. Which leaves open the question of just who exactly is going to unravel the story of how this White House set in motion an amazing skein of fund raising that ran from Washington to wherever Charlie Trie is holed up in China.

The press may stay on the case, though newspapers have no power of subpoena and of course a White House aide has already tried to intimidate one writer with a $30 million libel suit. Rep. Dan Burton's hearings in the House promise to keep the lights shining on some of the key players, and he wants Ms. Reno and Director Freeh to appear before his committee next Tuesday. And, of course, Louis Freeh might decide there is no choice but to ramp up the FBI's own investigation into these matters. What's the alternative?

The alternative on the table this morning is to let Janet Reno's Justice Department take care of everything. This would be the Justice Department that Independent Counsel Donald Smaltz blasted Monday in a remarkable public statement following the conviction won by his office of the former Agriculture Secretary's chief of staff. The Smaltz statement said:

Louis Freeh

"While I am of course very pleased with the verdict, I regret DOJ's decision not to prosecute defendant Blackley for his various crimes. Moreover, there was in my judgment no valid basis for DOJ's vigorous opposition to the application we filed with the Special Division of the U.S. Court of Appeals to confirm our right to prosecute. . . . DOJ's opposition significantly delayed our investigation and prosecution."

Miami lawyer David Barrett, serving as independent counsel for the Cisneros case, appears to have had similar problems. Mr. Barrett is the low-profile counsel who was appointed to investigate charges that then-Housing Secretary Henry Cisneros lied to the FBI about payoffs to a former mistress. Apparently Mr. Barrett's trek turned up suggestions of additional matters worth investigating, but according to recent reports in this newspaper and the New York Times, Justice blocked an expanded probe. Now Mr. Barrett wants to see phone records of calls made by the Justice Department's Public Integrity Section personnel.

So let's see—two independent counsels (at least), one FBI Director and one Congress all find themselves in conflict with the Clinton Justice Department and White House right now. It's not a pretty picture.

Meanwhile, political attacks by Clinton surrogates and others on the investigators continue unabated. Last week, unnamed Justice Department officials were in the Times blasting Judge David Sentelle, chief of the three-member Special Division, for political bias, and the independent counsels as "overzealous amateurs."

How now Justice? At her news conference Ms. Reno said, "These decisions do not end our work." What work? Does this mean Ms. Reno's professionals at Public Integrity will go back to focusing on the arcane issue of whether phone calls were made from the White House residence or offices, not broad evidence of conspiracy or conflict of interest? As Rep. Bob Barr has said, this is akin to scrutinizing a broken taillight on the 37th car in a 50-car pileup.

The Clinton campaign-finance pileup is still spread all over the political turnpike. Despite Ms. Reno's decision, we suspect it'll be awhile before the crowds disperse. Specifically, Congress now has two immediate matters to attend to. It should hear out FBI Director Freeh. And it should ask the independent counsels whether Justice has obstructed them.

Letters to the Editor

Obstructionism

Regarding "The Reno Decision" (Review & Outlook, Dec. 3): With the current administration we've all grown more than familiar with the legal term "obstruction of justice." But obstruction by Justice? Now that's new.

KATHRYN B. SLATTERY

New Canaan, Conn.

Editorial Feature

Anyone See a Republican As Tough as Reno?

Anyone who still doubts that Democrats play a rougher brand of politics than Republicans should consider this week's reaction to Janet Reno's nixing of an independent counsel.

Vice President Gore, who should have been relieved, talked trash to the same Republicans Ms. Reno had just dunked on: "Bear in mind that in the days and weeks and months ahead, there will continue to be partisan attacks, politically motivated."

Potomac Watch

By Paul A. Gigot

Janet Reno

Meanwhile, House Judiciary Chairman Henry Hyde, who should have been furious, sounded more like Dr. Jekyll. He found Ms. Reno's stonewall "very disappointing and disheartening" but was lost about what to do next.

"We're going to study the attorney general's response to our letter and all her enclosures," said Mr. Hyde. "We're going to hold further oversight hearings; if necessary, in executive session." Executive session—there's intimidation for you.

Give Mr. Gore credit for understanding what Republicans don't, which is that Ms. Reno has now made this a political battle. This week she may well have spared Mr. Gore and President Clinton from any legal liability for dubious fund raising in 1996.

But she also handed Republicans an issue—a politicized, Nixonian Justice Department—they could pound through 1998, if they have the nerve. Republicans have been so eager to pass the buck to a special counsel that they've forgotten how to hold the White House politically accountable.

This has been the pattern since the beginning of this campaign-finance saga. First Mr. Clinton discovered he could break the campaign laws to finance $40 million of unanswered attack ads making Bob Dole's middle name "Gingrich."

An opposition party that controlled Congress and was serious about power would make a president pay for winning like that. Instead the Democrats, even in the minority, have out-maneuvered Republicans. Fred Thompson went out of his way to be bipartisan in his Senate probe, but was rewarded with John Glenn's footprints on his back.

Another generous Republican, John McCain, has helped Democrats with their strategy of changing the subject to campaign-finance "reform." Mr. McCain has even been gracious enough to force a Senate vote this spring that could give some Democrats an issue in November. So here we are: Voters could yet blame Republicans in the next election because Mr. Clinton stole the last one.

Henry Hyde

Republicans offer various excuses for this predicament, but none are very convincing. One is that the press gives the White House a pass, which is sometimes true but isn't this time. The New York Times was harder on Ms. Reno this week than they were. Even the networks reported FBI Director Louis Freeh's break with Ms. Reno. Without a special counsel, the press may be more inclined to report what Congress discovers.

Another excuse is that Americans don't care, and thus probing scandal won't play in focus groups. But I doubt Al Gore would agree. Even without a special counsel, the story has already tarnished Mr. Clean and made other Democrats readier to challenge him in 2000.

And in 1998 the issue of politicized law enforcement will at least mobilize Republicans to vote. Turnout matters in nonpresidential elections, as Democrats learned to their glee in the Watergate election of 1974.

In any case, Congress has a constitutional obligation to oversee the executive, regardless of popularity. If Republicans believe what they say about the special counsel law, they have a duty to investigate why it's being flouted.

A system of checks and balances requires someone willing to do the checking. If the White House can spurn Congress this easily, it will only get more brazen. Congress can expect three more years of stonewalled subpoenas, overlooked videotapes and lost billing records.

If Ms. Reno were a Republican attorney general, says former Reagan Justice official Ted Olson, Democrat "John Dingell would have had the subpoena letter out before Janet Reno got to work Wednesday morning. And she gets to work early."

Mr. Olson says Republicans can invite Mr. Freeh to testify, as House Chairman Dan Burton plans to do next week. They can also probe the politicization of Justice's "public integrity" section, as well as use their spending and confirmation powers for leverage.

Republicans needn't impeach Ms. Reno, merely her undeserved reputation for independence. This is the same attorney general, after all, who fired all 93 U.S. attorneys in 1993 at the request of presidential pal Webster Hubbell. Then a year later, on the day he resigned, she called the soon-to-be-felon "a tireless crusader for doing justice, for doing the right thing." She added, "I don't believe he did a thing wrong."

Sure, oversight is hard. Democrats will shout "partisanship." Columnists will be scornful. But that's the price of power. If Republicans won't exercise that power, they might as well turn it over to people who will—the Democrats.

REVIEW & OUTLOOK

The Unknown Seaman

If there is a constant in Washington it is that any story involving the Clinton White House will always have a second act. Remember the stories last month over special dispensations and campaign contributions for burials at Arlington National Cemetery? White House spokesman Mike McCurry blamed "the hate-radio circuit" for inflaming a story that had "no basis in fact." Well, it appears more facts are starting to come in.

The most curious burial waiver went to Larry Lawrence, who died in 1996 while serving as U.S. ambassador to Switzerland. Burial at Arlington is normally accorded only to veterans with the highest military honors. The White House attacked as "scurrilous" the allegation that Mr. Lawrence's role as a former fund-raiser for the Clinton-Gore ticket could have been a factor. White House spokesman Lanny Davis said Mr. Lawrence had served in the Merchant Marine during World War II, where he had been "thrown overboard and suffered a serious head injury" that would have qualified him for a Purple Heart had he been in the Navy.

Yesterday Rep. Terry Everett, chairman of a House subcommittee on veterans affairs, reported that his committee's investigators have found no records that Mr. Lawrence ever served in the Merchant Marine much less was injured. The Associated Press, checking with Administration sources, reported yesterday that a State Department background check in 1993 also turned up no records of his service, but "because there were no contradictory documents, the department chose not to pursue it further, one official said."

Larry Lawrence was indeed close to Bill Clinton. The San Diego businessman gave $200,000 to candidate Clinton in 1992 and hosted him for a week long Presidential vacation at his home in 1994. His diplomatic appointment was controversial. His flubbed answers to questions during confirmation hearings caused a Democrat-controlled Foreign Relations Committee to send his nomination to the floor on a tie vote, without a recommendation. President Clinton delivered the eulogy at Mr. Lawrence's funeral in 1996.

Back after the Arlington burial tumult subsided, a closer second look appeared in a column by Arianna Huffington. Mr. Lawrence's executive assistant, Norma Niccols, told the syndicated columnist that his wartime injury wasn't in his biography when he hired her; it was added in the 1980s, after Ms. Niccols was told to research the names of U.S. ships damaged during World War II.

Now other questions about the 10 burial waivers that were granted over the objection of Arlington cemetery officials are surfacing. Last week, the Associated Press reported that Defense Secretary Bill Cohen intervened to help a Republican Congressional staffer bury his father in Arlington. Roland Charles, a staffer for GOP Rep. Dennis Hastert, used a Congressional letterhead to seek a private meeting with Secretary Cohen. Army Secretary West advised against such a meeting and repeated his opposition to a waiver. Two days later Mr. Cohen, a former GOP Senator, met with Mr. Charles, and by the end of that day Secretary West had reversed himself and granted the waiver. Both men insist Mr. Cohen did not intervene.

None of this means that the White House was selling sacred burial plots to campaign contributors, as some speculation ran last month. But by and large the rest of the press and various pundits have been content to accept on its face the White House's defense of the Lawrence case and the other Arlington waivers. Once again, however, flat denials out of the White House are beginning to turn into a pumpkin.

Most Capitol Hill Republicans timidly sidestepped the issue after they realized the scandal could be bipartisan. But veterans have a right to know what part favoritism played here for a scarce Arlington burial plot, and presumably Rep. Everett will see his probe through to a conclusion.

Letters to the Editor

My Father's Burial at Arlington

Your Dec. 5 editorial was inaccurate and highly offensive to my family and me. This painful-to-read editorial, in which I was incorrectly referred to as "Roland Charles," pertained to burials at Arlington National Cemetery, and cast in a negative light both my father and myself in the same space as the mysterious case of "The Unknown Seaman."

My father's case is so thoroughly opposite and unrelated, and my activities concerning his burial so completely within the waiver procedures in place at Arlington that I can only believe my family has been placed in the public eye because of my professional position as a Republican staff member in the House of Representatives. You did not initiate the story, but I was genuinely surprised that you repeated the incorrect assertions without attempting to contact me.

In 1962, Arlington Cemetery selected a site for my grandfather, who had served in the Navy. That site, in which my grandmother was also later buried, is near an oak tree. In this grave site, my father was expected to be buried with his father in vertical "layers." Like thousands of other military family members, my father wished to be buried with his parents. This entitlement has never been disputed by Arlington or anyone else, and was not related to my father's own eight years of Navy service.

On July 18, 1997, my father died after spending his last year in a Veterans' Hospital. As his eldest child, and because my parents had been divorced many years, the burial obligation fell to me. As I proceeded to have him buried, my initial call gave no hint of a problem. I was asked to fax the vitals of my father's death and his military papers to the cemetery. I did so, not on "congressional letterhead," but on the standard fax cover sheet used by the office. So the record is clear: I did not at any time "use a congressional letterhead to seek a private meeting with Secretary Cohen." I never wrote to Secretary Cohen seeking a private meeting on any stationery.

A return call from the cemetery revealed that the oak tree had expanded its root system during the intervening 35 years between my grandfather's and father's passings. The cemetery explained that the root system had thoroughly consumed my grandfather's and grandmother's site -- a situation that they said had "never before occurred in the history of the cemetery."

In view of my father's uncontroverted entitlement to burial at Arlington, I asked whether the roots could be snipped, a smaller casket used or burial effected beneath the root system. I was told that, for "protection of aesthetics," these were not options; the cemetery did not want to risk damaging the tree. I asked what could be done, and they instructed me that the White House or Pentagon can give a "waiver" when circumstances warrant, and that this was my only course of appeal. Thus, I called both the White House and the Pentagon to put in a waiver request.

I now know, based on an internal memo brought to my attention by the media, that former Assistant Secretary Sara Lister recommended to Secretary of the Army Togo West that the waiver be declined. Remarkably, Ms. Lister failed to put in the memo that the basis for the request was that a tree's root system had thoroughly consumed the pre-existing entitlement -- an unprecedented occurrence.

Eventually, because of the abnormality of the case, I was summoned to plead the facts to the Department of Defense. During that meeting, Secretary Cohen popped in briefly, listened to facts, gave no commitment, offered his sympathies and left. The most that I could learn, as I waited for a ruling, was that the secretary of the Army was continuing to consider the case. Eventually, I received a call from the cemetery and was told that Secretary West had reviewed the facts and, as he later stated at some length, believed -- after learning that a root system had consumed the gravesite -- "this family had a justifiable expectation" of the burial at Arlington.

ROBERT B. CHARLES

Chevy Chase, Md.

Review & Outlook

Steely Rectitude

When Janet Reno testifies in Congress today, she will have one strong thing going for her. She actually believes there are no grounds for appointing an independent counsel for the President, the Vice President and Hazel O'Leary. After all, she built her career on persuading herself of impossible things.

The 11th Circuit Court of Appeals is just now taking another look at one of Ms. Reno's landmark cases in her highest previous office, Dade County prosecutor. It has accepted an appeal of the conviction of former police officer Grant Snowden, who has spent the last 11 1/2 years in prison as the culmination of Ms. Reno's charge against alleged child molesters. Her performance here was equal to the most outrageous of any of the runaway sex-abuse prosecutions that ruined countless lives and reputations in the 1980s.

Those included the case against Bobby Finje—a devout, 14-year-old church worker. He was held for 20 months and portrayed as a depraved criminal on the basis of a single accusation from a child who said she was afraid of Bobby. It later turned out that she was afraid of loud games Bobby played. To ensure full media treatment, the state attorney decided to try young Finje as an adult. In this instance, Ms. Reno did not prevail, a jury having refused to convict.

Mr. Snowden, a law officer who had compiled a distinguished record, was also acquitted. But in the fever of molestation accusations yielding so much political opportunity for ambitious prosecutors, Ms. Reno and her eager prosecutors came up with newer charges and newer child witnesses. In the Finje case, the children said that the accused had eaten a newborn baby and danced naked on the roof. In the Snowden case, interviewer Laurie Braga—anointed by Ms. Reno as an "expert" who knew how to get children to testify—led a four-year-old child through a long series of sexual adventures played out on a doll. Previous to this, the child had never before had a word to say about any sexual act, but Ms. Braga persuaded a jury the exercise with the doll proved what Grant Snowden did to

Janet Reno

her. He was convicted and sentenced to no less than five consecutive life terms.

As her first act as Attorney General, Ms. Reno persuaded herself to summarily fire all sitting U.S. Attorneys, an unprecedented action that conveniently produced openings in Little Rock and the District of Columbia, jurisdictions of particular interest to the Clintons. But her gritty countenance won the hearts of TV viewers by accepting "responsibility" for the raid on the Branch Davidian compound in Waco, where 95 persons died in the most mismanaged law-enforcement operation in U.S. history. It developed that she'd been told child abuse was involved, and that during the crisis she'd delegated the task of talking to the President to Clinton crony Webster Hubbell. When Mr. Hubbell departed the Justice Department on his way to a felony conviction, she praised him as a "tireless crusader" and volunteered, "I don't think he did a thing wrong."

In Congressional hearings today, Ms. Reno will defend her finding that after a preliminary investigation no independent counsel is needed; that in the words of the statute, there are "no reasonable grounds to believe that further investigation is warranted." This will be a true prodigy of self-persuasion. After all, FBI Director Louis Freeh thinks there are plenty of grounds for further investigation; is he unreasonable? After all, Ms. Reno herself says that investigation will continue. Indeed, she says that she refuses to honor a Congressional subpoena for Mr. Freeh's memo because it would reveal details of an ongoing investigation.

The whole intent of this law is that if high officials "may have violated" federal law, any ongoing investigation should be given to an independent counsel. Yet no doubt the Attorney General will grit her way through this logical minefield, telling us that black is white with all of her usual steely rectitude.

It will not matter that the President headed a meeting at which John Huang was installed as a fund-raiser at the Democratic National Committee, where he clearly broke the law; there are "no reasonable grounds to believe that further investigation is warranted" into whether the President ordered or condoned the lawbreaking. It will not matter that the Vice President spoke at a Buddhist monastery; there are "no reasonable grounds to believe that further investigation is warranted" into whether he was dense enough not to understand the illegal sham taking place.

It will not matter that Johnny Chung said that Energy Secretary O'Leary thanked him for a $25,000 contribution to a favored charity, made after an Energy Department official told him the contribution was the price for meeting her. Mr. Chung's account is "little more than speculation," Ms. Reno has declared with her straightest face. Surely there are "no reasonable grounds to believe that further investigation is warranted."

Ms. Reno comes from a world that gives little standing to the precise words of a statute, or the precedent of letting U.S. Attorneys serve until their replacements had been named, or the implausibility of avidly coached child witnesses. She will choose which children to believe, and which laws should be followed. She is, after all, a woman of Javert-like mien and rectitude.

Editorial Feature

A Constitutional Campaign Finance Plan

By Michael W. McConnell

Janet Reno's refusal to seek an independent counsel to investigate Clinton fund raising is likely to refocus debate on systemic campaign finance reform. Senate Majority Leader Trent Lott yanked the McCain-Feingold campaign finance reform bill off the agenda for this year. But thanks to Democratic filibustering, the bill will be back before Congress next spring. The result will be the same. Republicans will refuse to support legislation unless it prevents labor unions from using coerced dues from workers; Democrats will refuse to support it if it does. Stalemate.

The disagreement over union money is only the public face of a deeper and more intractable problem. Everyone can agree that the present system needs to be changed, but most proposals for "reform," including McCain-Feingold, would probably make matters worse.

And such efforts to control political speech inevitably founder on the shoals of the First Amendment. It *may* be constitutional to restrict contributions to candidates or political parties (though most First Amendment purists doubt even this). But restricting direct contributions simply forces would-be contributors to find indirect means of supporting candidates . To be effective, therefore, the restrictions have to extend far beyond limits on contributions.

The Very Core

McCain-Feingold, for example, would make it a crime to run an advertisement stating your views on the candidate within 60 days of the election. Under no coherent reading of the Constitution could it be permissible to prohibit citizens and voluntary associations from attempting to persuade their fellow citizens how to vote. That is the very core of the First Amendment.

What's more, these proposals would make it even more difficult for challengers to mount effective campaigns against incumbents, who enjoy built-in advantages of media access, taxpayer-funded mailings, name recognition and constituent service. Nor would public financing solve the problem. There is no neutral formula for allocating funds, and most proposals would favor the candidates of the two major parties at the expense of all others.

We need to be clear about the problems with the current system and about the purpose of reform. The problem is *not* too much campaign speech. Nor is the problem that "special interests" are using their resources to influence public opinion. That's what freedom of speech is all about. Pro-lifers, environmentalists and free-traders have a right to make their opinions known to the public. All of us are "special interests."

John McCain

The problem is that elected officials use the powers of office to extract contributions and hence to perpetuate themselves in office. (That is why the prohibition on the use of publicly funded telephones, offices and computers for partisan fund raising is more than just a technicality.) The flip side of this is that contributors seek to influence public policy not by persuasion but by currying favor with officeholders. Roger Tamraz contributed hundreds of thousands of dollars to the Democratic Party not because he believes in its philosophy of government. He did it in hopes that the Clinton administration would return the favor.

As the Supreme Court held in *Buckley v. Valeo*, there is no constitutional barrier to laws designed to combat this kind of corruption. Americans have a First Amendment right to do what we can to sway public opinion, but not to buy privileged access to our leaders by giving money to their campaigns.

I have not seen any plausible comprehensive solution to this problem, and I suspect that no such solution exists. But there are reforms that would reduce the opportunities for official corruption without infringing free speech rights or further entrenching incumbents. Instead of repeating the McCain-Feingold standoff, I suggest that Congress consider more productive proposals.

First, Congress should enact tax credits for modest political contributions (refundable, so that the poor have equal opportunity). Limits of perhaps $250 per candidate, with a $1,000 annual cap per taxpayer, would be about right. This would make it easier for candidates to raise money from ordinary people, and easier for ordinary people to participate in politics through contributions. It would be the equivalent of partial public financing, but without government control over how the funds are divided. The cost would be small change in today's budget.

Second, Congress should abolish political action committees and raise limits on individual contributions. The wrongheaded campaign reforms of the 1970s placed strict limits on individual contributions— but allowed PACs to aggregate contributions and donate them to candidates in $5,000 units. This "reform" magnified the power of interest groups and lobbyists and restricted the influence of individuals.

Russell Feingold

Individuals have many different opinions and interests, and unless their contributions are large enough to warrant invitation to a White House coffee or its equivalent, the candidate does not necessarily know what those interests are. The interests of a PAC lobbyist, by contrast, are all too clear. It also bears mention that PACs give almost 13 times as much money to incumbents as to challengers—a sure sign that the purpose of the contribution is to buy influence rather than to persuade voters.

A more radical proposal is to create a mechanism for anonymous contributions above the ordinary legal limit. If a candidate does not know who made the contribution, then there is no possibility of improper influence. This would also bolster the argument that contribution limits are constitutional. If everyone is free (within certain generous limits) to contribute to the candidate of his choice, then the only question is whether there is a constitutional right to make one's generosity known to the candidate. That is not freedom of speech. The constitutional right is to persuade one's fellow citizens—not to make an officeholder grateful. To be sure, there may be practical problems in ensuring anonymity. Contributors are extraordinarily clever about evading the laws in this area. But I think campaign nondisclosure merits serious consideration.

Fourth, Congress should ban campaign contributions for a certain period—perhaps six months—after Election Day. The postelection fund-raiser, where lobbyists scurry to placate the winner, may be the most undisguised form of influence peddling in our entire system. It is particularly disgusting to see lobbyists who supported the loser suddenly switch sides. This abuse can be banned without injury to freedom of speech. Postelection contributions cannot possibly serve the function of persuading our fellow citizens how to vote. It is simply a way for the holder of public office to use his position for personal political advantage—and for lobbyists to curry favor without any danger that the other side might win.

Specified Period

An extension of this idea would be to require all political campaign contributions to be used by the recipient within a specified period (no longer than six months). This would prevent incumbents from amassing "war chests" to scare off potential challengers. It is hard to believe that contributions made years before the election, and before the contributor even knows who the opposing candidate might be, is a good-faith attempt to persuade. It is almost certainly an attempt to buy influence.

Another possibility is to prohibit contributors from giving money to both sides in the same election. Someone who gives money to both the Republican and the Democrat is not expressing his political opinions, but purchasing access to the future officeholder.

The common element in all of these proposals is that they prohibit forms of campaign fund raising that have little or no relation to legitimate persuasion, and seek to increase the role of ordinary citizens in our political process. They would not solve the whole problem. But they are a big improvement over McCain-Feingold, which cannot possibly pass Congress and would likely (and rightly) be struck down by the Supreme Court if it did pass. This is a test to see whether those members of Congress who say they want to reform the system are really serious.

Mr. McConnell is a professor of constitutional law at the University of Utah.

Letters to the Editor

Campaign Ad Funding Needs Full Disclosure

In his Dec. 11 editorial-page piece "A Constitutional Campaign Finance Plan," Michael W. McConnell says the McCain-Feingold campaign finance reform bill would "make it a crime to run an advertisement stating your views on the candidate within 60 days of the election."

McCain-Feingold does not prevent any person or organization from running any ad during a campaign season; it is only a question of how the ad is paid for and whether that expenditure is disclosed to the public. Under the legislation, if ads clearly advocate the election or defeat of a particular federal candidate, they will be covered by federal election law, meaning the funding must be raised under certain limits and must be fully disclosed. In addition, the bill provides that people who violate this law are subject only to civil fines and not criminal penalties.

The groups and organizations that sponsor multimillion-dollar attack ads in the closing days of an election should not be allowed to do so in secrecy. These ads should be subject to the same disclosure and financing laws as all other campaign commercials. It is the rule that candidates live by, it is the rule that political parties live by, and I believe it should be the rule that all groups involved in federal campaigns should live by.

SEN. RUSS FEINGOLD (D., WIS.)

Washington

* * *

The McCain-Feingold legislation stipulates that a broadcast advertisement referring to a clearly identified candidate 60 days before a federal election be paid for with hard money. In other words, ads that fit that description could not be financed with corporate funds or union dues, but could use in an unlimited fashion publicly disclosed hard dollar donations from individuals or political committees. No advertisement bans, no gag rules.

In fact, this provision of the bill is designed to deal with the very problem Prof. McConnell identifies as most in need of a remedy: contributors seeking to influence public policy not by persuasion but by currying favor with officeholders. By running a barrage of ads immediately preceding an election that savage a candidate's opponent, contributors can provide something of enormous value to an officeholder or candidate, while avoiding the court-upheld disclosure requirements and contribution limits that apply to contributions to candidates.

Unions, corporations and ideological groups know it is developing into one of the best ways to purchase policy results on Capitol Hill.

BECKY CAIN
President
League of Women Voters
of the United States

Washington

REVIEW & OUTLOOK

Acting Exercise

Maybe the only sensible thing to do for the next three years is accord the entire Clinton government "acting" status. With Bill Lann Lee now the acting head of Justice's civil rights division, he takes his place alongside the fellow who's served as "acting" head of the Clinton criminal division for about 2½ years now. When you think about it, the status of "acting" this or that is just about a perfect metaphor for this administration.

"Acting" means almost, sort of, kind of, not quite, like, I lied to my diary, I didn't inhale, to the best of my recollection, mistakes were made.

"Acting" means having your cake and eating it too, as when the President said yesterday that he couldn't get Bill Lann Lee through the confirmation process and he'd try again next year but, oh by the way, "he has the full authority of the office." Too bad Latrell Sprewell isn't working for Bill Clinton; he'd be in the starting lineup tonight.

This is a presidency that creates its own versions of reality and then asks the rest of the country to like it or lump it. The Supreme Court hands down a ruling called *Beck*, asserting that unionists can't be forced to contribute their dues to their parent union's political windmills, and the Clinton Administration decides not to enforce it.

Subpoenas from the second branch of government looking into the President's fund raising in Asia? Yawn. They're "political," so maybe we'll comply sometime next year.

The federal Vacancies Act says temporary positions can be filled for no more than 120 days. The criminal division head has been "acting" for more than two years, but the administration's lawyers have ruled the act doesn't apply to people who were already employees of a department. We guess this means Bill Lann Lee turns into a pumpkin in four months. But some pretense will be found.

Which explains why, incredibly enough, it required the mechanism of an independent counsel to swat the Henry Cisneros mosquitoes. Anthony Lewis of the New York Times was in the paper yesterday pointing out the absurd spectacle of appointing an independent counsel to investigate the truth of a federal officer's statements about his love life before he worked for the federal government.

We agree. It's pretty silly. We agree that a Cabinet officer suspected of lying to the FBI is something that the government itself, specifically Justice's Public Integrity Section, should be able to handle.

But this is an administration that whatever else its accomplishments, has established as a matter of policy that the enforcement and interpretation of laws and statutes is a *selective* process. Instead of any sort of recognizable consistency, the Clinton presidency is proudly *ad hoc*. Ask federal Judge Royce Lamberth, who's been round this track twice with administration lawyers, going back to their attempt to withhold the identities of the entire Health Care Task Force.

The idea that Mr. Cisneros should be prosecuted, a senior Justice Department figure tells us, was strongly opposed by Public Integrity. In other words, it hardly assaults reason to imagine that this Public Integrity Section—the one that could find no "covered persons" in the White House fund-raising mess—would listen to the FBI's reports of Mr. Cisneros's lies to them and conclude that his case didn't warrant prosecution. At which point the FBI's function is down the tubes. The FBI's investigative powers rest on the assumption that no one can get away with lying to them.

The danger in all this is that our government, rather than what we recognize as checks and balances, becomes a chaotic free-for-all. The chaos has already claimed Orrin Hatch. The Senate Judiciary Chairman, whose committee had just made clear it wouldn't confirm Bill Lann Lee, tossed away his authority like a used nose tissue Sunday by announcing that an "acting" appointment wouldn't be so bad. A great Beltwayesque compromise, but ruinous to the institutional powers of Congress.

Even stepping away from this particular corner of the Clinton administration, it is possible to see the effects of its free-for-all political philosophy. On the global warming treaty, for instance, environmental activists have suggested that Mr. Clinton merely start enacting it himself via executive orders. Jack Kemp has called on the President to submit this treaty to the Senate, as the law requires, so it can properly reject it. He is right.

No, folks, we don't think that Bill Clinton made Latrell Sprewell strangle P.J. Carlesimo. What we think is that Mr. Clinton has given the public life of this country a legacy of politics as whatever you can get away with. The instruments of this chaos have been the White House Office of General Counsel, attorneys employed by the Justice Department and the Attorney General. Altogether, it is an administration "acting" like a normal U.S. government. But not quite.

Warping the Law

As 1998 approached, the Journal focused attention on damage being inflicted on the institutions of government, particularly the legal institutions. It published excerpts from Federal District Judge Royce Lamberth's sanction against the White House for misconduct during litigation surrounding Hillary Clinton's attempts to cloak in secrecy meetings of her Health Care Task Force. The judge criticized government officials who had "run amok" and an Executive Branch that had been "dishonest with this court."

Judge Lamberth was not alone. In New York, Manhattan District Attorney Robert Morgenthau was raising concerns about senior Justice Department officials undercutting two of his investigations, including one centering on illegal contributions to the 1992 Clinton campaign. In Washington, Independent Counsel Donald Smaltz told a Congressional panel that he had "changed direction" in his investigation after Arkansas poultry giant Tyson Foods lobbied the Justice Department and the Attorney General summoned him for a meeting. Mr. Smaltz was not entirely deterred, however, and at year's end secured a guilty plea from Tyson for giving illegal gratuities to Agriculture Secretary Mike Espy.

Meanwhile, the House Government Reform and Oversight

Committtee had picked up the campaign-finance baton from the Senate, opening hearings into Interior Secretary Bruce Babbitt and the nexus between departmental policy and campaign contributions. The House hearings, chaired by Rep. Dan Burton of Indiana, would be marked by bitter partisan warfare.

Other matters bedeviled the Clinton Adminstration as well. In early January 1998, the Treasury Department confirmed it was investigating a claim by Arkansas native Paula Jones that she was the subject of an Internal Revenue Service audit because of her sexual harassment lawsuit against Mr. Clinton.

The Journal noted that Mr. Clinton had plenty of tax problems of his own, scarcely mentioned elsewhere. In particular, there was the matter of the debts of Whitewater Development Co., the Clinton share of which might amount to $58,000. As the late Vincent Foster prepared tax returns for the President and First Lady, Jim McDougal, their former Whitewater partner, paid the Clintons $1,000 for their share of the company. Mr. McDougal did not have the money, and the $1,000 was provided to him by Tyson Foods general counsel Jim Blair. Whitewater was deeply in debt, however, so Mr. McDougal in effect gave the Clintons a gift of $58,000, which they did not report as income to the IRS on their 1992 return. Clinton Attorney David Kendall offered a defense, but the lawyer who prepared the returns had died, a suicide.

On other fronts, Far Eastern Economic Review reporter Bruce Gilley reported on the ties of controversial Clinton campaign donor Ted Sioeng to a suspected Cambodian drug trafficker, Theng Bun Ma. And in what would prove to be one of the most fateful moves of his career, on January 17 Mr. Clinton drove to the office of his Beltway sex lawyer, Robert Bennett, to give a deposition in the Paula Jones harassment case. "We think it is a very big deal," the Journal wrote of the Jones matter. "We think it is a symptom of Mr. Clinton's recklessness with his private life and public office that he has allowed the Jones case to reach this point." But few could imagine just how reckless the President had been. That story would emerge in the coming weeks and months, in the person of a young former White House intern named Monica Lewinsky.

REVIEW & OUTLOOK

Thwarting Justice

With independent counsels so much under assault these days, the recent experiences of a determinedly independent New York prosecutor are instructive. In two cases this month, Manhattan District Attorney Robert Morgenthau has seen some of the same Justice Department figures involved in the sprawling campaign contributions affair thwart his own aggressive investigations.

Mr. Morgenthau's office disclosed Monday that earlier this year it had strong information about illegal campaign contributions and offered it to Lee Radek, head of the Justice Department's Public Integrity Section, only to be turned away. The disclosure came at a sentencing hearing for Jorge Castro Barredo, scion of a Venezuelan banking family that allegedly funneled $50,000 to the Democratic National Committee and state organizations in 1992. Earlier this year Mr. Morgenthau convicted Mr. Castro and family members on grand larceny charges involving the theft of millions from a Puerto Rican bank. Mr. Castro agreed to cooperate in exchange for a reduced sentence and offered information about the illegal contributions.

While details are murky, it appears that Mr. Morgenthau first presented his information to the U.S. Attorney in Miami—the Castro family's North American base of operations—but the case ended up with Mr. Radek at Main Justice. According to court filings and news reports this week, Mr. Morgenthau in April delivered his witness, bank records and a memo from a Venezuelan company laying out the contributions scheme. Justice spurned the information, and Mr.

Radek dispatched a letter saying "there is no further role for [Mr. Castro] to play in matters under investigation by the task force."

This week, with the possibility that this could become another storm cloud over the Public Integrity Section, Justice backtracked. The Venezuelan affair might yet be under investigation, Justice spokesman Bert Brandenburg indicated. Mr. Radek's letter "does not say anything about what we may or may not do in the future."

Our interest in the case extends as well to a friend of the Castro family, Charles Intriago, the publisher of the newsletter Money Laundering Alert. Mr. Morgenthau has noted in published reports that his office first began studying Venezuelan banks because of concern over drug-money laundering operations that might be connected to New York. In April 1996, Peter Truell of the New York Times reported that an investigator for Money Laundering Alert had obtained information about the suspicious routing of $3 billion from a Castro bank to the New York offices of a Madrid-based bank. Mr. Intriago rejected his investigator's findings.

Mr. Morgenthau

We should note that money laundering was not at issue in the Castro trial and that Mr. Intriago hasn't been charged with anything. But Mr. Intriago is well acquainted with the White House. A big Democratic Party contributor, he enlisted the help of Florida fund-raiser Charles "Bud" Stack in arranging a meeting at the White House between President Clinton and Orlando Castro Llanes—the central figure in Mr. Morgenthau's successful prosecution. Mr. Castro circulated a photograph of the occasion widely in Venezuelan newspapers. And Mr. Stack was proposed by Mr. Clinton for a seat on the 11th Circuit Court of Appeals, but the nomination foundered.

Meanwhile, the U.S. Attorney for the Southern District of New York, Mary Jo White, recently ran over Mr. Morgenthau's authority by unilaterally making a deal with a suspect who'd already been indicted by the Manhattan DA. In an extraordinary move, Ms. White involved her office in a major securities-fraud investigation by accepting a still-undisclosed plea agreement with a Morgan Stanley compliance officer charged in state court with 11 counts of theft of inside information and fraud.

Ms. White's rationale for cutting Mr. Morgenthau off appears to be the assertion of federal primacy in securities fraud cases. Ms. White says the pursuit of the case through state court "demeans" federal securities law. But the U.S. Attorney showed no interest in the case until newspaper accounts made it public, at which time she snatched it from Mr. Morgenthau.

Ms. White's assertions of federal primacy are especially shaky. The great majority of securities cases are handled by state and county officials, not the feds. Congress also has consistently upheld the right of state prosecutions not to be displaced by federal authority. Last year,

Mary Jo White

in amending the Securities Exchange Act, Congress reinforced the notion of state authority. A report of the House Commerce Committee specifically notes that the intent of the law is to "preserve the ability of the States to investigate and bring enforcement actions . . . in connection with any securities or any securities transactions. . . ."

From a crime-fighting perspective, Ms. White's move sends a terrible message. Facing the often sterner conditions of state justice, defendants can simply attempt to cut a deal with the U.S. Attorney. Mr. Morgenthau's leverage in his ongoing probe, needless to say, has been dramatically reduced.

Among its many tasks, Ms. White's office is responsible for the investigation into the improper financing of Teamster President Ron Carey's re-election campaign, including the possible involvement of DNC officials. We do not for a moment question Ms. White's professionalism or integrity, but the reality is that eventually her sensitive investigations will pass through Mr. Radek at Public Integrity in Washington and Attorney General Janet Reno's squad of advisers. Mr. Morgenthau's recent travails suggest there is more than one way to rein in an overly independent prosecutor.

REVIEW & OUTLOOK

Officials 'Run Amok'

The following is the concluding section of an opinion issued yesterday by Federal District Judge Royce Lamberth in Association of American Physicians and Surgeons, Inc., et al. v. Hillary Rodham Clinton, et al. The case concerned whether federal open meeting laws applied to the First Lady's Health Care task force, and a declaration by "Health Czar" Ira Magaziner that it was exempt because only federal employees were members of the task force. Judge Lamberth referred Mr. Magaziner for a perjury investigation; U.S. Attorney Eric Holder criticized the government but declined to prosecute. Mr. Holder is now Deputy Attorney General.

Because of government misconduct during litigation, the judge ordered it to pay the plaintiffs' legal fees of some $286,000. We note that there is growing concern about the standing of the Justice Department in light of Attorney General Janet Reno's decision not to seek an independent counsel in the campaign finance investigation. But aside from that, the judge's remarks need little amplification by us:

[I]t is clear that the decisions here were made at the highest levels of government, and that the government itself is—and should be—accountable when its officials run amok. There were no rogue lawyers here misleading this court. The court agrees with plaintiffs that these were not reckless and inept errors taken by bewildered counsel. The Executive Branch of the government, working in tandem, was dishonest with this court. . . .

The Department of Justice has a long tradition of setting the highest standards of conduct for all lawyers, and it is a sad day when this court must conclude, as did the United States Attorney in his investigation, that the Department of Justice succumbed to pressure from White House attorneys and others to provide this court with "strained interpretations" that were "ultimately unconvincing."

* * *

This court goes further than the United States Attorney, however, because this court cannot agree that the Department of Justice never relied on the "all employee" exemption for the working group. Having been presented the "all-employee" facts in the Magaziner declaration, the Court of Appeals specifically found that the defendants had made that argument. Neither the briefs on appeal, nor any transcript of the oral argument on appeal, was before this court. Yet the Department of Justice sat back and never told this court that it was not making, and had not made, such an argument, and never corrected any of the factual inaccuracies in the Magaziner declaration. The United States Attorney reported that this was a conscious decision because attorneys in the White House refused to allow any supplemental information to be provided to the court. It seems that some government officials never learn that the coverup can be worse than the underlying conduct.

Most shocking to this court, and deeply disappointing, is that the Department of Justice would participate in such conduct. This was not an issue of good faith word games being played with the Court. The United States Attorney found that the most controversial sentence of the Magaziner declaration—"Only federal government employees serve as members of the interdepartmental working group"—could not be prosecuted under the perjury statute because the issue of "membership" within the working group was a fuzzy one, and no generally agreed upon "membership" criteria were ever written down. Therefore, the Magaziner declaration was actually false because of the implication of the declaration that "membership" was a meaningful concept and that one could determine who was and was not a "member" of the working group. This whole dishonest explanation was provided to this court in the Magaziner declaration on March 3, 1993, and this court holds that such dishonesty is sanctionable and was not good faith dealing with the court or plaintiff's counsel. It was not timely corrected or supplemented, and this type of conduct is reprehensible, and the government must be held accountable for it.

* * *

The court adheres to its view, expressed at the August 11, 1995, hearing, that "it is remarkable that any United States Attorney would make comments to a court that are so sharply critical, frankly, of the government conduct of this litigation . . . ." The court adds that it is beyond remarkable, it is commendable, and it demonstrates adherence to the traditional role of the Department of Justice that justice be done rather than that a case be won at any cost. The elevation of United States Attorney Holder to be Deputy Attorney General is an encouraging and hopeful sign that this case was a rare aberration—never to be repeated in this court.

DECEMBER 19, 1997

Editorial Feature

The President on His Critics

Our letters editor had a nice conversation yesterday with Richard H. Mason of El Dorado, Arkansas, who had been called to our attention by an old friend, Bill Clinton. Mr. Mason had written to complain about our picking on the president and to cancel his subscription; Mr. Clinton quoted his remarks extensively in his Dec. 13 speech to a group of Arkansas Democrats visiting Washington.

Our editor had not seen the Dec. 2 letter, perhaps lost in the volume of correspondence, but Mr. Mason faxed another copy. We admire his feisty prose, but the president had already picked out the best parts. And in his remarks to fellow Arkansans, the president kind of came to our defense, but also complained about being picked on by Kenneth Starr and accused Republicans of trying to destroy the two-party system. So rather than run Mr. Mason's letter, we've decided that readers would be more interested if we let the president speak for himself, in the following excerpts of his remarks. —Ed.:

I probably shouldn't do this, but I'm going to try to acknowledge the Arkansans in the administration who are here. . . . I think it's important. I just want you to get a feel for how many people are here: Mack and Donna McLarty, of course; Bruce Lindsey; Nancy Hernreich; Marsha Scott; Bob Nash and Janis Kearney; Stephanie Streett, Mary Streett; Catherine Grundin; Patsy Thomasson; Anne and Grady McCoy. . . . And in the administration, of course, Secretary Slater and Cassandra; James Lee and Lea Ellen Witt;

Hershel Gober and Mary Lou Keener; Harold and Arlee Gist; Wilbur Peer; Gloria Cabe has done great work for us; and in the DNC, Carol and Joyce Willis; Lottie Shackleford; Mary Anne Salmon. . . .

I don't want to embarrass him, but about two hours before I came over here tonight I was finishing up some paperwork in my office. . . . And at the top of the folder was a letter that Richard Mason just wrote to The Wall Street Journal. And it said, I got as much chance of getting this letter printed as Dan Quayle does of getting elected President. (Laughter.)

But he went on to say he was a businessman, he had read the Journal faithfully for years. He said, for five years I've watched you bad-mouth my president and my state and say things that weren't true. And if your advice on business is as bad as your understanding of politics, I'll be in deep trouble if I keep reading this newspaper. (Laughter.) Please cancel my subscription. (Applause.)

I did what I always do. You know, I was saying, but Richard, you know, you can't blame the editorial page, they have good articles, all that kind of stuff. I was making my good-government argument. He said, look, the economy is better, the world is at peace, the crime rate is down, the country is in great shape—sooner or later some of those people that are trying to tear your guts out and lying about our state are going to have to fess up and admit it. Get over it, the country is in better shape. This is working. (Applause.)

Since under our new policy all these are covered by the press, they may have to run your letter now, Richard. (Laughter.) We'll see. . .

When I was getting ready to come over here, I was reliving many of the things that have happened since Oct. 3, 1991, when I declared for president. I remember how people sneeringly referred to me as the governor of a small Southern state. I remember how people talked about how we had failed to do all these things. I remember when I was pronounced dead before arrival in New Hampshire. . . .

I remember how surprised—the people that ran against me in '92 by and large are good friends of mine now, and I remember how surprised they were that we kept doing well in odd places. And it took them a long time to figure out that 25% of the voters in Chicago were from Arkansas. (Laughter.) That there was something to be said for being poor throughout the '30s, '40s, '50s and '60s. (Laughter.) I keep waiting any day now for all of them to be subpoenaed by Mr. Starr. (Laughter.) You know, a 50-year-old conspiracy to take over the

White House—(laughter)—which started with our running people out of Arkansas back in the '30s and '40s in a dark and devious way. (Applause.)

I came upon a little town outside Flint, Michigan, one day, full of auto workers. And literally 90% of them had roots in Arkansas, and I thought to myself today, those people are going to be called to testify any minute now. (Laughter.) There's a presumption there's something wrong with them; it was some dark plot.

I was in the Bronx—did you see the pictures? . . . So I get out, I shake hands with Ralph Porter; he's the current president of the Mid-Bronx Desperados, and we are walking down the street in the Bronx. He looked at me and he said, you know, my wife worked with your mother at Ouachita Hospital for 15 years. (Laughter.) And I graduated from Langston High School in Hot Springs. (Laughter.) I said, no, they'll never believe this. (Laughter.) I hope Ralph doesn't get a subpoena. . . .

And I'm telling you, it will take your breath away if you could walk down some of these streets—not just nice houses, but safe streets, clean streets, going to remodeled schools that are working where communities that were given up for dead are working.

And sometimes I think what our adversaries, that are almost pathologically obsessed with personal destruction, don't get is that that's what politics is about. That's what you taught me. That's why we're all here after five years and that's why the country is in better shape. Politics is about real people and their hopes and their dreams. So, to me, all this stuff—you all always say, gosh, I don't know how you put up with it. How do you put up with mosquitoes in summertime in Arkansas? (Laughter.) You just swat them and go on, it's part of living. That's what you do. . . .

I ran for a very clear reason: I thought our country was divided and drifting; that we were not succeeding; that we were clearly the greatest country in human history; and that we were too dominated, completely paralyzed and in the grip of the mosquitoes instead of the planting. That's what I thought then. And so we decided that we would endure the mosquitoes so that we could plant and reap. . . .

The reason it's important for you to be here is that part of the counterbattle, the mosquito biting, this year was a calculated, determined effort to use the hearing process and the legal process to force all the Democrats—and especially people associated with the party—

to hire a lawyer every 15 seconds in the hope that we'd never have another penny to spend on campaigns. (Applause.) Somebody pointed out I'd been to so many fund-raisers in the last year that I'd gotten tired a time or two, and I plead guilty to that. It's OK to get tired, you just can't give in. (Applause.)

So when you go home and people ask you why you did this, say because they tried to end the two-party system in America by forcing the Democrats to spend all their money hiring lawyers. And you think the two-party system is a pretty good idea, especially since one party, the one you belong to, was right about the deficit, was right about the economy, was right about crime, was right about welfare, was right about so many things, and that's why this country is in better shape today, and you think that's a pretty good indication about which party ought to be able to lead us into the new century. That's why you're here and that's why I'm very proud of you.

Let me just say, lastly, I wanted you to go back home and tell the people who aren't here what I said tonight. And remind them— because they're a long way away—never to get confused between the mosquitoes and the planting, because as soon as you do you won't be able to bring in the crop. We have brought in the crop and you made it possible and I'm very proud of you. Thank you and God bless you. (Applause.)

Editorial Feature

How Justice Tried
To Stop Smaltz

Earlier this month, in a case brought by Independent Counsel Donald Smaltz, a District of Columbia jury convicted former Agriculture Secretary Michael Espy's chief of staff, Ron Blackley, of lying to government authorities to hide $22,000 he received from Mississippi agribusinesses in 1993. Mr. Smaltz would not have secured this conviction had the Clinton Justice Department prevailed in its opposition to his effort to prosecute Mr. Blackley.

Rule of Law

By Terry Eastland

The jurisdictional struggle between Justice and Mr. Smaltz, which quietly occurred in the first months of 1996, was the subject of recent congressional testimony by the independent counsel and Attorney General Janet Reno. The conflict merits close attention for several reasons, not least because it may help explain Ms. Reno's steadfast refusal to seek appointment of an independent counsel to investigate campaign fund-raising abuses.

Mr. Smaltz was named in September 1994 to investigate whether Mr. Espy had violated any laws by accepting gifts from organizations and individuals with business pending before the Agriculture Department. His probe has so far resulted in convictions of seven individuals, four corporations and one law firm, a $1,050,000 fine of a major securities broker, and recovery of more than $4.5 million in fines and penalties. Mr. Espy is awaiting trial on charges involving his acceptance of gifts. During the course of his probe, Mr. Smaltz came across information pointing to Mr. Blackley.

Mr. Smaltz's original jurisdiction, as defined by the special division of judges within the D.C. Circuit Court of Appeals that appointed him, was quite broad. In fact, Mr. Smaltz believed it already encompassed the matters involving Mr. Blackley. But to insulate himself from jurisdictional challenges, Mr. Smaltz in late 1995 raised with Justice whether it might give him these matters by virtue of their "related" character under Section 594(e) of the independent counsel statute. That provision enables a counsel to ask either the attorney general *or* the special division to refer related matters. This is a significant "or," as will be seen.

Given his previous experiences with the Justice Department, Mr. Smaltz did not have great confidence that he could win its agreement. Early in 1995, having uncovered information involving Arkansas-based Tyson Foods, Mr. Smaltz asked Justice for a referral of Tyson as a "related matter" or, alternatively, for an expansion of jurisdiction to include Tyson. Justice said no.

Donald Smaltz

In late spring, Mr. Smaltz found himself summoned to meet with Attorney General Janet Reno and an assemblage of top officials, including the deputy attorney general, the head of the criminal division and her top deputy, and lawyers from the Public Integrity Section. This meeting took place after lawyers for Tyson had complained to Justice about Mr. Smaltz's work. The result of this meeting was that Mr. Smaltz, as he testified in Congress, "changed direction."

As it happened, the Justice Department was indeed unwilling to recognize Mr. Smaltz's claim to jurisdiction over Mr. Blackley. So in January 1996 Mr. Smaltz, taking the alternative route provided for in the independent counsel statute, asked the special division for a "related matter" referral. Justice then filed a vigorous brief in opposition. In April, the three-judge panel unanimously agreed with Mr. Smaltz, thus enabling his prosecution of Mr. Blackley.

Justice contended that Section 594(e) of the independent counsel statute must be read to require the concurrence of the attorney general before the special division can refer related matters to a counsel. It is easy to see why the department lost. The traditional view held by attorneys general (at least until Ms. Reno took office) was that the Constitution does not permit judges to assume the quintessentially executive task of defining prosecutorial jurisdiction. But the Supreme Court rejected this view in sustaining the independent counsel statute in the 1988 case of *Morrison v. Olson*. In light of *Morrison*, there can be little doubt that judges may interpret the reach of the jurisdiction they previously have defined—and thus determine whether a matter is related or not.

In rejecting Justice's argument, the special division observed that "to construe the statute as [the department] urges would amount to judicially rewriting it." The proper forum for Ms. Reno to submit her complaint is Congress.

There is, of course, not a little irony here. Like most Democrats, Ms. Reno upon taking office was largely satisfied with a statute that had been used mainly against Republican administrations. In 1993 congressional testimony, she enthusiastically supported reauthorization of the then-lapsed statute, expressing no separation-of-powers concerns about any provision, much less about 594(e).

Not incidentally, that provision had been amended during the previous reauthorization, in 1987, to make clear that the special division may indeed refer a related matter to a counsel without the concurrence of the attorney general. This clarification—further irony— was urged by House Democrats upset with what they regarded as too narrow enforcement of the statute by Attorney General Edwin Meese. Coincidence or not, it is only as several independent counsels close in on allies and associates of President Clinton that Ms. Reno's lawyers discover separation of powers and speak of "grave constitutional issues."

Some of those lawyers also have turned up in recent press accounts, spinning the notion that the attorney general's unwillingness to ask for a fund-raising counsel may be influenced by her "bad" experiences with Mr. Smaltz and other counsels. Example: Some Justice officials, reported the New York Times in late November, "regard four of the five independent prosecutors appointed under Ms. Reno as overzealous amateurs who have tried repeatedly to expand jurisdiction."

This campaign against Mr. Smaltz and other counsels (the special division also has been anonymously lambasted) is unworthy of the department Ms. Reno heads. And of course her view of Mr. Smaltz or any other counsel should have no bearing on how she evaluates evidence that could result in the appointment of a counsel in the fund-raising (or any other) matter.

Mr. Smaltz does not accuse Justice of trying to obstruct his investigation by opposing his effort to prosecute Mr. Blackley. But it is a fact that Justice's opposition considerably delayed his work, and that it has inspired targets of his probe to make similar jurisdictional challenges, producing more delays. Perhaps the wonder of this story is that Mr. Smaltz has stuck with the job as long as he has.

Mr. Eastland is publisher of The American Spectator and a contributor to Forbes Digital Tool.

Review & Outlook

Asides

There's the Outrage

"Where's the outrage?" was Bob Dole's complaint about Clinton Administration ethics during the 1996 campaign. Yesterday, Independent Counsel Donald Smaltz struck another blow for ethical accountability after Arkansas poultry giant Tyson Foods pleaded guilty to giving former Agriculture Secretary Mike Espy more than $12,000 in illegal gratuities. Tyson agreed to pay $6 million in fines and investigative costs. Mr. Smaltz's investigation, which has been under brutal attack lately, is about illegal gift-giving, doubtless for the purpose of influence, to a sitting member of the President's Cabinet. "Such conduct," Mr. Smaltz said yesterday, "must continue to invite outrage, never passivity, from those who are regulated, the public, and our lawmakers."

Editorial Feature

Executive Branch, Not Just Ira Magaziner, Is Found 'Dishonest'

By JOHN FUND

The Clinton administration is desperately trying to contain the controversy over federal Judge Royce Lamberth's dramatic levying of $286,000 in sanctions against it for what the judge calls a "cover-up" of efforts to keep Hillary Clinton's 1993 health care task force secret. The White House would like the public to view the dispute as one between Judge Lamberth and Ira Magaziner, the longtime Clinton friend who was czar of the ill-fated health care plan. But a close reading of the record indicates the real conflict could be summarized as The Facts v. the Clinton Administration.

Ira Magaziner

President Clinton says, "I am quite confident that Mr. Magaziner acted appropriately." He noted that in 1995 U.S. Attorney Eric Holder, since appointed by Mr. Clinton to the No. 2 slot at the Justice Department, found "no evidence that Mr. Magaziner intended to mislead the court." Mr. Holder therefore declined to prosecute Mr. Magaziner for perjury, a conclusion that Judge Lamberth says he "cannot disagree" with.

But this doesn't exonerate the White House from political or ethical responsibility for its actions. Mr. Holder himself said a March 1993 declaration drafted for Mr. Magaziner by the late Vincent

Foster, then deputy White House counsel, left Mr. Magaziner "open to charges that portions were inaccurate." The declaration claimed that federal open-meeting laws didn't apply because all health task force members were government employees. This was at a time when nearly half of the task force's members were in fact private citizens, including many who worked for managed-care interests with a stake in the outcome.

Mr. Holder also criticized White House and Justice lawyers who he found "persisted in an attempt to go back after the fact" and tried to reclassify outside consultants as government employees. Indeed, in an attempt to comply with the open-meeting law, Mr Foster even signed Federal Register notices for meetings that had already taken place. Mr. Holder concluded: "The declaration can be misleading if relied upon as a historical description of the entire working group process." At the time of Mr. Holder's 1995 decision not to prosecute Mr. Magaziner, Judge Lamberth observed that Mr. Holder's investigation "does not address whether there is evidence as to whether the White House or Department of Justice attorneys intended to mislead the court."

Royce Lamberth

Mr. Magaziner has defended himself by noting that he is not a lawyer and that he relied on White House and Justice lawyers in drafting his controversial declaration. Among the Justice lawyers who supervised the drafting were Webster Hubbell, now a convicted felon, and Beth Nolan, who has been appointed by President Clinton to head the Justice Department's Office of Legal Counsel.

Judge Lamberth has made it clear that while he found Mr. Magaziner's declaration "dishonest," his real concern is with the coverup that followed. That involves behavior not of Mr. Magaziner, but of top lawyers in the White House and Justice Department.

In awarding legal fees of $286,000 to the American Association of Physicians and Surgeons (AAPS), which originally challenged the secrecy of the health care task force, Judge Lamberth minced no words: "It is clear that the decisions here were made at the highest levels of government, and that the government itself is—and should be—accountable when its officials run amok.... The Executive

Branch of the government, working in tandem, was dishonest with this court." Judge Lamberth concludes, "It seems that some government officials never learn that the coverup can be worse than the underlying conduct." Despite White House spin, it is clear he isn't speaking of Mr. Magaziner, but of higher-ups.

The Clinton administration itself confirmed its untenable position in the case back in August 1994 when it offered to settle the case by making public all of the documents demanded by AAPS, a move Judge Lamberth called "total capitulation." The Administration also offered to pay $239,000 in legal bills to AAPS, a figure not far off the sanctions imposed by Judge Lamberth. AAPS declined to settle because Dr. Jane Orient, the group's president, felt the government wouldn't turn over all its records.

Judge Lamberth sided with Dr. Orient's view in his award of legal fees to AAPS. "The defendants did not properly provide public access to all the files of the participants of the working groups, as they had offered in settlement," he noted. "It took weeks of prodding by plaintiffs' new counsel, and inspections of produced material, to identify a number of discrepancies that led to further court hearings and orders before the court could finally declare the case was moot." Judge Lamberth concludes that "all of these working group documents would be safely tucked away in the National Archives had it not been for this litigation. It is only because of this litigation that they are now available for inspection."

Administration officials have privately attacked Judge Lamberth's ruling as out of the mainstream and have made much of the fact that it was Ronald Reagan who named him to the bench in 1987. But the 53-year-old Judge Lamberth has an unquestioned reputation for independence and fairness. His first major appointment was by Jimmy Carter, who named him chief of the civil division of the U.S. Attorney's Office for the District of Columbia.

While on the bench he has sometimes disappointed conservatives. In 1988, Congress required the Washington, D.C., City Council to enact legislation allowing religious educational institutions to discriminate against gays. The case stemmed from an incident in which Georgetown University refused to give homosexuals equal access to campus facilities. Judge Lamberth ruled Congress had infringed on the council members' First Amendment rights. He reasoned that their votes were a form of free speech and Congress could not force them to vote against their will. After his decision, council members drank a champagne toast to the judge.

After Judge Lamberth's controversial opinion last month sanctioning the Clinton administration, House Ways and Means Chairman Bill Archer called for Mr. Magaziner's resignation. A better approach is offered by Georgia Rep. Bob Barr. Back in 1995, he wrote to Attorney General Reno demanding that she investigate the role government lawyers played in misleading Judge Lamberth. As in her recent refusals to appoint independent counsels, Ms. Reno has been consistent; she did not act on Rep. Barr's request. Perhaps it's time for Congress to exercise its oversight function and step in where Ms. Reno has chosen not to tread.

Mr. Fund is a member of the Journal's editorial board.

Review & Outlook

'This Court Will Not Permit'

Last month federal Judge Royce Lamberth levied $286,000 in sanctions against the executive branch for "running amok" in a "cover-up" of Hillary Clinton's health care task force. The next day, we now learn, the other shoe dropped: The judge was back in court indicating he may impose sanctions in a *second* case against the Administration.

This one involves Filegate. It's an invasion-of-privacy lawsuit seeking $90 million for the White House's improper procurement of the confidential FBI files of up to 900 former Reagan and Bush appointees.

The case was brought by Judicial Watch, a conservative legal group, which wants to question First Lady Hillary Clinton, former White House security chief Craig Livingstone and his assistant Anthony Marceca about how the files came to be transferred in what FBI Director Freeh has called "an egregious violation of privacy." David Kendall, the first lady's lawyer, has objected to a face-to-face deposition for his client and instead wants all questions in writing. However, Judge Lamberth has given wide latitude for depositions, and so Mrs. Clinton may end up testifying. Rep. Chris Cox, a deputy White House counsel in the Reagan Administration, calls Filegate "the most underexplored of the Clinton scandals" and hopes Congress will pursue it.

In a Dec. 19 status conference on Judicial Watch's Filegate suit, Judge Lamberth observed that both the White House and FBI had asserted they would only produce relevant documents at some unspecified future date. Judge Lamberth responded that this was precisely the kind of behavior he had found "unacceptable" in the health care task force litigation. "This court has made it abundantly clear that such a practice will not be tolerated," he wrote in a December 22 order. He added: "This court will not permit such tactics to occur in this case either, as defendants' conduct in the instant case is equally improper. This court will entertain any motion for sanctions arising from this misconduct that plaintiffs may wish to file."

Sounds to us as if this White House's stonewall reflex has finally created a fairly significant federal-judiciary problem. A status conference on Judicial Watch's request for sanctions will be held next Tuesday at 10 a.m. in Judge Lamberth's courtroom.

Judicial Watch is becoming a veteran of the stonewall struggles. Its three-year-old lawsuit seeks documents to establish whether the late Ron Brown traded prize seats on trade missions for campaign contributions. In that case, Commerce lawyers capitulated last year and actually asked that "judgment should be entered against" their own client. Commerce admitted its record search had been incomplete and asked Judge Lamberth to order " a new and adequate search" and to have the agency pay all of Judicial Watch's legal fees and costs.

Judicial Watch chairman Larry Klayman declined the settlement and hopes to pursue the case. He notes that in the health care task force lawsuit, the government also offered a settlement only to have Judge Lamberth later rule that it "did not properly provide public access to all the files . . . as they had offered in settlement."

It's hard to see how anyone could be surprised that the Clinton Administration has enraged a federal judge. From lost billing records to the search of Vincent Foster's office to videotapes of White House coffees the Administration has never been able to get its story straight, though its operatives must have concluded they were nonetheless getting the best of the press, public and congressional committees. So why not stiff the judiciary as well? Lately, though, the courts have started to slap down the White House. The Supreme Court, for example, summarily rejected its attempts to block the Paula Jones lawsuit and withhold documents from Kenneth Starr.

Now Judge Lamberth has begun to levy sanctions against some of the Administration's tactics. It's somehow reassuring to see that the buck still stops somewhere in Washington.

REVIEW & OUTLOOK

Taxing Scandals

The taxman cometh to the Clinton scandals. On Wednesday, the Treasury Department confirmed it is investigating Paula Jones's claim that she is the subject of an IRS audit because of her sexual-harassment lawsuit against Bill Clinton. Separately, the Rutherford Institute, which is supplying much of the legal and financial fire-power for Ms. Jones's case, is fighting off a sub-poena from Clinton lawyer Bob Bennett seeking information on the group's nonprofit status. Yes, by all means, let's audit everybody with a legal defense fund—starting with the other party to the Jones suit.

Paula Jones

Last month, Mr. Clinton decided to close down his Legal Expense Trust, following a steep decline in donations. We're not privy to infor- mation about donations to Ms. Jones, but some- how we doubt her fund has seen the likes of Charlie Trie showing up with $460,000 in a brown paper bag, an episode that helped chill contributions to the Clinton trust. Undeterred, Mr. Clinton is exploring the formation of a new trust that would allow direct fund raising.

We recall that Mr. Clinton's friends came to the rescue as well in another taxing issue involving the messily settled Whitewater Development Co. In late 1992, Tyson Foods counsel Jim Blair, long-time Clinton friend and adviser to Mrs. Clinton in her spectacular commodities trades, brokered the signature of Whitewater partner Jim McDougal on a document releasing the Clintons from any obligations relating to Whitewater. In a document drafted by Vincent Foster, Mr. McDougal paid the Clintons $1,000—provided, it turns out, by Mr. Blair—for their shares in the Whitewater company.

It also turns out that the Clintons were in the hole to the tune of $58,000 to Mr. McDougal, money owed to the former S&L operator for their half of Whitewater Development Co. expenses. Mr. Blair getting Mr. McDougal's signature on an indemnity agreement releasing the Clintons from all obligations appeared to be a brilliant move. "In a single stroke," wrote John Hartigan on this page in August 1996,

David Kendall

"this canceled the Clinton's $58,000 debt without their having to pay the McDougals a nickel. But by the same token, it also obligated the Clintons to include the $58,000 they saved in the total annual income reported on their 1992 federal income tax return."

The Clintons did not report Jim McDougal's $58,000 debt cancellation, doubtless aware of the firestorm this particular favor from this particular friend would touch off. They have obfuscated the issue ever since. But being excused from paying a business debt is the economic equivalent of receiving the same amount in cash, and must be reported to the IRS as taxable income.

After Mr. Hartigan's article appeared, the Clintons' personal attorney, David Kendall, sent us a letter blasting it as "tendentious nonsense." Mr. Kendall wrote that once the Whitewater corporation was formed in 1979, "the Clintons became shareholders and their liability was accordingly limited." Furthermore, the Clintons "never suggested there was any legally binding agreement to contribute one-half the cash the McDougals (who ran the company) might decide to spend, and there was none. Arkansas contract law, to which Mr. Hartigan makes reference, does not support any different conclusion."

Mr. Hartigan fired back in a letter published two days later, calling Mr. Kendall's argument "nonsense and double nonsense." The Clintons, Mr. Hartigan wrote, "have both given sworn testimony that their original agreement with Mr. McDougal 'did not change over time,' and the courts of Arkansas have consistently held that incorporation of a business venture in no way excuses" agreements entered into prior to incorporation.

Surely the Internal Revenue Service can offer a clear resolution of the dispute between Mr. Kendall and Mr. Hartigan. If the agency is to have any hope of restoring some sense of public confidence, it should at least balance a close look at the President's enemies with a public report on the arguments advanced by his allies.

Editorial Feature

A Democratic Donor's Cambodian Connection

By Bruce Gilley

Cambodian tycoon Theng Bunma could barely suppress his grin as he stood on a stage in Phnom Penh's Inter-Continental Hotel on Dec. 20 wearing a scholar's mortarboard and gown. Mr. Bunma, who failed to complete high school, had just been awarded an honorary doctorate in business administration from a little-known American school, Iowa Wesleyan College. Mr. Bunma was the center of attention, not least because the controversial hotelier and trader has been barred from entering the U.S. due to suspected drug trafficking.

But another colorful tycoon was also on hand that day, and, as he has done for the past year, he was trying to avoid the media. Ted Sioeng, an Indonesian-born businessman at the center of the "donorgate" scandal over China's alleged attempt to influence the 1996 U.S. elections, remained in the shadows as a procession of dignitaries, including Cambodian Co-Premier Hun Sen, presented flowers to Mr. Bunma.

Mr. Sioeng's appearance in Cambodia was the first time he has been sighted by the media since questions arose about his role in the "donorgate" scandal. Though he stood carefully out of camera range in Phnom Penh, his trademark silver mutton-chop sideburns and the constant stream of instructions whispered to aides made him easy to spot.

Mr. Sioeng's role was anything but low profile that day, however. It was he who secured Mr. Bunma's Iowa Wesleyan degree, and he who arranged for the degree to be granted during a one-day conference on investing in Cambodia. The conference was cosponsored by Mr. Sioeng's U.S.-based Federation of Chinese Industrial & Commercial Organizations and the Phnom Penh Chamber of Commerce, the latter headed by Mr. Bunma. Further research reveals not only the depth of Mr. Sioeng's relations with Chinese officials at various levels, but also that he has been building close ties to Cambodia in general, and Mr. Bunma in particular, for several years.

Unwelcome Attention

Doing favors and building personal connections with government officials are unremarkable activities in the Asian business context. Even so, Mr. Sioeng's close links to Mr. Bunma may garner him unwelcome attention: The Cambodian is widely seen as the most unsavory tycoon in a country where corporate activity is frequently fueled by narcotics trading and illegal forestry. Moreover, in the U.S., the emerging evidence of Mr. Sioeng's close connections to Chinese officials is likely to fuel charges that China used foreign businessmen to try to buy political influence.

Mr. Sioeng's lawyers deny that he or his family has ever acted on China's behalf. But according to media reports, Mr. Sioeng's name was mentioned in U.S.-intercepted conversations among Chinese officials looking for a conduit into the American political system, beginning in 1995. Mr. Sioeng carries a passport from the small Central American nation of Belize, home of his flagship S.S. Group, even though his wife and five children are U.S. citizens. But in 1995 and 1996, he appeared at several glitzy Democratic Party fund-raisers in the U.S., usually accompanied by delegations of unidentified ethnic-Chinese businesspeople. On one occasion, he sat next to President Clinton, and on another with Vice President Al Gore. His family and businesses donated a total of $250,000 to the Democratic Party, according to official disclosure documents in the U.S.

U.S. federal agents are now combing Mr. Sioeng's bank records in Los Angeles in search of further details of a Chinese connection. But he has been lying low in Asia for more than a year. At a Senate committee hearing in October, Sen. Robert Bennett (R., Utah) described Mr. Sioeng as among a dozen witnesses who had "fled the country rather than be available for either this committee or the Justice Department." Others include Democratic Party fund-raiser Yah Lin "Charlie" Trie, who has been spotted in China.

Mr. Sioeng has long been buying influence in the U.S. in other ways too. In November 1995 he paid $3 million for a politically moderate Chinese-language newspaper in Los Angeles, the International Daily News, and gave it a more pro-Beijing flavor. A newly opened Hong Kong bureau of the newspaper is headed by Yeung Hong Man, a former editor of the territory's Beijing-run Wen Wei Po newspaper. The International Daily News, which also distributes an American edition of Wen Wei Po as a free "bonus" for its readers, is run by Mr. Sioeng's eldest daughter, Jessica Elnitiarta. It was in her name that one of the major donations was made. (Mr. Sioeng's children use their mother's Indonesian surname; he is a native Indonesian who was adopted by Chinese parents.)

It was through the former publisher of the newspaper, Simon Chen, that Mr. Sioeng was introduced in 1994 to Robert Prins, president of Iowa Wesleyan College. With a modest contribution for scholarships to the college, which has a full-time student body of just 430, Mr. Sioeng was awarded an honorary doctorate and placed on the college's 29-person board of trustees that year.

Mr. Sioeng's main business is tobacco, his initial connection with China. He has the world-wide rights to China's Red Pagoda Mountain cigarettes, which his Singapore company, World Wide Golden Leaf, produces with tobacco giant B.A.T. One prominent business partner based in Phnom Penh says most of the Red Pagoda Mountain cigarettes made in Singapore—50,000 cartons a month, worth a total of $5 million—are sold back to China, where demand is insatiable and the "Made in Singapore" label fetches a premium.

The cigarette venture has also helped Mr. Sioeng cement his ties with Indonesia's powerful Tanuwidjaja family. Last May, a company partly owned by the Tanuwidjajas, the Hong Kong-listed Millennium Group, bought 25% of World Wide Golden Leaf for $34 million. The acquisition was a profitable one for Millennium since at the time of the transaction, World Wide Golden Leaf revealed that it expected to make profits of not less than $30 million in the year to March 1998. The Tanuwidjajas are another ethnic-Chinese Indonesian family with business in China whose name has come up in investigations about Democratic Party fund raising. There is also a family bond: Mr. Sioeng's daughter Laureen recently married Subandi Tanuwidjaja.

But Mr. Sioeng's China connection goes beyond cigarettes. His business card lists him as an "economic adviser" to no fewer than six Chinese provinces or regions—Yunnan, Guizhou, Guangxi, Jilin, Heilongjiang and Inner Mongolia. This is an honorific usually reserved for major investors or other "patriotic" overseas Chinese.

Mr. Sioeng got his start selling secondhand cigarette-making machinery to China, where he now has a $5 million tobacco-machinery joint venture with the Guizhou government. (Shen Yongfen, general manager of the venture, Hangao Industries, attended the Phnom Penh conference.) But Mr. Sioeng has since expanded into other businesses, including a Guizhou brewery, Billion Beer Industries, and a nationwide real estate investment firm, Lucky Property Estate Investment. Mr. Sioeng also chairs a fund for mainland-Chinese students in the U.S.

Most of Mr. Sioeng's Asian investments are coordinated and financed by his Hong Kong company, World Seal, chaired by his youngest son, Yopie Elnitiarta. Perhaps because Mr. Sioeng has spent more time in the region since leaving the U.S., he has recently leased a large office in a new building in Hong Kong's Wanchai district. The corporate logos of the S.S. Group, World Seal and the International Daily News are all displayed in the reception area, flanked by an ornate, three-foot-long jade sculpture. Yopie Elnitiarta answered the telephone there recently; the next day, however, a staff member declined to open the glass door, saying all the executives were away.

In 1996, Mr. Sioeng began to investigate building his own cigarette plant in Cambodia. When completed this year, it will produce a local brand and will be run by one of his sons, he told the Far Eastern Economic Review at the Phnom Penh conference. One of Mr. Sioeng's first acts as he planned the investment was to prevail upon Iowa Wesleyan President Prins to confer honorary law degrees on Cambodian leader Hun Sen and his chief of cabinet, Sok An. "I was very impressed with the work Hun Sen was doing in Cambodia," Mr. Sioeng says. Mr. Prins made the presentations in Phnom Penh in October 1996. The following month, Hun Sen attended the wedding of Mr. Sioeng's daughter Laureen and Subandi Tanuwidjaja in Hong Kong. Mr. Bunma was also present.

In March 1997, Mr. Sioeng urged Mr. Prins to confer an honorary doctorate on Mr. Bunma, whom Mr. Sioeng had met two years earlier. "Ted told me that Theng had built roads, donated rice to the poor and provided funds for farmers," Mr. Prins says. Mr. Bunma indicated that he intended to donate $10,000 a year for Cambodian students to study at Iowa Wesleyan, whose motto is "Real World Learning." Recruiting Cambodians is a pet project of Mr. Prins, so he agreed, despite the fact that Mr. Bunma had by then been banned from the U.S. because of suspected involvement in the drugs trade. (U.S. State Department spokesman Nicholas Burns said last year that Washington had "reliable reporting that he is closely and heavily involved in drug trafficking in Cambodia." Mr. Bunma denies any involvement in the trade, saying it is a business that "everyone in the world hates.")

Theng Bunma

"I only met Theng the night before the ceremony, but he seemed like a decent person," recalls Mr. Prins, who says he was not aware of the entry ban or the drug allegations. "I have learned you should check more than just what you're given on someone."

Messrs. Sioeng and Bunma also came together in November at an international conference of ethnic Chinese in the Southern Chinese city of Chaozhou. The conference was presided over by Chinese Communist Party Politburo standing committee member Li Ruihuan, who appealed to the overseas Chinese to act as a bridge between China and the world. It was then that the pair decided to hold the Phnom Penh conference and couple it with the degree ceremony.

Mr. Bunma's Hong Kong company, which shares the name Thai Boon Roong with his Thailand-based flagship, handled all the arrangements for the conference, according to organizers and conference documents. The Chinese embassy in Phnom Penh, meanwhile, provided support staff and sent several officials to the conference early in the morning to help with preparations. (When the early-arriving diplomats discovered a Taiwan flag at the chair of a delegate from the island republic, they demanded it be removed; it was.) A dozen provincial officials from the provinces Mr. Sioeng advises also attended the conference—all their expenses being paid by the conference organizers. "Mr. Sioeng takes very good care of us," commented Li Lu, deputy director of the business-registration bureau for Yunnan Province, one of those attending.

The speed with which Messrs. Sioeng and Bunma struck up a partnership surprises some. But Jeffrey Ung, a prominent Chinese-Cambodian businessman in Phnom Penh, says Mr. Sioeng saw Mr. Bunma as a potential partner the moment they met. "Ted goes by instinct," says Mr. Ung, whose company, Cambodia National Merchants, plays a key role in China-Cambodia relations. "When he meets someone and feels he can get along with them, he acts fast."

'Business to Do'

Mr. Sioeng, like others, says he was impressed with Mr. Bunma's sway in Cambodia. Mr. Bunma is used to getting his way: He once shot out the tires of a Cambodian airliner in a fit over some lost luggage. His influence was never more apparent than the day after Hun Sen ousted his rival co-prime minister, Norodom Ranariddh, in July's bloody coup. Fearing that the Inter-Continental Hotel, which he owns, would be used by Hun Sen's troops as a command post, Mr. Bunma phoned the prime minister and demanded the soldiers leave the capital. (Mr. Bunma told this story himself at his dinner table after the Dec. 20 conference.) Hun Sen, though incensed, according to Mr. Bunma's recollection, agreed to withdraw the troops in return for $1 million from Mr. Bunma. "After all," Mr. Bunma explained at dinner, "I had business to do."

Mr. Sioeng is now a regular visitor to Cambodia, though he spends most of his time shuttling between Hong Kong, Singapore and China. Besides the new cigarette factory in Cambodia, World Seal is also considering new investments there. Since December, the new managing director of World Seal has been Didi Kurniawan, the Indonesian-born husband of another Sioeng daughter, Sandra Elnitiarta. The couple attended the Phnom Penh conference. Mr. Sioeng, 52, says his recent flurry of activity in Cambodia and China is a means of laying the groundwork for his children's future. "Now that I am retired, I want to give the younger generation a push and just enjoy myself," he says.

Mr. Sioeng's graciousness to Mr. Bunma may not pay off, however. Mr. Prins is now conferring with the U.S. State Department as well as elders of the Methodist Church, which oversees Iowa

Wesleyan College, about whether Mr. Bunma's doctorate should be revoked. "I'm taking a lot of flak for it," Mr. Prins says from Mount Pleasant, Iowa. If taken back, it would be a serious blow to Mr. Bunma, who has told colleagues in Phnom Penh since the ceremony that he finally feels like a "complete person." Says one colleague: "Everyone here is calling him 'Doctor' now, just like they call Ted Sioeng 'Professor.' "

Iowa Wesleyan is not likely to make a public announcement either way. Says Mr. Prins: "We don't want to reopen this wound."

Mr. Gilley is a Hong Kong-based reporter for the Far Eastern Economic Review, a Dow Jones & Co. publication, in whose Jan. 15 issue this article first appeared.

REVIEW & OUTLOOK

'Someone Else's Politics'

This Saturday morning, Bill Clinton will travel a block down Pennsylvania Avenue to the office of his Beltway superlawyer Robert Bennett to give a deposition in Paula Jones's civil suit against him for sexual harassment in a Little Rock Hotel room in 1991. Up to now, there's been a loose consensus that the case would be settled somehow, if only to avoid a lurid spectacle. It now appears that the Clinton team intends to take the case to trial.

Unless we miss our bet, the Clinton team started thinking seriously about taking the case to trial about the time a jury bought

Paula Jones

Hunter Tylo's preposterous argument that pregnancy shouldn't impair her role as a seductress on "Melrose Place." The Clinton side may have concluded that given today's jump-ball jury logic, a he-said/she-said litigation offers good odds, perhaps a chance to turn the politics of the Jones case in its favor.

Mr. Clinton himself signaled this tack in telling U.S. News that the case is "probably" going to court. He also suggested the underlying strategy of going for a victory at trial when in the same interview he characterized the Jones case as "someone else's politics." If Mr. Clinton emerged from such a public cauldron with a decision in his favor, he could argue that the jury's verdict constituted a generalized people's rejection of the credibility of all the Administration scandals (unless of course another shoe drops that sweeps the Paula Jones case off center stage).

Mr. Clinton's defenders by now seem to have convinced themselves that the whole skein of events has all been merely "someone else's politics"—Whitewater, the $100,000 commodities miracle, Travelgate, Filegate, Judge Lamberth's sanctions, the string of failed memories under oath, the Foster suicide, the Espy case convictions, the Jim Guy Tucker conviction, the Hubbell guilty plea, the Cisneros independent counsel, the Ron Brown investigation, the Babbitt case, the Lincoln Bedroom, the whole fund-raising story and whatever the Starr investigators talked to Hillary about yesterday.

Skeptics may snicker, but one hard fact ought to be kept front and center amid this morass: Bill Clinton holds the office of the American Presidency. This, we imagine, has to be regarded by Mr. Clinton's litigators as his trump in any Jones trial. Even allowing for the American instinct that no man is above the law, it is at least arguable whether any jury, much less from Arkansas, would hold a President guilty of these particular charges.

It's a risk, of course, since Mrs. Jones's case is not a trivial one, as Stuart Taylor detailed in the American Lawyer piece that made the mainstream press take another look. But then, Mr. Clinton has spent his lifetime talking his way out of ethical scrapes ranging from independent counsels to draft boards. Why not one more?

Well, the fact is that we live in the age of the Simpson and Albert cases, and Jones v. Clinton would become a national spectacle quite unhinged from the conclusions of any mere jury. Our brief against Bill Clinton is that he has abused the powers of his office. Even his apologists reformulate this charge into the argument that the American people know all of this about Bill Clinton and have shown they don't care. But does this mean they don't care about him or about the office of the Presidency itself? If most people have by now written off even the Presidency as just another compromised American institution, then airing out the laundry of Governor Clinton's behavior in and around the Arkansas capital is no big deal.

But we think it is a very big deal. We think it is a symptom of Mr. Clinton's recklessness with his private life and his public office that he has allowed the Jones case to reach this point. He should have called off the Carville counterattack and settled promptly. He should have recognized that the dignity of this or any Presidency is not something that should be chewed over by the sharks of national television who will surely swim through the blood of this trial night after night until the climactic irrelevancy of the jury's thumbs up or down. In the predictable circus, some will accuse "the media" of undermining the dignity of the office, but protecting that dignity is first and foremost the duty of the man who holds the office.

To recognize the potential damage to the institution of the Presidency, one would have to acknowledge there is a distinction between the office itself and whichever mortal occupies it. Whatever else we've learned from the campaign fund-raising affairs, the Lincoln Bedroom rentals and the rest, the office is currently in full service to one man. In other words, someone else's politics.

Editorial Feature

That'll Be $43 Billion
For the Next Three Minutes

By P.J. O'ROURKE

Last Thursday the president of the United States telephoned the president of Indonesia to discuss the worsening economic crisis in Asia.

These two gentlemen have something in common: Both hold views on economics that are, shall we say, interesting. President Clinton's first major act in office was to propose price controls and rationing in a "health care reform plan" that showed magnificent ignorance of economic principles. President Suharto has indulged in wanton corruption and gross budgetary malfeasance, thus devastating what was one of the most promising economies in the developing world. Every student of economics is eager to know what these two thinkers had to say to each other. Unfortunately, the transcript of the conversation has not been released. We have to imagine it:

PRESIDENT CLINTON: President Suharto, I just want you to know how bad I feel about what's happened to the rupiah. I understand the hurt, the disappointments and the dashed hopes that can result from a currency devaluation. I remember when I was a boy in Hope, Ark., the U.S. currency lost all its value, and suddenly my family and I and all our neighbors had money that was worth nothing. Just to buy a loaf of bread, we needed to load bundles of this money into wheelbarrows and . . .

PRESIDENT SUHARTO: Was this during the Carter regime?

MR. CLINTON: President Suharto, Jimmy Carter faced political challenges just as you are facing them now and he overcame those challenges. Today, he is one of the world's most respected statesmen. Have you considered becoming involved with Habitat for Humanity? Maybe you could spend a few hours every week helping to build housing for the disadvantaged.

MR. SUHARTO: Is this one of the demands the IMF is making upon Indonesia?

MR. CLINTON: The IMF is a vital institution, a bulwark of freedom and democracy, and I want you to know that I support its goals. But I must be frank when I say that, although the United States is fully committed to aiding Indonesia, the Republican-dominated Congress is making a shortsighted move to obstruct full funding of the . . .

MR. SUHARTO: I understand we have some mutual friends. You remember the Riadys. They own the Lippo Group. Very kind people, very generous . . .

MR. CLINTON: Is $43 billion enough?

MR. SUHARTO: It is hard to say. What Mr. Huang gave at the White House coffee meetings, was that enough?

[A portion of the imaginary transcript has been lost from the administration's imaginary files.]

MR. CLINTON: Have you considered raising taxes? During my presidential term the American economy has undergone its largest expansion in history. This is because we raised taxes.

MR. SUHARTO: Huh?

MR. CLINTON: It has been my policy to "spread the wealth around."

MR. SUHARTO: How can you spread the wealth around? You have only one child.

Suharto

MR. CLINTON: Have you considered increased social spending? Social spending is an investment in the future.

MR. SUHARTO: We have been investing, mainly in the Cayman Islands.

MR. CLINTON: Have you considered raising the minimum wage?

MR. SUHARTO: Mostly we are considering exporting everything to you. My son Tommy has a very excellent automobile, the Timor, that he is planning to manufacture. Perhaps you would like 300,000 of them?

MR. CLINTON: My commitment to free trade is well known. But the Republican-dominated Congress has made a shortsighted move to obstruct. . . . Have you considered blaming everything on the Republican-dominated Congress?

MR. SUHARTO: I have not checked on these things recently, but I do not believe we have a Republican-dominated Congress in Indonesia. We are, however, thinking about blaming everything on the ethnic Chinese.

MR. CLINTON: The Chinese are among the greatest peoples on earth, a bulwark of freedom. My commitment to . . .

MR. SUHARTO: Yes, they donate a lot to my election campaigns, also.

MR. CLINTON: Which reminds me, congratulations on your re-election this coming March.

MR. SUHARTO: Thank you. But these elections are so expensive. And the raising of funds is so time-consuming. Perhaps I could ask you, is Albert Gore free? I understand that the vice president might be wishing to go on a long foreign visit.

MR. CLINTON: Actually, Al is pretty busy—you know, traveling to the funerals of foreign dignitaries . . .

Voice in Background on Air Force One: Like Suharto's!

MR. SUHARTO: Excuse me, what was it you said?

MR. CLINTON: Hillary did real well with cattle futures. Have you tried that?

MR. SUHARTO: Water buffalo are trading at a very low rate just now. We were thinking of selling short the Dow Jones index. We have calculated that, if Indonesia collapses completely, this would lead to . . .

MR. CLINTON: How about $50 billion? This kind of thing worked great for Mexico.

MR. SUHARTO: Did Mexico pay back the money?

MR. CLINTON: Yes. That's why the bailout was such a success. We saved the Mexican economy, and Mexico paid back the money with interest. Everybody was happy.

MR. SUHARTO: Mexico paid back the money? Plus interest?

MR. CLINTON: Yes.

MR. SUHARTO: With all respect, President Clinton, I must tell you that you have a great deal to learn about the "Asian Miracle."

Mr. O'Rourke is international affairs desk chief for Rolling Stone.

Review & Outlook

The Democratic Tribe

This morning Rep. Dan Burton's House committee begins several days of hearings on Interior Secretary Bruce Babbitt and the nexus between contributions to the Democratic Party and Indian policy. The Babbitt tale is noteworthy because it resonates on a number of levels.

There is first of all the issue of whether the Interior Secretary's case merits the appointment of an independent counsel. The relevant question might be put this way: Are there any conceivable circumstances under which Janet Reno would call for an independent counsel to investigate any member of the Clinton Administration? If she passes on the Babbitt case, the answer would have to be no, that there will be no more ICs for any reason for any conceivable covered person over the next three years.

Bruce Babbitt

The essential details of the Babbitt case are fairly straightforward—almost a he-said/he-said dispute between Mr. Babbitt and a lobbying Democratic lawyer—but the fact remains that enough public detail has emerged that someone has to resolve whether federal law was violated. Mr. Babbitt is a member of the President's Cabinet, heretofore a "covered person" under most anyone's interpretation of the independent counsel statute.

Rep. Burton's detractors will continue to charge that somehow his hearings don't count because "it's someone else's politics." From this we may conclude that their view of how the system of accountability should properly function is that Mr. Burton should drop his "political" hearings and all the rest of us should just, you know, take Bruce Babbitt's word that it was all a slip of the tongue.

Problem is, you don't need Dan Burton to generate political heat over the Babbitt case and the other Indian casino incidents. Politically, the most interesting thing about the Indian casinos is that they have the potential to open fissures inside the Democratic tribe itself.

In the Babbitt case, involving the Chippewa Indians, it looks as if someone is going to have to take a fall. Beyond Mr. Babbitt's legal difficulties, however, there is the matter of the Democratic Party's self-image. This, after all, is a party whose members generally have assumed a moral purpose superior to that of their opponents. But what we seem to have here is this particular party trying to beat money out of relatively poor Indian tribes. This is supposed to be something liberals would never do, but it is at the center of the controversy involving the Cheyenne-Arapaho tribe.

Today there are 11,000 Cheyenne-Arapaho, 63% of them unemployed. According to the Bureau of Indian Affairs, the average income of those who have jobs is $6,074 a year. In May 1996, Michael Turpin, a Democratic fund-raiser, told the tribe that if it contributed $100,000 it would be given a chance to pitch President Clinton directly on the return of 7,500 acres seized in 1883. The next month, Charles Surveyor, the Cheyenne tribe's chairman, found himself one of seven guests at a private White House luncheon.

Mr. Clinton listened for 20 minutes as Mr. Surveyor made his case. After the meeting, Mr. Surveyor remembers President Clinton saying, "We're going to help you." Right after the lunch, Clinton-Gore finance chair Terry McAuliffe told Mr. Surveyor and tribal leader Tyler Todd that "the President has given his word and you're going to get your land back." Mr. McAuliffe has issued denials in matters relating to tribal fund raising.

The tribe was overjoyed and agreed within days to send $87,675 from its welfare fund to the DNC. Through an "oversight" the contribution wasn't reported to the Federal Election Commission for eight months. The tribe was told they still owed some $12,000, which they couldn't afford, and were also encouraged to give $20,000 for a

Presidential birthday dinner in August 1996, which they did scrape together. Then after the November election, says Richard Grellner, the tribe's lawyer, the Democrats "completely dropped us off their radar screen until December when the DNC called and wanted more money, including $250,000 for Mr. Gore to come to Oklahoma."

Frustrated, the tribe asked a veteran Democratic professional named Mike Copperthite to help, and he became an unpaid adviser to the Cheyenne-Arapaho tribe in December 1996. Not much came of Mr. Copperthite's efforts other than demands to give the DNC more money.

Mr. Copperthite has begun talking about the experience recently, mostly, he says, out of disgust. "If they took money from impoverished Indians, whose money didn't they take?" he asks. "What Clinton-Gore did in 1996 was worse than anything I've ever seen in politics," he told us. "Everybody doesn't do it."

On the one hand, that's reassuring. On the other hand, with Janet Reno concluding that none of it merits an independent counsel and with the remaining oversight efforts such as the Burton hearings derided by the Beltway, the odds are good that in the future, many more people in politics will indeed be doing it.

Editorial Feature

'The Election Was Decided By Early 1996'

The following is excerpted from former Senate Majority Leader Bob Dole's written testimony last week to the Senate Governmental Affairs Committee, which is investigating campaign finance illegalities during the 1996 election campaign:

When I resigned from the Senate in June of 1996, my reputation for personal honesty and integrity was intact and I wish to keep it that way. The pundits will tell us the general public either doesn't care about, or has given up on, politicians. I disagree and continue to believe that while not one of us is faultless, most Americans expect and respect honesty and integrity in the political process.

Bob Dole

As the Committee knows, I offered to appear before the Committee voluntarily and testify under oath about any and all of my activities during the 1996 presidential campaign. I was and am now concerned about the untrue allegations leveled against my campaign during the course of the Committee's proceedings. During the 1996 election cycle, I believe that I complied with all campaign laws then in effect.

Two principal allegations about the Dole for President campaign surfaced during the Committee's hearings. First, some have suggested that our campaign conspired to evade the spending limits imposed under federal election law by improperly running so-called issue advertisements through the Republican National Committee ("RNC"). Second, some have alleged that our campaign misused certain nonprofit organizations by improperly coordinating the political activities of those groups for the benefit of our campaign.

Permit me to respond to each of these false allegations.

*   *   *

In the fall of 1995, even before the Republican primaries had begun, the Democratic National Committee ("DNC") began an extensive advertising campaign substantially paid for by "soft money" raised in unlimited sums from corporations, unions and wealthy individuals. Almost without exception, the advertisements depicted the President working in the Oval Office and praised him for his leadership on key public issues. The ads contained ominous looking images of me (then the Senate Majority Leader), joined me at the hip with Speaker Newt Gingrich (who had a very low favorability rating at the time), and mischaracterized my positions on issues. The DNC reportedly spent in excess of $40 million running these ads in key electoral states. As the President stated in one of the White House videotapes, belatedly turned over to your Committee, this sustained barrage of advertising by the DNC was instrumental in shaping positive public opinion about the President and negative public opinion about me. History will show that, because of the ad campaign, the election—for all practical purposes—was decided by early 1996, long before Republicans had a nominee.

The DNC's so-called issue ads were particularly damaging because, unlike the President, I faced a difficult multi-candidate primary challenge. While our campaign spent precious resources in key primary states, the Clinton/Gore campaign spent little throughout 1995 and early 1996 while the DNC, under White House direction and control, continued to relentlessly promote the President's candidacy.

Some have argued that, since each party sponsored issue ads supporting its presidential candidate, there was no difference between the two ad campaigns. The facts do not support such a view. It is beyond dispute that the DNC ran a longer, more sustained ad campaign than did the RNC. The $40 million spent by the DNC on the President's behalf dwarfed the amounts spent by the RNC. The RNC's effort, minimal as it was, was in fact an act of self-defense since everyone knew from polling data the adverse impact the

Presidential-DNC ad barrage was having on Republican electoral prospects across-the-board.

More importantly, there was a major difference between the issue ads sponsored by both parties. Unlike the President, I did not direct and control the ads produced by the Republican National Committee nor did I coordinate with RNC officials to ensure that the ads provided maximum benefit to my campaign. Frankly, I was dissatisfied with much of the ad content and failed to understand the RNC's strategy on airing the spots.

As your Committee's investigation has amply documented, the President reviewed, drafted and edited most of the DNC ads. As [former Clinton campaign adviser] Dick Morris has noted in his book:

"[T]he president became the day-to-day operational director of [the DNC's] TV-ad campaign. He worked over every script, watched each ad, ordered changes in every visual presentation, and decided which ads would run when and where. He was as involved as any of his media consultants were. The ads became not the slick creations of ad men but the work of the president himself. . . . Every line of every ad came under his informed, critical and often meddlesome gaze. Every ad was his ad."

Other accounts are consistent with Morris's account. In his book *The Choice*, author Bob Woodward concludes:

"Clinton personally had been controlling tens of millions of dollars worth of DNC advertising. This enabled him to exceed the legal spending limits and effectively rendered the DNC an adjunct to his own re-election effort. He was circumventing the rigorous post-Watergate reforms that were designed to limit and control the raising and spending of money for presidential campaigns."

There is no indication that the DNC ever exercised any control over the advertising campaign—indeed, every aspect of the ad campaign was reviewed, approved and controlled by the President. As Fred Wertheimer, former president of Common Cause, explains:

"The President and his campaign aides determined how the money would be distributed—which state parties received it, how much they got, when they got it and how they spent it. It was all done to re-elect the President. Democratic Party officials at the national and state levels did not control the money or the ads. They were the equivalent of a corporate shell through which the President and his aides ran the second track of the campaign."

Mr. Chairman, I can assure you and the Members of this Committee that there was no "second track" to the Dole for President campaign. I did not draft, edit or even preview the RNC ads that began running in mid-1996 long after the $40 million advertising onslaught by the President through the DNC.

Of course, there is nothing illegal or improper about national party committees running ads highlighting issues important to their respective constituencies. If the DNC and RNC want to sponsor advertisements urging voters to support policies that also happen to reflect the views of their respective presidential candidates, that's appropriate. In my opinion, however, controlling legal authority does not permit a presidential candidate to *direct and control* a national party's ad campaign *with the intent* to advance his or her own prospects for election. That's why my campaign did not engage in this practice and that's why we filed a complaint with the Federal Election Commission against the Clinton/Gore campaign on this very issue. This complaint is still pending before the FEC.

The bottom line is that when a presidential candidate, using "soft money," directs and controls his party's issue ads, these ads become campaign expenditures—not party outlays—and they effectively render the presidential spending limits of federal election law meaningless.

This is a crucial point because both the President and I agreed to accept public matching funds during the primary and general election campaigns. As a condition of receiving the public's financial support, we both agreed to abide by the rules on direction, control and spending set by federal law.

* * *

The other allegation relates to our campaign's purported misuse of nonprofit groups. Some have implied that our campaign improperly coordinated the election activities of several nonprofits. To the contrary, I never personally directed, controlled or coordinated the election activities of any nonprofit group during the 1996 election, and I have no knowledge of my campaign participating in such conduct.

I understand that campaign staff had occasional contact with leaders of nonprofit organizations that were ideologically sympathetic to the goals of my campaign. To my knowledge, however, there is nothing illegal or improper about such contact. Absent some evidence that the activities of these groups were directed, controlled or coordinated by my campaign, I strongly object to the baseless accusation that my campaign acted improperly or illegally.

*   *   *

I would also like to address—with the benefit of hindsight—some of the problems that I see in the current presidential campaign finance system. First, as demonstrated by the 1996 election cycle, it is unfair to provide a presidential candidate public matching funds in a primary if that candidate is unopposed or virtually unopposed—as was the case with the President in 1996. Unlike the President, Republicans held a bruising and costly primary contest for the presidential nomination.

Even though the President had no primary challenger, his primary campaign received roughly $37 million in public matching funds—in addition to the $40 million of in-kind contributions received from the DNC in the form of issue ads. With no primary challenge, the President was able to focus his primary campaign on me long before I became the Republican nominee. Lacking the resources to respond to the President's negative attacks, my general election campaign started at an enormous disadvantage. In the future, I believe Congress should limit the availability of public funds in primary campaigns to those candidates who actually face significant primary opposition.

There is nothing partisan about this suggestion: While the Republican nominee in 1996 was harmed by the President's receipt of public funds despite the lack of primary opposition, a similar situation could arise in the future in which the Democratic nominee would be adversely affected by an unopposed Republican nominee whose campaign is awash in public funds.

Another aspect of campaign election law that I find particularly troubling is the audit process conducted by the Federal Election Commission. These audits are too costly and too long. Furthermore, I believe it is inappropriate to hold a presidential candidate personally liable for the inevitable minor infractions that are the product of these audits. In most cases, a losing presidential campaign is broke and it is simply unfair to hold the candidate personally responsible for the misdeeds of a sprawling campaign unless the candidate participated in, or had direct knowledge of, any misconduct.

*   *   *

Finally, Mr. Chairman, let me make a few general suggestions as

-181-

to how we can reform the current campaign finance system.

First, the systematic laundering of foreign money that we saw in last year's presidential campaign must never occur again. To help prevent these abuses, our campaign law should be amended to reflect a simple principle: "If you can't vote, you can't contribute."

Second, a reasonable cap should be placed on the amount of labor, corporate, and individual "soft money" that the national political parties may legally accept, and a five-year phase-out period should be established after which all "soft-money" contributions would be banned.

Third, with organized labor playing an enormously potent role in last year's elections, fairness dictates that no union member should be forced to finance political activities to which he objects. To give teeth to the Supreme Court's *Beck* decision, federal law should be amended to require unions affirmatively to receive permission from their members before using forced dues payments for political purposes.

More generally, I believe the best way to untie the Gordian Knot of campaign finance reform is to remove this issue from politics altogether. As we have seen over the years, both political parties will inevitably succumb to the urge of trying to rig the rules to favor their own interests. That's why Congress and the President should establish an independent commission of outside experts to develop a comprehensive reform plan. Congress would then consider the plan through an "up-or-down" vote without amendment, or with a limited number of amendments by each party, and follow procedures similar to the way Congress has considered the recommendations of the Base Realignment and Closure Commission.

Meet Monica

A Clinton firestorm arose on January 21, 1998, with a bombshell report in the Washington Post. Independent Counsel Kenneth Starr, with the approval of a three-judge panel of the U.S. Court of Appeals following a request by Attorney General Reno, had expanded his investigation to cover allegations of suborning perjury, false statements and obstruction of justice involving the President and a 24-year-old former White House intern named Monica Lewinsky. Another former White House aide, Linda Tripp, had provided Mr. Starr with hours of audiotaped conversations between Ms. Tripp and Ms. Lewinsky. In the tapes, the Post reported, Ms. Lewinsky not only graphically recounted sexual liaisons with the President, but also described efforts by him and others to direct false testimony in the sexual harassment lawsuit brought against Mr. Clinton by former Arkansas state employee Paula Jones.

The story riveted the nation. A media conflagration exploded around the White House and speculation about the President's resignation or impeachment careened through the airwaves. In an editorial titled "Bonfire of the Presidency," the Journal noted that "From the first, we have written of 'Arkansas mores'—not in denigration of that state's good people but in depicting the political habits Mr. Clinton carried to Washington. In this sense the Lewinsky crisis is of a piece with Whitewater, $100,000 commodity strikes, the coverup after the Foster suicide, the Travel Office firings, the misappropriated FBI files, and the campaign finance mess. Whenever and however Mr. Clinton leaves office, we will spend a long time discovering what damage his mores have done to our institutions, and a longer time repairing them."

Review & Outlook

The Outrage Arrives

If they're true, they're not only politically damaging, but could lead to impeachment proceedings.

— George Stephanopoulos, ABC News

Five years and a day into the Presidency of Bill Clinton, the outrage has arrived. As the details spill out everywhere of allegations that Mr. Clinton had an affair with White House intern Monica

Monica Lewinsky

Lewinsky and then asked her to lie about it under oath, political voices from George Stephanopoulos to Henry Hyde are raising the possibility of impeachment. As the useful saying goes, Who'da thunk it?

After all that's happened the past five years, the Clinton Presidency teeters on a sex scandal. We don't mean to diminish the seriousness of this matter. Mr. Clinton is old enough to be her father. And though it'll likely get buried in the tumult, Independent Counsel Kenneth Starr's interest doesn't have to do with whatever was going on between them, but whether the President suborned perjury from her.

Either way, the core issue is the same as in the first months of Mr. Clinton's tenure; it's about character.

This is exactly the same issue that came up over the draft board letters and the "I didn't inhale" statement. But back then the political cognoscenti, for reasons they may explain to the rest of us someday, waved away those red flags as irrelevant to the conduct of the Presidency. And they kept right on waving—through all the details of the Whitewater land schemes, revelation of Hillary's long-shot jackpot in the commodities pits, the Travelgate and Filegate scandals, the Thompson campaign finance hearings.

Bob Dole finally asked, "Where's the outrage?" The consensus answer that came back from the press: Voters know all this about Bill Clinton, and they don't care. Blow after blow after blow to the integrity of our institutions by this Administration elicited condemnation only from a handful of editorial pages, magazines dismissed as partisan and obsessional, and a few reporters in the mainstream media. Until the Washington Post and Los Angeles Times broke the intern story yesterday.

So now comes the outrage, pouring out of the mouths of every Beltway pundit with access to a TV talk show. The ceiling is suddenly caving in on Mr. Clinton's Presidency on the testimony of two or three courageous women. All of this was smoked out by the Paula Jones lawsuit, and the crucial tape recordings of conversations with Ms. Lewinsky were made by longtime civil servant Linda Tripp. Yesterday the President went on TV to say "there is no improper relationship," but his press spokesman refused to define "improper."

Add as well former White House aide Kathleen Willey, whose deposition was reported in yesterday's Post. She testified to Ms. Jones's lawyers that she went to Clinton about a better job, he grabbed her and started groping and kissing her, saying, "I've always wanted to do that." We guess this means Mr. Clinton has violated the Packwood Standard; Senator Packwood was driven from office for trying to cadge kisses and the like from nonconsenting women.

This story now proceeds on two tracks—the independent counsel's investigation and television.

Mr. Starr's request for an expansion of his mandate was approved over the weekend by two separate overseers. He could have gone directly to a special panel of three federal judges who monitor all independent counsel, but stopped along the way to consult Janet Reno's Justice Department. Both approved his request quickly.

As for television, here is a medium whose news divisions by and large couldn't be bothered with the Clinton scandals; only Fox Cable

News, for example, carried the campaign-finance hearings live. But with the scent of Presidential sex in the air, they're calling anchormen back from covering the Pope in Cuba to handle the story.

Someday Bill Clinton may muse on his long, reckless run with Lady Fortune. No matter how serious the charges the past five years, he was safe so long as he was able to restrict the judgment calls on his conduct of the Presidency to the sophisticates in the Washington political establishment. In Washington nowadays, no act is so gross that it can't be reduced to mere "partisanship," and no one makes judgments independent of "the polls."

Now, however, Mr. Clinton finds himself at the tender mercies of TV programmers who have a story they know how to tell—sex and lies about it. Bill Clinton is about to enter into that same land recently visited by Marv Albert and Mike Tyson, where an event whose relevant details can be described in five minutes will be talked about unto prime-time eternity.

Again, if this Presidency has to go to the brink of dissolution, we'd have preferred for the sake of Mr. Clinton and our politics that it be over such matters as lying about tax returns, lying to Congress or lying to the federal judiciary. Instead it totters over asking a starstruck girl to lie. It would be nice to think the American system could do better than rough justice, but for the moment, it looks as if that's what we've got.

Editorial Feature

This Is Why
We Have Impeachment

By BOB BARR

Independent Counsel Kenneth Starr's recent authorization to investigate allegations that President Clinton conducted a sexual affair in the White House with a 21-year-old intern, then attempted to tamper with a witness, to obstruct justice, and to induce her to commit perjury has drawn wide attention, as it should. The matter once again raises the troubling question of how best to hold the president accountable for his actions.

Some might now argue that this scandal, as it has developed in the past few days, shows that the independent counsel statute has teeth

Bill Clinton

and the Justice Department has integrity. But in fact we know that such important matters deserve a forceful political reaction—including possible impeachment proceedings—if only because the independent counsel law, so beloved inside the Beltway, has proved unworkable.

Following public revulsion on a mass scale over the Watergate scandal, Congress in 1978 passed legislation to allow "independent counsels" to investigate and prosecute top executive branch officials suspected of wrongdoing. The law has been used, on the whole, quite effectively, resulting in many successful prosecutions, such as those of former Arkansas Gov. Jim Guy Tucker and Tyson Foods Inc. It has also served as a potent encouragement for top officials to follow the law.

Lately, however, this well-intended law has ceased to serve its purpose, and is now working to hide the wrongdoing it was meant to expose. Rather than a sword to fight corruption, the independent counsel statute is being used as a shield to protect a rogue executive by a complicit Justice Department. Justice is thwarted and corruption becomes the norm.

An egregious example concerns the multiyear effort to camouflage the true composition of Hillary Rodham Clinton's 1993 Health Care Task Force. A recent opinion by U.S. District Judge Royce Lamberth declared in unusually blunt language that the White House successfully pressured the Justice Department to participate in a coverup on behalf of presidential aide Ira Magaziner. Eric Holder, then the U.S. attorney for the District of Columbia and now the No. 2 official at Justice, refused to prosecute Mr. Magaziner. To further complicate matters, immediately after Judge Lamberth's opinion was released, the top Justice Department internal watchdog—whose job it is to prevent misconduct such as departmental participation in covering up perjury—resigned amid charges of petty bureaucratic theft and bullying in his office.

The independent counsel law presupposes a Justice Department sufficiently objective, competent and uncorrupted to trigger the law when specific and credible evidence exists. But these recent experiences give the lie to this optimistic assumption. Time and again in recent months, a handful of investigative reporters have outperformed a Justice Department task force of hundreds of investigators and attorneys. These repeated embarrassments are enough to make one wonder whether top Justice officials are capable of pursuing the evidence if they even wanted to.

In fact, the independent counsel statute is now being twisted to provide cover for the Clinton administration. By reducing her inquiry to incredibly technical questions, and then refusing to appoint an independent counsel in the campaign finance mess after months of inquiries, Attorney General Janet Reno has allowed the statute to be used as a mechanism for issuing clean bills of health for an obviously corrupt administration. The statute has lost all credibility, save for that garnered as a result of the few continuing investigations—concerning Whitewater, Mr. Espy and former Housing Secretary Henry Cisneros—that began their work before this Justice Department became the defense firm for the Clinton-Gore campaign.

In the present case, Ms. Reno and a three-judge panel of the D.C. Circuit Court of Appeals acted promptly on Mr. Starr's request to expand his mandate to cover the president's role in allegedly suborning perjury from Monica Lewinsky, who claims to be his former lover. But it's doubtful whether Mr. Starr can indeed gather evidence sufficient to prove a criminal case against the president, and even more unlikely that under our Constitution a sitting president can be prosecuted through the courts for criminal conduct.

The question then becomes: How do we fight corruption at the highest levels of government without special prosecutors? The answer is simple: We do what we did before 1978. We use the mechanisms provided in the Constitution, including if necessary the process of impeachment. Even before the news about the former White House intern, Mr. Clinton had provided sufficient grounds for the House to begin a debate on drawing up articles of impeachment. His alleged conduct with Ms. Lewinsky, if true, only adds to an already imposing mountain of evidence against the president.

Because history does frequently repeat itself, Congress may indeed be moved by public outcry to enact a new version of the independent counsel statute. But for now, this law should be removed from the books. Keeping it while openly and brazenly refusing to enforce it does too much harm to the credibility of federal law enforcement. Instead it's time for Congress to step into the breach and perform its constitutionally mandated role to root out corruption in the executive branch.

Rep. Barr (R., Ga.) serves on the House Judiciary and Government Reform committees. He was the U.S. attorney in the Northern District of Georgia under Presidents Reagan and Bush.

REVIEW & OUTLOOK

POTUS on Wall Street

If current difficulties keep Bill Clinton in Washington the next little while, inhabitants of Manhattan will live a little easier. POTUS has been making a local nuisance of himself lately, running up police bills and snarling traffic on three fund-raising forays in the past six weeks, counting his visit to Jesse Jackson's personal tree-shaking. Indeed, in New York alone the President raised an estimated $2.5 million toward a $10 million winter drive.

Even local Democrats are complaining. They worry that with the President shipping all the money back to Charlie Trie and the Buddhist nuns to pay off DNC debt, there won't be anything left for, say, Geraldine Ferraro to pick over in her effort to oust Al D'Amato. N.Y. State Democratic Party Chairwoman Judith Hope told the local press, "Virtually all of my major donors are the same as their major donors. When I'm making phone calls, and they've just been here, I hear, 'I just gave a $25,000 check to the DNC, and I can't give to you for a while.' " The state party wants a 25% cut of the gate.

Everyone understands, of course, that when POTUS visits Hollywood he's after copyright protection money, that when he visits Silicon Valley he's garnering funds from adherents of the Microsoft antitrust suit, and that in Texas he's seeking leave-us-alone money from the tort liability bar. In the canyons of Wall Street, it's equally clear, he's prospecting for, well, Wall Street money.

Lo and behold, the Presidential attention to New York has coincided with a drive to immunize big Wall Street firms from state prosecution by Manhattan District Attorney Robert Morgenthau. When Mr. Morgenthau indicted a compliance officer from Morgan Stanley, the defendant's lawyers managed to cut a plea bargain with federal prosecutors. What's more, U.S. Attorney Mary Jo White proclaimed a principle: "Securities frauds affecting the national and international markets should be charged federally." Mark Pomerantz, chief of the criminal division in her office, elaborated in an interview with

the New York Times, "We are charged with enforcing Federal securities laws, and in major securities fraud cases affecting the national markets, we need to prevent end runs around the generally tougher Federal laws and sentences."

While Ms. White formally reports to Main Justice in Washington, we've previously noted her considerable reputation for independence. In particular, she won speedy guilty pleas from three associates of former Teamster President

Mr. Morgenthau

Ron Carey, an action that could not have been pleasing to Democratic Party officialdom in Washington. Her prosecutors also said the AFL-CIO treasurer was involved, and Treasurer Richard Trumka took the Fifth Amendment when questioned by the master overseeing the Teamsters. He remains in office as the number two in the AFL-CIO, which recently spent $25 million trying to elect Democrats. In accepting guilty pleas, we note, Ms. White's prosecutors got promises of cooperation in a continuing investigation.

Yet Ms. White loses a few of the Teamster points, at least in our book, by declining any on-the-record discussion of her declaration of federal supremacy in prosecuting insider trading at big Wall Street firms. We guess we can say that she says she doesn't want to perpetuate the argument with Mr. Morgenthau, but this leaves her sweeping comments to the Times the last thing on the record.

Some whom we respect agree with this position, but more think it's bunk. The Securities and Exchange Commission was asked to support federal pre-emption, for example, but decided it would not take sides in an argument between two often-useful allies. A District Attorney in East Podunk might indeed defer to more knowledgeable federal authorities if he stumbled across an insider-trading case, but the Manhattan District Attorney's office can surely handle these cases—at certain times better than the U.S. Attorney's office, which in the Giuliani era won convictions repeatedly reversed by the Second Circuit.

More broadly, Mr. Morgenthau is an "independent counsel" in a way that Kenneth Starr and the like never can be. He derives his authority through an entirely different route, not appointment by the Department of Justice but by election by voters of Manhattan. The Founding Fathers called this the principle of Federalism. Independent authorities provide checks and balances, so that oversights, incompetence and abuse can be more easily identified and corrected.

With financial crime, the Manhattan District Attorney is clearly the most important law-enforcement official outside of federal lines of authority, and Mr. Morgenthau has often been a thorn in the side of Washington, as in pushing the BCCI cases harder than federal authorities deigned to. This kind of independence should be protected, particularly when we have a Washington Justice Department like the current one. This is certainly not the time to proclaim a rule that the state authorities can prosecute the little traders, but only federal authorities can prosecute the big contributors.

Editorial Feature

It Turns Out Character Does Matter

It's impossible to make sense of this latest Bill Clinton scandal without flashing back to an eerily similar scene six winters ago.

We reporters were shivering on a suburban driveway in New Hampshire. Before us stood then-Gov. Bill Clinton and his wife, holding hands. James Carville worked the bigfeet one by one. Mr. Clinton put on his aggrieved face and told us and the world that Gennifer Flower's "story is just not true."

Potomac Watch

By Paul A. Gigot

Six years later almost to the day, Mr. Clinton has now reportedly told a different story himself. Several sources say he told Paula Jones's lawyers in his deposition last Saturday that he did in fact have an affair with Ms. Flowers. That was under oath. His earlier line was merely under pressure.

Yesterday the besieged White House spokesman, Mike McCurry, refused to deny the reports about Saturday. But he claimed, incredibly and without elaboration, that the president's 1992 and 1998 statements "are not at odds." When asked repeatedly if that meant Mr. Clinton didn't have an affair with Ms. Flowers, Mr. McCurry begged off.

Ms. Flowers has told the Washington Post this is "vindication." But how foolish should the rest of us feel? The truth is that just about everyone in the press corps thought Mr. Clinton was lying even then, but we let it slide. Ms. Flowers had her own audiotapes, but we dismissed them as "doctored."

The tapes revealed Mr. Clinton intimating that she should lie, but she had sold her tale for money and so she couldn't be believed. "If they ever hit you with it just say 'no' and go on, there's nothing they can do," Mr. Clinton said to Ms. Flowers as recorded on tape. But we said the voters didn't care, even apparently about lying.

Monica Lewinsky

So now this history is repeating itself as tragedy instead of farce, and Washington is shocked. We forgave Mr. Clinton his personal recklessness as a part of the past, but are now stunned to see it return with a vengeance that jeopardizes his presidency. We said character didn't matter, but now we discover it may be the only thing that matters.

All of this past explains why Mr. Clinton's denials are being treated so skeptically in the case of former White House intern Monica Lewinsky. After five years, even friendly reporters have learned to look for the weasel word, the legalistic evasion.

About Harry Truman or Jimmy Carter or Ronald Reagan, no one would have believed something like this. But about Bill Clinton, we have learned to wait for the other stiletto heel to drop. So when Mr. Clinton tells PBS's Jim Lehrer that "There is not a sexual relationship," even Clinton friends note with caution that he repeatedly used the present tense. Or they wonder how he defines "sexual."

None of the familiar White House scandal defenses seem likely to work this time, either. This isn't a memory out of Arkansas, but allegedly took place last year in and around the Oval Office. It doesn't involve a platinum blonde on the make but a woman only a few years older than Chelsea. The charges don't involve partisan enemies but former employees. And the tape-recordings weren't made by the Star tabloid, but by the FBI at the behest of independent counsel Ken Starr.

All of which means that the Clinton presidency as we've known it is over. If Ms. Lewinsky surfaces today or soon and insists that what she said in those tapes was delusional, then the story will go away. But if she corroborates even half of what's on tape, the political damage for the president will be severe. The Tabloid Presidency will have arrived.

This will be so even if Mr. Starr finds the more serious charges of obstruction of justice and suborning perjury impossible to prove. The mere fact of a president having an affair with a 21-year-old in the White House would be damaging by itself.

This is no simple case of adultery. It is the definition of a boss in a position of power exploiting someone young and easily swayed. It shows arrogance and recklessness of the kind that ran Gary Hart from the presidential race in 1987 and Bob Packwood from the Senate in 1995. And there is the risk of perjury if he lied about it under oath (as opposed to on TV).

Already the networks are relating the alleged details of the Clinton-Lewinsky relationship like evidence in the O.J. trial. There are reports of special courier deliveries from Ms. Lewinsky to the Oval Office; phone calls from the president to her home; frequent admissions to the White House; and of course the salacious tape transcripts that are sure to leak. All of which would be mere prelude to the Paula Jones trial in May, media event of the century.

A friend of mine says Bill Clinton has benefited all these years from "the Harry Truman effect." This is the American faith that anyone can rise to the challenges of the presidency and should be absolved of his past once elected. It is a democratic conceit that has sometimes served us well.

But such faith always hangs on character. David McCullough ends his biography of Truman by quoting Eric Sevareid, the late TV newsman, observing that the essence of any presidency is "character, just character."

A scandal like this one is what we get for ignoring that wisdom in electing this president. We can't say we weren't warned.

Editorial Feature

Even Houdini

By MARK HELPRIN

Houdini succumbed, at the peak of his fame, to a blow from an unexpected quarter. After a long career of living dangerously, bursting from handcuffs, shedding straitjackets, and emerging in triumph from chained coffins, he failed by a fraction of a second to lock his abdominal muscles before the impact of a punch delivered by a young man whose enthusiasm and timing he had misjudged, and that killed him. Even Houdini was no match for the continual pressure of fate. No one is. The truth, which is indestructible, has a way of accumulating against pride and arrogance, and then sweeping them from its path.

The same reporters, commentators and columnists who, sharing his politics, have dismissed the vast accumulation of damning evidence against President, Governor, and just plain Bill Clinton, have in the past few days felt what they themselves characterize as the explosive force of the Lewinsky Affair. It is explosive to them because it is unfamiliar. It is unfamiliar because they have not seen it. They have not seen it because they have been blind. And they have been blind because they have wanted to be blind.

Jolted From Somnambulism

The question now is whether, having been jolted from its somnambulism, the press will stay awake or go back to sleep. It will certainly be tempted with sleep. Although the president and even his snapping turtle, James Carville, seemed stunned by the new peril, his strategy is clear. Not only does he have only one course to follow other than resignation, but he has enunciated the plan himself, in his own words, in his own voice, on tape. The following is a direct quotation of Bill Clinton, explaining how to lie his way out of an affair of which he has been accused before the entire nation. "Well, that's what I mean. You know, if all the people who are named . . . deny it. . . . That's all, I mean, I expect them to come looking into it and interview you and everything, uh, but I just think that if everybody's on record denying it you've got no problem. . . . . I wonder if I'm going to be blown out of the water with this. I don't see how they can . . . if they don't, if they don't have pictures."

This was his advice to Gennifer Flowers in 1991. It worked as predicted, despite the fact that she played the tape at a news conference. On national television, Mr. Clinton gave a lawyer's denial that he had had a 12-year affair with her, having in mind perhaps 11.5 years. Though he has now admitted it, why should he be discouraged? Having been caught in a conspiracy to lie about it, having lied about it, and then confirming under oath that he lied about it and (by implication) conspired to lie about it, he is still the president of the United States; he still has a 62% approval rating; he has come through this kind of thing in this way many times before; and he knows that if he, Vernon Jordan, and Monica Lewinsky hang tight, he may have no problem. After all, Monica Lewinsky's potentially incriminating voice on tape is just a voice on a tape, as was Mr. Clinton's own voice on Gennifer Flowers's tape. This would not be the first time the president bet either his candidacy or his presidency on the fact that the American people have moved away from the word, even the spoken word, and find it difficult to come to a conclusion or make a judgment "if they don't have pictures."

To date, the president has come through because he begs for his transgressions to be overlooked on account of the peace and prosperity that he has inherited, and the press and people have answered this prayer. But as the tangled web has gotten slowly heavier, its very nature has changed. Now the president must fight circumstantial evidence in light of testimony given under oath, and all that this implies. If the accusations are true, he must rely upon the character of two very different people to determine his fate, and he cannot know what they will do.

But he can know what his partisans will do, or most of them anyway. They will almost undoubtedly make a last-ditch effort to turn this latest scandal as upside down as it has recently turned them. They will deny the facts, they will counterattack, and they will claim according to habit that sexual scandals are unworthy and irrelevant. Even though slandering their opponents and "smelling rats" has redounded against them, as soon as the ringing stops in their ears they will excoriate anyone who dares offer a challenge. Expect it.

But keep in mind that this is not merely a sexual scandal. Nor is it just a matter of legal technicalities along the Kafkaesque lines of a conviction for resisting false arrest. It is, rather, a fundamental question put to the American people, and the power of recent events stems from this rather than from the fact that it comes packaged with sex, lies and audiotape. Like the Paula Jones case, which many, even among the president's detractors, mistakenly find to be petty, embarrassing, or merely a provocation, the Lewinsky Affair is about the essentials not only of jurisprudence but of governance. Paula Jones and Monica Lewinsky are

Bill Clinton

two inconsequential women who, in the manner of democracies, have become gravely consequential. And the heart of both their cases is whether truth can be denied by power. Can the king declare, in the blinding light of midday, that it is night, and can he compel his subjects to accept what he declares?

The answer, of course, is clear, and it is an answer that is not elicited only once. Every now and then, we are put to the test, which is the fundamental test of English and American history, and perhaps the fundamental test of Western civilization. The answer must be that the king cannot compel a lie. The answer must be that power cannot compel a lie.

Is it not exceedingly strange that Paula Jones and Monica Lewinsky are the nails in the shoe of the horse in the skirmish in the battle in the war for which, wanting them, Western civilization may be, to some degree, lost? It is, indeed. It is embarrassing, unseemly, and a lot less dignified than, say, the Battle of Britain. And why is that? Is it because, according to the voice of the snapping turtle, a bunch of hyperpartisan conservative extremists could find no better way to embarrass a great president other than to drag hundred-dollar bills through trailer parks?

Or is it that investigation of matters of far greater consequence is suppressed by the very powers that complain of inconsequentiality? On the one hand, the president receives money from half a dozen agents of influence allied to the People's Republic of China, and, on the other, he decides upon the transfer of supercomputers, advanced military machine tools, and nuclear technology to the Chinese. This is not an inconsequential matter, but his attorney general refuses to appoint an independent counsel. The president and his men, his cabinet and his assistants, violate campaign laws, raise funds illegally, convert government property, suborn FBI files, lie under oath, take bribes, and shake down pathetic and impoverished Indian tribes. Nor are these inconsequential matters, and yet, in most cases, the attorney general refuses to appoint independent counsels.

Many Curators' Labor

A museum of this administration's lies and transgressions would be as big as the Louvre, would require the labor of many curators in its many departments, and would spread through so many rooms and in so many exhibits that it would be overwhelming. And yet, most rooms are closed, and the public has not yet clamored for them to be opened.

The Lewinsky Affair is not in itself of minor importance, as it will be characterized in the days to come. Far from it. But it is by no means the heart of the matter of power subverting truth. No incident stemming from sexual indiscipline, even from the breaking of vows, even from the betrayal of a wife and daughter, can be as grave as similar betrayals of the whole people in matters of state. These are still the heart of Whitewater and all that it means. That the inquiry, investigation, and impulse toward justice have been expressed of late and very powerfully in sexual exposés is the result of truth held at bay and then finding its own level as it rises in whatever channels are available. Would that all the channels were open. But, then again, history is the story of blows from unexpected quarters.

Mr. Helprin, a novelist and Journal contributing editor, is a senior fellow of the Hudson Institute.

Editorial Feature

A Watergate Scorecard

With the White House embroiled in the most wide-ranging scandal since Watergate, it's useful to recall that a single, small event can reverberate widely, with consequences for many people, both small fry and bigwigs. In Watergate, a burglary and the subsequent coverup profoundly changed the lives of many men and women, including the following, most of whom went to jail:

Richard Nixon

Alfred Baldwin: Lookout at the Watergate. Turned state's evidence.

Bernard Barker: Led the Cuban-American break-in teams at the Watergate and at Daniel Ellsberg's psychiatrist's office. Served 12 months in jail.

Rule of Law

Dwight Chapin: Nixon's appointments secretary, 1969-72; served eight months in jail.

Charles Colson: Special White House counsel, 1969-73. Found guilty of obstruction of justice; served seven months in jail.

John Dean III: White House counsel, 1970-73. Turned whistleblower. Served four months in jail.

John Ehrlichman: Chief domestic policy adviser to the president. Found guilty of conspiring to obstruct justice; served 18 months in jail.

Virgilio Gonzalez: Lockpick of the Watergate break-in team. Served 15 months in jail.

H.R. Haldeman: White House chief of staff, 1973-74. Served 18 months in jail.

E. Howard Hunt Jr.: CIA veteran; White House consultant; member of the White House Special Investigations Unit know as the "Plumbers"; recruited the burglars; member of the Watergate break-in team and of the team that broke into the office of Daniel Ellsberg's psychiatrist. Served 33 months in jail.

Herbert Kalmbach: Nixon's personal lawyer; raised hush money. Served six months in jail.

Richard Kleindienst: Attorney general, 1972-73. Received a suspended one-month sentence.

Egil (Bud) Krogh Jr.: John Ehrlichman's deputy; White House Plumber. Served four and a half months in jail.

Frederick LaRue: Chief adviser to John Mitchell. Served five and a half months in jail.

G. Gordon Liddy: White House Plumber; counsel to Nixon's re-election committee; architect of break-ins into the Watergate and Ellsberg's psychiatrist's office and head of the White House "dirty tricks" operation. Refused to cooperate with prosecutors; served 52 months in jail.

Jeb Stuart Magruder: Deputy director of the 1972 re-election campaign. Guilty of obstruction of justice; served seven months in jail.

Eugenio Rolando Martinez: Member of the Watergate and Ellsberg psychiatrist break-in teams. Served 15 months in jail.

James McCord Jr.: Longtime CIA officer; one of the Watergate burglars; wrote a letter implicating higher-ups. Served four months in jail.

John Mitchell: Attorney general, 1969-72; head of Nixon's 1972 re-election campaign. Served 19 months in jail.

Richard Nixon: President, 1969-74. Pardoned.

Herbert (Bart) Porter: Assistant to Jeb Stuart Magruder. Served 30 days in jail.

Donald Segretti: Nixon campaign dirty trickster. Served 4.5 months in jail.

Maurice Stans: Secretary of Commerce 1969-72; finance chairman of Nixon's re-election committee. Fined $150,000.

Frank Sturgis: Member of the Watergate break-in team. Served 13 months in jail.

Anthony Ulasewicz: Private eye for the White House; former New York cop; made hush money drops. One year on probation for failing to declare expenses for income tax.

David Young: Aide to Secretary of State Henry Kissinger, 1969-71. White House Plumber. Granted immunity from prosecution in return for testimony on the break-in into Ellsberg's psychiatrist's office.

* * *

Editor's Note: We relied on a number of sources to refresh our memory, notably Fred Emery's "Watergate: The Corruption of American Politics and the Fall of Richard Nixon" (Simon & Schuster, 1994).

Letters to the Editor

Maurice Stans Wasn't A Watergate Villain

Your listing of Maurice H. Stans in "A Watergate Scoreboard" (Rule of Law, Jan. 26) was unfair. While Secretary Stans was investigated by the Watergate special prosecutor, his "crimes" had nothing to do with the break-in at the Watergate and the coverup that followed.

As so ably set forth in his book "The Terrors of Justice," Stans was prosecuted for activities that were overlooked or ignored when engaged in by committees for other candidates. Stans ultimately agreed to plead guilty to five misdemeanors, and a total fine of $5,000 (not $150,000 as you reported), for things such as non-willful receipt of illegal contributions and late reporting of contributions, not because he felt he was guilty, but to finally stop an investigation that had already gone on for two years and would have cost additional hundreds of thousands of dollars in legal fees if it had continued.

What happened to Maurice Stans, both then and now with your mention of him in "A Watergate Scoreboard," is a perfect example of the kind of guilt by association that so often happens in situations such as Watergate. Secretary Stans deserves an apology.

PATRICK J. ALLEN
River Forest, Ill.

REVIEW & OUTLOOK

Bonfire of the Presidency

With Bill Clinton's presidency in the balance, the country waits to hear what Monica Lewinsky finally says. We hope it will also ponder whether the issue is a purely personal peccadillo, or the ultimate revelation of Mr. Clinton's conduct of office.

The White House is reduced to the hope that Ms. Lewinsky will stand by the account Vernon Jordan's statement outlined, and dismiss her taped comments to Linda Tripp as youthful delusion. This is the only conceivable exculpatory theory, but it seems increasingly

Bill Clinton

stretched. ABC News now even reports there was an unnamed eyewitness to a sexual act, just prior to Ms. Lewinsky's transfer from the White House to the Pentagon. Did a delusional 24-year-old make up the point about perjury not often being prosecuted in civil cases, or draw up the talking points in the note she provided Ms. Tripp on how to doctor her testimony? Witness tampering is a serious felony, opening charges against Ms. Lewinsky and opening the question of what principal she represented.

William Ginsburg, who's taken over Ms. Lewinsky's defense, is a family friend and clearly has her interests at heart. In bargaining for immunity with Independent Counsel Kenneth Starr, his first proffer—to testify to sex but not to the crime of witness tampering—was understandably rejected. Negotiations continue, and their tenor is suggested by Mr. Ginsburg's remark, "We will not go south like Susan McDougal and refuse to talk nor will we have any lapses of memory like Webb Hubbell. If my client is granted immunity we will tell the truth and nothing but the truth to the office of Independent Counsel."

Given all this, it is unlikely Ms. Lewinsky's ultimate testimony will lance the boil. It is far more likely, indeed, that the coming week will see further damage to the President—more revelations concerning Ms. Lewinsky and possibly other women as well. Indeed, the Lewinsky furor has obscured what would otherwise be a bombshell revelation that Kathleen Willey testified that she was the object of unwelcome presidential advances. And of course, the Paula Jones court case ticks along.

The President, meanwhile, has retreated to a White House bunker, surrounded by Mrs. Clinton and his personal lawyers, calling back Harold Ickes and Mickey Kantor for advice and dispatching James Carville and Paul Begala to represent him on Sunday talk shows. His inability to mobilize the entire resources of the executive branch in his defense is already an important victory for Mr. Starr, who won a court battle giving him the right to subpoena notes of government employees. (It may also help protect the unfortunate employees—see the list of Watergate casualties in Rule of Law nearby.)

Yet the real issue of the week is what goes on in Mr. Clinton's mind. The White House defense has been curiously tepid. There are reasons for that in Mr. Starr's subpoena precedent and Ms. Lewinsky's pending testimony. But the passiveness could also reflect a more profound personal collapse, some inner presidential recognition that the game is in its final moments. In this case, resignation could come quickly, without the protracted agony of Watergate, if further revelations mount. Leon Panetta, Mr. Clinton's former chief of staff, has already raised this possibility.

It might also be, however, that Mr. Clinton would simply refuse to leave, a course the group now gathered around him might well support. He has, after all, overcome crisis after crisis through perseverance and an amazing ability to compartmentalize his life. Clearly we are not dealing here with a normal personality; indeed, the roots of this crisis lie somewhere in the psyche shaped by Mr. Clinton's genes, troubled childhood and life experiences.

Of course, national leaders are seldom normal. At least a democratic system protects us from outright psychotics such as Hitler, Stalin or Mao. Yet other presidents have also had curious psyches; Nixon intimate Leonard Garment has remarked "the presidential gene is filled with sociopathic qualities." Someone with antisocial personality disorder, as psychiatrists now call it, displays a total lack of respect for the standards of society, an ability to lie without shame, twisted sexual relationships, an invariably charming affect and an ability to avoid depression when it might be objectively appropriate. In Mr. Clinton's case a strict diagnosis does *not* hold, but such traits have built his success and now threaten his failure.

From the first we have written of "Arkansas mores"—not in denigration of that state's good people but in depicting the political habits Mr. Clinton carried to Washington. In this sense the Lewinsky crisis is of a piece with Whitewater, $100,000 commodity strikes, the cover-up after the Foster suicide, the Travel Office firings, the misappropriated FBI files and the campaign finance mess. Whenever and however Mr. Clinton leaves office, we will spend a long time discovering what damage his mores have done to our institutions, and a longer time repairing them.

Editorial Feature

Sex and the Presidency

By Marvin Olasky

Compartmentalization: That was the conventional Washington answer up to last week. Repeatedly we were told that a president's personal life has no relation to his public activities. But a study of presidential history shows a link between lying about adultery and lying about other matters.

Woodrow Wilson is a classic example. Until age 50 he was an upright if slightly dull Presbyterian professor and long-married university president. Then he had an affair with Mary Hulbert Peck, which he covered up so well by paying her off financially that he was elected governor of New Jersey in 1910 and president in 1912, both times running as a candidate of private and public integrity. Adultery and its coverup contributed to a theological transformation in Wilson. He spent the rest of his life liberating himself from other commandments that he now regarded as suggestions.

The new Wilson broke faith with the American people in three ways. In 1916 he won re-election with the effective slogan "He kept us out of war," while privately telling cabinet members, "I can't keep the country out of war." One month after his second inauguration, Wilson led the U.S. into World War I.

Then he lost the peace by refusing to compromise with Senate leaders who agreed to adopt the League of Nations treaty only with reservations that would preserve American sovereignty. Finally, when Wilson had a major stroke that left him unable to exercise the duties of the presidency, he refused to step down. Instead he and his aides pretended that he was able to work, and his second wife was effectively the president during Wilson's last year and a half in office.

Or consider the case of Warren Harding. His sexual coverup (he hid his affairs with Carrie Phillips and Nan Britton) presaged his administration, one of the most corrupt in American history. In contrast, Jimmy Carter's faithfulness in marriage, so great that he needed to confess publicly that he had lusted in his heart, was also a marker: His administration would be open and above-board, even if not entirely competent.

Franklin Roosevelt successfully covered up affairs with Lucy Mercer and Missy Le Hand, and used the same techniques to cover up affairs of state. Turner Catledge of the New York Times told friends that Roosevelt's first instinct was always to lie; sometimes in midsentence he would switch to accuracy because he realized he could get away with the truth in that particular instance. FDR, for instance, ran against Herbert Hoover in 1932 promising to reduce the size of government, before turning around and launching the New Deal. Roosevelt was a great president, but the doublespeak he first developed while hiding an affair grated on reporters who were not yet accustomed to presidential falsehood.

On the other hand, Grover Cleveland showed how private truth-telling led to public conscientiousness. In 1874, 10 years before he was elected president, Cleveland fathered a son out of wedlock. He gave the child his last name and arranged for adoption. This became an issue in the 1884 campaign, with Republican opponents chanting, "Ma, ma, where's my pa? Gone to the White House, ha, ha, ha." But this didn't sink his candidacy. Cleveland by then had become known as the "veto governor" of New York because of his willingness to stand up to special interests, and he became the "veto president," opposed by some but respected for his honesty.

Woodrow Wilson

A flawed presidential character is not always bad for the nation. John F. Kennedy's success in keeping unreported his record-setting flow of young women into Senate bedchambers and then the White House probably led him to think he could get away with other quasi-secret activities, such as the Bay of Pigs and numerous Castro assassination plots. And yet the emotional detachment he showed in using women as he did made him into a fine Cold War poker player. He could coldly go to the brink of nuclear war without being unnerved by a normal man's sensitivities.

Amid charges and countercharges, we need to remember two points if the likelihood of future presidential scandals is to be reduced. First, there is no immoral equivalence ("everyone does it"). One guest on Geraldo Rivera's show last week stated that George Washington probably left splinters from his wooden teeth in someone's thigh, but no one was looking to report such matters then. Not true: British and some Antifederalist journalists looked hard for dirt in his past (especially in his early friendship with Sally Fairfax), yet Washington was spotless. Throughout most of American history there have been Matt Drudges—journalists looking to dig up dirt—but the overwhelming majority of presidents have been clean, at least in the White House.

Second, journalists and voters who do not scrutinize candidates' sexual flings are negligent. Faithfulness to a wife is no guarantee of faithfulness to the country; look at Richard Nixon. Faithlessness, however, is generally a leading indicator of trouble. Small betrayals in marriage generally lead to larger betrayals, and leaders who break a large vow to one person find it easy to break relatively small vows to millions.

Mr. Olasky is a University of Texas professor and author of the forthcoming "God, Sex, and Statesmanship: American Leaders From Washington to Clinton" (Free Press).

Editorial Feature

A Clinton Resignation Won't Shatter World Order

Tonight is the president's State of the Union address, an event that has ballooned in recent years from a rather modest constitutional requirement into a celebration by all of Washington's principal actors of their fame and power. The world will be focused this time, however, not on the pomp and circumstance or indeed on the union itself, which is in good shape. It will focus on the state of the presidency, which clearly isn't.

Global View

By George Melloan

Indeed, it will take all the sublimation of reality the star-studded cast can muster to keep this from being the most embarrassing party ever thrown inside the confines of the Beltway. A president accused of turning the American seat of government into his personal bordello will have to go before a TV audience, Congress, Supreme Court justices, cabinet officers and ambassadors from throughout the world and try to appear presidential.

The sordid tape-recorded descriptions by a former White House intern of her alleged romps with Bill Clinton in his office, along with allegations that he asked her to lie under oath, undermine even without absolute proof the dignity of the presidency. The president's denials would be more believable were it not for his long, long record of artful replies to accusations of a wide variety of mischiefs. It hardly seems necessary at this point to recite the whole list of charges, but of course sexual misconduct has had a prominent place on the docket. The man seems to have a special problem with that kind of thing.

The role Mr. Clinton is expected to perform tonight goes to the heart of the problem these latest accusations pose for the American presidency. If a man elected to that office cannot maintain the dignity his job demands, a case can be made that he has disqualified himself from serving. Should he resign, or, failing that, should the two parties in Congress mutually agree to remove him from office through impeachment? Would that pose a grave danger to the nation and the world? There is a simple answer and it is no.

Many of those who think otherwise cite as their reason the argument that the American president is the "leader of the free world" and hence his fall from power must always raise the danger of adventures by well-known thugs lurking in places like Iraq and Libya. The pompous description of his importance does have at least some measure of validity. The U.S. president commands the most effective single military force in what is clearly the world's most powerful military alliance. So in the primitive world of power politics, he rises above all the rest.

But the American president is only the leader of the free world to the extent that he has followers. Mr. Clinton is an adroit politician. His ability to ad lib policy without putting a foot wrong sometimes amazes his peers. He also has remarkable skill at playing the chords that keep him in tune with his audience. But how can a man who is constantly being accused of violating the very laws he is supposed to be enforcing continue to command the respect of those he wishes to lead?

Further, it is the American presidency, not Bill Clinton, that the world looks to for leadership. If Bill Clinton steps down and turns over the office to Al Gore, the world will turn to Al Gore. That's what happened, under the far more dangerous circumstances of a closely fought Cold War, with Lyndon Johnson and Gerry Ford. In the latter case, it could be argued that the office itself was strengthened by the demonstration that a president—even one who had recently been elected by a large margin—could be brought down for abusing the powers of the office. It is the American presidency, the American system of government and all the people who make the system work—which means just about every citizen—that the world so often admires. It is not a man from Arkansas who managed to get himself re-elected in a placid period when less than half the eligible voters went to the polls.

It also will be argued that Mr. Clinton still has important work to do in his presidency. That must be judged from the perspective of the entire American electorate, not merely those who think they might benefit from some new government handout. The work Mr. Clinton and his wife have in mind consists of spending a projected budget surplus as quickly as possible on projects that will buy votes for the Democratic Party. His typically grandiose plans include such things as expanding the already huge, and potentially unmanageable, obligation of the U.S. government to future clients of Medicare. In short, the work Mr. Clinton has mapped out is essentially irresponsible, much like the programs he proposed when he first came into office but that fortunately were largely blocked by Congress.

During Mr. Clinton's presidency there has been a marked decline, according to opinion polls, in the confidence of the American people in the ability of government to do good works. As the light election turnout suggested in 1996, a lot of Americans are turned off by political posturing. They know from their own personal experience that private efforts, by individuals, community groups and business organizations, work more smoothly and achieve more than those of the government. They have had it up to here with Bill Clinton grabbing credit for achievements that he had little to do with, such as reducing crime. His promise to improve education is belied by a long history of federal involvement in education that has not reversed, and may have contributed to, a decline in quality. Most Americans know that if education is to be improved it will have to be done by parents and teachers working together at the local level.

It also is argued that there is a crisis in the Mideast that demands the full attention of the president. Saddam, indeed, is challenging a president who has never demonstrated great resolve, but there is no clear and present danger. Saddam isn't going anywhere and his weapons sites can be dealt with when the U.S. has a president who can command the respect of both his friends and his enemies. As to the Mideast "peace process," it has never been a peace process at all, but instead a continuation of long-running negotiations over the control of territory.

It is not pleasing to witness a crumbling American presidency. But change is the essence of progress and quite likely change is needed now.

White House Counterattacks

After several days of stunned silence following the Monica Lewinsky revelations, the White House fired back, mounting an unprecedented assault on Independent Counsel Starr. On "Meet the Press," Clinton adviser James Carville declared "war" on Mr. Starr. On the "Today," show, Mrs. Clinton blamed the President's problems on a "vast right-wing conspiracy." Mr. Clinton's lawyer filed a complaint against Mr. Starr alleging illegal news leaks of grand jury proceedings. And despite earlier promises of a quick and complete revelation, the President ignored the subject in his State of the Union address and for months thereafter.

In a February editorial titled "Trashing the System" the Journal wrote that the White House strategy was clear: "to put in the public's mind that all of the criticism of the Administration's conduct is politically motivated. That is, they're trying to diminish their enemies. Mrs. Clinton's interview suggests they've concluded it may also be necessary to cut down public respect for the judiciary as well. Whether the Clintons survive, they are leaving behind cynicism and rubble."

In the campaign finance controversy, Attorney General Reno requested an independent counsel to examine the narrow question of whether Interior Secretary Bruce Babbitt lied to Congress in testimony about a license for an Indian casino in Wisconsin. Mr. Babbitt would be the fourth Clinton Cabinet member to be investigated by a special prosecutor, after Agriculture Secretary Mike Espy, Housing Secretary Henry Cisneros and Commerce Secretary Ron Brown. Ms. Reno continued to resist calls for an independent counsel with a broad mandate to probe the sprawling allegations growing out of the 1996 campaign. But in February her Department of Justice task force delivered its first indictment, of longtime Clinton friend Charlie Trie. Mr. Trie, who fled the United States in 1996, returned to Washington after hiding out in Macau and China, and was charged with 15 election-fraud counts.

REVIEW & OUTLOOK

Surreal State

We'll say this for President Clinton's State of the Union address Tuesday night: He left no part of the body politic unmassaged. Any voting bloc with even the slightest request for a federal handout got something.

That's especially true of the liberal Democratic interests who've sometimes felt neglected by this President. Now he's paying them back, and all the better politically that he is able to do it under cover of a suddenly "balanced budget." Republicans John Kasich and Newt Gingrich should feel foolish for making a fetish out of a goal that now allows Mr. Clinton to refire the engine of big government.

Bill Clinton

Thus the President promised a third minimum wage hike in three years to Ted Kennedy, an expansion of Medicare for the AFL-CIO, cash to build more schools for the teachers' unions, child-care subsidies for parents who work (but not for those who stay at home), housing subsidies for mayors and builders, new water regulations for the Sierra Club, and on and on as far as the American public could stay awake. Mr. Clinton even policy-wonked his way to telling the nation's educators how small their class sizes should be. And don't forget the new $1.50-a-pack tobacco tax.

All of this serves the political purpose of rallying Democrats in this election year. It also doesn't hurt to appease them on policy if he needs their support later, on, say, the House Judiciary Committee.

Yet Mr. Clinton still tried to placate public skepticism toward Washington by claiming that "we have the smallest government in 35 years." This is false if you measure government by federal taxation's share of the American economy, which at about 20% of GDP is the highest since 1969, the year of LBJ's Vietnam surcharge. If Mr. Clinton is referring to the number of federal employees, then he should add that most of the reduction has come from defense and winding down the savings-and-loan bailout.

The President's boldest play at preserving big government is his proposal to preserve any surplus for Social Security. This will make it harder for Congress to return the surplus to the people who created it, i.e., the taxpayers. It also makes it sound as if the surplus is going to be held in some pot in the U.S. Treasury for safekeeping.

This is preposterous. Social Security is already running a surplus, which is being spent on current programs. Does anyone seriously think Congress—this one, or any other—is going to let any more of this cash alone? Social Security's real problem is its future liabilities, that is, what is owed Baby Boomers when they retire. Those liabilities aren't changed by setting aside a few extra billion dollars now.

Yet now that Mr. Clinton has opened the subject, reformers in both parties should leap at the chance to make retirement more secure. This can only mean changing Social Security into a system based more on individual responsibility and private-market returns. We doubt Mr. Clinton will allow any such thing, and his history on Medicare is to double-cross Republicans. But the opportunity is too great to ignore, and some Democrats (Nebraska Senator Bob Kerrey) are thinking anew as well.

All of this assumes of course that Mr. Clinton somehow retains the moral authority to govern after Monica Lewinsky tells her story. It's surreal to hear this President lecture the country on words like "accountability" and "responsibility" when he can't even tell us what he did with an intern in the Oval Office. The one titter we heard in the crowd was when Mr. Clinton said, "We must set a good example."

We wonder how that sounded to parents who've lately had to block their 10-year-olds from watching the evening news. At least Mr. Clinton didn't talk about the V-chip.

REVIEW & OUTLOOK

Who Is Robert Litt?

As we mentioned the other day, we will all be a long time discovering and repairing the damage the Clinton Presidency has done to our institutions of government. The prime example is the Department of Justice. And within Justice, the prime example is one Robert Litt.

As Principal Associate Deputy Attorney General, Mr. Litt is the most powerful behind-the-scenes figure in Janet Reno's fiefdom, the new Webster Hubbell. Asked for a photo of him, the Department tells us that none exist! In all of this, Mr. Litt and his sponsors have not been deterred by the failure of his nomination to be head of the Criminal Division; the nomination was quietly pulled by Justice before the 1996 election.

The top post in the Criminal Division, which is to say the division that might be investigating such matters as the campaign finance imbroglio, has been vacant since August 1995. Its current head serves on an acting basis, despite the provisions of the Vacancy Act, which limits such temporary appointments to 120 days. So just why Mr. Litt's nomination was withdrawn is of no little moment. Rumors in fact have circulated privately in Washington circles. We are hard put to understand why the public shouldn't know the facts.

Mr. Litt's resume is stellar. In 1993-94, he served as a Special Adviser to the Assistant Secretary of State for European and Canadian Affairs. Before that he was a partner at Williams & Connolly, where the President's personal attorney, David Kendall, also is a partner. He served as an Assistant U.S. Attorney in the Southern District of New York. Along this professional trail he developed a friendship with Mark Pomerantz, chief of the Criminal Division for the Office of the U.S. Attorney for the Southern District of New York. These pages have chronicled recently the disputes between Manhattan District Attorney Robert Morgenthau and federal officials policing the securities industry.

In late 1995, President Clinton nominated Mr. Litt—then a Deputy Assistant Attorney General—to be chief of the Criminal Division. But the nomination hit a shoal, which was never explained. There were no Senate confirmation hearings and the nomination was withdrawn. Then in 1997, immediately after being nominated as Deputy Attorney General, Eric Holder elevated Mr. Litt to the principal associate's job, a post that does not need Senate confirmation. This effectively makes Mr. Litt the third most powerful figure in the Department.

What happened? We learned from two independent sources with firsthand knowledge that Mr. Litt's nomination to the Criminal Division was withdrawn due to the FBI's sharp objections. Mr. Litt, our sources said, lied to the FBI about past marijuana use in a background check. Marijuana is not the relevant issue here. The relevant issue is lying to the FBI, which is a serious offense. The Cisneros case involved allegations of lying to the FBI, and an aide to Agriculture Secretary Mike Espy was recently convicted of this offense.

Yesterday both Mr. Litt and Mr. Holder provided the Journal with explanations for the withdrawal, and we print both in the columns nearby. If this is all there is to it, let's immediately reschedule the confirmation hearings to sort all this out. But as matters now stand, the larger point about the withdrawn Litt nomination is left unresolved: It is that someone who couldn't be confirmed is nonetheless working as one of the Department's highest officials.

This circumstance is precisely what the Vacancies Act was intended to prevent. It degrades the principle of accountability, which is indeed the role of Senate confirmation or a statute such as the Vacancies Act. A report this month on the Vacancies Act by the Congressional Research Service cites a 1991 Supreme Court decision on Executive appointment powers: "The 'manipulation of official appointments' had long been one of the American revolutionary generation's greatest grievances against executive power." Further,

"The Framers understood that by limiting the appointment power, they could ensure that those who wielded it were accountable to political force and the will of the people."

To whom or what is Mr. Litt accountable? Or for that matter Bill Lann Lee, or whatever functionary has been running the Criminal Division for two years?

The Clinton Justice Department has flouted these procedures with a ruling that it was OK for someone to serve longer than the Vacancies Act permitted, so long as it was someone who came out of the bowels of Justice rather than from the outside. The Senate should now correct the balance here. Senator Hatch's Judiciary Committee should take up the appointments of both Mr. Litt and Bill Lann Lee, make an issue of them, and if warranted vote them down. The worry that weak-kneed Republicans would hand him a defeat is much less now than two weeks ago.

But the major responsibility lies with Mr. Clinton. The Department of Justice is chief among the institutions corrupted by the Clinton Presidency. The Vacancy Act violations follow on top of the Hubbell appointment, a travesty, in hindsight; the 1993 Justice reversal of its position in the Rep. Harold Ford corruption trial, causing several Department resignations; the firing of all 93 U.S. attorneys; and the indefensible refusal this year to appoint an independent counsel on the campaign finance issue.

The Department of Justice, like the rest of government, is supposed to be a public trust, not someone's personal law firm or political machine. In the end, Justice's many defenders tell us, the Department always rises to the occasion. But its abuse breeds cynicism about government. As matters now stand, Robert Litt is serving Bill Clinton. His nomination, whatever the particulars, should be resubmitted to the Senate so that he can serve the people of the United States.

Letters to the Editor

You've Tarnished A Respected Man

I know Bob Litt well enough to know your Jan. 29 editorial "Who Is Robert Litt?"—to the extent it sought to raise any issue of Mr. Litt's character—was far off the mark. I fear you have tarnished a man for whose intellect and character I have the highest regard. Mr. Litt and I have represented mutual clients, and I know of no other attorney whose judgment I would trust as much as his. Moreover, I have the utmost respect for his integrity, which I believe distinguishes him from a number of other high administration officials.

Concerning the manner of appointments being made at Justice and other departments: I agree that the administration's action with respect to Bill Lann Lee, making a recess appointment after it was clear the Senate would not approve his appointment as chief of the Civil Rights Division, amounted to game playing. Mr. Litt's appointment, however, was withdrawn, and he was hired for another job that does not require Senate confirmation. The two cases are not the same. Moreover, the alleged character issue you raised lacks any substantive basis.

You framed the issue bearing on Mr. Litt's character in general terms, whether Mr. Litt lied to investigators concerning his marijuana use. That makes the issue sound ominous. Both Mr. Holder and Mr. Litt, however, framed the issue in their responses with specificity: what is the reason for the discrepancy between Justice and State background reports, each of which apparently indicate that Mr. Litt admitted that his last marijuana use was at least 23 years ago, with one pegging that last puff at 27 years ago.

You imply Mr. Litt was less than honest in his background interviews on the issue of marijuana use. Yet, if he admitted smoking marijuana, as did virtually everyone who attended college in the 1970s, that was the key and honest admission. There is simply no motive for anyone to dissemble on the question of whether his last puff was in 1971 or 1975—even assuming he could remember—and you posited no such motive.

Whether it was 23 years ago or 27 years ago, it was so long ago as to have no materiality to his qualifications. I find it reprehensible you would raise an issue of such triviality to attack someone's character undeservedly. There is certainly a lot to criticize with respect to the judgment being exercised in the Justice Department, including why children in the Waco compound were tear-gassed with a flammable agent; how the FBI's Hostage Rescue Team came to shoot a woman holding a baby at Ruby Ridge; and why despite clear and convincing evidence of a conspiracy to abuse the campaign finance laws, the attorney general fails to appoint a special prosecutor. To the extent Mr. Litt had any involvement in these or other issues, it is fair to question his judgment and thinking. Whether Mr. Litt last used marijuana in 1971 or 1975 hardly has any significance, however, other than to smear a man who I know exhibits personal integrity, which should be a model for government service.

GEORGE L. LYON JR.

Washington

Editorial Feature

Litt's Reply

Statement of Robert S. Litt, principal associate deputy attorney general:

You have asked whether I made any false statements to the FBI in the course of a background investigation. I did not. I have never made a false statement to background investigators.

Because background investigations are supposed to be kept confidential as to the nominee as well as the public, I have never seen the relevant documents. However, my understanding is that there is an inconsistency between two background investigations—one prepared by the Department of State in 1993 and one prepared by the FBI in 1995—concerning whether I said that I last used marijuana 24 years ago or 27 years ago. I told the truth about this issue at all times. From what I have been told I believe that any discrepancy exists because the State Department investigator misunderstood what I told him. I also understand that senior career employees at the Department of Justice have reviewed my entire file and have found nothing that would adversely affect my continued employment by the Department of Justice.

Although I am confident that any discrepancy in the background investigation was due to an inaccuracy in the report, I nevertheless decided to withdraw my nomination to head the Criminal Division after this issue surfaced. I was told that, in the political climate at the time, it was likely that the inconsistency between the two reports would lead to a messy political battle that would ultimately be harmful to me and to the Department, however baseless the charges were. I saw no reason to put myself, the Department and my family through that.

*   *   *

Statement of Eric Holder, deputy attorney general:

After I became Deputy Attorney General, I decided to hire Bob Litt as my Principal Associate Deputy Attorney General. Merrick Garland was not a candidate, nor was I ever contacted by anyone at the White House regarding my selection.

When a discrepancy between Mr. Litt's two background investigations arose regarding when he last used marijuana, several senior career Justice Department employees reviewed his background files. All of them found nothing that would affect Mr. Litt's employment at the highest levels of the Justice Department. They concluded that he was suitable for the job, and for the Department's highest security clearance.

When I learned of the discrepancy I reviewed the matter and was satisfied that Mr. Litt had not lied. Based on my own review and that of the career employees, and upon Mr. Litt's outstanding record and qualifications, I chose to hire him. For many years, under Republicans and Democrats, the federal government has had to deal with the issue of prior drug use by federal employees. I did not believe that a discrepancy as to whether his last marijuana use was 24 or 27 years ago should disqualify him from office.

The government's ability to recruit good people depends in part on the confidentiality of background investigations. Selected excerpts and characterizations from confidential files can result in someone's record being mischaracterized. That's what has apparently happened here, and I am disturbed that misleading leaks to the press are being used to smear an outstanding public servant.

REVIEW & OUTLOOK

Assaulting the Messenger

When James Carville announced on "Meet the Press" last Sunday there would now be "war" between the White House and Kenneth Starr, one of the first things we wondered is: Whose side are the Secret Service and FBI supposed to be on in this war? By the end of the week, Bill Clinton's lieutenants had provided an answer. The Secret Service agents will fight with General Carville against the

Ken Starr

independent counsel. We guess this makes the Secret Service's agents a kind of Praetorian Guard, loyal first to a single man, and if it's OK with the lawyers then maybe also to the institutions of the government or the established legal system.

We suppose you could argue it the other way around, and in the current climate, just about any old argument will do as a philosophy of government. Not that long ago, the institution of the Office of Independent Counsel was seen generally as a necessary arbiter of alleged wrongdoing involving the combatants in the relentless political pits of modern Washington. Now every Beltway solon has climbed out of the pits, taken a shower and is appearing on camera or in print to solemnly question the independent counsel's "role." Or as will be asked on weekend TV from Friday night till midnight Sunday: "Has Ken Starr gone too far?"

We're happy to entertain conflicting views on that matter, too.

Just one proviso: If you hear or read one of these wisepeople going on like this without once mentioning the words "White House stonewalling," feel free to laugh.

It is just too rich. Here you have a Presidency and its appointees who since the Administration's first weeks have taken the legal position that they don't have to tell anyone what they don't want to tell—not Congress, not the Courts, not any independent counsel, not the press and most certainly not the American people.

A long parade of witnesses suffered memory collapse before the D'Amato committee, or lied to their diary. Administration lawyers for Hillary Clinton's health care task force temporized so egregiously in court that a federal judge denounced them from the bench. When Justice Department lawyers showed up after Vincent Foster's suicide, White House counsel told them to get lost. Subpoenas have been resisted for every scandal this White House has produced—Whitewater, Travelgate, Filegate and campaign fund raising. Mr. Starr had to fight for one subpoena all the way up to the Supreme Court. Prospective witnesses? Fled the country or taking the Fifth. The Journal's Glenn Simpson reported yesterday that the White House is now considering claiming executive privilege over internal administration meetings on the Lewinsky scandal.

Somehow across five years, none of this *omerta* has moved the conscience of the Beltway. But Mr. Starr puts a wire on a witness and the men and women who have seen or heard everything in politics are suddenly "shocked."

So rather than come to grips with Mr. Clinton's conduct of the Presidency over his full term, we are asked to pull over to the side of the road and muse on the prosecutor's tactics. In this endeavor the First Lady gets to play the bad cop, going on the "Today" show to not only accuse Mr. Starr of being "politically motivated," but to also make a remarkable attack on the judiciary, ripping into the three federal judges who appoint all independent counsels. And the whole five years has been a right-wing fantasy.

Impugning the motives of anyone who questions them is familiar territory for the Clintons. Recall that back in December 1993 a New York Times headline read, "First Lady Defending President Denounces Attacks. She Hints At Conspiracy to Damage Clinton." The Office of White House Counsel prepared a 331-page report titled "Communication Stream of Conspiracy Commerce." It alleged that "right-wing groups" were behind phony scandal stories in the media. When our Micah Morrison revealed the existence of the report last year, the White House, including the President, backed away from it.

But it's a handy smoke bomb. After Mrs. Clinton lobbed "a vast right-wing conspiracy" into the TV talk shows, the White House got busy again passing out to friendly journalists updated copies of the media-conspiracy report that it had deep-sixed a year ago in embarrassment.

For all the diversions this week, a plain reality remains: The Independent Counsel Act is on the books, courtesy of Bill Clinton's renewal of it, and it is the only instrument we have now to deal with the current corruptions. The Congress is obsessed with following the polls. The Democratic Party is unwilling to confront the President it elected. The Justice Department? Only last month it was being roundly hooted for seeing no cause to appoint an independent counsel in the campaign finance scandal.

For sure, the assault on Mr. Starr and inconvenient women will continue. What doesn't change is that some institution—whether the Office of Independent Counsel, the press or the judiciary—has to account for the acts of the Clinton Presidency that went beyond the boundaries of normal or acceptable political behavior.

Editorial Feature

Starr 'War':
Back to Smash-Mouth Defense

President Clinton should fire Kenneth Starr.

First Lady Hillary Rodham Clinton this week all but accused Mr. Starr, the court-appointed special counsel, of fomenting a coup d'etat.

"We get a politically motivated prosecutor who is allied with the right-wing opponents of my husband," she told NBC's "Today" show. That evil man is "scratching for dirt, intimidating witnesses, doing everything possible to try to make some accusation against my husband."

Potomac Watch

By Paul A. Gigot

Mrs. Clinton is saying she believes Mr. Starr is coercing people to lie. That is a crime. Does her husband believe it, too? Because if the president does, he has a duty to order Attorney General Janet Reno to fire Mr. Starr. Mr. Clinton is sworn to faithfully execute the laws, and his wife is saying, presumably on his behalf, that Mr. Starr is breaking the law.

This president isn't about to give those orders to Ms. Reno, of course. He knows the political price would be too great, as Richard Nixon learned.

Mr. Clinton knows that unleashing his wife to attack Mr. Starr is politically so much craftier. This defense lets the first lady play the role of a wounded but stalwart Tammy Wynette, a public favorite. It creates a "partisan" foil against whom he can rally his supporters. And it provides a theory of how 24-year-old Monica Lewinsky could be induced to say such lurid things about the president she worshiped like a rock-star groupie.

The beauty of this defense is that it might work whether or not Monica Lewinsky cooperates with Mr. Starr. If she doesn't, then White House spinners can tear into Mr. Starr for tormenting an innocent young thing (who nonetheless is recorded on tape asking another woman to lie for her). But if she does cooperate, the spinners can claim she was coerced by Simon Legree into lying to avoid a jail term. (Never mind that Paul Begala and other White House defenders-without-facts are kept away from the real truth by the lawyers.)

Hillary Clinton

Granted, this is a long shot, but what other choice do they have? Clearly the first couple is hunkering down for a long and nasty fight. And if the Clintons are going to be run back to Fayetteville, they're going to take a few other reputations down with them. As first spear carrier James Carville says, this is "war."

Smash-mouth defense has always worked before for the Clintons, though we now know at a fearsome future price. Their strategy of deny, delay and attack got them past two elections and every congressional probe. It induced in both press and public a kind of ethical numbness. But it has also kept the investigative machinery alive long enough to stumble across Monica's tapes.

Had Mr. Clinton not delayed the Paula Jones trial so long, her lawyers wouldn't have been around to subpoena other women. Had his agents not smeared Paula Jones, maybe she'd have settled her suit long ago. Had superlawyer Bob Bennett not said Linda Tripp wasn't believable, maybe she wouldn't have taped her friend Ms. Lewinsky. But most of all, had the Clintons not stonewalled so long and successfully on Whitewater, Mr. Starr wouldn't threaten them today.

The White House wants Americans to believe Mr. Starr is just digging up adultery. But the real linchpin of his request to Ms. Reno to expand his probe was Webb Hubbell, of Whitewater fame. The former first friend had once pledged to cooperate with Mr. Starr but suddenly clammed up. Later Mr. Starr discovered that Mr. Hubbell had been steered toward big money by other friends of Bill. One of those friends was Vernon Jordan, who took him to a Revlon-affiliated company that paid Mr. Hubbell some $63,000.

Maybe this was just a case of Mr. Jordan's legendary generosity. But when the names Jordan and Revlon both showed up on tape helping Ms. Lewinsky, Mr. Starr was duty-bound to pursue the case for a pattern of witness tampering. My sources say Mr. Starr gave Ms. Reno's department the option to investigate this itself, or along with him, but she quickly told him to do it. Mr. Starr's decision to wire Ms. Tripp before he got permission to expand his probe is standard prosecutorial procedure.

This all helps explain why Mr. Starr seems willing to drive a hard bargain over immunity with Ms. Lewinsky now. He wants to avoid another Hubbell-like memory lapse. He'd like her to take a polygraph and perhaps to plead to a crime herself. And he knows her testimony isn't the sole basis for an obstruction of justice or perjury case against the president.

Mr. Starr has made mistakes as special counsel, but they've been political, not legal. He should have dropped his other clients to avoid even the appearance of partisan taint. His Pepperdine detour was a fiasco, as he quickly recognized. And he underestimated how much this White House would resist his probe—and assault him personally.

But all of this has also had the ironic effect of preparing him, and his office, for this current fight. When he was first appointed, Mr. Starr was every Democrat's favorite Republican lawyer, the type who thought everyone played politics by Marquess of Queensbury rules. He's learned the hard way that this White House doesn't. If he's now a threat to the Clinton presidency, Mr. Clinton has made him so.

REVIEW & OUTLOOK

Trashing the System

Perhaps the most interesting thing about Hillary Clinton's ruminations on "a vast right-wing conspiracy" were the remarks she made just beyond that point. She went on to impugn the integrity of the panel of three federal judges who appoint all independent counsel: "The same three-judge panel that removed Robert Fiske and appointed him [Mr. Starr], the same three-judge panel that is headed by someone who was appointed by Jesse Helms and Lauch Faircloth." She added that "we are using the criminal justice system to try to achieve political ends in this country."

Mrs. Clinton was on TV primarily in reaction to the allegations of lurid sex around the Oval Office. But in terms of Mr. Starr or the judges, the sex isn't the issue. That's plain from a reading of Attorney General Janet Reno's letter to the three-judge panel requesting an expansion of Mr. Starr's jurisdiction. There's nothing at all

Hillary Clinton

in there about sex. Ms. Reno's letter indicated she had received information that Ms. Lewinsky "may have submitted a false affidavit and suborned perjury from another witness in the case. In a taped conversation with a cooperating witness, Ms. Lewinsky states that she intends to lie when deposed. In the same conversation, she urges the cooperating witness to lie in her own upcoming deposition."

Now what were Ken Starr, Janet Reno or the three judges supposed to do with this? Is Mrs. Clinton, a Yale Law graduate, seriously suggesting that the special panel should have ignored Attorney General Reno's letter? They did what they should have done: referred the matter for investigation to the FBI agents and career prosecutors who work for Judge Starr.

But Mrs. Clinton wants the public to infer from her suggestions that the three-judge panel is part of "an entire operation" out to get her husband. To diminish the credibility of David Sentelle, the D.C. Circuit Court of Appeals judge who heads the panel, she says he was "appointed by Jesse Helms and Lauch Faircloth," the two GOP Senators from North Carolina.

Federal appeals court judges are appointed by Presidents, not Senators. In fact, Mr. Faircloth was nowhere near the Senate when David Sentelle was named a judge in 1985. He was still a *Democrat* and had just left a job as Democratic Governor Jim Hunt's secretary of commerce.

The three-judge panel that Judge Sentelle heads includes Peter Fay, an apolitical judge appointed by Gerald Ford. The third member is John Buntzel, who was appointed to the bench by Presidents Kennedy and Johnson. All the decisions of the panel on independent counsels have been unanimous, though judges can dissent from any majority opinion.

Mrs. Clinton should think some before trashing the criminal justice system as little more than a tool of someone else's politics. Recall the embezzlement prosecution of Billy Dale, the director of the White House Travel Office, who was acquitted in two hours. Or the delivery of confidential FBI files on Republican appointees to Craig Livingstone. Recall the improper perjury investigation of two Secret Service agents by Treasury Department Inspector General Valerie Lau after they testified before Congress on Filegate. Ms. Lau had to apologize to the agents and resigned under pressure last month.

Clearly the White House's strategy is to put in the public's mind that all of the criticism of the Administration's conduct is politically motivated. That is, they are trying to diminish their enemies. Mrs. Clinton's interview suggests they've concluded it may also be necessary to cut down public respect for the judiciary as well. Whether the Clintons survive, they are leaving behind cynicism and rubble.

REVIEW & OUTLOOK

The Clinton Poll Paradox

We have to admit we're pretty happy with the angst over Bill Clinton's poll numbers, ascending like a Roman candle in the wake of the Lewinsky affair. Yes, Roman candles burn out and fall to earth, but that's not the important point. What's wonderful is that in a political culture that wouldn't cross the street unless someone took a poll to see if the public approves, everyone in Washington agrees the Lewinsky polls don't add up.

It turns out that the pollsters' drones, interrupting the quotidian lives of folks at home with their phone calls and tidy little list of questions, can't plumb the higher moral and political calculus of America in the late 20th century.

Thus, what historians may someday call the Clinton Poll Paradox—voted the most popular boy in the political class even though you wouldn't let your daughter go out with him—is forcing everyone in politics this week to do something they did all the time before the era of polls: Think for themselves. That is the first good thing to come of the Clinton Paradox.

The next good thing may be that the American people are telling us that they don't want a U.S. President run out of office by a media frenzy and these polls.

As compared with the past two weeks' torrent, it's worth recalling that there were reporters trying to dig out the truth about the Clintons as far back as the '92 campaign. The stories then were about land deals, commodities trading, political cronies in the

Justice Department or unpaid tax liabilities. For their efforts, many of these reporters were sniffed at by their peers or had to plead with editors to put these stories in the paper. TV couldn't be bothered because such stories don't fit easily into television's model of journalism. Political professionals couldn't be bothered because the polls didn't pick up any negative feedback from the stories, which weekend TV pundits ridiculed as "arcane" or "political."

But the Lewinsky story fit the model just fine. As with the O.J. Simpson trial, Princess Di's death or Marv Albert, the Bill and Monica tale qualifies for the kind of journalistic Xtreme Games staged by TV's talk shows and their guests. So maybe the polls' respondents are saying, Don't expect us to vote thumbs down on a Presidency just because TV has staged a vocal orgy for two weeks. What was wrong with the system of righting wrongs that we used to have? The one that decided guilt or innocence after something called due process.

Bill Clinton

That said, one has to quickly add that the Clinton circle's modus operandi doesn't make it easy for the traditional system to function. They've proved since the Administration's first months that what they're most schooled in is due *non*-process—legitimate subpoenas fought or ignored, high IQ memories gone blank, phony jobs found for Webster Hubbell on his way to prison, the fund-raisers' activities concealed behind Fifth Amendment claims.

At bottom, many people in the media no doubt also wish a system other than rush-to-judgment would sort out all these charges. The fact remains, however, that a lot of people around the Beltway have spent five years with successive Clinton scandals, all the while noting that none of it has been conclusively proved; the independent counsel has "conflicts of interest," the Republicans are "partisan," and most of the charges are generated by the President's "critics." But when allegations of seducing an intern become the last straw for these same Washington's sophisticates, they profess shock that the American people haven't jumped to a conclusion that the sophisticates have talked them out of for five years.

The polling numbers mean that the voters aren't going to let sensationalism or cynicism take control of the American political system. Instead, the existing institutions of law and politics—for all their imperfection, imprecision and timidity—are still going to have to produce the truth about the Clinton Presidency. Kenneth Starr's investigation, despite the sniping, is doing serious work, but will have to offer some considered proof against its eventual targets. The courts will arbitrate the process. And when that happens, the system better find a way to cope with the Clintons' certain attacks on anyone likely to sit in judgment on them—from judges to witnesses.

Beyond the law, there is also the fact that later this year the American people will go to the polls—not Mr. Gallup's polls but the ones in which individuals do in fact work out the complex calculus of the nation's life and then pull levers for candidates and their parties. It adds up to a judgment. There is the palpable sense around the political community now that the system badly needs to have some such legitimate judgment rendered—again—about this Presidency. When that comes, it almost certainly will be about more than sexual relations. It will be about Bill Clinton's tenure and conduct in office, a subject on which it now appears the American people intend to remain resolutely focused.

Letters to the Editor

Why Clinton's Ratings Are So High

Your Feb. 3 editorial "The Clinton Poll Paradox" highlights the upside of the Clinton controversy: Clinton's soaring poll ratings have spurred creative thinking among Beltway politicians and have demonstrated the American public's refusal to allow media hype to undermine our political system. But the present debacle also highlights an unmentioned downside.

Often the universal response to a political emergency is myopic. The populace does not want to accept that its leader squandered the public trust and the leader's closest advisers do not want to admit to dedicating their career to a man and a cause that proved utterly false.

William Manchester, author of "The Last Lion: Alone," the second portion of his tripartite biography of Winston Churchill, writes: "In politics the squeaky wheel gets little grease. . . . The mass distrusts controversy. Reluctant to reconsider its convictions, superstitions and prejudices, it rarely withdraws support from those who are guiding its destinies. Thus inertia becomes an incumbent's accomplice. So does human reluctance to admit error. Those who backed the top man insist, against all evidence, that they made the right choice." (p. 407) The passage describes the 1939 British public's reaction to Neville Chamberlain, prime minister of Great Britain from 1937-40, whose appeasement of Nazi Germany left Britain dangerously ill-equipped to defend itself. While today's crisis is far different from the one Mr. Manchester describes, both

Clinton and Chamberlain have benefited from the "inertia" of incumbency.

I trust that the American public is not lending high marks to the president out of an aversion to responsibility, but out of an inclination to weigh the facts and act when it counts: at the ballot box. However, if the American people continue to be fed only half-truths from its leaders, as Britain was in the 1930s, choosing the best leaders becomes impossible.

MARTA E. HUMMEL
Research Director
U.S. Term Limits

Washington

* * *

The Clinton Poll Paradox is no paradox. The public is simply saying that there is so much cynicism over politicians that what is understoodabout Mr. Clinton is safer than what is not known about others. Every intimate revelation pulls the voters closer to this individual, who is now perceived as being comprehended so well. Mr. Clinton has a desire to be accepted as every person's best friend, and Ken Starr is assisting him in accomplishing that.

STANLEY HERZ

Somers, N.Y.

REVIEW & OUTLOOK

Charlie Trie's Return

Monica Lewinsky flew home to her father Tuesday, free for the moment of that den of iniquity known as Washington, D.C. Of course, Bill Clinton presides over Washington right now, which means if nothing else that the story line never stops. At about the very hour that Ms. Lewinsky took off, Charlie Trie, the former Little Rock restaurateur who worked his way up to Clinton colleague, landed at Dulles Airport to turn himself in to the Department of Justice. It turns out that Mr. Trie was holed up all these weeks in one of the world's certified dens of iniquity, Macau, the Chinese appendage known mainly for gambling, women, gang murders, Portuguese restaurants and, more recently, contributions to the Clinton-Gore re-election campaign.

Charlie Trie didn't flee to Beijing and Macau because he was too fainthearted for the Beltway's rough and tumble. Charlie Trie was a go-to guy for the Clinton-Gore team. He knows a lot about their glob-alized fund-raising strategies. Some of those fund-raising activities were the basis for an indictment Justice obtained against him last week. After his arrest Tuesday, Mr. Trie posted $200,000 bond and turned in his passport. Yesterday's coverage immediately raised the question of precisely how much sentence reduction Mr. Trie may get after cutting a deal with Justice.

Charlie Trie's hoped-for Justice deal is the first order of business here. Some of us went on record as skeptical of this Justice Department's ability to referee political malfeasance back when Mr.

Clinton gave Little Rock colleague Webster Hubbell the run of the place. Mr. Hubbell's felony guilty plea removed him from Justice, but not our doubts. Serious people now say that federal prosecutor Charles La Bella can be trusted to prosecute any fund-raising crimes without fear or favor, including the Trie case.

We're still deeply skeptical, and it's hard to see how one couldn't be. For one, the hard calls on any involvement by Messrs. Clinton or Gore aren't part of Mr. La Bella's portfolio. And in disposing of two recent cases, that of the Lums and Ron Brown's son, the Department did deals for guilty pleas in return for essentially nothing. The one prosecutor who hasn't caved in before all this *omerta* is in fact the independent counsel, Kenneth Starr, who works beyond Justice's walls and who's been willing to let convicted felon Susan McDougal sit in a cell and do TV turns until she says simply that Bill Clinton did lie or did not lie under oath about Whitewater. And of course in recent days Mr. Starr's office has refused to cut a deal with Monica Lewinsky in return for nothing more than tales from the Clinton Decameron.

Charlie Trie

If Justice merely wants a scalp, it could narrowly define Charlie Trie's role in return for his cheerful pleas to a little brown bag's worth of campaign-finance peccadilloes. But to a prosecutor willing to more broadly define his value as a witness, Charlie Trie becomes a gazetteer of the Clinton/Gore/DNC overseas ventures.

For instance, Mr. Trie's most recent address, Macau, is also home to Ng Lap Seng, or Mr. Wu, one of the most intriguing, unexplained pipelines for cash into the re-election campaign. If Mr. Trie fled to seedy Macau, why there, of all places? Charlie Trie's activities touch James Riady of Indonesia's Lippo Group, John Huang, and two additional Little Rock Clinton colleagues and Asian-based rainmakers, Joe Giroir and Mark Middleton.

In short, who appropriately should prosecute Charlie Trie? Prosecutorial appropriateness is a big subject just now, and a good one. What makes the issues at hand here so difficult is that no possible system of accountability could have foreseen the breadth of institutional politicization that Bill Clinton has brought to Washington. Everything, it seems—Justice, the FBI, the Secret

Service, the Lincoln Bedroom, the interns—somehow gets subsumed into Mr. Clinton's political corpus. It suggests a blurring of the national leader's public and private selves more common to the Middle Ages. And indeed an army of courtiers works full time merely to hold the whole, blurred political entity together.

In this unique environment, can Janet Reno's Justice Department take on Charlie Trie and the campaign-finance labyrinth? We doubt it.

Instead, with Mr. Trie now in hand, Congress should resubmit a request to Attorney General Reno that she formally seek the appointment of an independent counsel to investigate and if necessary prosecute campaign-finance violations. In declining to do so the first time, Ms. Reno argued she saw no credible evidence that a covered person committed a crime. Charlie Trie, under oath, should be able to resolve that issue in a 10-minute conversation.

The fig leaves against invoking the independent counsel statute for these matters are falling. Get on with it.

REVIEW & OUTLOOK

The Casino Decision

Attorney General Janet Reno must decide by this Wednesday if all the curious details in Interior Secretary Bruce Babbitt's rejection of a Chippewa Indian casino in Hudson, Wis. should trigger the independent counsel law. The stakes are high. Insofar as the Indian casino decision involves President Clinton and top White House officials, an independent counsel could find the trail leading to a larger campaign-funding conspiracy. Also, the same White House that is discussing invoking executive privilege against Ken Starr in the Monica Lewinsky case has already invoked it selectively to keep its memos on the casino issue from being made public.

The Administration appears to be on increasingly weak ground in insisting there was no link between the casino rejection and nearly $300,000 in campaign contributions from nearby tribes who felt the new casino would threaten their own gaming. A draft report recently came to light showing that in June 1995 the Indian Gaming division of Interior was making a strong case for *approval* of the casino— less than a month before Secretary Babbitt rejected it, overriding both members of his staff and his Minnesota regional office.

But what the Indian Gaming staff apparently didn't know is that days before their favorable draft report was prepared, an aide to then Deputy White House Chief of Staff Harold Ickes was told by Heather Sibbison, a special assistant to Secretary Babbitt, that it was "95% certain the application would be turned down."

The official whose name appears on the report, George Skibine, then director of the Indian Gaming division, claims the document didn't represent his views. He also admits he decided not to turn over the document as part of a lawsuit the losing Chippewa Indians filed against Interior. In January 1996, Mr. Skibine told the court that in turning over documents, "I included all substantive internal communications except those to or from legal counsel." He now claims the draft report, which didn't involve legal counsel, didn't need to be submitted to the court. Mr. Skibine insists the casino rejection was made by him "on the merits."

But stubborn facts keep emerging. Tom Schneider, a friend of President Clinton and a paid lobbyist for the Indians opposing the Chippewas' bid for the Hudson casino, received word that the President himself was looking into the matter. Mr. Schneider hosted a fund-raiser for President Clinton on July 13, 1995, at which the two men sat next to each other. The event raised $420,000 for Mr. Clinton's re-election campaign. The date is significant, because the decision to reject the Hudson casino was made the next day.

Bruce Babbitt

Paul Eckstein, an old friend of Secretary Babbitt and a lobbyist on behalf of the Chippewas, has testified that during a meeting with Mr. Babbitt on July 14 he was told that Mr. Ickes had directed the secretary to issue the decision that day, and that "tribes" opposed to the casino had contributed about half a million dollars to the Democrats. Mr. Babbitt first told Congress he never made the Ickes comment, but then told Senator Thompson that he had made it up as a way of getting Mr. Eckstein out of his office quickly. As for the contribution comment, Mr. Babbitt said carefully to Senator Thompson: "I am stating under oath that I have no recollection of any conversation of that kind."

One large reason the persistent Indian casino case is significant is that it highlights the extent to which the Clinton Administration politicized nearly everything it touched. Yes, there are invariably going to be political considerations of a sort when a bureaucracy has to sign off on competing interests in a matter such as this. But it is another level of hyperpoliticization altogether when decisions out of the bowels of the Interior Department get siphoned into the Clinton-Gore re-election effort, dragging along lobbyists, a senior White

House aide and Bruce Babbitt.

Consider also how the Justice Department has been driven into a corner. It is defending the Interior Department against claims brought by the Chippewas that improper political influence was involved in the rejection of their casino. Fine. But it is also supposed to be investigating the matter to determine if an independent counsel should be named. It is thus acting as both defense and prosecution in the same case.

When GOP Rep. Steve Horn questioned Ms. Reno about this recently, she replied there are times "when we might be investigating a prison guard, but at the same time, defending the lawsuit against him." She added: "We tried to build an appropriate structure that will permit that."

It is hard to be persuaded that such contortions will ensure accountability in the government. But we'll hear more about this from Ms. Reno with Wednesday's decision.

REVIEW & OUTLOOK

Spinning Starr

Today, a generation after Watergate, we still do not know the identity of Deep Throat; the editors of the Washington Post say they will name the inside source confirming so many of their leaks only after he dies, or gives permission. But in Whitewater, the current attack on Independent Counsel Kenneth Starr runs, the important thing is the source of leaks, not the conduct of the President.

What passes for logic from Clinton mouthpiece David Kendall is that there have been leaks, they have been damaging to the President, and therefore Mr. Starr must be responsible. In an age when instant communication has toppled the Soviet empire, they ask us to believe in a hermetic seal around a case involving the President of the United States receiving oral sex from a 21-year-old intern. Get real.

Mr. Kendall offers no evidence beyond newspaper clippings that the leaks come from Mr. Starr or his office, though a court filing might produce more. This could be, of course, but is far from the only possibility. Indeed, the interest of a prosecutor is usually to assemble his case and present it at a swoop. On the record Mr. Starr was trying to delay or stop the publication of the first leak, Newsweek's scoop of the Lewinsky tapes. This popped up in the Drudge Report on the Internet after Mr. Starr had presented his evidence to the Justice Department, now full of Clinton loyalists such as the unconfirmable Robert Litt. The furor was a warning not only to Ms. Lewinsky, but to other potential witnesses Mr. Starr would have liked to approach privately.

As to the alternatives: Conceivably, though barely so given the current cast of characters, there is a Deep Throat in the White House, at Justice or even at Williams & Connolly who thinks the public should know the truth. The public prints already are full of liberals grossed out by this Presidency; why not those on the inside?

Possibly the White House or lawyers for various parties think  there is some advantage in confusing Mr. Starr's investigation. Was Presidential secretary Betty Currie debriefed after her testimony, were memos written and who received them? Who, by the way, arranged for and paid her lawyer? In the normal course of a big defense effort, scores of people in Washington would likely have known of her testimony before it appeared in the New York Times.

Ken Starr

And possibly, as the House's Rep. Dan Burton says has happened with his investigation, White House tacticians are leaking precisely because they calculate that the other side will be blamed. Clearly, after all, the White House is in campaign mode to besmirch Ken Starr. Events of recent days suggest that an analysis by Mr. Clinton's legal team has concluded that their strongest strategy is not to meet on the battlefield of facts and law, but to conduct a *political* offensive against the IC and his staff.

For those familiar with Mr. Starr's public career, it is amusingly ironic to hear the likes of Paul Begala pillory him as the ultimate partisan. To the contrary, when Mr. Starr was George Bush's Solicitor General in the early 1990s, many conservatives thought him professorial to a fault, and privately criticized his seeming reluctance to push hard to overturn liberal court precedent. These same doubts about Mr. Starr's toughness resurfaced when he first got the IC appointment.

And in light of Mr. Starr's current mad-dog reputation, it's ironic to recall the Pepperdine University episode. By some interpretations, Mr. Starr's decision to resign his post and retire to Santa Monica suggested at the time that the former judge didn't have the fortitude to see through an investigation of the nation's highest public official. Still, ever alert to spin opportunities, the Clinton side seized on philanthropist Richard Scaife's financial support of Pepperdine as evidence that Mr. Starr was a pawn of the far right. This did not prevent an invitation to a White House dinner last month, approved by Mrs. Clinton, to this same Mr. Scaife for another of his right-wing philanthropies, the fund to preserve the Presidential residence.

On our reading, the Clinton geniuses have managed to turn Judge Starr not into a foaming partisan, but something far more dangerous to their interests, a real prosecutor. When he took the job, the brainy Mr. Starr had no credentials as a prosecutor. He knew it, so he recruited a staff that amounts to a Special Force Team of career prosecutors, with strong reputations for convicting high public officials of political and financial crimes. No one, including a President, would choose to take on this particular prosecution team.

In a way, this makes the Clinton tactics hard to understand as a calculation, though predictable as a habit. No matter what opposition they've encountered—Paula Jones, Linda Tripp, Kathleen Willey, Fred Thompson, Judge Royce Lamberth—the Clinton side has always chosen the same strategy of stonewalling, smash-mouth lawyering. This brazen strategy has in a sense "worked," culminating in the current joke that if Mr. Clinton had been the Titanic the iceberg would have sunk.

But it is a strategy that enrages and hardens nearly all of Mr. Clinton's presumed enemies; witness Paula Jones's refusal to settle or Linda Tripp's tape recordings or Judge Lamberth's denunciations of their legal tactics. The most plausible explanation for Ken Starr's behavior is that the relentless Clinton stonewalling and public demagoguing have finally made him as aggressive as the more experienced prosecutors on his staff. This may produce poor polling numbers for Mr. Starr, but at a purely legal level simply can't be good news for the White House.

If in fact we are expected to take Mr. Kendall's accusations seriously as a matter of legal ethics, Mr. Clinton should begin the process of firing Mr. Starr, as laid out in 28 U.S.C. Sec. 596. This requires "the personal action of the Attorney General," who must submit the facts and grounds for removal to the court and to the House and Senate Judiciary committees. The removed IC then may appeal to the U.S. District Court for D.C. Given this prospect, don't expect President Clinton or lawyer Kendall to pursue the logic of their claims against the independent counsel.

Their PR offensive is winning in the polls, which look increasingly to be a last redoubt; in May of 1973, two months after Judge

John Sirica blew Watergate open, 64% of Americans in a Harris poll thought of Richard Nixon as a man of high integrity. The Clintonites' past success with the smash-mouth strategy has come mainly against other politicians or defenseless women. In Mr. Starr they may finally be meeting someone beyond their experience, someone who cares less about the polls than about his duty.

REVIEW & OUTLOOK

'Leon, What's the Deal?'

After ignoring its provisions as the campaign finance scandal has built for the last 18 months, Attorney General Janet Reno has just triggered the law for the sixth time in the Clinton Administration on the narrow issue of whether Interior Secretary Bruce Babbitt lied before Congress.

That charge is not nothing. But the larger issue that should be investigated is whether political influence led to the rejection of an application by impoverished Indian tribes to open a casino in Hudson, Wis. But Ms. Reno's proposed charter for an independent counsel is so narrowly drawn that one former Interior lawyer calls it "the eye of a needle."

Any serious investigation of the matter would likely widen into a full-scale look at 1996 White House fund-raising practices. The three-judge panel that oversees independent counsels has the final say in the wording of a charter; in 1986, at the request of Democrats in Congress, it expanded the reach of Lawrence Walsh's Iran-Contra probe to include an inquiry into U.S. funding of the Nicaraguan contras. In addition, any independent counsel can ask to have his mandate broadened. Justice opposed such a request from Donald Smaltz, counsel in the Mike Espy case, but the three-judge panel expanded it anyway.

White House political fingerprints are all over the sudden rejection of the casino in July 1995. That April President Clinton and deputy counsel Bruce Lindsey met with Patrick O'Connor, a former

Democratic National Committee treasurer hired to kill the casino. Mr. Clinton then told Mr. Lindsey to "talk to O'Connor here about his concerns about tribes that he represents," according to a deposition by Mr. O'Connor. Days later DNC Chairman Don Fowler met with casino opponents and contacted Interior as well as White House deputy chief of staff Harold Ickes.

Depositions filed in federal court show that on May 25, 1995, Mr. Ickes called the Interior Department about the casino. About the same time, lobbyist Larry Kitto spoke with Vice President Gore. Mr. Kitto was asked in his deposition: "You were hoping to solicit Al Gore's direct communication with Secretary Babbitt, is that correct?" He replied: "That's correct."

A busy President Clinton also kept tabs on the obscure casino decision. The latest issue of Human Events reproduces a handwritten note from Clinton to chief of staff Leon Panetta that reads: "Leon, what's the deal on the Wisconsin tribe Indian dispute?" The note was turned over to Sen. Fred Thompson's committee after the White House first tried to claim executive privilege to block its release.

Secretary Babbitt claims he came under no pressure from the White House, though he overrode both his own Minnesota regional office and a draft report prepared by his staff. Before that favorable draft report was completed, an aide to Mr. Ickes was told by Heather Sibbison, an assistant to Secretary Babbitt, that it was "95% certain the application would be turned down."

Interior officials have tried to explain that the casino rejection was done by the book, but evidence has just been uncovered by Rep. Dan Burton's oversight committee that the Hudson casino rejection represented a new policy by Interior.

On December 16 last year, Ms. Sibbison e-mailed Interior spokesman Michael Gauldin that "it has been our position, first articulated in Hudson, that expressed opposition from local elected officials essentially is prima facie evidence of detriment" to the community. A Justice lawyer defending Interior in a lawsuit against its decision admits that "the Department appears to have changed in this case its past policy of requiring 'hard' evidence of detriment to the community."

The Reno decision to restrict a small piece of the Babbitt casino controversy to an outside investigator won't end Justice's conflict of interest. Justice is defending Interior in a civil suit brought by casino proponents at the same time it is investigating the allegations of White House involvement in the decision. Ms. Reno's "eye of the needle" mandate for an outside counsel will only inspire confidence if it is expanded so that Justice no longer is acting as both defense and prosecution in the case.

Editorial Feature

Making Sense of the Polls

By JAMES Q. WILSON

There are two main criticisms of what is taken to be the American view of President Clinton's sexual behavior. The first, voiced loudly by European critics but echoed by many Americans, is that we are hopelessly Puritanical—obsessed with sex and unwilling to take the sophisticated view that private life and public conduct are two different matters. The second, expressed especially by critics of the president, is that Americans are hopelessly pragmatic—indifferent to morality and preoccupied with the state of the economy and their own material condition.

There are elements of truth in both views, but I think neither quite captures what is suggested by a close reading of the polls. (I will not cite the poll data here, but all of my descriptions of particular American beliefs come from a variety of recent surveys.) While it is true, as some Europeans complain, that Americans think the president should have strong moral values, Americans define these values rather carefully. A majority do not think that in evaluating a president it is important to know whether he has had an extramarital affair, fathered a child out of wedlock or is homosexual. But they care strongly whether he has used drugs, failed to pay debts, been an alcoholic or had a gambling problem.

Most Americans think Mr. Clinton had an affair not only with Monica Lewinsky but probably with other women since becoming president. They are skeptical of the claim that such allegations are part of a right-wing conspiracy, but do feel that his private life is a private matter. They take seriously his legal obligations, however. If he lied under oath, or urged Ms. Lewinsky or others to do the same, he ought to resign. If he fails to resign, impeachment is in order.

These opinions are not very different from those that so-called sophisticated Europeans urge us to have. But they are deeply disturbing to people who believe such views are morally ungrounded. To them, Mr. Clinton has refused to discuss candidly the many alleged examples of sexual misconduct in office, even though questions about such behavior now intrude on his ability to hold a serious press conference with a foreign leader. It is pointless to lay the blame for all this on the media; they live off sex and violence.

Monica Lewinsky

From the available poll data, those who take Mr. Clinton's conduct more seriously have one thing in common—they are Republicans. By very large margins, Republicans are more likely than Democrats to have a low opinion of Mr. Clinton and a high one of Independent Counsel Kenneth Starr, to believe that Mr. Clinton had an affair with Ms. Lewinsky and told her to lie about it, and to think that the country faces a moral crisis in which the president displays lower moral standards than the average married man. We do not know whether these views would be reversed if a Republican president faced similar charges. But to some unknown degree, there would no doubt be a party-linked shift.

Because of this partisan division, the country is about evenly divided over the central question—whether we should care about Mr. Clinton's personal life or only about how well he "runs the country." This split—deeply troubling to many people—is not part of the American psyche but a feature of our political orientation.

Bear in mind what Americans mean when they say they approve of how a man, about whose credibility there are growing doubts, is "running the country." No president "runs the country." He may nudge it in good or bad directions, but the U.S. has long placed economic markets and private arrangements over state leadership. A sad consequence of the growth of the federal government is the new belief among many people that it creates our wealth or solves our problems. Except in a few cases, it does neither. What Americans probably mean is that they will give good marks to whoever is in office when things are going well and poor marks to whoever holds office when things are going badly.

This is a rational way for people to think. Politics is not very important to most of us, and so we think about it using this retrospective shorthand: "Vote for good times and against bad ones." If we cared passionately about politics, we would instead ponder party platforms, take seriously the State of the Union address, and infer future behavior from present conduct.

Europeans, for whom party politics is more important than it is here, tend to take a different view. Party loyalties matter more in Europe, in part because only by party involvement can one have much influence (if any at all) on a parliamentary government that lacks a separation of powers. But to the extent that party rule is all-important, people must devise a system for protecting a regime from the natural frailties of human life. Too much is at stake in a centralized government for it always to be vulnerable to sexual misconduct. One way to manage that risk is to deny it—that is, to say that having a mistress or publicly cavorting with other women is a "private" matter. It is, of course, exactly the opposite; it is very public matter. But one must act as if it were private in order to preserve the stability of the governing regime.

I think Americans are right to believe that the normal frailties of human life should not affect our judgment of a president. If he acquires a mistress in response to tension between himself and his wife, as Franklin D. Roosevelt did, it is none of our business. If he has an affair with a woman before becoming president, it should not affect our judgment greatly, provided he is honest about it.

But if a president is sexually reckless, arranging liaisons with many women, most of them significantly younger than he and many of them vulnerable to the power and romance of presidential stature, he is revealing himself to be a self-serving thrill-seeker whose conduct abuses an office that today is supposed to stand for a public reaffirmation of the importance of family life. Not many corporate CEOs could keep their jobs if what has been alleged about Mr. Clinton were alleged about them, and corporate executives are not expected to preach from a bully pulpit.

What troubles me about the polls is not that people think truly private matters should remain private, but their unwillingness to link two beliefs they now profess: They believe Mr. Clinton had an affair with Ms. Lewinsky, and they believe that if he did and lied about it he should resign. But since Mr. Clinton has denied an allegation most Americans think is true, then he has in their minds lied about it. And if he has lied . . .

Americans do not think they are being inconsistent; they think they are waiting for proof. But though they wait, they already think they know the truth yet profess not to care about it. To me, the public has yet to align its beliefs into a coherent whole. In large measure, that reflects their tolerance, the absence of concrete proof, and their difficulty in taking politics all that seriously. These are decent attitudes.

It would be better if people said that they are waiting for proof, and until it appears they do not wish to act on their suspicions. Instead they are saying that they don't want the investigation to continue (why wait for facts if you don't want facts to appear?), they don't trust the media or Mr. Starr (who else will get any facts?), and they think that lying under oath is worse than lying to the people (how can one lie be worse than the other?).

Americans are neither Puritans nor pragmatists. We are partisan, and confused.

Mr. Wilson is the author of "Moral Judgment" (Basic Books, 1997) and "The Moral Sense" (Simon & Schuster paperback, 1997).

REVIEW & OUTLOOK

Asides

The Whole Truth?

The father of and attorney for Monica Lewinsky have joined the assault on Independent Counsel Kenneth Starr being conducted by White House spinmeisters. Their obvious agitation is intriguing, since presumably they are adult enough to understand that their daughter/client faces no serious legal jeopardy so long as she's willing to tell the whole truth.

Also intriguing is the sudden plea bargain by Jim Guy Tucker, Mr. Clinton's successor as Governor of Arkansas, who agreed Friday to cooperate with Mr. Starr's original Whitewater investigation. Perhaps Jim Guy is decamping the Presidential stonewall because he doesn't read the impact of the Lewinsky episode the way the pollsters do. And in his case, the whole truth includes what transpired in two meetings with the President in October of 1993. This was just after the White House learned, through a series of "heads ups," that a criminal fraud referral by investigators probing the Whitewater S&L, Madison Guaranty, had named Governor Tucker and the Clintons as possible beneficiaries.

REVIEW & OUTLOOK

Starr Struck

In terms of sheer tactical skill, you have to admire the Clinton scandal squad. On the Sunday before the State of the Union address, James Carville goes on TV to declare "war" on Mr. Starr, on Tuesday morning Hillary Clinton waves the "vast right-wing conspiracy." By the weekend, they managed to change the subject from whether the President suborned perjury to whether Independent Counsel Kenneth Starr stepped on a crack in the pavement. Bravo and yuck.

This week the Beltway media professed shock when Mr. Starr struck back by subpoenaing White House aide Sidney Blumenthal, who "monitors" media coverage of the scandals, to ask about his press contacts. There is of course a legitimate issue about prosecutors probing into journalistic sources, but Mr. Starr also has a legitimate interest here. He complained yesterday that his office "has been subjected to an avalanche of lies."

For example, his office received some 30 phone calls pursuing a plant that one of his deputies was fired from a university job—which turned out to be untrue. And 18 U.S.C. Section 1503 makes it a crime to try "to influence, intimidate, or impede" any officer of the court through "any threatening letter or communication." Journalists owe little to sources who tell them lies, and it would help if they started to report such incidents. As Mr. Starr said yesterday, "the First Amendment is interested in the truth."

And after all, it was Clinton lawyer David Kendall who demanded that Mr. Starr start investigating leaks. Mr. Kendall's purpose was to suggest all leaks come from Mr. Starr, but that is by no means the case. The Washington Times noticed, for example, that the White House sent out aide Ann Lewis on "Good Morning America" to blame Mr. Starr for leaks to Newsweek about the testimony of Ashley Raines, Ms. Lewinsky's fellow intern. But at the same hour, Newsweek writer Michael Isikoff pointed out on the "Today" show that he had attributed his account to "sources close to the President's defense." In short, the White House leaked the bad news so it could blame Mr. Starr.

Then there's the little matter of dirt diggers, especially since George Stephanopoulos warned/threatened that Clinton defenders would expose sexual sins by others. Last Sunday, the White House issued a blanket denial that anyone had been hired "to look into the background of . . . investigators, prosecutors or reporters." But that statement proved "inoperative" within 48 hours as it was revealed that the President's lawyers have been paying investigator Terry Lenzner to dig up background information on Whitewater and Paula Jones since 1994. White House spokesman Mike McCurry explained the discrepancy by saying there is a difference between "the kind of leg-work" investigators do for lawyers and "looking up dirt on prosecutors and reporters."

Ken Starr

Mr. Lenzner was also called before the grand jury this week, quite possibly to flesh out that distinction. Once a Democratic Congressional staffer who investigated the Watergate scandal, he now runs a firm, Investigative Group Inc., that has done opposition research for many liberal politicians as well as business figures such as Michael Milken. Former IGI investigator Michael Moroney says some of its research while he was there "went into sexual peccadilloes." Mr. Moroney told the Washington Times that IGI could unearth damaging information. "They can now target all the Congressmen on the Judiciary Committee and how many of them have had affairs," Mr. Moroney said. "I mean, this is ripe for that kind of arm-twisting."

Reporters have also uncovered clues that Jack Palladino, the private investigator who quelled numerous "bimbo eruptions" for the 1992 Clinton campaign, is back on the job. A former '60s radical, he did investigative work for lawyers for the Black Panthers. He boasted recently of how he has avoided subpoenas from Paula Jones's attorneys. Sandra Sutherland, his wife and partner, describes their approach as "the honest con." This means, according to the New Yorker's Jane Mayer, "they believe that it is acceptable to use subterfuge and outright lies in the service of a larger truth about a client's case."

This week, a House committee subpoenaed the Teamsters union for information on the $130,000 of work Mr. Palladino did for them in 1994 at the behest of Charles Ruff, then the union's lawyer. Mr. Ruff is now White House Counsel and the Teamsters are in the middle of the 1996 campaign fund-raising scandal. Joe DiGenova, who is working for the committee, complained eloquently on Sunday about the investigation of himself and his wife.

The outrage here is not Mr. Starr's tactics, but Mr. Clinton's. As White House aides keep saying, we should get back to the important business of the nation, which emphatically includes Mr. Starr's mandate—inquiring whether the President has upheld his Constitutional duty to see that the laws are faithfully executed.

Macau Again

In March, the Senate Governmental Affairs Committee voted out a lengthy report on the 1996 campaign finance scandal. Among the conclusions by the GOP majority under Senator Fred Thompson: six pivotal campaign players—Charlie Trie, John Huang, James and Mochtar Riady, Maria Hsia and Ted Sioeng—had ties to Beijing. The Riadys, longtime supporters of Mr. Clinton, "have had a long-term relationship with a Chinese intelligence agency," the report noted. Ms. Hsia—the central figure in Vice President Al Gore's controversial fund-raiser at a Buddhist temple in California—"has been an agent of the Chinese government."

Noting that so many roads led to tiny Macau, the Journal's Micah Morrison paid a visit to the wide-open gambling entrepot. He reported on Ng Lap Seng, Mr. Trie's moneybag. Mr. Ng, a shadowy Chinese businessman with interests in Macau gambling spots, had funneled more than $900,000 to accounts controlled by Mr. Trie and had visited the White House 10 times. Mr. Morrison reported on Mr. Ng's extensive contacts in the triad organized crime underworld, his ascending power in the interlinked worlds of Macau and China politics, and Mr. Clinton's other friends in the lawless enclave.

Back in Washington, the White House assault on Independent

Counsel Starr continued. Four former attorneys general released a statement supporting Mr. Starr and expressing "concern that the severity of the attacks" seemed to have "the improper purpose of influencing and impeding an ongoing criminal investigation." Yet the Clinton Administration and outside advisers such as James Carville pressed on, targeting not only Mr. Starr but his deputies, federal judges, critics and women who raised allegations against the President. Mr. Clinton continued to ride high in the polls on the strengths of a good economy, his personal charm and a powerful White House spin machine. Mr. Starr dwelled in poll purgatory.

"Serious people should recognize the damage being wrought to institutions developed over centuries to uphold the idea that civilization means something more than the sentiment of the passing moment," the Journal warned. "If poll ratings are all that matter in the nation's capital, a President can perhaps sustain them with a prosperous economy and a winning television manner, or as the Romans said, bread and circuses. Mr. Carville's war and Mr. Starr's polls give us a glimpse of one possible evolution of our political system in an era of instant communications. The issue is whether we will be governed by men or by laws."

Editorial Feature

The Macau Connection

BY MICAH MORRISON

MACAU—A visitor to Macau—with its seedy downtown and decadent atmosphere redolent of "Casablanca"—may start to look around for Humphrey Bogart. The Portuguese-administered territory an hour's hydrofoil ride from Hong Kong may be the most lawless six square miles on earth. Its major industries, legalized gambling and prostitution, spawn other pursuits such as money laundering, extortion, drugs and violence. Lately it's been in the grip of "triad wars"—with the rival crime syndicates battling for control of the rackets—that have claimed at least 24 lives in the past 14 months, and taken a sharp bite out of casual tourism.

While it's a long way from Arkansas, mysterious Macau has been a star setting for the campaign-finance controversy swirling around President Clinton. Charlie Trie, the Little Rock restaurateur turned Clinton fund-raiser, took refuge here before deciding to return stateside to fight his indictment for funneling illegal foreign funds to the 1996 Clinton-Gore campaign. The majority report from Sen. Fred Thompson's Governmental Affairs Committee says Mr. Trie was one of six individuals identified by the CIA and FBI as having ties to China's intelligence apparatus. Rep. Dan Burton's House committee had scheduled further hearings on Mr. Trie this week, but they were canceled because two key witnesses were unavailable. Mr. Trie himself has invoked the Fifth Amendment and was not scheduled to appear.

Mr. Trie's choice of Macau as a refuge was scarcely an accident, since it is the base of his business partner Ng Lap Seng. (Mr. Ng is also known as Mr. Wu, since the Cantonese and Mandarin dialects have different pronunciations of the ideograph for his name.) The Senate report finds that Mr. Trie and Mr. Ng collaborated in a scheme to funnel "hundreds of thousands of dollars in foreign funds" to the Democratic National Committee. Mr. Ng wired in a total of more than $1 million from accounts in Macau and Hong Kong to Trie accounts in the U.S. The report says that Mr. Trie's "bank records and tax returns reveal that he received little or no income from sources other than Ng Lap Seng."

Mr. Ng's largesse won him 10 visits to the White House between

A greeting for Ng Lap Seng

1994 and 1996, including at least one with President Clinton, according to White House entry logs. Mr. Ng and Mr. Trie were seated beside the president at a February 1996 fund-raiser at the Hay Adams Hotel in Washington, and in October 1995 they organized a reception for then Commerce Secretary Ron Brown at Hong Kong's Hotel Shangri-La. Given all this activity, questions naturally arise: Who is Ng Lap Seng, and what did he want?

Mysterious Figure

According to several well-informed sources in Hong Kong and Macau, Mr. Ng is a mysterious figure with extensive business in China, where he also held a minor post as a member of the Chinese People's Political Consultative Conference in his hometown of Nan Hai in Guangdong province. In Macau, his most visible interest is his ownership of the Fortuna Hotel, a garish high-rise in the gambling district, featuring a 20,000-square-foot nightclub with "table dancing" by strippers, as well as a massage parlor and, according to its brochure, "over 30 independent karaoke rooms, all luxuriously decorated with the most advanced sound system for any one interested in performing his favorite songs." The brochure also boasts "attractive and attentive hostesses from China, Korea, Singapore, Malaysia, Vietnam, Indonesia and Burma together with erotic girls from Europe and Russia, certainly offer you an exciting and unforgettable evening with friends or business associates."

Sources in Macau say Mr. Ng's nightclub is frequented by officials of China's People's Liberation Army. And also that its private VIP karaoke rooms are known hangouts for the Wo On Lok Triad, which is involved in gambling, loan sharking, protection rackets and prostitution. The Wo On Lok and its main rival in Macau, the 14K Triad, are at the center of the continuing gang war. "The 14K is one of the world's biggest organized crime syndicates," Agence France-Presse noted in a January report. "The 14K and Wo On Lok have more than 400,000 members around the world between them, intelligence officials in Hong Kong say, ranging from couriers and street corner thugs in London to corporate chiefs in New York."

The triads play a complex role in Macau and elsewhere in Asia. According to a 1995 report by Jane's Intelligence Review on organized crime and money laundering, most of the triads are based "in Hong Kong and Macau, from where they maintain their international links." Jane's adds, "Chinese organized crime is extremely powerful and their contacts extend to large, respectable businesses and even into government circles in many countries in East Asia." And, according to Jane's, "the so-called Triads or Secret Societies" handle the heroin trade out of the Golden Triangle. "Western anti-narcotics agents in Southeast Asia emphasize that it would be impossible for drug traffic to operate without the cooperation of local officials in the producer as well as transit countries."

The triads also exercise a political influence often more subtle, say, than the cocaine killers of Colombia or the terror bombers of the Italian Mafia. Controversy erupted in Hong Kong last year when Wong Man-fong, a former deputy secretary general of China's Xinhua News Agency, disclosed that he had met with triad chieftains prior to the signing of the 1984 Sino-British Declaration on Chinese rule. "I told them that if they did not disrupt Hong Kong's stability, we would not stop them from making money," he told a forum at Hong Kong's Baptist University.

According to a May 1997 report in Hong Kong's South China Morning Post, Mr. Wong "refused to say if the idea for the meeting had been instigated by Beijing." But after the agreement was reached, China's security minister said, "Not all of the Triads are bad. Some of them love the Motherland."

With Macau's tourist trade suffering, some efforts have been made to contain the triad wars. The Morning Post reported in August that local "police raided several hotels including the show-piece Lisboa, the Grande and the Fortuna. The raids came as part of a move to clean up the enclave's image. Prostitution is not illegal in Macau but orga-nized crime laws introduced late last month forbid solic-iting in public and give the authorities powers to imprison pimps."

Advertisement for Fortuna Palace night club owned by Ng Lap Seng.

The Chinese characters translate /God of Wealth Palace's Magnificent Dance Stage/ Macao—All Night City/ Most magical table dancing/ Asia's Pioneering Electrical Extending Stage/ Fully equipped with luxuri-ous decor and the most advanced lighting and sound/ Working dance stage shower/ Tens of thousands of dollars in fine craftsmanship/ Address: Macau New Port Fortuna Hotel 6th floor/ Operating Hours: 6:30 p.m. continuous performances until 2 a.m.

Following a New York Times report in October linking him to organized crime, the Morning Post caught up with Mr. Ng. It reported that he declared: "I am very upset, especially about this allegation that I am linked to organized crime. It is absolutely untrue and has no basis in fact." Mr. Ng did not respond to repeated requests by the Journal for an interview on the matter.

In Macau it is not unusual to find "black businessmen," involved in both legal and illegal activities. Mr. Ng is unusual for the Macau business community because of his extremely low profile. "Ng does a lot of business in China," says a Macau "big brother," or triad asso-ciate. "But no one really knows where his money comes from. Even in Macau, he is a mysterious figure."

From Nan Hai, near Guangzhou city, Mr. Ng arrived penniless in Macau around 1979, locals say. He began working in the local gar-ment industry as a middleman, reselling cheap cloth from China to factories in Hong Kong and Macau. Trade with China is Macau's way of life, and by the early 1990s Mr. Ng was a wealthy man. In addition to the Fortuna Hotel, he owns a small commercial center linking the hotel to the Lisboa Casino, the flagship of casino magnate Stanley Ho. In partnership with Mr. Ho and mainland concerns, Mr. Ng also has a major stake in what seems a fitting gamble for a gambling town—a grandiose $1.4 billion development project called Nam Van Lakes.

The development involves the conversion of Macau's harbor into two inland lagoons surrounded by apartments, hotels and resorts. Launched during a regional boom in 1992, Nam Van Lakes became a favored site for wealthy Chinese to move "hot money" out of the neighboring wealthy Guangdong province into the more stable precincts of Macau. Late last year, Mr. Ho announced plans to take the project public in Hong Kong by 1999. But with the Macau property market weak, prospects appear dim. The project is scheduled for completion early in the next century, and it is not clear how the investors will fare. But today thousands of empty apartments rise from the site, with no visible signs of life.

Mr. Ng has also made efforts to expand his business empire to Arkansas. In October 1994, Mr. Trie incorporated San Kin Yip International for Mr. Ng in Little Rock; the Senate report says its bank records "revealed neither earnings nor any genuine business activity." In early 1994, Mr. Ng also appeared as an outside investor in Mr. Trie's bid to buy the Camelot Hotel in downtown Little Rock. According to testimony by FBI Special Agent Jerry Campane before the Senate panel last July, Mr. Ng arrived in Little Rock with a suitcase full of cash. "There was a meeting in a hotel room," Mr. Campane testified, "and an eyewitness told us that Charlie Trie turned to Mr. Wu [i.e., Mr. Ng] and said, 'I need some money for expenses.' And Mr. Wu opened a suitcase, which was described as full of cash, and handed Charlie Trie approximately $20,000 in cash."

In a rough debate before the Little Rock Board of Directors, a city commissioner raised questions about the source of Mr. Trie's capital and the Chinese drug trade. Little Rock deal maker and attorney Joseph Giroir, a close associate of the Clintons and former head of the Rose Law Firm, protested the "offensive remark," but Mr. Trie lost the bid.

Mr. Trie next enlisted the help of Lehman Brothers investment banker and DNC fund-raiser Ernest Green, who wrote a 1995 letter offering to raise money for investment in Van Dam Lakes if the Macau government approved his investment concept. Mr. Green told Senate investigators that Mr. Trie approached him, and that he traveled twice to Macau to meet with Mr. Ng and other investors. In a videotape pried out of the White House by the Senate investigation, Mr. Green is shown introducing Mr. Ng to President Clinton at a November 1995 forum in Georgetown. Mr. Green told the president that Mr. Ng was "very helpful" in arranging an event for then Commerce Secretary Ron Brown in Hong Kong.

Meanwhile, Mr. Ng was working his new White House connections. According to White House entry logs, Mr. Ng visited Mark Middleton, an Arkansas aide to then Chief of Staff Mack McLarty, six times between June 1994 and February 1995. In one instance, Oct. 20, 1994, Mr. Middleton met in the Roosevelt Room of the White House with his brother, Stephens Inc. investment bank executive Larry Middleton, as well as Mr. Trie and Mr. Ng, according to Mark Middleton's White House calendar. That same day, $100,000 was wired from Mr. Ng's Macau account to Mr. Trie.

Mark Middleton left the White House in February 1995 to pursue a career as an Asian deal maker and by July was receiving a $12,500 retainer from Mr. Giroir—the Arkansas operative who had risen to the defense of Mr. Ng in the Camelot Hotel bid. Mr. Giroir, closely associated with Mochtar Riady's Lippo Group, gave a deposition to Senate investigators, but Mr. Middleton invoked the Fifth Amendment and refused to testify. As with most things touched by the hapless Mr. Trie, the deal never materialized. When the media began exposing the Clinton campaign-finance connections, Mr. Ng dematerialized back into the vaporous intrigues of Macau, shunning requests for interviews and making no public appearances.

"The source of Ng's funds and what he or those behind him hoped to gain through Trie remains unknown," the Senate campaign-finance report concludes. From here on the streets of Macau, there would seem to be various possibilities, none of them reassuring.

Listening Post

Macau has for decades also been a listening post and staging point for the world's spy agencies. The Senate Committee accepted that the Chinese government had a plan to infiltrate American politics, though the Republican majority and Democratic minority disagree on whether it had any actual effect. The triads, so prominent locally, also have world-wide interests. In an article reprinted here Jan. 13, Bruce Gilley of the Far Eastern Economic Review reported that Ted Sioeng, another fugitive Clinton fund-raiser, showed up in the

Cambodian capital, Phnom Penh, in the company of Theng Bunma, a controversial businessman who has been barred from entering the U.S. due to suspected drug trafficking. Of course, it may be hard to discern where criminal societies end and various Asian governments and intelligence agencies begin.

China has long exercised de facto control of Macau, but is now preparing to assume formal rule in 1999. Asked whether gambling and prostitution will remain legal, a Chinese diplomat invokes "one country, two systems." Last month the Chinese government honored Mr. Ng with a big promotion from his Nan Hai post to the national Chinese People's Consultative Conference in Beijing. Two other Macau figures were also named to the Beijing Conference—Stanley Ho, the dominant figure in the Macau economy, and Macau legislator Chen Kai-kit. Both have also crossed paths with President Clinton.

Mr. Morrison is a Journal editorial page writer.

FEBRUARY 27, 1998

Editorial Feature

The Macau Connection — II

By MICAH MORRISON

MACAU—In a self-published biography, Macau businessman and legislator Chen Kai-kit brags that many international figures have paid him tribute, including President Clinton, who "presented Mr. Chen with a signed photograph."

Indeed, local reporters here say that the photograph of Mr. Chen with the president was featured prominently in television advertisements during Mr. Chen's successful 1996 campaign for a seat in the Macau legislature. In a story about the presidential encounter that appeared in the Macau Daily, Beijing's semi-official mouthpiece in the enclave, Mr. Chen was quoted as saying that Mr. Clinton was "very concerned" about Macau. Mr. Chen, who also uses the name Chio Ho Cheung, declined to make himself available for an interview for this article.

Mr. Chen's claims about his connections with the president, however, are unimpeachable. He sat at the head table with Mr. Clinton at a dinner at Washington's Sheraton Carlton Hotel on May 13, 1996. Also at the head table was Mr. Chen's business partner, Elsie Chan, a former starlet. "This is a fund-raising dinner for the Democratic National Committee," notes a briefing memo for then DNC Chairman Don Fowler. "The attendees are some of the top supporters of the President and the Democratic Party from the Asian-American community." A partial guest list for the event, forwarded by a Lippo Group operative to DNC fund-raiser John Huang, identified Mr. Chen and

Ms. Chan as the president and managing director, respectively, of the Ang-Du International Corp. Also at the head table were Charlie Trie and Ted Sioeng, familiar names in the campaign finance scandal.

The president's ties with Macau are not merely the matter of his Little Rock friend Charlie Trie and the mysterious Ng Lap Seng, detailed in yesterday's article. There are also Mr. Chen and Ms. Chan. In addition, Wong Sing-wa, another controversial businessman, is reported to have a photograph of himself with the president—and as the photo nearby testifies, he clearly visited the White House in the company of Macau casino magnate Stanley Ho and others. For that matter, Mr. Ho's Seng Heng Bank of Macau was previously owned by a partnership between Mochtar Riady's Lippo Group and Stephens Inc. of Little Rock.

A photo from "The Biography of Anna Chennault," by Hu Sin, published in Taipei in 1995. The caption in upper left reads, "1995 at the White House participating in President Clinton's breakfast meeting, from the left: Wong Sing-wa, Loretta Fung, Stanley Ho, Anna Chennault, Yip Wai-ki." Mrs. Chennault, the widow of the legendary World War II head of the Flying Tigers, raised money from Asians for the Franklin Delano Roosevelt memorial.

Speck of Soil

This set of connections is amazing given the obscurity of this speck of Portuguese soil set to revert to China in 1999. Across the mouth of the Pearl River from Hong Kong, Macau maintains a casino economy and is in the midst of "triad wars," with Chinese organized crime gangs fighting for control of loan-sharking, prostitution and extortion rackets. An example of local flavor: With triad gunmen fighting it out on the streets last year, Macau's senior security minister sought to reassure the jittery tourism market with the odd claim the attacks were simply the work of "professional killers who never miss their targets."

The career of Chen Kai-kit is a local success story, though one marked by controversy. His election to the 23-person legislature was marred by allegations that he benefited not only from the president's photograph, but also from the support of the 14K Triad at 1,500 Hong

Kong dollars (US$195) a vote. Mr. Chen vigorously denied the stories, and a Macau government probe found no evidence to support the charges.

President Clinton's table mate at the Sheraton Carlton built his business career on the success of the Thai Palace, a "no-hands" restaurant. In such establishments, naked waitresses hand-feed patrons, leaving the hands of paying customers unencumbered for other pursuits. (Prostitution is legal in Macau.) Mr. Chen is also said to have business interests in organized gambling junkets. Local triads often prey on hard-up gamblers, engaging in loan sharking, and in kidnapping and extortion when the gamblers don't pay up. Here in Macau, Mr. Chen is called "Thai Chen," for both his restaurant and his roots in Thailand. With the success of the Thai Palace, Mr. Chen expanded into other "entertainment" facilities, as well as exporting wooden doors and latex gloves. He made a fortune, his biography says, by foreseeing "a huge demand for latex gloves caused by the widespread fear of AIDS in Europe and the United States."

Chen Kai-Kit

Ang-Du International, which Mr. Chen and Ms. Chan head, also operates in Thailand. One of its functions, local sources say, is supplying Macau with Thai women. Ms. Chan herself is a minor celebrity in the region. In 1986, she won the Miss Peace prize in the Miss Asia beauty contest. She made a mark in the Hong Kong television and film industry, and is credited with establishing a trend toward full-bodied women in the local entertainment media. After her star began to fade, she told a Hong Kong entertainment magazine, she quit the business to become a manager in an unnamed international business firm in Macau—presumably Mr. Chen's. Ms. Chan described the firm's work as mostly in fashion, tourism, cigarettes and construction material. Her specialty, she said, was "personnel." Ms. Chan's office said she was not available for an interview for this article.

Wong Sing-wa—according to local sources a partner with Mr. Chen and others in a new casino in Macau's Mandarin Hotel—operates a travel agency. In particular he issues visas for North Korea and is Pyongyang's honorary consul in Macau. Presumably he would have information on North Korea's activities here, where that nation has long maintained a presence through the Zokwang Trading Co. This would be of interest to the U.S. Secret Service, which traced large sums of remarkably high-quality counterfeit $100 bills to Zokwang accounts. Five North Koreans were arrested in conjunction with the counterfeiting here in 1994 but were released after pleading ignorance.

Earlier this month, the Lisbon-based weekly newspaper Independent protested Mr. Wong's presence in a Macau delegation to the Portuguese president. The paper cited a Macau security official, who said Mr. Wong had "no criminal record, but we have registered information that links him to organized crime and gambling in Macau." The security official added that Mr. Wong also was known to be linked to "one of the VIP rooms of the Lisboa Casino," a room allegedly controlled by the 14K Triad. Mr. Wong did not respond to the allegations, and calls by the Journal to a Macau phone number listed to him were not answered.

In 1995, Mr. Wong posed for a photograph on the doorstep of the White House with Mr. Ho, Anna Chennault (widow of Flying Tigers legend Claire Chennault), Loretta Fung (Mrs. Chennault's sister) and Yip Wai-ki. A caption on the photo says it was taken after a breakfast meeting with President Clinton. Mr. Ho donated $250,000 to the Franklin Delano Roosevelt Memorial Commission; according to a report by the MSNBC cable network, he gave his check directly to Mr. Clinton, the honorary chairman. Mr. Wong and Mr. Yip are also FDR memorial donors. Mrs. Chennault raised money for the memorial from Asians. According to the Washington Post, she said Mr. Ho gave $500,000 but asked that his name not be engraved with other donors of that amount; the executive head of the commission said she had received only $250,000.

As reported in this space yesterday, Mr. Ho, Ng Lap Seng and Chen Kai-kit have recently been named to the national Chinese People's Consultative Conference in Beijing. Mr. Ho is managing director of the Sociedade de Turismo e Diverserões de Macau, which has held an exclusive franchise for Macau gambling since 1962, and which licenses individual casinos. The STDM dominates the local economy, supplying the Macau government about $600 million a year, or roughly half its budget. However, the STDM monopoly is to end in 2001, two years after Macau formally comes under Chinese rule.

The Macau legislature—a special body elected to serve as a

"through train" past the China handover and into the twilight of the STDM franchise—will play a significant role in both events. The Communist regime in Beijing, of course, will call the final shots; but longtime observers of the scene say the reality on the southeast China coast is that corrupt local officials on both sides of the border, in league with organized crime, will carve up the pie. A local journalist predicts "one country, no system."

The current triad wars, sources speculate, are essentially about local gangs staking out territory in anticipation of the end of the STDM franchise. Mr. Chen is said to support a breakup of the STDM monopoly. "Nobody really knows where Chen Kai-kit and Wong Sing-wa get their money," says a triad "big brother," who does not think their local investments are sufficient to generate their evident wealth. "Their money is not from Macau. Chen, we know, is positioning himself for the future, for China. He wants to be the future governor of Macau."

'Special Consultant'

In 1994, Mr. Chen's ambitions got him in hot water with U.S. authorities. According to his biography, the U.S. Congress passed "Decree 101" naming him "special consultant to the U.S. Congress." The biography continues: "Mr. Min-cai Gan, envoy of the U.S. Congress came to Macau to preside over a ceremony presenting him with the letter of appointment and a U.S. national flag which was once raised at the White House; this would be the only U.S. national flag officially allowed to be raised in Macau." This, it continues, "meant that the voice of Macau could be directly heard by the U.S. Congress and could play a role in its decision-making." The biography notes that "trade issues should not be linked to human rights issues" and that Mr. Chen "wished to make arrangements for visits by important U.S. Senators and Congressmen."

Mr. Chen took out newspaper ads in Macau and Hong Kong, featuring himself in a photograph with Rep. Esteban Torres (D., Calif.). In February 1994 the U.S. Information Service in Hong Kong issued a press release authorized by Rep. Torres. It said the U.S. counsul general in Hong Kong had asked Mr. Chen "to stop identifying himself as a 'Congressional Special Advisor.'" It said that Mr. Chen had inquired about being designated a special adviser, and Rep. Torres responded that congressional rules do not permit it. It branded as unfounded any claims by Mr. Chen "to represent the U.S. Congress or the U.S. government, or to have a special status with regard to the U.S. Congress."

Two years later, Mr. Chen was dining with the president at the head table at the Sheraton Carlton Hotel, part of a series of connections between Mr. Clinton and this remote and vice-ridden enclave. By all appearances the president was seeking political contributions from Macau, but the mystery is what Macau was seeking from the president.

Mr. Morrison is a Journal editorial page writer.

Editorial Feature

The Agony of Being Mike McCurry

So you think your job is lousy. Try being spokesman for a president who won't speak.

That's the miserable duty of Mike McCurry, who daily plays press-corps piñata for a president who won't

Potomac Watch

By Paul A. Gigot

tell him, much less the country, what really went on with Monica Lewinsky. Consider it another example of how President Clinton will sacrifice the reputation of everyone around him in order to save his own.

Richard Nixon's lies turned Ron Ziegler, his spokesman, into a laughingstock. His evasions—"inoperative"; "third-rate burglary"—remain political classics. Mr. McCurry has so far avoided Ziegler status because he's so well liked by the press corps. Count me in that club. He's always played straight with me, our ideological differences notwithstanding.

Mike McCurry

That's why it's painful to see his credibility abused by his boss now. A White House press secretary is supposed to serve two masters—the president, and the public via the press. It's never an easy job. But it's become impossible now that Mr. McCurry is out of the Monica loop, as he has admitted. By turns he's being made to look ridiculous, dissembling and disloyal.

The ridiculous came when the Washington Post reported that Mr. Clinton, in his Paula Jones deposition, had finally admitted an affair with Gennifer Flowers. Mr. McCurry didn't deny the Post story. Instead he said Mr. Clinton believes his denial of an affair during the 1992 campaign and his deposition testimony are somehow "not at odds." No elaboration, thank you.

The dissembling happened this week after Republican Joe DiGenova declared Sunday that he and his wife were being investigated by Clinton operatives. Later that day Mr. McCurry's office issued a categorical denial. It said neither the White House nor "any of President Clinton's private attorneys has hired or authorized any private investigator to look into the background" of investigators, prosecutors or journalists. The accusations were "blatant lies."

Not exactly. Somehow that denial had, er, overlooked the hiring by Mr. Clinton's lawyers of notorious dirt-devil Terry Lenzner. Mr. McCurry, in piñata mode, had to explain to incredulous reporters that the "legwork" done by the likes of Mr. Lenzner is different from probing "backgrounds." Tell that to Paula Jones, or to Independent Counsel Ken Starr's deputies now fielding calls about their pasts.

Mr. McCurry's biggest problem is that there are now two White House media operations. His is supposed to provide the wry, reassuring face of cooperation and public trust. The other, led by liberal former journalist Sidney Blumenthal, is kicking the teeth out of anyone who threatens Mr. Clinton.

You could see this coming when Mr. Blumenthal and Paul Begala were recruited last

Sid Blumenthal

year. This column called them "black belts in the Clintonian black art of offensive defense." Mr. Begala has become the sound-bite Savonarola, calling Mr. Starr "corrupt." Meanwhile, Sid Vicious works the phones backstage. While the media have played up Mr. Starr and his staff as the main targets, this dirt-throwing also serves to warn potential witnesses that they too can be ruined.

When Mr. Starr took the bait and hauled Mr. Blumenthal before the grand jury this week, Mr. Blumenthal claimed to be "outraged." But you could see the pleasure in his courthouse smirk. He was living his own "vast right-wing conspiracy" theory.

That Mr. McCurry has personal qualms about all this seems apparent. He has some fealty, as anyone would, to a president who gave him such a prominent job. He's also a loyal Democrat. But his doubts about his boss's nonstory came through in a recent interview with the Chicago Tribune.

Regarding Mr. Clinton and his intern, he said, "Maybe there'll be a simple, innocent explanation. I don't think so, because I think we would have offered that up already." In epic understatement, he added, "I think it's going to end up being a very complicated story."

Some read that as a trial balloon for a presidential apology. But most McCurry-watchers detected the Freudian slip of a man trying to maintain his dignity in a mosh pit. It must be excruciating, and the speculation is that he won't be long in the job.

At a Harvard forum recently, someone asked Mr. McCurry when he might feel compelled to resign. "At the point where I don't believe anything that I've been instructed to say," he replied, adding that he didn't expect that day to come.

That's being a good soldier, but you have to wonder how long he can retain his self-respect playing Mr. Clinton's Sgt. Schultz ("I know nothiiiiing!"). This Tuesday, a reporter asked Mr. McCurry, "Are you confident that the people to whom you address the questions are giving you full, complete, truthful answers?"

"Yes," Mr. McCurry replied. "And God help them if they're not."

The press room erupted in laughter.

Editorial Feature

Life Inside the Gilded Bunker

Money has been pouring into Bill Clinton's fund-raising chapeau since he began lying about his relationship with Monica Lewinsky.

These are not five- and 10-dollar donations from ordinary Americans, who keep telling pollsters they are reluctant to pass judgment on the president. Know a man by his friends: Bill Clinton's America has become a very small place.

Business World

By Holman W. Jenkins Jr.

His golden panhandling takes him from Hollywood and New York to New York and Hollywood. His most conspicuous supporters nowadays are our age's most restless social climbers. A wounded president has become their ornament.

Old friends have been carried from the field as casualties or have sunk below the parapets. But new friends have stepped into the breach. Tina Brown, the New Yorker editor, attending a dinner for Britain's Tony Blair, has discovered in Mr. Clinton "a man in a dinner jacket with more heat than any star in the room."

She is not gaga over the man, of course, but over the symbol he has become in the wake of the Lewinsky scandal. The presidency since Mr. Clinton has become a totem of unbridled adolescent entitlement, much as it was under Kennedy.

James Brolin, Barbra Streisand's escort, emerged from the same dinner quipping, "He's the most fun president we've ever had"—another post-Lewinsky perspective.

But to no one, seemingly, has Mr. Clinton more commended himself than to Jeffrey Katzenberg, at whose Utah vacation hideaway the Clintons were skiing last week.

Once known for his animation work at Disney, he has become more famous for his catfights with other Hollywood personalities, like Michael Ovitz and Michael Eisner, and for his DreamWorks camaraderie with David Geffen and Steven Spielberg—camaraderie being the narcissist's simulacrum of friendship.

In a New Yorker article he's portrayed as "chortling" because the president likes to refer

Jeffrey Katzenberg

to him as the "one who's broke"—i.e., not a billionaire. Next we find Mr. Katzenberg in a Time magazine photo, gamboling in the White House with Elton John, Al Gore and the first lady. They were the very picture of self-conscious hilarity, by people who calculate every effect and know when a photographer from Time happens to be in the room. It was exactly as they would have wanted to be seen.

Every president needs supporters drawn from the nation's powerful and wealthy. Hollywood and the world of celebrity are the ones rallying around Bill Clinton in his hour of crisis. They have stepped forward as refuge and crutch to his social standing even as his leadership on matters of importance to the country becomes more and more a bad joke.

All their lives they have known how to be where attention is focused, and how to cut loose when attention moves on. They only have eyes for themselves, of course, but his self-indulgence in the Lewinsky matter has given him a kind of reckless glamour. Another president might have surrounded himself with people next to whom the words "service" and "duty" would not seem out of place. But Mr. Clinton cannot find any. He surrounds himself with a different elite, one known for its love of self and a belief in its entitlement to live beyond the rules that lesser mortals live by.

Even Vernon Jordan has sent up smoke signals to the Washington commune, letting the town know he intends to survive and be around long after this president is history. In serious circles, Mr. Jordan, who once considered it advantageous to let it be known that he was sharing "locker room" talk with the president, is a leading indicator. So is the Washington press corps, which has turned on Mr. Clinton in a cold fury.

Mr. Clinton's social repositioning has gone on against the background of a country preparing for war against a mad dictator in Iraq. It would have taken the lives of American pilots and the lives of many innocent Iraqis who grub for a living among the shambles of Saddam Hussein's society. It would have been a tragic but necessary war, and would have taken real leadership to explain. In another of the narrow escapes that Mr. Clinton's career has been made of, the job of leadership has been abdicated to Kofi Annan, while our Peter Pan president, who skitters across the surface of everything, runs into the arms of the Hollywood friends who understand him.

Knowing little else about it, to them the presidency represents a more rarefied celebrity even than their own. Michael Ovitz, when he found the agent's role too small for him, gazed longingly on the White House. But when popularity has to be sacrificed for leadership, they'd want no part of it. Mr. Clinton wants no part of it either. Celebrities have always wanted to be president. Mr. Clinton wanted to be president to become a celebrity.

Americans are not a censorious people, and have been waiting on the judgment of leaders they trust about whether his private foibles have put the country in danger. This president may have lost the professional pols, the policy wonks, the elder statesmen, the names and faces associated with one school of traditional leadership or another. But he can still scrape up a bottom-of-the-barrel elite for support and validation, made up of individuals for whom notoriety, almost any kind of notoriety, is a value, as long as it represents someone getting away with something and being rewarded for it.

His fund-raising endeavors have put this notoriety up for sale, and they fetch larger sums than he managed to spring loose when he had actual policy initiatives to offer. "I have more people supportive today than I ever expected to get," a Manhattan real estate impresario, David Steiner, told the New York Times on the eve of a $25,000-a-plate dinner at his mansion in New Jersey a few weeks ago. "Everyone seems to be higher on the president now."

The New York Observer, a weekly that follows the media culture, assembled a panel of literary females to applaud the president for being "alive from the waist down." Ron Perelman, the Revlon CEO, reached into his fulsome pocket to give Webb Hubbell a $100,000 consulting contract, and was primed to put Monica Lewinsky on the payroll when Mr. Jordan and Mr. Clinton had reason to want her out of town. A Revlon adviser was quoted in the Washington Post denying that any policy agenda attached to Mr. Perelman's support: "His basic value is making money, money, money and collecting women."

These are the supporters on whom Mr. Clinton's "political viability" depends these days. Every president needs allies out there in the world, and after disappointing anyone who was susceptible to being disappointed, this is what Mr. Clinton is left with.

REVIEW & OUTLOOK

Try Again

Janet Reno has three times refused to appoint an independent counsel in the campaign finance scandal. But new information keeps cascading forth, and the appropriate members of Congress have a duty to give her yet another chance.

Senator Fred Thompson's investigating committee voted out its report yesterday, for example, with the majority identifying six individuals in the campaign finance mess with ties to Beijing— Charlie Trie, John Huang, James and Mochtar Riady, Maria Hsia

Janet Reno

and Ted Sioeng. The Riadys, for instance, "have had a long-term relationship with a Chinese intelligence agency," based on "mutual benefit." The committee report said that Ms. Hsia, the central figure in Al Gore's Hsi Lai Temple fund-raiser, "has been an agent of the Chinese government, that she acted knowingly in support of it and that she attempted to conceal her relationship with the Chinese government."

The principals deny this, of course, and the Democratic minority contends that the evidence isn't conclusive. Both sides agree there's evidence that the Chinese government had a plan to influence the elections, but the Democrats say nothing happened. But the issue Ms. Reno keeps trying to define away is not whether everything is pinned down, but whether there is enough evidence of high-level skullduggery to warrant an independent investigation.

In two reports last week, our Micah Morrison put flesh and bones on this concern by tracing fund-raising connections through Macau, the Portuguese enclave across the Pearl River estuary from Hong Kong. Macau, where Mr. Trie took refuge while evading subpoena, is a hot-bed of vice, with gambling, prostitution and "triad wars" between competing Chinese gangs. Mr. Trie's patron, and the source of money he handed out so freely that much of it had to be returned, was one Ng Lap Seng, a nightclub owner with connections to both a triad and the People's Liberation Army. Last month the Chinese gave him a big honor, naming him to the Chinese People's Consultative Conference in Beijing.

It further turns out that Mr. Clinton also entertained other Macau figures, Chen Kai-kit, Elsie Chan and Wong Sing-wa. Chen Kai-kit used a photo with the U.S. President in running for the Macau legislature; he and his business partner Ms. Chan were entertained at a Washington fund-raiser, though the American consulate in Hong Kong had earlier put out a statement repudiating Mr. Chen's attempts to insinuate himself as a special adviser to the U.S. Congress. Mr. Wong, a White House visitor, has official connections with North Korea, which apparently used Macau to distribute counterfeit U.S. currency.

These connections, in short, are even seamier and even more pervasive than has been generally understood. Mr. Sioeng, by the way, turned up back in Asia in the company of Cambodian tycoon Theng Bunma, who has been barred from entering the United States because of suspected drug trafficking. It is true that all of this is circumstantial. We do not have tape recordings forging a chain from Chinese intelligence through the various triads through the DNC to the President. This is what investigations are for.

From the first, the case for an independent counsel rests on a Presidential-led conspiracy to violate the campaign finance laws. The President, for example, was at a key meeting on September 13, 1995, with James Riady, Bruce Lindsey and Arkansas-Indonesian businessman Joe Giroir, at which it was decided to move Mr. Huang from the Commerce Department to a fund-raising post at the DNC. The violations followed, including not only the Asian money, but the total obliteration of the legally required distinction between the DNC and Clinton-Gore campaigns.

Ms. Reno has repeatedly and implausibly rejected this argument, asking for evidence of some petty violation by "covered persons," rather than the grand crimes of conspiracy and obstruction of justice. Her own investigation has started to show some signs of life, with the indictment of Mr. Trie, Ms. Hsia and, yesterday, California businessman Johnny Chung. Republican Haley Barbour may get thrown in for balance. It is hard to imagine, though, a Justice Department investigation pressing whether the profusion of Democratic violations all flow from a Presidential font.

There is plenty of evidence—in the Thompson Committee report and elsewhere—that the President not only set the illegal fund-raising in motion, but may have carried it to an extent that jeopardized the national interest. Such an investigation is what the independent counsel law is all about, and as further evidence mounts, Congress should keep calling on Ms. Reno to deal with it.

REVIEW & OUTLOOK

Asides

Dumpster Politics

Independent Counsel Kenneth Starr has been under remarkably harsh assault. Monica Lewinsky's father likened him to Hitler. The White House describes his approval ratings as on a par with Saddam Hussein. Discourse from the dumpster is commonplace nowadays. Yesterday, however, produced a retort from four attorneys general who served three presidents: Griffin Bell, Ed Meese, Richard Thornburgh and William Barr. They released a statement supporting Mr. Starr as "an individual of the highest personal and professional integrity." As former chief law enforcement officers in the nation, they added, "we are concerned that the severity of the attacks on Independent Counsel Kenneth Starr and his office by high level government officials and attorneys representing their particular interests, among others, appear to have the improper purpose of influencing and impeding an ongoing criminal investigation and intimidating possible jurors, witnesses and even investigators."

Editorial Feature

Why It Matters

By WILLIAM J. BENNETT

In the matter of Bill Clinton and Monica Lewinsky, almost everything points to the conclusion that something unseemly happened: the tapes; Ms. Lewinsky's 37 visits to the White House; Mr. Clinton's morning-after-the-deposition meeting with his secretary, Betty Currie; the gifts; the talking points; Vernon Jordan's many activities; the job offer from United Nations Ambassador Bill Richardson; the president's stonewalling; his initial, unconvincing denial; his refusal to explain what happened; Press Secretary Mike McCurry's remark that the relationship is probably "very complicated"; and White House surrogates' declaration of "war" against the independent counsel.

Nevertheless, many Americans think the scandal—even if true—is either "none of our business" or not worth the effort to inquire about. This apparent indifference is surprising and unsettling. It is therefore important to respond to the most common arguments made by those who believe that a president's sexual involvement with a 21-year-old intern, and the ensuing suspected coverup, are essentially irrelevant to our national life:

• *We shouldn't be judgmental.* At a recent speech before an organization of religious broadcasters, I criticized the president's unwillingness to explain what happened in the Lewinsky matter. A member of the audience took me to task for "casting stones." I responded that it shows how far we have fallen that asking the president to account for possible adultery, lying to the public, perjury and obstruction of justice is regarded as akin to stoning. This is an example of what sociologist Alan Wolfe refers to as America's new "Eleventh Commandment: Thou shalt not judge."

Lost Its Way

Even the Rev. Billy Graham declared yesterday: "I forgive him. . . . I know how hard it is, and especially a strong, vigorous, young man like he is; he has such a tremendous personality. I think the ladies just go wild over him." Mr. Graham, perhaps the nation's most admired religious figure, apparently is willing to shrug off both adultery and lying, without any public admission or apology on Mr. Clinton's part. This is what the theologian Dietrich Bonhoeffer called "cheap grace."

Monica Lewinsky

All of us are in favor of tolerance and forgiveness. But the moral pendulum in America has swung too far in the direction of relativism. If a nation of free people can no longer make clear pronouncements on fundamental matters of right and wrong—for example, that a married, 50-year-old commander-in-chief ought not to have sexual relations with a young intern in his office and then lie about it—it has lost its way.

The problem is not with those who are withholding judgment until all the facts are in, but with the increasing number of people who want to avoid judgment altogether. For it is precisely the disposition and willingness to make judgments about things that matter that is a defining mark of a healthy democracy. In America we do not defer to kings, cardinals or aristocrats on matters of law and politics, civic conduct and moral standards. We rely instead on the people's capacity to make reasonable judgments based on moral principles. Our form of government requires of us not moral perfection but modest virtues, and adherence to some standards. How high should those standards be? Certainly higher than the behavior alleged in this case.

Those who constantly invoke the sentiment of "Who are we to judge?" should consider the anarchy that would ensue if we adhered to this sentiment in, say, our courtrooms. What would happen if those sitting on a jury decided to be "nonjudgmental" about rapists and sexual harassers, embezzlers and tax cheats? Justice would be lost.

Without being "judgmental," Americans would never have put an end to slavery, outlawed child labor, emancipated women or ushered in the civil-rights movement. Nor would we have mobilized against Nazism and communism.

Mr. Clinton himself put it well, in a judgment-laden 1996 proclamation he signed during National Character Week, which said that "individual character involves honoring and embracing certain core ethical values: honesty, respect, responsibility. . . . Parents must teach their children from the earliest age the difference between right and wrong. But we must all do our part."

• *A president's private behavior doesn't matter.* In a recent Wall Street Journal/NBC News poll, 57% said that private character doesn't matter at all or matters only if it interferes with his ability to do the job. Of course, if Mr. Clinton did have sexual encounters with Ms. Lewinsky, it involves at least adultery and lying to the public—and probably lying under oath as well. In any event, the attempt to rigidly compartmentalize life in this way is divorced from the real world. A mother would not accept from her son the explanation that his drug habit doesn't matter because he did well on the Scholastic Assessment Test; a police commissioner should not dismiss the raw bigotry of a detective because he has a good arrest record.

Yet in the name of "compartmentalization," many now seem willing to accept raunchier behavior from our president than we would from any CEO, college professor or Army drill sergeant. Housing Secretary Andrew Cuomo put it this way: "Let's remember what's important here. The lives of the American people are more important than the personal life of the president." But Mr. Clinton is a laboratory test case of why private character is relevant. Prevarications typify his private and public life. A seamless web of deceit runs through the man and through his administration.

John Adams held a far different view than Mr. Cuomo does. Adams wrote that the people "have a right, an indisputable, unalienable, indefeasible, divine right to that most dreaded and envied kind of knowledge; I mean, of the characters and conduct of their rulers. Rulers are no more than attorneys, agents, and trustees, for the people; and if the cause, the interest and trust, is insidiously betrayed, or wantonly trifled away, the people have a right to revoke the authority that they themselves have deputed."

To better understand the limits of the "private-public" argument, imagine the storm that would engulf a president who privately supported a whites-only membership policy at a country club. Most voters would rightly deem this private sentiment to be of intense public interest. Why, then, are we supposed to accept a man in the Oval Office whom many parents would not trust alone with their daughters?

• *The only thing that matters is the economy.* "What we should be talking about is that we are going to have the first balanced budget in more than three decades," says one citizen, who voted against Mr. Clinton in 1996. "That's going to impact our children, not this sleaze that is masquerading as news." This sentiment reveals an arid and incomplete understanding of the presidency. More than any other person, the president symbolizes America. He stands for us in the eyes of the world and of our children, who inevitably learn from his example. Whether or not Bill Clinton escapes impeachment, his legacy will be one of pervasive deceit, squandered trust, a reckless disregard for the truth, heightened cynicism and a nastier political culture.

A Rogue in Our Midst

This corruption matters a great deal. Even if the Dow Jones breaks 10000. Even if Americans get more day care. Even if the budget is balanced. It matters because lessons in corruption, particularly when they emanate from the highest office in the land, undermine our civic life. Children are watching, and if we expect them to take morality seriously, they must see adults take it seriously. As C.S. Lewis wrote: "We make men without chests and expect of them virtue and enterprise. We laugh at honor and are shocked to find traitors in our midst."

Today we find not a traitor but a rogue in our midst. Of course, rogues have been with us forever, and the corruption of people in power is at least as old as the Scriptures. But in America today, more and more citizens seem to be complicit in that corruption. One worry of the Founders was that luxury and affluence might dull our moral sensibilities. The next few months will go a long way toward determining how strongly we believe in something we once revered as "our sacred honor."

Mr. Bennett is author of "Our Sacred Honor: Words of Advice From the Founders in Stories, Letters, Poems and Speeches" (Simon & Schuster, 1997).

Editorial Feature

Yes, You Can Indict the President

In the next few weeks Kenneth Starr is likely to find himself at a particularly vexatious fork in the legal road he has been traveling these past four years. From the earliest Whitewater fraud investigations, through Travelgate and Filegate, to the allegations of possible perjury and witness tampering emanating from the Monica Lewinsky matter, Mr. Starr will have to decide where to go with whatever evidence of presidential wrongdoing he has uncovered.

Rule of Law

By Gary L. McDowell

One path, undoubtedly the smoother one, would lead him to the House of Representatives under the independent counsel statute, which obligates him to inform that House of any impeachable offenses. The other more treacherous way would take the independent counsel directly to a criminal indictment against President Clinton. Unfortunately, he is not likely to find much guidance in most of the recent discussions of these weighty matters.

The past few weeks have focused public attention on impeachment for the first time since Watergate, but this most basic and straightforward constitutional provision has been the subject of great confusion at nearly every level of public discourse. From the commonplace assumption that the constitutional standard of "high crimes and misdemeanors" means whatever Congress says it does (it does not; the phrase was a common law term of art to the Founders with a reasonably precise meaning) to the idea that a president cannot be indicted before he is impeached, history has been the victim of political calculations. This is especially troubling on the issue of whether indictment may precede impeachment.

The argument that a sitting president may not be indicted prior to impeachment derives not from the Constitution or even from a judicial decision as a matter of constitutional law. Rather, it originated in a memorandum prepared in 1973 by then-Solicitor General Robert Bork in the matter of Spiro Agnew. In that report, Mr. Bork drew a distinction between indictment of the president and indictment of the vice president and all other civil officers. In the case of Agnew, Mr. Bork concluded, there was no reason he could not be indicted prior to impeachment; such was not the case for the president, however, who would have to be impeached first. The basis of this distinction was certain institutional attributes peculiar to the presidency that Mr. Bork found "embedded" in the structure of the Constitution.

Robert Bork

The problem with this interpretation is that it elevates an argument that might be reasonably inferred from the Constitution's overall design and structure over the clear language of the document itself. When the provisions of the Constitution dealing with impeachment are viewed in light of the history that inspired them, it is clear that there is no immunity from indictment conferred on the president or any other officer of the government. Nor is there any demand that impeachment must precede such an indictment.

The Constitution lays out the mechanics of impeachment, including the limits of the sanction, in Article I, 3: "Judgment . . . shall not extend further than to removal from office and disqualification to hold and enjoy any office of honor, trust or profit under the United States: but the party convicted shall nevertheless be liable and subject to indictment, trial, judgment and punishment according to law."

Later, in Article II, 4, the Constitution provides that the president, vice president and all civil officers "shall be removed from office on the impeachment for, and conviction of, treason, bribery, or other high crimes and misdemeanors." To make clear that impeachment is a political rather than a legal process, the Constitution specifically precludes the right to a trial by jury or the possibility of a presidential pardon or reprieve in cases of impeachment.

As Alexander Hamilton put it in The Federalist, echoing British constitutional history, impeachable offenses are those that "proceed from the misconduct of public men, or in other words from the abuse and violation of some public trust," what Sir William Blackstone had termed "maladministration." Such political sins would include neglect of duty, abuse of power, or subversion of the Constitution. Although indictable offenses are not necessary for an impeachment, they may surely be deemed sufficient grounds to proceed. This is especially so in the case of the president, in whom any criminal behavior would likely be seen as a clear failure to "take care that the laws be faithfully executed."

Alexander Hamilton

Indeed, the language of the Constitution—"the party convicted shall nevertheless be liable and subject to indictment, trial, judgment and punishment according to law"—was designed for just such a possibility. Should there be evidence of criminal acts, and should that give rise to a successful impeachment and removal from office, the Founders did not wish to shield the person impeached from further legal proceedings under any notion of double jeopardy. High office offers no immunity from the ordinary rigors of the criminal law.

But neither does that constitutional language demand that impeachment must precede indictment. As legal historian Raoul Berger showed long ago, there is only one place in the Constitution where immunity is conferred on public officials, and that involves not holding members of the Senate and House liable to arrest for anything they may say or do in their respective chambers or "in going to and returning from the same." Even then the Founders did not include the more serious offenses, making clear that such immunity extended to "all cases, except treason, felony or breach of the peace."

As Mr. Bork pointed out in his memorandum denying immunity to the vice president, "[s]ince the Framers knew how to, and did, spell out immunity, the natural inference is that no immunity exists where none is mentioned." This logic applies equally to the president. Had the intention been to demand impeachment before indictment, the Framers would have spelled that out.

When Mr. Starr comes to that fork in the road he may well decide, on the basis of what would be best for the country, to turn it all over to the House Judiciary Committee and leave them to it. But that would be a political choice, not a constitutional one. There is no constitutional roadblock keeping him from taking the road directly to criminal indictment. Given the Republican majorities in both houses and the high poll ratings he now enjoys, Mr. Clinton might even thank him for it, preferring a jury of his peers to facing what Hamilton described in The Federalist as that "awful discretion" the Constitution gives to the political court of impeachments.

Mr. McDowell is director of the Institute of United States Studies at the University of London.

REVIEW & OUTLOOK

The Borking of Starr

We blink every time talking heads discuss Kenneth Starr's low approval ratings; we hope we aren't the only ones taken a bit aback by the very idea of conducting opinion polls about judicial officers. In the judicial branch, we thought, the game was about statutes and precedents and scholarly qualifications, not about popularity. But perhaps this useful distinction too is being obliterated in the current climate.

If so, the corner was turned with the campaign against Robert Bork's nomination to the Supreme Court. Precisely because his scholarly attainments and intellect were the cream of his generation, his opponents feared his views would dominate a new crop of jurists. So they mounted a campaign to drive down his poll ratings, and thereby frighten the Senators weighing his nomination. They succeeded, but the cost to American institutions becomes clearer and clearer with the passage of time.

Ken Starr

We have arrived at a point where a James Carville goes on television to declare "war" on Kenneth Starr. Mr. Starr is an official of the U.S. government, duly appointed by a panel of three judges pursuant to laws passed by the U.S. Congress and signed by Bill Clinton. Presumably this means he is not the local football coach, removable by mob sentiment. If Mr. Starr is abusing his powers, that same law provides that the Attorney General can remove him, and she should do so.

Instead, Mr. Clinton's Attorney General has expanded the scope of Mr. Starr's investigation at least three known times. Four former attorney generals, including Griffin Bell of the Carter Administration, have testified to Mr. Starr's longstanding personal reputation for integrity and judicial temperament. (Since their statement has not been widely covered, we reprint it in its entirety nearby.)

None of this matters in Mr. Carville's war, and we're confident none of it is explained to people when the pollsters put their questions.

What we have here is a public relations offensive intended to turn the public against a court official going about his work and not in a position to reply to every criticism. In the March 2 New York Times an obviously confident White House aide casually describes "our continuing campaign to destroy Ken Starr."

This "continuing campaign" hasn't been restricted to Mr. Starr, himself a former appeals court judge. Judge David Sentelle of the three judge panel has been diminished by Clinton operatives as merely a tool of Senator Helms. Other troublesome judges can expect to be similarly targeted. This is, in effect, an attack on the judicial branch if not indeed the law itself.

In this campaign, the President of the United States avails himself of his own personal Praetorian Guard of dirt-diggers, personified by Terry Lenzner's Investigative Group Inc. Back in 1994, the President's private attorneys, Robert Bennett and David Kendall, retained IGI's services in the Paula Jones and Whitewater cases. Jack Palladino, hired in the first Clinton Presidential run to help with Betsey Wright's "bimbo eruptions," has also appeared on the scene, bragging about his success in avoiding subpoenas. Mike McCurry, spokesman for the Presidency who's doubling inappropriately as flack for Mr. Clinton's own lawyers, said the President was aware that his private lawyers had hired outside investigators but that the detectives weren't looking for "personal derogatory information."

Yet somehow derogatory information, some of it plainly false, keeps popping up. Former prosecutor Joseph DiGenova said last month on "Meet the Press" that journalists told him that both he and his wife were being probed after they'd given interviews critical of Mr. Clinton in the Lewinsky scandal. Mr. Starr's private life has also been investigated, with all involved denying a White House connection. Mr. Starr's perhaps impolitic subpoena of White House spinner Sidney Blumenthal came after the IC's office started receiving reporters' calls asking for comment on destructive rumors about staff prosecutors. Wire stories, for example, suggested that prosecutor Bruce Udolf had been fined 10 years ago for violating a defendant's civil rights in Georgia. A former federal judge defended Mr. Udolf against the implication that he could be expected to abuse the law.

Richard Nixon's Watergate "Plumbers" offended mainly because the President, who has authority over a powerful national security apparatus, had created a private posse to investigate his enemies, unchecked by professional pride and the mores of an ongoing institution. It's now evident that the Clintonites learned two things from Watergate: Burn the tapes, and put your plumbers in your personal law firm to acquire attorney-client privilege.

No doubt the White House is proud of its success in Borking Mr. Starr. Yet serious people should recognize the damage being wrought to institutions developed over centuries to uphold the idea that civilization means something more than the sentiment of the passing moment. If poll ratings are all that matter in the nation's capital, a President can perhaps sustain them with a prosperous economy and a winning television manner, or as the Romans said, bread and circuses. Mr. Carville's war and Mr. Starr's polls give us a glimpse of one possible evolution of our political system in an era of instant communications. The issue is whether we will be governed by men or by laws.

Letters to the Editor

The Attack Dogs Are Borking

Your superb March 11 editorial "The Borking of Starr" identifies perfectly my concerns about the damage being inflicted on our system of government and our country. Kenneth Starr will continue to carry out the dictates of his office. The White House, at the president's direction, appears willing to destroy the credibility of our judicial process in its misguided efforts to obfuscate the issue of the president's failings. Mr. Clinton's narcissism is such that he appears willing to sacrifice his country's well being in order to salvage what remains of his tattered political career.

Mr. Clinton can begin the nation's healing process by stepping down, and that is what he should do, "sooner rather than later."

ADDISON GARDNER

Atlanta

* * *

Now politics and attack dogs will be the norm in our courts. Long live Mr. Clinton, and may history tell our ancestors what he and his attack dogs have done to this country. Conservatives need to get their act together and start Borking.

RICK WILSON

Dallas

* * *

I think your comparison of Robert Bork with Kenneth Starr is not just unfortunate, but ridiculous. One is an outstanding scholar (who of course creates ideological enemies) while the other is a wholly owned subsidiary of the Republican fringe. And you keep referring to Mr. Starr's integrity. Where is this evidenced? In his securing all the part-time jobs for his law firm and himself while being paid by the taxpayers? In his representing wacko positions in Wisconsin while trying to take tax dollars for religious schools?

Or do you seriously argue that a temporary special counsel who spends his entire time rummaging through Bill Clinton's panty collection is comparable to Robert Bork? An unrestrained special prosecutor is not in America's tradition; in fact, it violates every tenet of our beliefs.

If it weren't for the good jokes developing from Mr. Starr's inquisition and subpoenaing everyone in the world at taxpayers expense, we might actually concentrate on the campaign financing atrocities.

Bork got "Borked," as did Ollie North, but Mr. Starr will have a Pepperdine sinecure while everyone else will have paid a high price for his fetid fetishes.

JEREMY LYNCH

Hales Corners, Wis.

* * *

Thank you for the editorial on Mr. Starr and the abuse he must suffer in silence as he carries out the job given him by the attorney general and the three-judge panel.

How is it that the law is not more definitively applied to the likes of Messrs. Carville, Blumenthal and Clinton? Long term it will only harm our nation if the rule of law is so easily cast aside and destruction is undertaken of those who seek to uphold the law. I hope Mr. Starr will realize that many Americans are behind him and hope he maintains his goal of seeking truth. I salute him.

M.J. LEARNED

Peoria, Ill.

* * *

Your editorial is a lily of truth in a rain forest of misleading deceptions by almost all the other media. I am truly frightened by the mass of uninformed people willing to be duped by the media and this administration. How long can our orderly society and rule of law surviveunder this corruptive onslaught?

Remember when a cabinet member (Sherman) in the Eisenhower administration was forced to resign because the origin of his wife's fur coat was in question? In the current administration, with the adoring White House reporters, such an event would not even be newsworthy.

GALE NEWMAN

Naples, Fla.

Editorial Feature

Let Starr Do His Job

The following statement was issued last Thursday by four former U.S. attorneys general. A related editorial appears on page 312.

As former attorneys general of the United States, we oppose the Independent Counsel Act. We believed in the past, and we believe now, that the United States Department of Justice is capable of investigating all criminal and civil matters involving the United States government. We also believe that the Independent Counsel Act raises serious constitutional issues involving, among other things, separation of powers and due process. However, we also believe in the

Ken Starr

rule of law. In *Morrison v. Olson*, the United States Supreme Court ruled that the Independent Counsel Act is constitutional. Moreover, in 1994, after the law had lapsed, Congress reauthorized the Independent Counsel Act, and President Clinton signed it into law. Therefore, the Independent Counsel Act is today the law of the land, and it must be enforced.

As former attorneys general, we are concerned that the severity of the attacks on Independent Counsel Kenneth Starr and his office by high government officials and attorneys representing their particular interests, among others, appear to have the improper purpose of influencing and impeding an ongoing criminal investigation and intimidating possible jurors, witnesses and even investigators. We believe it is significant that Mr. Starr's investigative mandate has been sanctioned by the Attorney General of the United States and the Special Division of the United States Court of Appeals for the District of Columbia.

Further, Mr. Starr is effectively prevented from defending himself and his staff because of the legal requirements of confidentiality and the practical limitations necessitated by the ongoing investigations.

As former attorneys general, we know Mr. Starr to be an individual of the highest personal and professional integrity. As a judge on the United States Court of Appeals for the District of Columbia and Solicitor General of the United States, he exhibited exemplary judgment and commitment to the highest ethical standards and the rule of law.

We believe any independent counsel, including Mr. Starr, should be allowed to carry out his or her duties without harassment by government officials and members of the bar. The counsel's service can then be judged, by those who wish to do so, when the results of the investigation and the facts underlying it can be made public.

GRIFFIN B. BELL

Attorney General for President Jimmy Carter

EDWIN MEESE III

Attorney General for President Ronald Reagan

RICHARD L. THORNBURGH

Attorney General for Presidents Ronald Reagan
and George Bush

WILLIAM P. BARR

Attorney General for President George Bush

Editorial Feature

Whitewater Figure Laid to Rest, But Probe Goes On

By MICAH MORRISON

ARKADELPHIA, Ark. -- In a hilltop tableau that doubtless would have pleased the Southern raconteur and rogue banker, James Bert McDougal was sent to his eternal reward Friday surrounded by 100 friends and former adversaries, his literary agent, his ghost writer, and television cameras. A Dixieland band played him out.

McDougal -- owner of the failed Madison Guaranty Savings & Loan, at the heart of the Whitewater inquiry -- was eulogized by W. Hickman Ewing Jr., the federal prosecutor who put him in jail. In May 1996, McDougal was convicted on 18 fraud and conspiracy charges in a Whitewater prosecution that also saw the conviction of his wife, Susan, and then-Arkansas Gov. Jim Guy Tucker. Facing more than 80 years in prison, McDougal agreed to cooperate with Independent Counsel Kenneth Starr in exchange for a lighter sentence. He got three years and the devoted attention of Mr. Ewing and his staff. But he died in a Texas prison on March 8, following a heart attack. He was 57.

"Lord, we thank you for Jim McDougal," Mr. Ewing said at the graveside ceremony, a cool breeze stirring the nearby trees. "Jim McDougal became very transparent" toward the end of his life. "I mean, there are some things that I don't think he really wanted to come out. But Jim McDougal at one point said, 'I'm tired of certain things.' "

In an April 1997 interview with NBC, Mr. McDougal said that

then-Gov. Bill Clinton was present at a meeting where a fraudulent $300,000 loan for Susan McDougal was discussed. Mrs. McDougal was convicted on four fraud counts relating to the loan and sentenced to two years in prison. Asked why he was no longer claiming -- as he had at trial -- that Mr. Clinton wasn't involved in the fraud scheme, Mr. McDougal said, "I just got sick and tired of lying for the fellow."

In a McDougalism later widely cited, he added, "I think the Clintons are sort of like tornadoes moving through people's lives. . . . I'm just one of the people left in the wake of their passing by there, but I have no whining or complaining to do, because I have lots of company."

McDougal cut a colorful swath through Arkansas political life. A Democratic political operative, he served as a local staff member for Sen. William Fulbright in the late 1960s and early 1970s, meet-

Jim McDougal

ing along the way an ambitious young politician named Bill Clinton. By the mid-1970s he was doing "dirt deals" -- converting rural real estate into home-building tracts -- and passing along some of the bounty to his political friends.

In 1978, the McDougals and the Clintons purchased a 230-acre tract along Arkansas's White River for development and named it Whitewater. Four years later, Mr. McDougal bought Madison Guaranty S&L and began a period of rapid expansion. He lived the high life, driving a baby-blue Bentley and throwing his S&L's money at increasingly extravagant real-estate projects. But soon it would all come crashing down.

By 1985, the Federal Home Loan Bank Board was raising questions about Madison's financial stability and lending practices. In actions that later would come under scrutiny by Mr. Starr and Congress, Gov. Clinton one day jogged by McDougal's office and asked that Hillary Clinton be steered some money, according to McDougal's later account. Mrs. Clinton began to receive a $2,000-a-month retainer at the Rose Law Firm. Within eight weeks of the first payment, she dispatched a recapitalization offer for the foundering Madison to the Arkansas Securities Commission, headed by a longtime associate of her husband. The plan was approved but never implemented. McDougal was removed from the S&L's board of directors, and in 1989 federal regulators shut down Madison at a taxpayer loss of $60 million.

In 1990, McDougal went on trial a first time, for bank fraud. Prosecutors focused on two alleged sham transactions involving a land development called Castle Grande. Suffering from heart trouble and diagnosed as a manic-depressive, McDougal nevertheless mounted a vigorous defense and was acquitted. He wasn't so lucky the second time around, in 1996.

Today, Mrs. Clinton's involvement in other Castle Grande transactions is a central part of Mr. Starr's inquiry. McDougal's death is expected to have only minor impact on Mr. Starr's case.

After the 1990 trial, the Clintons had little use for McDougal; the tornado was moving on. A year later, Mr. Clinton announced his candidacy for president, denouncing "S&L crooks." Broke and embittered, McDougal survived on the kindness of friends, living in an Arkadelphia trailer home provided by Bob Riley, a former Arkansas lieutenant governor. In 1992, Jeff Gerth of the New York Times showed up in town asking questions about Mr. Clinton's finances.

The rest is history. Mr. Starr has gone on to secure guilty pleas or convictions of 13 people, including Mr. Tucker and former Associate Attorney General Webster Hubbell, triggering a widespread cleanup of corrupt practices in Arkansas and establishing a record as one of the most successful independent counsels ever.

But as Jim McDougal went into the Arkansas earth last week, there was little talk of Whitewater. The wind over Arkadelphia was growing colder, and in Little Rock and Washington the Clinton tornado was claiming new victims.

As the mourners departed, some of those who knew McDougal in his last year said that he had achieved a kind of happiness in prison -- that the truth, finally, had set him free.

Amen to that.

Mr. Morrison is a Journal editorial page writer.

All the
President's Women

As spring 1998 arrived in Washington, the Journal noted a "torrent of troubles headed toward the White House." The President battled Independent Counsel Starr in the federal courts, invoking executive privilege for top aides and claiming a new "protective function" privilege for the Secret Service in an effort to prevent testimony in the Lewinsky affair. Attorney General Reno moved closer to naming a fifth special prosecutor to investigate yet another Cabinet official, Labor Secretary Alexis Herman. Ms. Reno's troubled campaign-finance task force netted more midlevel players, indicting Buddhist temple fund-raising figure Maria Hsia and obtaining a plea-bargain with California fund-raiser Johnny Chung, but calls for an outside prosecutor continued. And on "60 Minutes," another woman, former White House volunteer Kathleen Willey, said that President Clinton had made crude sexual advances to her in the Oval Office and that several of his associates had later sought to pressure her to keep silent.

The President got some good news in early April when an Arkansas judge dismissed the Paula Jones sexual harassment lawsuit, ruling that Mrs. Jones had failed to make a case of emotional or career harm, and that even if true, her accusations did not reach the required level of "outrage." Earlier, in January, the judge had excluded all material relating to Monica Lewinsky from the Jones civil case, saying pursuit of the Lewinsky evidence would disrupt Mr. Starr's criminal probe. Following the April ruling, the White House declared "vindication" for Mr. Clinton. Mrs. Jones's attorneys announced they would appeal.

Mr. Starr's inquiry, exploring issues of perjury and obstruction of justice by Mr. Clinton and Ms. Lewinsky in the Jones matter, was unaffected by the April ruling in Arkansas. Yet the dismissal of the Jones case, the Journal noted, "clearly takes some of the impetus out of the drive to hold the President accountable, certainly in the tabloids and perhaps in Congress. But at the same time, dismissal may make the issues clearer. The root issue has never been about sex. It has always been about abuse of the powers with which the President is entrusted."

REVIEW & OUTLOOK

Beyond Sex

Most children of the '60s call the music they listened to way back then "oldies," a culture they set aside for the more serious rigors of adulthood. Bill Clinton, however, seems to be still living it. The famous Steppenwolf anthem, "Born to Be Wild," comes to mind. Now, five years into the wild ride that has been this Presidency, the country finds itself in an extraordinary crackup of sex, politics and uncertain mores. Amid the confusion, the one thing that the American people all seem to agree on is that they still honor the institution of the Presidency. Beyond this, what's honorable anymore is hard to say.

Try to connect these dots: Within a week we have Kathleen Willey telling 60 million or so of her intimate friends that the President of the United States was ready to party for about as long as it was going to take the Treasury Secretary to make it up from the front door to the Oval Office; we have a military jury acquitting Sgt. Major Gene McKinney in the face of sexual harassment charges by six female soldiers; we have the Secretary of Defense suggesting that the answer to sexual tensions in the armed forces is to set up barracks barriers of some sort on land and sea.

Meanwhile, feminist theologian Patricia Ireland announces that Monica Lewinsky was "consensual," whereas Kathleen Willey may have been "sexual assault." And the relevant analysis of Paula Jones's lawsuit over whatever Governor Clinton proposed in a hotel room is that it probably doesn't include the number of angels now required to dance on the head of a sexual-harassment pin.

This is all no doubt endlessly fascinating and maybe even important, as proven by the ratings of the many evening talk shows dedicated nowadays to establishing the prevailing etiquette of sex and the Presidency. Still, we're not much taken with refashioning the Presidency as a kind of personal magical mystery tour. The Presidency, after all, is the office once held by the likes of Washington, Jefferson, Lincoln, Roosevelt, Truman and Reagan who, whatever their deficiencies as mere mortals, recognized they had come into possession of their political system's most hallowed

Bill Clinton

institution. They all may have run political risks, but none routinely risked the integrity of the institution itself.

All the talk now is about how sexually confused Bill Clinton appears to be. But the greater Clinton confusion has been his misunderstanding of the office, a misunderstanding that has resulted in significant abuse and which was apparent from the earliest days. It is not Bill Clinton's personal sins or appetites that set him apart, but his potential for degrading this institution.

We don't mean to be demure about presidents and their baser political instincts. Others abused the FBI or IRS. Mr. Clinton, however, seems to have uniquely ascended to this office on the assumption that it exists to serve his needs first, with the affairs of the nation tagged on as some second or third order of concern. The campaign-finance story is emblematic—flouting laws and even common sense so as to transform the President's daily schedule, the White House itself, his Vice President, American policy and the DNC apparatus into his re-election cogs.

Historically, struggles within the executive or between the branches of government have been almost entirely over matters of politics and policy, as with a Vietnam or Iran-Contra. But from the start, every corner of the government has been on daily call to defend Mr. Clinton against the consequences of reckless actions that have had nothing to do with the affairs of the nation. Whitewater mobilized Treasury and White House counsel on his behalf; Travelgate mobilized the FBI and the Justice Department, which brought a vengeful lawsuit against Billy Dale; Filegate mobilized the FBI and Secret

Service; the objectivity of the Justice Department's Public Integrity Section was so doubtful as to become a Washington laughingstock.

So now, tumbling to the existence of a problem in the sixth year of this Presidency, denizens of the Beltway are agog that the American people won't denounce Bill Clinton for what they have made known about his treatment of two women. Why should they? The oath Mr. Clinton swore was to "faithfully execute the Office of the President of the United States." If the American people are hesitant to conclude that a sexual circus is violation of that oath, it is in no small part because their watchdogs—Members of the Congress and the media—have not sounded the alarm about a pattern of abuse of authority and law over the past five years. Until eyes are raised to Mr. Clinton's most damaging actions, the office he holds will continue to wither.

Editorial Feature

A Kiss Is Still a Kiss, But a Grope Can Be a Felony

By JAMES TARANTO

"This is not just sexual harassment," Patricia Ireland, president of the National Organization for Women, said Sunday of Kathleen Willey's story. "If it's true, it's sexual assault." Ms. Ireland added, however: "It's extremely unlikely that a prosecutor would take that kind of case to court."

Tell that to Stanley Feinstein, a 65-year-old former worker's compensation judge from Los Angeles. Three years ago, Mr. Feinstein was convicted of felony sexual battery in a case that eerily echoes President Clinton's current adultery-and-assault scandals.

On March 28, 1994, then-Judge Feinstein met in his chambers with a female lawyer who had business before his court. According to the lawyer, Judge Feinstein pushed her against a wall, grabbed her breast and forcibly kissed her.

Six days later Judge Feinstein surrendered to police, after learning a warrant had been issued for his arrest. He was charged with false imprisonment and sexual battery, both felonies. In short order, the California Department of Industrial Relations, which oversees the workers' compensation court, removed him from the bench—not for sexual wrongdoing but for refusing to cooperate with the department's internal investigation. "Even though he is innocent, he didn't want to compromise his rights in the criminal case," Mr. Feinstein's lawyer, Philip Israels, told the Los Angeles Times. "We said we'd cooperate fully, but to let us take care of the criminal matter first." Mike McCurry couldn't have said it better.

Judge Feinstein, for his own part, declared himself the innocent victim of a political conspiracy, orchestrated by lawyers unhappy with his rulings. (Unlike Mr. Clinton, however, he made the case himself, rather than delegate the job to his wife.) "They are using me to send a message," he told the Times the day of his arrest. "The message is: If you don't do what we want in the workers' compensation system, we will find you, and we will get you. There has been a history of attacks against workers' compensation judges."

Asked by the Times why this woman would file a complaint, the judge seemed, well, bewildered: "You have to go into their minds and find out why they are doing this." Later Mr. Feinstein's lawyers claimed she was out for money, filing a false police report in preparation for a civil lawsuit.

In a preliminary hearing, Municipal Court Judge Mary Waters reduced the charges to misdemeanors, but prosecutors were determined to try Mr. Feinstein on the more serious charges.

Kathleen Willey

They asked a judge of the California Superior Court, one Lance Ito, to reinstate the felony charges; he refused. But the California Court of Appeal saw things the prosecutors' way and overruled Judges Waters and Ito. In April 1995 Mr. Feinstein went before a jury.

Although the defendant did not take the stand, the jurors did get to hear from him—on tape. The day after their initial encounter, Judge Feinstein's accuser had visited his chambers again. On the advice of the Los Angeles Police Department, she was wearing a wire.

On the tape, the accuser told Judge Feinstein that she was "freaked out about what happened yesterday." He replied: "I will not do anything like that again," and added, "I assure you, if you ever appear before me, you will be treated decently."

The jury convicted Mr. Feinstein of the battery charge, carrying a maximum penalty of four years in prison. Owing to his age and lack of prior convictions, prosecutors asked for only a six-month jail term. But Superior Court Judge Darlene Schempp sentenced him to twice that. "When a judge abuses trust, a serious punishment is appropriate," she said in court, quoting a Los Angeles Times editorial.

She refused to release him on bail while he appealed the conviction. So he went to the Los Angeles County Jail's special ward for high-risk inmates; Lyle Menendez was in the next cell, awaiting retrial on charges of murdering his parents. He spent a month there, whereupon he was released, for reasons he does not know and the Los Angeles County Probation Department, citing confidentiality laws, will not disclose.

Mr. Feinstein appealed the verdict and lost. The accuser also filed a civil suit, which he settled for "about $30,000." In an interview yesterday, he maintained his innocence, blaming his "harsh treatment" on the Times editorial Judge Schempp quoted in sentencing him.

When I first heard about this case, it struck me as an example of prosecutors gone mad. (Full disclosure: Mr. Feinstein's son is a friend of mine.) The behavior alleged certainly was piggish and unprofessional, good cause for ostracism and removal from the bench. But felony prosecution and imprisonment seemed to me wildly excessive.

The jury didn't see it that way, however. Juror Jeanne Wiczek of Northridge told the Los Angeles Daily News: "Someone in his position should know better."

It's a good point—and one that applies all the more forcefully to the president of the United States.

Mr. Taranto is deputy features editor of the Journal editorial page.

REVIEW & OUTLOOK

Laying Down the Law

It seems that Federal Judge Royce Lamberth has some old-fashioned views on intentional obfuscation. He just sentenced Ronald Blackley, the chief of staff to former Agriculture Secretary Mike Espy, to 27 months in prison for making false statements. "Our democracy depends upon trust between the people and government officials," Judge Lamberth noted. The judge's recent experience presiding over several lawsuits against the Clinton White House has clearly made him wise to the many ways officials try to evade responsibility.

At the sentencing Judge Lamberth also raised an eyebrow at legal experts who downplay the chances of anyone being prosecuted solely for perjury. Referring to tireless TV pundit and Monica Lewinsky chaperone William Ginsburg, he said: "A lawyer, who must have been on another planet—actually he was just from Hollywood—recently claimed that no one is ever prosecuted for false statements under oath in a civil proceeding. . . . This Court has a duty to send a message to other high level government officials that there is a severe penalty to be paid for providing false information under oath."

Mr. Blackley was convicted last year of lying on his financial disclosure forms and then to several federal investigators. A jury found he failed to disclose $22,000 he'd received from Mississippi farmers. In one instance, Mr. Blackley actively intervened to protect a subsidy going to an associate, an act that strikes at the heart of the principle of equal treatment under the law.

Clearly, the Blackley case was a serious matter, just like the coming trial of Mr. Espy on related charges. But when in 1996 Independent Counsel Donald Smaltz asked to expand his probe into Mr. Espy's ties to agribusiness, he was opposed by the Clinton Justice Department. Justice argued in part that the Blackley matter wasn't sufficiently related to his original jurisdiction. A three-judge panel of federal judges disagreed and so, ultimately, did a jury. Last year, the D.C. Circuit Court of Appeals ruled the White House couldn't withhold documents from Mr. Smaltz in the Espy case. That opinion was written by Patricia Wald, leader of the D.C. Circuit's liberal bloc.

Royce Lamberth

This isn't the first time Judge Lamberth has expressed his displeasure with the drawbridge-raising reflexes of the White House. Last year, he levied $286,000 in sanctions against the executive branch for a "coverup" of Hillary Clinton's health-care task force. The judge also found a pattern of stonewalling and evasion in a lawsuit filed by Judicial Watch seeking documents on trade missions led by the late Ron Brown. Finally admitting that it hadn't properly looked for the documents, government lawyers asked the judge to order a new document search by stating "the Department of Commerce moves the court to enter judgment against the Department of Commerce."

In his no-nonsense approach to such behavior, Judge Lamberth may be stepping into the shoes filled by Judge John Sirica during Watergate, when he imposed provisional 40-year sentences on the Watergate burglars, which helped lead to an uncovering of the coverup. For this White House's aides and allies, the judiciary's new stern message of zero tolerance is not going to make for a balmy spring.

Editorial Feature

Feminism: What NOW?

By BARBARA AMIEL

If you want to appreciate the dilemma feminists face these days, click on to the National Organization for Women's Web page. Up comes a picture titled "A vision of what a true Women-Friendly Workplace should look like."

There are seven people in this picture, and they do not actually appear to be working at anything apart from perfecting their power salutes. Of the seven, the only person wearing a skirt is the black lady carrying that very desirable workplace accessory—a small child. The only person resembling a white male is in a wheelchair, presumably the best place for Caucasian males in NOW's view.

NOW's Women-Friendly Workplace certainly does not match the West Wing of the White House as described by a number of women workers of late. That building seems short on power salutes and long on short skirts. But what's a good feminist to do? Bill Clinton promised to be the strongest advocate of NOW's programs, from affirmative action to sexual harassment policies. It would have been unnatural not to give him the benefit of every doubt, especially when his accusers were not respected members of what I call the "new matriarchy."

Legal Privilege

Most people describing themselves as feminists simply hold the classical liberal belief of equal treatment for all regardless of sex. But our academic, media and political elites have been almost entirely taken over by this new matriarchy. They openly demand a position of legal *privilege* for women and are busy re-engineering American institutions, from the military to private business, on this basis.

In the new matriarchy, when a man is charged with a "gender" crime, any attempt to defend himself against the allegation is itself a crime. What feminists never anticipated was catching one of their own. Their rules were designed to trap a Wilbur Mills or a Clarence Thomas, not a Bill Clinton. In the legal landscape feminists have created, the accused is deprived of most normal safeguards. *Mens rea* (guilty intent) is of reduced relevance. The accused is guilty until proven innocent—and feminists proudly announce this reversed onus. As evidentiary rules are whittled away to protect accusers, one can't help feeling that we might as well dispense with trials and send men postcards telling them where to serve their sentences.

Then there is Kathleen Willey. Previous accusers of the president were American parodies. Paula Jones is of a class American feminists have never seen. Monica Lewinsky has the appearance of a spoiled Beverly Hills girl. Ms. Willey, on the other hand, with the right sort of fine lines in her face and minimalist style of dress, is central casting's ideal victim. Feminists must react to her or they create a serious credibility problem.

As it is, women tend to believe Mr. Clinton, men to believe Ms. Willey. This is attributed to political affiliation (more women are Democrats, men Republicans), but I cleave to a simpler interpretation: Men know they sometimes grope; women know they sometimes lie. Even the warm letters Ms. Willey wrote to the president after the alleged grope don't exculpate Mr. Clinton from the standpoint of feminist ideology, which holds that victims of sexual manip-

Kathleen Willey

ulation may be trapped in a sort of Stockholm syndrome with an attachment to their tormentor. Besides, what the hell, she needed a job.

At the time of the Anita Hill/Clarence Thomas hearings, mainstream America hadn't quite grasped what was behind the feminist agenda to banish sexual harassment from the workplace. It sounded apple-pie enough: To grope female employees against their will under threat of dismissal is unequivocally un-American. The reality was that under the rubric of "sexual harassment," feminists actually wanted to criminalize normal sexual behavior and outlaw the ordinary routines of flirting, dating, office relationships, even sexual banter.

The majority of Americans have resisted feminist attempts to rewire sexual responses, and perhaps that's why they seem to have taken the allegations against the president pretty much in stride. I'd say eight out of 10 American males carry on girl-watching, while the same percentage of women carry on preening, and everyone goes through the same little rituals of display and courtship. But the 20% who have swallowed the feminist line holus-bolus can be an epoch-altering number. These are the people who have bought into the hatred and confusion of the gender wars and are its causalities. They have the "recovered memories"; they are involved in the witch trials; they are the people who charge sexual harassment when normal flirtation takes place.

And our epoch has been altered. The feminist movement has been successful beyond its wildest dreams or this madness in Washington would never have got off the ground. The very notion that a Paula Jones can win damages by proving that some other woman who succumbed to the president's advances had a better career than she did is madness. You can only posit this in a society that has caught a whiff of insanity and undergone something akin to the Chinese Cultural Revolution.

What will happen? In the short run, it is simply a matter of whether or not the president's accusers are telling the truth. If they are, then it is remotely possible that the president suffers from a male version of what 19th-century novelists genteelly called "furor uterinus" when they actually meant nymphomania. Such a medical condition would be no moral failing but could interfere with his work and concentration. If it turned out—and there is no proof of this—that a portion of the White House staff had to spend time procuring, controlling or cleaning up the situations created by this condition, it would be a matter of public interest.

Future Looks Iffy

If the allegations are not true, why this outbreak of lying women? Accusations can create a climate of mass hysteria rather like a revival meeting, in which certain types of women feel impelled to come forward and invent, reinvent or blow up events for psychological or economic reasons. I can't speculate on the motives, for example, of Ms. Willey, but her temerity in using the Oval Office as her employment agency is staggering. Such a person might bring to the table the sort of behavior that could be misinterpreted when asking the president to find her a paying job.

For those of us who hope to see common sense prevail, the future looks iffy. One hopes that we'll come to our senses and reassert that while male and female sexuality are not totally the same, they are both valid and should be allowed to operate within reasonable limits, free of ideology. If the accusations and revelations had gone no further than Gennifer Flowers, Monica Lewinsky and Paula Jones, the silliness of it all might have created a backlash against the excesses of feminism. But if Mr. Clinton turns out to be a truly priapic personality, then the feminists may desert him just as they deserted Bob Packwood. Indeed, both Messrs. Clinton and Packwood could then become symbolic. Perhaps one day we will call up our NOW Web page to see their pictures with the caption "Even the best of them are beasts."

Paula Jones

Ms. Amiel is a columnist for the Daily Telegraph of London.

REVIEW & OUTLOOK

William Milhous Clinton

So William Jefferson Clinton becomes the second President in history to invoke executive privilege against a subpoena from a grand jury probing possible crimes in the White House. This is a sure sign that, despite the Monica-sex furor of past weeks, the worst is yet to come.

• To take the issue of executive privilege first, the White House has just set itself up for a series of courtroom defeats. Yes, executive privilege does exist, invoked most often in political tussles with Congress with the courts as referee. Resisting a criminal investigation is another matter, as President Nixon found in the Watergate scandal. *U.S. v. Nixon* was a unanimous opinion written by Chief Justice Burger and with Justice Rehnquist recused. It respected confidentiality to the extent of providing *in camera* inspection of the subpoenaed tapes and documents. But it flatly rejected an executive privilege from court subpoenas "absent a claim of need to protect military, diplomatic or sensitive national security interests."

Richard Nixon

Today President Clinton is seeking to protect conversation on his personal behavior with top aide Bruce Lindsey and—hold your breath—top hit man Sidney Blumenthal. Independent Counsel Kenneth Starr's subpoena to Mr. Blumenthal has been condemned in the press as a mistake, but the big whispering campaign against Mr. Starr's office did stop. And the executive privilege claim now raises an issue of whether the press was overly credulous in accepting Mr. Blumenthal's breathless account of what happened in the grand jury room. It will also be interesting to learn whether this frivolous claim was signed by the President personally, as has been customary in executive privilege cases. The argument will win delay, but in all likelihood at the expense of a string of rebuffs in court.

• The Administration has also discovered an entirely new privilege, Secret Service privilege, contending that agents can't protect a President if they feel they may be questioned about his possibly criminal acts. If the President out of boredom or madness decides to rob a bank, the supposed logic runs, Secret Service agents should protect him from the guards. This too is a sure loser. The most interesting question concerns Treasury Secretary Robert Rubin, who commands the Secret Service; will the Administration's last white hat get spattered by the Clinton muck?

• The Starr investigation ticks away, under a statute instructing the independent counsel to report to the House if impeachable offenses "may" have been committed. A report on Lewinsky et al. clearly impends, no doubt focusing on Presidential perjury and attempts to suborn perjury and obstruct justice. Fresh sexual embarrassments may be disclosed, but more important, the raw scandal has allowed prosecutors to penetrate the pattern of stonewalling that has kept them from connecting the dots on more substantive matters. Proof of obstruction over Lewinsky would be important evidence on such issues as the vindictive Billy Dale prosecution or hush money for Webb Hubbell.

Bill Clinton

• Clinton mouthpiece Bob Bennett hopes to end the President's troubles with something that can be spun as a "win" in the Paula Jones case. In fact, Mr. Bennett is going the wrong way on a one-way street created when Judge Susan Webber Wright ruled that the Lewinsky material can't be introduced. If Mrs. Jones wins, she wins. If she loses, either on summary judgment or on trial, her appeals will keep Monica in the headlines another couple of years. Even Judge Wright conceded the Lewinsky material was relevant, but barred it to prevent Mrs. Jones's lawyers from interfering with the Starr investigation. The sweeping ruling was far more than Mr. Starr asked for, and will do anything but bring the case to a speedy conclusion. Given any opportunity to avoid likely reversal on so spectacular a case, Judge Wright would be wise to think again.

• A new independent counsel now takes the field, with Carol Elder Bruce named to investigate decisions on Indian casinos by Interior Secretary Bruce Babbitt, also a former white hat. While the initial focus of the inquiry is whether Secretary Babbitt lied to Congress, the most interesting line of questioning concerns a conversation between an involved lobbyist and President Clinton, with apparent follow-up by Mr. Lindsey and Harold Ickes. Both Janet Reno's request and the Special Division charter, however, include the phrase "whether any violation of federal criminal law occurred" in conjunction with the decision. Knowledgeable lawyers say this gives Mrs. Bruce plenty of latitude to look at the President's own involvement.

• Attorney General Reno has asked for more time to study whether another independent counsel should be appointed concerning allegations that Labor Secretary Alexis M. Herman illegally accepted cash to help business interests while she served as a White House aide. Five independent counsels have already been appointed to investigate high Clinton Administration officials, and Mr. Starr's mandate has been expanded at least three times.

• The Justice Department campaign-finance probe is showing life under prosecutor Charles LaBella, who has now indicted Charlie Trie and Maria Hsia and won a plea-bargain cooperation agreement from Johnny Chung. Mr. LaBella is winning respect from Clinton investigators in Congress, but he operates under guidelines from Justice's Public Integrity division. At one point the Washington Post reported that the guideline meant investigators couldn't ask whether a crime had been committed by higher officials covered by the Independent Counsel Act. Senator Hatch or Congressman Hyde should ask Mr. LaBella whether he can question Mr. Chung or Mr. Trie about Presidential actions, or whether an independent counsel is needed after all.

Those with a sense of the torrent of troubles headed toward the White House keep asking themselves, what will happen? The White House tactics will both win delay and dig deeper problems. The economy is good, and even President Nixon's poll ratings held up well enough until the tapes were discovered. Presidents should not resign easily, and we further doubt that Mr. Clinton has the residue of conscience that led Mr. Nixon to leave when the time came. But the Presidency is weakened, and will be weakened further. The closest parallel may be President Woodrow Wilson, who spent nearly the last 18 months of his tenure bedridden after a stroke. Efforts to protect him from anxiety left Presidential decisions to his wife.

Editorial Feature

What If Judge Sirica
Were With Us Today?

By Douglas Caddy

The Clinton scandals, with all the claims of coverup and executive privilege, are certainly reminiscent of Watergate. But there is a crucial difference: This case lacks a John Sirica, the chief judge of the U.S. District Court for the District of Columbia who played such a crucial role in Watergate. The untold historical record reveals that the early actions of Sirica, who assigned the Watergate case to himself, helped spur the subsequent coverup and obstruction of justice that ultimately led to the resignation of President Nixon and the criminal convictions of many Watergate figures.

The Watergate scandal began at 2:30 a.m. on June 17, 1972, when Washington, D.C., police arrested five men on burglary charges at the Watergate office building. At 3:05 a.m. E. Howard Hunt phoned me from his White House office and asked if he could come immediately to my Washington residence. I had been Hunt's personal attorney for several years.

Hunt arrived half an hour later and informed me what had transpired earlier at the Watergate. He retained me to represent him in the case and then called G. Gordon Liddy, who also hired me. At that time, about two hours after the burglary, both Hunt and Liddy requested I also represent the five people arrested, four Cuban-Americans and James McCord, who were by then incarcerated in the D.C. jail.

On June 28—11 days later—while working on the case in the federal courthouse in Washington, I was served with a subpoena, bearing the name of Chief Judge Sirica, to appear "forthwith" before the federal grand jury investigating the case. Assistant U.S. Attorney Donald Campbell grabbed me by the arm and pulled me into the grand jury room.

From June 28 until July 19 I was to appear before the grand jury on six occasions and answer hundreds of questions. I drew the line, however, on the advice of my own legal counsel, at answering 38 questions we felt invaded my clients' Sixth Amendment right to counsel and the attorney-client privilege. A typical question: "Between the hours of Friday at midnight, June 16, and 8:30 a.m. Saturday, June 17, did you receive a visit from Mr. Everett Howard Hunt?" We believed answering such questions would incriminate Hunt and Liddy, who had not been arrested, and would violate their constitutional rights.

Judge Sirica

Judge Sirica, rejecting such arguments out of hand, threatened to jail me for contempt of court. When I went before the grand jury on July 13, I refused to answer the 38 questions. Within an hour I was back before Judge Sirica, who immediately held me in contempt and ordered me to jail. Five days later, on July 18, the U.S. Circuit Court of Appeals upheld the contempt citation and ordered me to testify under threat of being jailed again. The opinion, which I found gratuitously insulting, declared: "Even if such a relationship does exist, certain communications, such as consultation in furtherance of a crime, are not within the privilege."

In his July 19, 1972, Oval Office tape, Nixon is recorded as expressing dismay to John Ehrlichman: "Do you mean that the circuit court ordered an attorney to testify?"

Ehrlichman replied, "It [unintelligible] me, except that this damn circuit that we've got here, with [Judge David] Bazelon and so on, it surprises me every time they do something."

Nixon then asked, "Why didn't he appeal to the Supreme Court?"

The answer is that my attorneys and I believed we had built a strong enough court record that if Hunt, Liddy and the five arrested individuals were found guilty, their convictions could be overturned on appeal because of Sirica's and the appeals court's abuse of me as their attorney.

However, Judge Sirica's actions had an unintended consequence. Hunt and Liddy, seeing their attorney falsely accused by Judge Sirica of being a participant in their crime, realized early on that they were not going to get a fair trial, so they embarked on a coverup involving "hush money." As Hunt has written: "If Sirica was treating Caddy—an Officer of the Court—so summarily, and Caddy was completely uninvolved in Watergate—then those of us who were involved could expect neither fairness nor understanding from him. As events unfolded, this conclusion became tragically accurate."

Liddy appealed his conviction to the U.S. Circuit Court of Appeals, claiming that my being forced to testify denied him his Sixth Amendment right to counsel. The court upheld his conviction: "The evidence against appellant . . . was so overwhelming that even if there were constitutional error in the comment of the prosecutor and the instruction of the trial judge, there is no reasonable possibility it contributed to the conviction." Neither Judge Sirica nor the appeals court acknowledged that their assault on the attorney-client privilege helped spur the ensuing coverup and obstruction of justice.

I was never indicted, named an unindicted co-conspirator, disciplined by the Bar or even contacted by the Senate Watergate committee or the House Judiciary Committee, whose staff included a young lawyer named Hillary Rodham.

Now the issue of attorney-client privilege is again being raised, this time by Monica Lewinsky's first lawyer, Francis D. Carter, who has been subpoenaed to appear before the grand jury and bring the notes he took while representing Ms. Lewinsky. Mr. Carter got involved when Vernon Jordan referred Ms. Lewinsky to him in January. On March 4 Mr. Carter's attorney, Charles Ogletree, argued before Chief Judge Norma Hollaway Johnson that the subpoena should be quashed: "Once you start to allow the government to intrude on the attorney-client relationship and allow them to pierce the attorney-client privilege, clients will no longer have a sense of confidence and respect that lawyers should have."

Coming days will reveal how Mr. Carter fares in his fight to protect Ms. Lewinsky's constitutional rights and what effect this will have on the case's ultimate outcome. To date, at least, Judge Johnson has shown a restraint that her predecessor Judge Sirica did not.

Mr. Caddy is a Houston lawyer.

REVIEW & OUTLOOK

More Testimony

The sense grows that the ice is melting and cracking at the edges of the thick Clinton defenses. Former Arkansas Governor Jim Guy Tucker has testified before the Starr grand jury. Asian fund-raiser Johnny Chung has plea-bargained. And now on Monday Nolanda Hill, a former business partner and confidant of the late Commerce Secretary Ron Brown, sat in Federal District Court Judge Royce Lamberth's courtroom and talked about the world of Clinton trade junkets.

All these folks are in big trouble, and yes, under those circumstances people start looking for ways to minimize their legal exposure. This is the way the justice system works as it moves inexorably toward a resolution. Ms. Hill testified under oath that seats on Commerce "trade missions were used as a fund-raising tool for the Clinton-Gore presidential campaign." Among the officials she links to the sale of seats is Labor Secretary Alexis Herman, once a political aide to Mr. Brown, who worked in the White House until last year. Ms. Herman is currently the subject of a Justice probe over allegations of influence-peddling. Attorney General Reno faces a May 11 deadline to decide whether to appoint an independent counsel in her case.

Ms. Hill says that shortly before Mr. Brown's death in 1996 he showed her Commerce Department documents that linked seats on trade missions to minimum contributions of $50,000 to the Democratic National Committee. She claims that Mr. Brown told her on several occasions that the sale of seats had originated in the White House's "panic" for campaign dollars that followed the Democrats' loss of Congress in 1994. When the legal watchdog group Judicial Watch filed a Freedom of Information Act lawsuit for trade mission documents, she says that White House aides "instructed Mr. Brown to delay the case by withholding the production of documents prior to the 1996 elections, and to devise a way not to comply with the court's orders."

White House aides denied the charges this week and cracked back at Ms. Hill. They note, for instance, that she was indicted last week on separate charges that she embezzled money from companies jointly owned with Mr. Brown. True enough, but the timing of this indictment is indeed curious.

Ms. Hill first said these things in an affidavit given to Judicial Watch in January. In it she expressed concern that if she came forward with information about a FOIA document coverup, the "Justice Department will try to retaliate against me." Ms. Hill was indicted without first receiving a "target letter" informing her she was in peril, which is highly unusual. Her attorney in the criminal case is Courtney Elwood, who also represents private investigator Terry Lenzner, who has worked for President Clinton's attorneys on the Whitewater and Paula Jones cases since 1994. Since that affidavit, Ms. Hill has in fact *resisted* testifying in Judicial Watch's FOIA case and unsuccessfully tried to take the Fifth Amendment.

As to the trade-junket documents described by Nolanda Hill, the Commerce Department already has asked Judge Lamberth to enter judgment against itself in Judicial Watch's FOIA case, thus conceding its clear failure to search for relevant documents. With the Monday deposition completed, it now falls to Judge Lamberth to decide how to handle Ms. Hill's accusations of a broader White House coverup of Commerce's controversial trade missions.

REVIEW & OUTLOOK

Some 'Vindication'

The Independent Counsel shall have jurisdiction and authority to investigate to the maximum extent authorized by the Independent Counsel Act of 1994 whether Monica Lewinsky or others suborned perjury, obstructed justice, intimidated witnesses, or otherwise violated federal law . . . in dealing with witnesses, potential witnesses, attorneys, or others concerning the civil case Jones v. Clinton.

President Clinton claims "vindication" in Judge Susan Webber Wright's dismissal of the Paula Jones case. Even if it's true that he exposed himself and asked for oral sex, she ruled, that doesn't qualify as sexual harassment. Some vindication. And the vindication extends as well, the President's spinmeisters tell us, to perjury, obstruction of justice, fund-raising dinners with Asian lowlifes, hush money for Webb Hubbell, the ravaging of FBI files, shakedowns of Indian tribes, the Travel Office firings, the Rose billing papers, bogus loans to the Whitewater account and Hillary's $100,000 commodities coup.

In short, Bill Clinton once again displayed his main talent, dodging the bullet. Judge Wright in effect wrote that it's time for Mrs. Jones to grow up, and that everything nasty isn't an actionable tort. There is some sense to this reading, but it must leave thousands of men wondering where to apply to get their jobs back. Employers across the land are routinely faced with buying out discrimination suits based on allegations of far less reprehensible behavior than ascribed to Mr. Clinton. Mrs. Jones' mistake was not running immediately to the plaintiff bar. Conceivably such litigation will now abate, but it's more likely that Judge Wright has established a lenient reading of the discrimination law as a Presidential *droit du seigneur*.

Parlaying this coup into a blanket exemption, though, would be an even more amazing dodging act. Independent Counsel Kenneth Starr, after all, has all along been investigating the original Whitewater case, the Travel Office firings and the use of FBI files. Even in the Jones case, it pays to notice above what he has been specifically chartered to investigate. Not sexual misconduct or even

Kenneth Starr

simple perjury, but possible suborning of perjury, witness intimidation and obstruction of justice (and in the next paragraph of the judicial panel's mandate, conspiracy toward these crimes). Attempts to suborn perjury and obstruct justice are serious crimes standing alone, in no way wiped out by the conclusion of the civil case that may have occasioned them.

Intriguingly too, Monica Lewinsky is the only person specifically named in Mr. Starr's mandate. On the face of it, she did attempt to suborn perjury by delivering the infamous "talking points" to Linda Tripp. Bradford Berenson, a Washington white-collar defense lawyer writing in the Los Angeles Times, has suggested that Mr. Starr simply indict Miss Lewinsky and call the President as a witness. Mr. Berenson subscribes to the argument that a sitting president probably cannot himself be indicted, and writes, "A Lewinsky trial may be the only way the president ever would be required to answer the charges against him under oath, without immunity, in detail and in public."

The crimes Mr. Starr is investigating here are anything but personal peccadilloes, but go to the heart of the presidency, which is constitutionally charged to "take care that the laws be faithfully executed." Obstruction of justice, indeed, was point one of the bill of impeachment that forced President Nixon to resign. The theme of impeding justice runs through the gamut of Clinton offenses, from RTC investigation of the original Whitewater matter to the use of FBI files to the firing of Travel Office employees.

Beyond Mr. Starr's mandate, the theme appears again in the campaign finance controversy. The big issue there is not whether Johnny Chung or Charlie Trie broke the campaign finance laws, but whether they were agents of a presidentially chartered conspiracy to shred them. We still want to know whether, in the absence of an independent counsel, Justice Department investigator Charles LaBella is even permitted to put this question to Mr. Chung or Mr. Trie.

As tempting as it might be to dismiss Mr. Clinton as a passing rogue, he will establish the precedent for future presidents. Is it the duty of the Secret Service, for example, to cover up presidential crime? Can the President act through his personal law firm to charter a gang of plumbers to investigate and intimidate his opponents? Will Mr. Clinton's breathtaking assertions of executive privilege win another courtroom coup insulating future presidents from accountability not only to the Congress but the courts as well?

Dismissal of the Jones case clearly takes some of the impetus out of the drive to hold the president accountable, certainly in the tabloids and perhaps in the Congress. But at the same time, dismissal may make the issues clearer. The root issue has never been about sex. It has always been about abuse of the powers with which a president is entrusted.

Editorial Feature

Win a Case,
But Lose a Presidency

"I think the president is pleased to receive the vindication he's been waiting a long time for."

—WHITE HOUSE SPOKESMAN MIKE McCURRY

One thing the Clinton presidency never lacks is audacity. Only this White House could take the wreckage left by the Paula Jones case and call it a triumph.

Consider the fruits of famous victory:

- an admission under oath by Mr. Clinton that he indeed slept with Gennifer Flowers, meaning he lied to the country when he denied it in 1992;

Potomac Watch

By Paul A. Gigot

- an admission, by former beauty queen Elizabeth Ward Gracen, that she was asked by the Clinton campaign in 1992 to lie about her tryst with Mr. Clinton;

- the revelation of an unusual, to say the least, "relationship" in the Oval Office with a White House intern barely older than his daughter;

- tape-recorded statements by that intern, Monica Lewinsky, that the president suggested she could deny their relationship, and that Mr. Clinton himself has lied under oath about it;

- the ruin of Hillary Rodham Clinton as a plausible feminist spokeswoman, given her silence at the many accusations of harassment against her husband;

- and the assertion of executive privilege, both for White House aides and for Mrs. Clinton, far broader than even Richard Nixon dared to claim.

All of these uplifting facts, and many more, have become public record as the result of Paula Jones's charges. OK, nobody's perfect. But does any of this sound like something Harry Truman would call "vindication"? Merely recounting the list shows how much the Jones case has made a shambles of Mr. Clinton's moral leadership.

Bill Clinton

And the damage is a long way from done. Judge Susan Webber Wright's dismissal spares the president the spectacle of a sex trial next month. But he may miss the Jones case before his ordeal is through. By clearing away the fog about sex, Judge Wright has now forced everyone to confront the harder legal facts about perjury and witness tampering.

Sex has been Mr. Clinton's ironic political shield. Many Americans seem to buy the White House spin that presidential adultery is a private matter—even if it's conducted in the Oval Office study. Americans have also developed a healthy skepticism about sexual accusations of all kinds. They certainly won't impeach a president for them.

Monica Lewinsky

But Kenneth Starr is building a criminal and not a sex case, as the White House well knows. That's why it unleashed its spinners so ferociously on him after the Jones dismissal. Their new strategy is a public-private whiplash: In public, berate Mr. Starr for taking so long. But in private, make privilege claims (especially for confidant/fixer Bruce Lindsey) that will take months to reach the Supreme Court.

That's also a public signal to Ms. Lewinsky and her erratic attorney, William Ginsburg, that they can delay cooperating too. Mr. Ginsburg seems willing to jeopardize his client's future rather than have her explain what's on those tapes. His gamble seems to be that without Ms. Lewinsky, Mr. Starr has no good case against the president and so won't indict either one.

But Mr. Starr's case against her seems very strong. What if Mr.

Starr sends his report to Congress, while indicting her and naming the president an unindicted co-conspirator?

It's true Republicans may not consider that enough to impeach. But Congress also has other options. Republicans are now considering what Georgia Rep. John Linder calls "informational hearings" that could let Mr. Starr make his case in public over several days. The sight of the bookish, methodical ex-judge laying out evidence of lying would take the public far away from sex.

Sooner or later, Linda Tripp's tapes will also emerge—and those too will be educational. "I think the fish has to be out there long enough for the American people to see how rotten it is," says Mr. Linder, who leads the House GOP re-election effort this fall. Landing in summer or fall, such facts might help voters render their own judgment on Mr. Clinton's behavior this November.

So the president is likely to survive, but at the price of a broad public disdain for his honesty and ethics. And maybe that's the best way to perceive his "vindication" in the Jones case.

When Paula Jones first made her charges, I doubted her in this space. I'm suspicious of late hits and believe in the presumption of innocence. But nothing she's said has damaged Mr. Clinton more than his own responses to her. His agents smeared her, his lawyers sought to deny her a day in court, and he is suspected of obstructing justice.

Now her case has been dismissed—not because a jury found her charges untrue, but because a judge found they didn't reach the Arkansas legal standard of a "claim of outrage." What a proud moment in presidential history.

Editorial Feature

Was Wright Wrong?
Who Knows?

By Eugene Volokh

What does Wednesday's dismissal of Paula Jones's lawsuit against President Clinton mean for the future of sexual harassment law? And what effect will it have on Kenneth Starr's investigation of the president? In both cases, the answer is almost certainly: Not much. Sexual harassment law will remain hopelessly muddled, and Mr. Starr's investigation will go on.

* * *

What is sexual harassment? Courts have been struggling with this for 20 years, and still haven't really figured it out. In *Jones v. Clinton*, Judge Susan Webber Wright held that it isn't sexual harassment for an employer to expose himself indecently to an employee and explicitly ask her for sexual services. Even if Ms. Jones's charges are true, Judge Wright concluded, Mr. Clinton's conduct wasn't "severe" enough to create a "hostile environment." No need for a jury trial about the facts—as a matter of law, the behavior that Mr. Clinton was charged with isn't harassment.

Not all judges are so forgiving, however. Six weeks ago, the New Jersey Supreme Court held that a single epithet said by a supervisor to a subordinate could be harassment, if a jury so finds. Indecent exposure, of course, is much more serious than a slur—after all, indecent exposure is a crime, while epithets are not. Presumably, then, if one of the New Jersey justices had sat in Judge Wright's seat, the Jones decision would have gone the other way.

Likewise, two weeks ago the Second U.S. Circuit Court of Appeals held that harassment cases should go to the jury if the legal issues are a close call. "Today, while gender relations in the workplace are rapidly evolving," the court wrote, "a jury made up of a cross-section of our heterogeneous communities provides the appropriate institution for deciding whether borderline situations should be characterized as sexual harassment."

Other appellate courts, on the other hand, set the bar higher. Trial judges, they say, should throw out harassment cases unless the alleged conduct is considerably more severe than it would have to be in the Second Circuit. But even these appellate courts have never decided how "severe" indecent exposure is.

Paula Jones

So was Judge Wright right or wrong? As a practical matter, that question will be decided by the Eighth Circuit Court of Appeals, to which Ms. Jones will almost certainly appeal Judge Wright's ruling. But in terms of the law, the terms "right" and "wrong" may make little sense when we're talking about hostile environment harassment decisions. The law is so mushy that it really is a matter of which judge or jury you draw.

Hostile environment harassment law doesn't require evidence of sexual extortion. (Another form of harassment, "quid pro quo harassment," does require such evidence, and Judge Wright was probably right to conclude that Ms. Jones didn't have enough evidence for her quid pro quo harassment claim.) Hostile environment law doesn't require evidence of tangible career damage, or even of psychological injury.

The only test is whether a "reasonable jury" could find that someone's speech or conduct was "severe" enough to create a "hostile, abusive or offensive work environment" for the plaintiff and for a reasonable person, based on the plaintiff's sex, religion, race, national origin, veteran status, age, disability or any of a growing list of other categories. What exactly do "severe," "hostile," "abusive" and "offensive" mean? Nobody knows. Judge Wright's guess is as good as any.

This sort of vague, subjective law is a recipe for injustice. It makes it impossible for both employees and employers to tell what's legal and what's not. Setting aside indecent exposure, is it illegal for people to tell sexually themed jokes, perhaps ones about Bill Clinton, at work? I've read several articles in which employment experts have suggested that Clinton-Lewinsky jokes might indeed qualify as harassment. Is it illegal to put up reproductions of classical paintings depicting nudity? To make sexist political statements in the lunchroom? Nobody knows until the case goes to court.

Vague laws make it easy for the result to turn on a judge's or a jury's prejudices, whether conscious or not. It's always tempting to excuse conduct by those you like, and condemn conduct by those you dislike—and protean words like "severe" or "abusive" abet this unfortunate impulse.

We tell judges and jurors to set aside their personal views and follow the law, but how can they do so when there's no tangible law to follow? Judge Wright may have decided the case entirely objectively. But the law certainly didn't help her do that.

* * *

What about the Starr investigation? Does Mr. Clinton's courtroom victory render obstruction-of-justice allegations moot? Clearly not. A strong legal case does not provide a license to lie under oath or interfere with the administration of justice. If Mr. Clinton committed perjury or urged other witnesses to commit perjury, Judge Wright's decision won't scotch any possible prosecution.

Perjury is defined as a false, material statement made under oath. To be "material," a statement in a deposition must touch on a matter that's relevant to the case, or that can lead to discovery of relevant information. Answers to completely tangential questions don't qualify. If you're on trial for speeding and you lie about whether you're wearing a toupee, that's probably not material.

But the test is whether the matter is relevant—that is, potentially capable of influencing the result of the case, even indirectly. It is not whether the matter *actually* influences the result. Perjury laws are meant to protect the integrity of the justice system by ensuring truthful testimony; their effect would be weakened if one could get off the hook whenever, in retrospect, it turned out that the lie didn't help. In this case, of course, it's not even clear that it didn't. Suppose Mr. Clinton and other witnesses did lie in their depositions and affidavits in the Jones case. Maybe if the whole truth had come out, Ms. Jones's lawyers could have used it to discover extra evidence strengthening their case—or maybe not.

In any case, we have a pretty good idea of what perjury is. If Ms. Jones's factual allegations against Mr. Clinton are true—of course a huge "if"—then he has perjured himself and suborned perjury. We can then decide if that's the sort of president we want to have.

Meanwhile, of course, we're in the middle of a huge national muddle about the meaning of "sexual harassment." No one—not employers, not employees, not plaintiffs, not defendants, not judges and not juries—knows what the term really ends up covering. And no one knows how much he can legally say in the lunchroom about the conduct of our very own president.

Mr. Volokh teaches at UCLA Law School.

Editorial Feature

Have the Harassment Rules Changed?

By WALTER OLSON

According to the Rev. Jesse Jackson, last week's dismissal of the Paula Jones lawsuit was "planned by God." Mr. Jackson is not the first to confuse federal judges with deities. But his surmise of divine intervention does recall the old saying that God looks after drunks, children and the United States of America—or in this case leaders of the United States of America who are alleged to have behaved like drunken children. At any rate, now that Judge Susan Webber Wright has thrown out the world's most famous employment lawsuit, what can we conclude about the future course of harassment law? In particular, what does it mean for managers worried about their own organizations' liability exposure?

On the one hand, the case has prompted a vast public debate about the dangers and excesses of this newly grown branch of the law, and the public's newfound skepticism about harassment law is likely to be helpful over the long run to employers, as well as to individuals targeted by poorly founded harassment claims. On the other hand, it would be rash to read too much significance into the details of last week's ruling, which (1) doesn't signal any particular change of direction in harassment law, and (2) offers little guidance or precedent for anyone seeking to avoid such charges—an unsurprising fact, given that the Jones case was never very typical of the harassment docket.

Pundits are busy offering a host of supposed lessons of last week's ruling, most of which should be received with great skepticism:

• *From now on, it's one free flash or grope per employee.* It's "open season on women here in this country," claims Jones spokeswoman Susan Carpenter-McMillan. "Sleazy bosses popping corks all across America" ran the headline over Andrea Peyser's New York Post column.

But as most commentators have realized, Ms. Jones lost not because the judge declared any sort of blanket immunity for the general category of behavior charged, but because of the defects in her particular case. Ms. Jones's outrage-related charges were weak because she had trouble showing that she had reacted with the severe distress that most women would presumably experience if they encountered a flasher. Her employment-related charges were weak because she had trouble showing that her later job conditions were affected. Either hurdle might have been overcome had Ms. Jones taken relatively simple steps during her employ with the state, such as visiting a counselor. A would-be harasser would be foolish to imagine he can count on his victims' doing nothing to document their discomfiture.

• *Something must have been going on with this judge.* To the editorialists at the New York Post, the judge's "shocking and questionable" ruling "raises the suspicion that she was trying a bit of jurist nullification." But other editorialists on the right sharply differed: "In fact, Judge Susan Webber Wright was simply striking a blow for legal sanity in sexual harassment cases," wrote the impeccably conservative Detroit News, while the Chicago Tribune agreed that the judge acted "properly and courageously."

Mr. Clinton may not have been suspiciously lucky to draw this particular judge, but he was lucky. One of the open secrets of our court system is that judges differ enormously one from the next in their willingness to screen cases out at the summary judgment stage. Had Mr. Clinton been sued in many other federal courtrooms around the country, or in many state courts where employment defendants almost never win summary judgment, he would today still be headed for a nightmare trial.

• *Now other women will hesitate to press their claims.* If they draw the right conclusions from this case, they'll do the reverse of hesitating: They'll file earlier. Most of the distinctive weaknesses in Ms. Jones's case sprang from her extreme tardiness in getting a case together. The statutes of limitation had run out on many of her prospective legal claims, she'd done little or nothing to document key elements of her case, and she'd allegedly said and done a number of things that worked to undercut her eventual claims. Had she consulted a lawyer early on, she would certainly have been instructed to keep a diary, visit a counselor and take other steps aimed at documenting both emotional distress and difficulties encountered on the job.

• *Companies are going to feel less under the gun on the issue.* Harassment law was full of frightening and unpredictable legal exposure before Wednesday, and none of it has gone away. Employers do win many victories at the summary judgment stage, but such cases are hard to turn into reliable precedent that keeps them from getting sued in the future: Prevailing Supreme Court doctrine encourages lower courts to look at the "totality of the circumstances" in each case anew, rather than developing definite rules that clearly assign or reject liability given a particular pattern.

If a business's operations are confined to one part of the country where federal judges are known as relatively friendly to the dismissal of weak cases at the summary judgment stage, it may have some mild cause to nod with approval. But national employers by definition have to be prepared to be sued anywhere, and would be very ill-advised to relax even if they believe their conduct is beyond reproach.

• *See, the system works after all.* Defenders of the American litigation system are sure to trot this one out, as they did after the O.J. Simpson civil case. But many others will draw a rather different conclusion: Even if the defendant wins in one of these cases, he loses.

Among employment lawyers, a widely observed rule of thumb is that if a case is destined to get past summary judgment, the defendant should offer a substantial settlement. But the lesson of *Jones v. Clinton* is that even cases that aren't strong enough to make it to a jury can inflict ruin on defendants' reputations and pocketbooks. For months experts have criticized Mr. Clinton's refusal to settle the Jones matter with a cash payment at an early point. Mr. Clinton still looks unwise not to have done so, given the damage his reputation has suffered as a result of the "discovery" process. Even if Bob Bennett had been clairvoyant enough to know for certain that the case would be disposed of last week, he would still have been well-advised to recommend paying Ms. Jones almost any sum she wanted. What does this tell us about the economics of modern American litigation?

• *Now that the president has experienced firsthand the plight of defendants in our legal system, maybe he'll start supporting reforms.* Don't count on it. The Jones affair points up the unfairness of any number of rules in our litigation system: the ultraliberal discovery procedures that encourage fishing expeditions, the misbegotten evidence rules that permit harassment complainants to probe the sexual histories of the men they're accusing even if a judge finds the information irrelevant, and the lack of a loser-pays principle. (In harassment law, as in discrimination law more generally, plaintiffs can collect legal fees from defendants if they win, but not vice versa.) In a rational world, we would now proceed to a national debate about how to change those rules so as to protect more defendants against ill-founded claims. But any such reform movement will almost certainly have to proceed without help from the Clinton administration, which now as ever is wedded to the notion of giving litigators the most expansive powers possible.

Clinton adviser David Strauss, a law professor at the University of Chicago, had one of the best analyses of the case's aftermath. "I think we should resist the temptation to say that this shows the system works," he told National Public Radio. "I think it shows something closer to the opposite, which is even a baseless lawsuit that never should have been brought tied up the presidency for many months, dragged his name through the mud, dragged lots of other people's names through the mud, and turned out to be groundless. . . . That just shows the problem with allowing civil litigation to be used as a weapon against the president."

Or, he should have added, against anyone else.

Mr. Olson, a fellow at the Manhattan Institute, is author of "The Excuse Factory: How Employment Law is Paralyzing the American Workplace" (Free Press, 1997).

Great Walls

President Clinton's troubles continued to grow through the spring of 1998. In mid-April, the New York Times reported that he had approved the transfer of missile guidance technology to China at the behest of a major Democratic Party contributor, Loral Space & Communications chairman Bernard Schwartz. The report touched off a new round of Congressional probes and renewed demands for an independent counsel in the campaign finance matter. The calls increased later in April, when news filtered out that the recently installed head of the Justice Department's troubled contributions task force, Charles La Bella, would be departing. "Why in the world would an ambitious prosecutor such as Mr. La Bella walk away from this kind of probe?" the Journal asked. "The most likely answer is frustration."

In the Lewinsky affair, the Clinton stonewall was crumbling. Chief U.S. District Judge Norma Holloway Johnson, overseeing the Starr grand jury, rebuffed White House privilege claims. She refused to create a special "protective function" privilege for Secret Service agents guarding the President, ordering agents to testify. She also ruled that Mr. Starr's need for testimony from Clinton aides Bruce Lindsey and Sidney Blumenthal outweighed White House claims of executive privilege and attorney-client privilege. The White House announced plans to appeal the rulings. In a high-stakes legal show-down, Mr. Starr would soon be headed to the Supreme Court—and into the Oval Office itself.

Review & Outlook

China Syndrome

President Clinton approved the transfer of missile guidance technology to China at the behest of the largest personal contributor to the Democratic Party. He granted the needed waiver despite an ongoing Department of Justice criminal investigation of the same company's earlier transfer of similar technology: a Pentagon study concluding that in the earlier episode "United States national security has been harmed."

That is the essence of a report yesterday by Jeff Gerth of the New York Times (who also reported the original Whitewater story in 1992) concerning satellite launch technology provided by Loral Space and Communications and Hughes Electronics, a subsidiary of General Motors. Loral Chairman Bernard L. Schwartz topped the personal contributions list in 1997; his 1994 trip to China with Commerce Secretary Ron Brown was quickly followed by a memo to the President from Harold Ickes saying Mr. Schwartz "is prepared to do anything he can for the Administration." Lobbying jointly with Hughes Chairman C. Michael Armstrong, who has gone on to head AT&T, Mr. Schwartz succeeded in softening licensing requirements for export of guidance technology to China.

At one level, this is another round in ongoing disputes over technology exports. In the commercial space satellite business, Loral and Hughes want to use low-cost Chinese launch capability, and of course want the launches to succeed. But the technology they have provided for this purpose will help make military missiles more accurate. The usual arguments revolve around the military importance of the technology, the size of the commercial interests and, probably most significant, whether the same technology is available elsewhere. Within the government, there are nearly always legitimate arguments on both sides of such issues.

Expectations that a President will resolve such issues on the merits, though, have been deeply muddied by the ongoing controversy over the Clinton contributions scandal and Chinese money. The Justice Department is reportedly upset that Mr. Clinton's waiver decision undermined its criminal probe. Perhaps, but this is the same Justice Department that has repeatedly refused to appoint an independent counsel to investigate the Chinese connection. The Gerth story is only the latest reminder that the time for an independent counsel is long past. After all, consider the record:

Janet Reno

Senator Fred Thompson's Governmental Affairs Committee has been in a running controversy over illicit Chinese political contributions. In March it voted out a report identifying six individuals in the campaign finance mess with ties to Beijing—Charlie Trie, John Huang, James and Mochtar Riady, Maria Hsia and Ted Sioeng. The Riadys "had a long-term relationship with a Chinese intelligence agency," the report noted. Ms. Hsia, the central figure in Al Gore's Hsi Lai Temple fund-raiser, was identified as an "agent of the Chinese government."

The Justice Department campaign finance probe has secured indictments of Mr. Trie and Ms. Hsia, and a plea agreement with Democratic Party fund-raiser Johnny Chung on various schemes to funnel money into the 1996 campaign. But these are low-level actions, and there is no sign that they will move the inquiry up the food chain in either Washington or Beijing.

In February 1996, Mr. Trie played White House escort for Wang Jun, head of China's main overseas investment operation, Citic (China International Trust & Investment Corp.). Mr. Wang is also president of China Poly Group Corp., an arms-trading company owned by the People's Liberation Army and connected to military research and development including strategic missile programs. Mr. Wang denies connections with the political contributions.

More than $1 million of the money Mr. Trie funneled into the Clinton campaign came from mysterious Macau entrepreneur Ng Lap Seng. Mr. Ng, our Micah Morrison reported in March, runs a Macau nightclub frequented by officers of the PLA, as well as the Wo On Lok triad crime syndicate. In January, Mr. Ng was rewarded by Beijing with an appointment to the Chinese People's Consultative Conference in the capital; two other Macau figures who have visited with President Clinton, casino magnate Stanley Ho and Macau legislator Chen Kai-kit, received the same honor.

Ted Sioeng, another campaign contributor named in the Thompson report, turned up back in Asia in the company of Cambodian tycoon Theng Bunma, who has been barred from entering the United States because of drug trafficking. And then there is John Huang, the former Riady employee with a high-level security clearance who spent 18 months reading raw intelligence data while working as a Commerce Department official and then transferred to the Democratic National Committee after a meeting with the President and others on September 13, 1995.

In all of these contacts, Mr. Clinton was interested in campaign contributions; the question is what the other side wanted. The significance of the Gerth report is that it may have not been merely face-time or intelligence on commercial negotiations; national security issues were also in play. If the Justice Department is really alarmed by the President undercutting an investigation, it's time for Attorney General Janet Reno to do the right thing in chartering an independent counsel to take over the whole contributions issue.

Editorial Feature

What We Know

By WILLIAM J. BENNETT

Whenever the subject is scandal, President Clinton's apologists argue that his critics fail to distinguish facts from "mere allegations." The public, they aver, should withhold judgment until the facts are in. Implicit is the notion that there is no empirical basis from which to draw inferences and render reasonable judgments. In the wake of Judge Susan Webber Wright's dismissal of the Paula Jones lawsuit, the Clintonites have been emboldened; they are frantically claiming that we know nothing.

But in fact we know quite a lot. There are many important questions, arising from facts, about whether our president has (among other things) committed perjury, suborned perjury and obstructed justice. Given that the Clinton administration employs a nonstop, dust-in-your-eyes machine, it is important to recapitulate what we know:

• *Monica Lewinsky.* We know the president has denied, under oath and in public statements, any criminal wrongdoing and any sexual relations with "that woman." But we also know there are 20 hours of tape recordings between Ms. Lewinsky and her erstwhile colleague Linda Tripp, in which Ms. Lewinsky goes into detail about her affair with the president, and in which, according to people who have heard the tapes, she claims Mr. Clinton directed her to testify falsely in the Paula Jones case. We know, too, that Ms. Lewinsky's lawyer, William Ginsburg, gave Independent Counsel Kenneth Starr a "proffer" of testimony in which Ms. Lewinsky reportedly confirmed a sexual relationship with Mr. Clinton.

Extensive Personal Attention

We know that Ms. Lewinsky told others about her encounters with the president, and that others claim to have heard Mr. Clinton's messages left on Ms. Lewinsky's home answering machine. We know that under oath Ms. Tripp said she was told by Ms. Lewinsky to "lie and deny," and that Ms. Lewinsky passed along to Ms. Tripp three pages of "talking points" giving her instructions on how to lie under oath.

We know the president gave Ms. Lewinsky gifts that have been turned over to investigators, and that she sent courier packages to the president. We know that, according to lawyers familiar with Ms. Lewinsky's proffer who were quoted in the New York Times, the proffer says the pres-

Monica Lewinsky

ident told Ms. Lewinsky she would not have to turn over the gifts, subpoenaed by Ms. Jones's lawyers, if she did not have them in her possession. We know that Ms. Lewinsky turned the gifts over to Mr. Clinton's personal secretary, Betty Currie, who subsequently gave them to Mr. Starr's investigators. And we know that many former and current Clinton aides do not believe the president when he says that nothing sexual happened between himself and Ms. Lewinsky.

We know that Ms. Lewinsky, a former intern, made at least 37 visits to the White House after she was reassigned to the Pentagon, and that Mr. Clinton met with her after she was subpoenaed by Ms. Jones's lawyers. We know that Ms. Lewinsky received extensive personal attention and job-placement help from Vernon Jordan, a Washington power broker and Clinton confidant. We know that Ms. Lewinsky told Ms. Tripp that until Mr. Jordan got her a job, she would refuse to file her affidavit declaring that she never had sexual relations with the president, according to lawyers familiar with the case. We know that Ms. Lewinsky received a job offer from Revlon after Mr. Jordan personally called Ron Perelman, chairman of Revlon's parent company, on her behalf.

We know that Ms. Lewinsky received a job offer from U.N. Ambassador Bill Richardson after meeting with him at the Watergate complex, where Ms. Lewinsky lives. We know that according to Ms. Lewinsky's proffer, as reported in the Times, Mr. Clinton told her that if she were in New York, she might be able to avoid testifying in the Jones lawsuit. And we know that Ms. Lewinsky's job offers came from New York.

● *Betty Currie.* We know that on a Sunday in January, the day after his deposition in the Paula Jones case, Mr. Clinton met with Betty

Betty Currie

Currie. According to lawyers familiar with her testimony, he posed and answered a series of questions to guide her through an account of his relationship with Ms. Lewinsky. We know that in his deposition the president placed Betty Currie at the center of all Lewinsky-related matters, and that Mr. Clinton told Ms. Lewinsky (according to those familiar with her proffer) that she could explain her White House visits as trips to see Ms. Currie. And we know Mr. Clinton took Ms. Currie, one of the crucial witnesses in the Starr investigation, on his recent trip to Africa.

● *Kathleen Willey.* We know that when Ms. Jones's lawyers subpoenaed any letters from Kathleen Willey, Mr. Clinton falsely denied that

he had any such documents. Two months later, after Ms. Willey went public on "60 Minutes" with her allegations of presidential groping, Mr. Clinton personally approved the release of 15 notes and letters in an effort to discredit her. We know Mr. Clinton claimed through his lawyer that he had "no specific recollection" of his meeting with Ms. Willey, and later said that he "has a very clear memory" of the meeting. We know that according to Ms. Willey's sworn statement, she was sexually molested by the president. We

Kathleen Willey

know that two months after Ms. Willey was subpoenaed in the Paula Jones case, Democratic fund-raiser Nathan Landow flew her to his estate, where, according to sources familiar with Ms. Willey's grand jury testimony, Mr. Landow pressed her not to say anything about her encounter with Mr. Clinton.

● *Gennifer Flowers.* We know that Hillary Clinton told "60 Minutes" in 1992 that "part of what I believe with all my heart is that the voters are tired of people who lie to them." We know that during the same interview Mr. Clinton denied that he had an affair with Gennifer Flowers. And we know that six years later, when asked under oath if he ever had sexual relations with Ms. Flowers, Mr. Clinton answered yes. We know that on the matter of the affair, Mr. Clinton is on tape telling Ms. Flowers: "Deny it." And we know Ms. Flowers is on tape telling Mr. Clinton: "The only thing that concerns me . . . at this point, is the state job," to which Mr. Clinton replies, "Yeah, I never thought about that. . . . If they ever ask if you've talked to me about it, you can say no." And we know that Ms. Flowers testified under oath that when she told Mr. Clinton she had lied to a grievance committee, he said, "Good for you."

• *Stonewalling.* We know that while publicly pledging cooperation, the White House has followed a strategy of stonewalling and blocking inquiries from both Ms. Jones's lawyers and Mr. Starr's office. We know that for weeks the president made the fictitious claim that he could not comment on the Lewinsky matter because he was legally required to keep silent. We know that in January the president said of the Lewinsky matter: "You and the American people have a right to get answers. I'd like for you to have more rather than less, sooner rather than later. So we'll work through it as quickly as we can and get all those questions out there to you." And we know that in February, after having answered almost none of the key questions surrounding the Lewinsky story, Mr. Clinton said, "I've told the American people what is essential for them to know about this."

• *Executive privilege.* We know that Mr. Clinton has invoked claims of executive privilege that are even broader than Richard Nixon's—claims few legal scholars defend. We know the president is now claiming his lawyers are asserting executive privilege without his knowledge: "The first time I learn about a lot of these legal arguments is when I see them in the paper," Mr. Clinton told a reporter. We know that in 1994 Mr. Clinton said of asserting executive privilege, "It's hard for me to imagine a circumstance in which that would be an appropriate thing for me to do." And we know that in 1994, then-White House counsel Lloyd Cutler wrote a memorandum in which he said it is White House practice "not to assert executive privilege" in circumstances involving communications relating to investigations of personal wrongdoing by government officials.

• *Procuring and silencing women.* We know that state troopers who served on Mr. Clinton's Arkansas security detail have sworn under oath they procured women for then-Gov. Clinton; that Mr. Clinton acknowledges that he spoke to the troopers' former supervisor, Buddy Young, about their disclosures; that three state troopers have testified under oath that they or their families were threatened by Clinton associates if they talked; and that Dolly Kyle Browning said under penalty of perjury that her own brother, a 1992 Clinton campaign worker, warned her that if she talked about her alleged sexual relationship with Mr. Clinton, "we will destroy you." We know that people have testified under oath that Mr. Clinton helped secure government jobs for women with whom he had affairs, and that lawyer John B. Thompson has said under oath that his friend M. Samuel Jones told him Mr. Jones was paying women for their silence.

• *Private investigators and attempts to discredit the independent counsel.* We know that on Feb. 22 the White House issued a categorical denial that it "or any of President Clinton's private attorneys has hired or authorized any private investigator to look into the background of . . . investigators, prosecutors or reporters." We know that the next day Terry Lenzner said that his firm, Investigative Group Inc., had been retained by the law firm representing Mr. Clinton in Mr. Starr's investigation, and that Mr. Lenzner said if his investigators were looking into the backgrounds of members of Mr. Starr's staff, "I'd say there was nothing inappropriate about that." We know that James Carville declared "war" on the independent counsel, something no one acting on behalf of an administration had ever done before. And we know White House officials have talked about "our continuing campaign to destroy Ken Starr."

We know, too, that if the president is innocent of the felony allegations against him, a vast number of people, representing all points on the political spectrum, must have committed perjury.

The steady march toward impeachment hearings is not surprising; abuse of power, obfuscation, thuggery and an ends-justify-the-means mentality are the coin of the Clinton realm. In 1992 Mr. Clinton promised us "the most ethical administration in the history of the republic." Since then, five independent counsels have been appointed to investigate high administration officials; Attorney General Janet Reno has asked Mr. Starr to expand his mandate on three separate occasions; and even before the latest scandals broke, Mr. Clinton presided over one of the most scandal-plagued administrations in the history of the republic.

The infamous acts include the improper acquisition of some 900 FBI files; the mysterious reappearance (in the Clintons' private living quarters) of subpoenaed billing records, crucial to a Federal Deposit Insurance Corp. investigation, that had purportedly been missing for two years; the administration's misrepresentation about Mrs. Clinton and her commodity trades; the half-million-dollar payments to Webster Hubbell after he was forced to resign in disgrace (including $100,000 from one of James Riady's Hong Kong companies and, with Mr. Jordan's help, $63,000 in "consulting fees" from a holding company controlled by Mr. Perelman); the selling of the Lincoln bedroom; the illegal fund-raising calls made from the White House; the president's videotaped statement to donors that, contrary to his previous denials, he was illegally raising soft money to pay for re-election ads; the White House's failure to turn over to congressional investigators videotapes of Mr. Clinton's coffees with political donors until months after they were requested; its failure to turn over subpoenaed notes by White House aide Bruce Lindsey until the day after the Senate's Whitewater Committee's authorization expired; the improper use of the FBI to bolster false White House claims of financial malfeasance in the firing of the White House Travel Office; and the efforts to obstruct the Resolution Trust Corp.'s investigation of the failed Arkansas thrift, Madison Guaranty Savings & Loan.

Salt in the Soil

The effects of the Clinton scandals will be severe—particularly if the president, because of public indifference and congressional diffidence, escapes accountability until the history books are written years from now. If that happens, it will undercut efforts toward the moral education of the young, increase cynicism and further erode public trust in our political leaders. Indeed, Mr. Clinton has already devalued the office of the presidency. It is axiomatic that the actions of the president strongly influence what the nation talks about; consider, then, the nature of our public discourse these days. He is bringing us down. Through his tawdry, reckless, irresponsible conduct, he has plowed salt in America's civic soil. For that, and for much else, he has rightfully earned our obloquy.

Mr. Bennett is author of "Our Sacred Honor: Words of Advice From the Founders in Stories, Letters, Poems and Speeches" (Simon & Schuster, 1997).

REVIEW & OUTLOOK

Hale Storm

Kenneth Starr formally has the support of editorialists at the New York Times, though they get prissy whenever the independent counsel's critics find something to criticize. So when he subpoenaed White House hatchetman Sidney Blumenthal, the Times saw it as "an attack on press freedom and the unrestricted flow of information."

This week there's a new flurry of criticism, concerning allegations that some money from The American Spectator may have reached David Hale, a potential Whitewater witness against President Clinton. Attorney General Reno unjudiciously told her press conference that yes, this needs to be investigated. Her deputy, Eric Holder, released a tendentious letter to Mr. Starr asserting that while the independent counsel had jurisdiction, he had conflicts. U.S. District Court Judge Henry Woods down in Arkansas also has taken it upon himself to demand an investigation, echoing the usual crew at the White House.

So we have the U.S. government marshaling its powers to investigate how a magazine spent its money reporting stories highly critical of the incumbent Administration. The Spectator, while accepting money from Richard Scaife, is clearly a bona fide publication, with a circulation of more than 200,000. But so far as we've been able to see, none of the publications reporting this story sees any attack on press freedom here. The Times decrees, "These charges need to be examined quickly."

The charges about the Hale money came from an Internet magazine called Salon (paid circulation zip), based on quotes from somebody's former girlfriend. We do not believe all the folks writing about this happened across Salon while browsing the Web. It seems to us, rather, that the flurry of stories has Mr. Blumenthal's fingerprints all over it. And it's not about the Spectator. The press is missing the free press angle, and also the real point of the matter. To wit, that Mr. Hale goes on trial next week in Arkansas.

The Hale trial is a story in itself. Mr. Hale is, of course, the key witness in one of the most damaging allegations against President Clinton—that he cooked up an illegal $300,000 loan and funneled some of the money to the Clinton-McDougal Whitewater land deal. He's being charged under state law for insurance fraud. His attorney David Bowden asserts, without contradiction that we've seen, that in "the entire history of Arkansas, no one other person has ever been prosecuted under the statute utilized against Mr. Hale."

David Hale

When the insurance-fraud charges were first suggested, Mr. Starr noted that Mr. Hale was one of his cooperating witnesses; ultimately he was instrumental in the conviction of former Governor Jim Guy Tucker and Susan and Jim McDougal. The independent counsel wrote that it would be "highly unusual, if not unprecedented, for a state prosecutor to initiate separate criminal charges against an individual cooperating in an important federal investigation, during the course of that person's cooperation."

Nonetheless, Mark Stodola, then prosecuting attorney for Pulaski County, insisted on pressing the charges. At the time he was one of three candidates in the Democratic primary contending for an open Congressional seat; he was defeated in a runoff. His former deputy, Larry Jegley, is now continuing the prosecution.

In his letter to Attorney General Janet Reno, Hale lawyer Bowden charged that Mr. Stodola received campaign contributions from Charlie Trie and William Kennedy III, both Clinton friends. And also from Truman Arnold, the Texas millionaire who was a big Clinton backer. Why, Mr. Bowden asked, would Mr. Arnold "be making such large contributions to a local prosecutor in Central Arkansas?" Sam Dash, the former Watergate prosecutor who serves as Mr. Starr's ethics adviser, met with Mr. Stodola in January 1996, and told the Arkansas Democrat-Gazette that the prosecutor appeared to be under "heavy political pressure."

"Mr. Hale has provided information that is damaging to the President of the United States," Mr. Starr wrote in the letter to Ms. Reno he released yesterday, saying this means the Justice Department has its own conflicts, and suggesting a meeting to set up "alternative" investigatory mechanisms. Yet it seems to us that this new flurry of charges against an adversary magazine and an adversary witness lies smack in the middle of Mr. Starr's mandate. What we have here is the use of prosecutorial powers in Arkansas, and also the Justice Department in Washington, to protect Bill Clinton against David Hale; what needs to be investigated is further abuses of the power invested in the President of the United States.

Editorial Feature

Chile Con Carey: What Bill Did For the Teamsters

So you want to sign a treaty with Uncle Sam? Better hope the Uncle who's signing hasn't cut an under-the-table deal with the Teamsters to help himself win a second term.

That's what Latin American leaders may be thinking this weekend in Chile as they listen to President Clinton promote "free trade for the Americas." It's a fine vision. It ought to be part of his legacy.

But this is also the same president who has quietly reneged on part of his most recent American trade deal, the one with Mexico. Thus do other leaders understand how White House scandal has damaged U.S. foreign policy, even if most Americans avert their eyes.

Potomac Watch

By Paul A. Gigot

This too-little-known tale starts with Mr. Clinton's Nafta achievement of 1993. While the pact was George Bush's idea, this president did well to sell it to his own hostile Democratic coalition. One of Nafta's most important planks was to allow full and easy access by U.S. and Mexican truckers across the border. Commerce would be speeded up, transport costs reduced, living standards raised.

"We're unequivocally ready for December 18th," said then Transportation Secretary Federico Peña, just two weeks before the cross-border trucks were supposed to roll in 1995. He must have been out of the loop. Because on Dec. 18, the very day of implementation, the White House unilaterally backed out. It postponed the trucking deal because of concern about "safety."

This was odd. Mr. Peña had discounted the safety worries just two weeks earlier. Every Mexican truck would be subject to the same rules as U.S. trucks. Texas alone had hired 109 new troopers and opened four new inspection stations for the job. All four U.S. border-state governors were eager to move ahead.

So what really happened? All signs suggest this was part of the quo that Mr. Clinton paid for the quid that the Teamsters provided during the 1996 election campaign. The evidence is piled higher than the Himalayas in the Senate's recent report on campaign fund-raising.

Keep in mind that the Teamsters had long been the one big union that sometimes backed Republicans. But with new (and since defrocked) president Ron Carey at the helm in the mid-1990s, the Clinton team saw a chance to make the union a wholly owned subsidiary.

"We are in a good position to rekindle the Teamster leadership's enthusiasm for the Administration," says a 1995 set of "Teamster Notes" underlined by chief political fixer Harold Ickes. "But they have some parochial issues that we need to work on."

Work they did. One issue was the trucking deal, which would open U.S. roads to nonunion Mexican truckers. A memo from then-Teamster political director William Hamilton says he expressly brought up Mexican trucking in a meeting with Vice President Al Gore. Another Hamilton document includes "stopped the Nafta border crossings" on a list of White House favors performed.

What did Mr. Clinton get in return? Almost certainly lots of cash and thousands of man-hours to help re-elect him and fellow Democrats. Exact numbers aren't known, because the Teamsters are still refusing to turn over most of their own documents to Congress.

But we do know that the U.S. attorney for Southern New York has already won guilty pleas from Teamster consultants for breaking campaign laws. Especially suspect is a "contribution swap scheme" hatched between the Teamsters and the Democratic National Committee in 1996. Democrats hunted for a big donor to

Mr. Carey's re-election campaign while Teamster cash flowed into Democratic coffers.

We also know that Mr. Hamilton took the Fifth rather than testify before Congress. And we know that a House committee investigating the Teamsters has turned up evidence suggesting that a union with net worth of some $150 million in the early 1990s is now all but broke. Wonder where all of that money went?

Odder yet, even this long after his re-election, Mr. Clinton still hasn't budged on Nafta trucking. Mexico has protested to no avail, despite a Clinton visit last year. Border-state congressmen who ask questions, such as GOP Texas Rep. Henry Bonilla, get the runaround.

My guess is that as long as the threat of scandal hangs over him, Mr. Clinton figures he can't afford to upset his union allies. Especially not anyone who could cooperate with investigators. That's also why the president won't try again to get fast-track trade power passed this year, though he claims he wants it. There's also Mr. Gore's election in 2000 to think about—he'd like Teamster help too.

*   *   *

All politicians do favors for friends. But no president until this one has dared to trade a hard-won national commitment merely for campaign cash. Nafta was a sovereign U.S. promise, made by no less than Mr. Clinton himself. To renege on even part of it hurts not just his credibility but also America's.

Such behavior has consequences. In Chile this weekend, Brazil's president will sign trade deals that mean something, but America's president won't. Mr. Clinton will talk a lot and pose for photographs. That's one legacy of selling a chunk of American foreign policy to the Teamsters.

Editorial Feature

When Susan McDougal Almost Talked

BY CHRIS VLASTO

"I know where all the bodies are buried."

Those were the words that Susan McDougal said to me long before any pundits decided to call her a martyr, something likely to continue after her scheduled appearance today in front of the Whitewater grand jury in Little Rock.

We were sitting in a trailer in Arkadelphia back in the winter of 1994. Ms. McDougal, at the time, was overshadowed by her husband. She shunned the spotlight but at the same time wanted to be pursued. From Little Rock to Los Angeles, Ms. McDougal kept me on a string. She would intrigue me with a cryptic clue and then walk away, leaving me guessing at what she meant to say. Giving only little bits of information, always off-the-record, Susan McDougal was one of the more mysterious characters in the Whitewater saga.

Susan McDougal

It took three years and a felony conviction for her to agree to do an interview. It came suddenly. She called in August 1996 and said she was ready to tell all. She wanted to come to New York without her lawyer's knowledge to be interviewed by Diane Sawyer.

She flew up to New York alone. We met at the Essex House bar to discuss the areas we were going to cover in the interview. The conversation was off-the-record, but at the time she promised she was going to answer all the questions on television.

Overnight, everything changed.

After the arrival of her brother, Bill Henley, and her fiancé, Pat Harris, in the wee hours of the morning, Ms. McDougal began singing a different tune. With the cameras rolling, Ms. McDougal was constantly interrupted by the two men when Ms. Sawyer asked her sensitive questions involving President Clinton. She couldn't get a word in when Ms. Sawyer asked her whether Mr. Clinton knew anything about the illegal $300,000 loan she received from David Hale. The president has denied under oath knowing anything about that loan.

Here's how the interview went:

Ms. Sawyer: "Did Mr. Clinton know anything about your loan?"

Ms. McDougal: "That's probably something that my attorney would not want me to talk about." [To Messrs. Henley and Harris: "I hate that, guys!"] "God, I hate this, Diane! Sorry!"

Ms. Sawyer: "Did he?"

Mr. Henley: "That's a perfect answer."

Ms. McDougal: "Jeez, I hate that though!"

Mr. Henley: "That's the only answer you have."

Ms. McDougal: "That's the only answer I have."

I was confused by her silence. I knew she was angry at Independent Counsel Kenneth Starr, but we at "Prime Time Live" weren't the prosecutors. I asked her fiancé why she wouldn't answer the questions. He said "we have to save something for the prosecutors, we have to give them something." I concluded that she must know something incriminating about Mr. Clinton, and reluctantly accepted her silence.

Ms. McDougal went back to Little Rock to face the federal grand jury. Five days after the taping of our interview, she was cited for contempt of court. I watched Ms. McDougal outside the courthouse stridently declare she wasn't going to answer Mr. Starr's questions, which got her 18 months in jail.

I know she met with her attorney Bobby McDaniel and talked with Alan Dershowitz after our New York interview. But that Wednesday in Little Rock, I saw a completely different Susan McDougal. She no longer told her intriguing tales. After countless conversations, there was silence. Did someone get to her, or was she playing a game with me all along?

She will go before the same grand jury today, to be asked the same old questions. Wherever they are, the bodies are buried deep.

Mr. Vlasto is an investigative producer at ABC News.

Editorial Feature

Praetorian Privilege

They were called the Praetorian Guard. Roughly the same size as the 2,000-member Secret Service, the Praetorians protected the lives and secrets of emperors of Rome and their families. These ancient bodyguards came to mind last week when the Clinton administration asked a federal court to create a sweeping new "protective function" privilege. If the court agrees, the Secret Service would be transformed from a law enforcement organization into something close to a palace guard. These new Praetorians would come with dangerous legal and historical implications.

Rule of Law

By Jonathan Turley

Many presidents have longed to convert the Secret Service, if only in appearance, into a more imperial image. In 1970, Richard Nixon ordered the White House guards to wear Graustarkian uniforms with braided epaulets and helmets. While there was no legal change to match substance to appearance, there was such a public outcry that the uniforms were eventually given to the Southern Utah State College marching band. Under the Clinton plan, the Secret Service would keep their drab uniforms and plain clothes but take on an imperial legal status.

Before considering the imperial Secret Service of the future, it is useful to review the professional Secret Service of the past. Founded in 1865 to fight counterfeiting, the Secret Service was fashioned as a law enforcement agency. In 1901, after the assassination of President McKinley, it was given responsibility for protecting the president and, later, other high U.S. and foreign officials. The Secret Service performed these tasks through various wars and social upheavals, including Watergate, without any special privilege. Quite the contrary; as law enforcement officers, Secret Service members were compelled to share any possible evidence of criminal conduct in their possession. This all changed in 1998. The Secret Service has dealt with dictators and crazed assassins but never before had it encountered the likes of Kenneth Starr.

The president has testified that he did not have a sexual relationship with Monica Lewinsky and never molested Kathleen Willey, despite their statements to the contrary. Since either the president or these women have committed perjury, Mr. Starr wants to question the agents about their White House visits to establish who is lying. That is when the Secret Service suddenly discovered the new privilege that would move its agents outside the legal line of fire.

The Secret Service has never had either a legal or historical commitment to confidentiality. Unlike many government agencies, the Secret Service does not require its agents to sign confidentiality agreements. To the contrary, agents have repeatedly supplied information in criminal and congressional investigations. During Watergate, the Secret Service gave testimony on the taping system in the Oval Office and later supplied documents. During the Bush administration, the Secret Service supplied information clearing Mr. Bush of "October surprise" allegations by showing that he did not meet in Paris with Iranian leaders to delay the release of hostages in Iran.

At times, the Secret Service has more resembled Kitty Kelly than Dudley Do-Right. Presidents from Harding to Clinton have faced the release of personal details from their security staff. Most recently, President Kennedy's sexual escapades were documented by Seymour Hersh with the assistance of Secret Service agents, who supplied the most lurid details.

The new privilege would not, of course, halt such disclosures. It notably doesn't cover former agents or the many White House employees with access to the same information as Secret Service agents. Presidential barbers and pantry staff often hear presidential communications. Are we now to expect a "pantry privilege" for people serving meals and drinks in the Oval Office? Absent such a privilege, the president might refuse sustenance as well as security in order to protect his privacy. In the end, the argument for a new privilege misses a salient point: We shouldn't want the president to feel comfortable speaking about possible criminal conduct in front of public employees.

It is notable that the Clinton administration is attempting to craft a new privilege rather than extend the doctrine of executive privilege. The president cannot use executive privilege to refuse to answer questions of criminal conduct in office. Likewise, White House lawyers cannot use attorney-client privilege to bar questions of criminal acts committed in their presence or with their cooperation. The proposed new privilege for the Secret Service would be broader than both these privileges.

It is worth noting that the Clinton administration's proposed privilege would significantly limit the inquiry called for under the Independent Counsel Act. An independent counsel can be appointed when a president is involved in credible allegations of criminal conduct, but he would be barred from questioning central witnesses in order to protect the president from such intrusive inquiries. Only in Washington can such logic find its way into legal papers.

Now, back to the Praetorians. Fiercely loyal to their masters, they often carried out the secret activities of emperors against the Roman Senate. As an independent and powerful organization, the Praetorians became increasingly direct about their view of good government, including killing Emperor Caligula, whose sexual exploits and depravities shocked even ancient Rome. Ultimately, under Tiberius, the

Praetorians controlled the daily operations of the government by controlling the physical seat of government. While there is a leading alternative model—the eunuchs of the Chinese emperors—this would be understandably less attractive for the Secret Service (though, given the current allegations, perhaps more suitable).

As with the Praetorians, a special privilege for Secret Service agents would create a dangerous concentration of power in this small agency. It is the job of Secret Service agents to reduce access to the president, which only increases the need for their testimony in the absence of other witnesses.

The very function and access of the Secret Service places its members at continual risk of becoming willing or unwilling participants in criminal conduct by executive branch officers. In such circumstances, it's not hard to see how agents could play an active role in assisting a coverup of a criminal act by a president and then insist on immunity from any testimony about their knowledge. It is essential that these federal officers must not be free to refuse to testify about possible criminal acts. Otherwise, the Secret Service could all too readily evolve into a Secret Police.

Mr. Turley is a professor at George Washington Law School in Washington, D.C.

REVIEW & OUTLOOK

Call La Bella

Attorney General Janet Reno blandly confirmed Friday that Charles La Bella, installed only seven months ago to inject some credibility into the Justice Department's listless campaign-finance investigation, is departing to become interim U.S. Attorney in San Diego. The weekend press took this as a face-value yawn; with the Paula Jones trial sex charges off center stage, we guess, no one can see anything going on.

Yet the La Bella departure is a stunning development—all the more so since his FBI counterpart, Charles Desarno, is also departing. Also on Friday, Presidential boyhood pal Thomas (Mack) McLarty tearfully severed his last official ties with the White House. We also learned that with the AFL-CIO having served as the Democrats' moneybag, Richard Trumka, its number-two man, invoked the Fifth Amendment in refusing to testify before a House panel headed by Rep. Peter Hoekstra. And on Saturday, Independent Counsel Kenneth Starr conducted his sixth interrogation of Hillary Clinton, pointing toward the conclusion of the Arkansas phase of his investigation.

The self-evident collapse of Justice's campaign finance probe is worth attention on its own. Ms. Reno first turned down Congressional requests for an independent counsel on campaign finance in November 1996, when she was under attack by anonymous White House sources for not being a "team player" and after saying out loud she wanted to keep her job in a second term. Relieved from what accounts called "political limbo" after a December 12 visit with the President, she went on to reject two further requests as ever more information cascaded into public view.

It has long been clear that what needs investigation is the appearance of a Presidentially led conspiracy to shred the campaign finance laws. The President's agents—John Huang, Charlie Trie, James Riady, Mark Middleton, etc.—are at the center of a maze of illegally raised money. The President himself launched Mr. Huang's career as a senior Democratic National Committee fund-raiser at a September 13, 1995 White House meeting that included Mr. Huang, Mr. Riady, senior fixer Bruce Lindsey and Arkansas wheeler-dealer Joseph Giroir. The Vice President also led an illegal fund-raiser at the Hsi Lai Buddhist Temple in California. Despite this record, and despite the urging of FBI Director Louis Freeh, Ms. Reno has consistently asserted there is no "specific" and "credible" allegation of a crime.

Charles La Bella

Mr. La Bella's appointment was intended to smooth over this record by reinvigorating Justice's own probe. We initially expressed skepticism over his spectacular loss in the Imelda Marcos racketeering case but, as we've more recently remarked, he has won the respect of Congressional investigators. And he did finally indict Mr. Trie and Maria Hsia, the central figure in Mr. Gore's temple fundraiser, and obtained a guilty plea from fund-raiser Johnny Chung.

Up the food chain from these small fish, much evidence hints at real national damage. For example, Senator Fred Thompson's investigating committee voted out a report, based in part on classified intelligence briefings, that identified six campaign finance figures as having ties to the Communist government in China. The Beijing Six include James Riady, who "had a long-term relationship with a Chinese intelligence agency," and Ms. Hsia, who "has been an agent of the Chinese government." The others are Mr. Huang, Mr. Trie, Lippo Group patriarch Mochtar Riady, and businessman Ted Sioeng. The principals deny the accusations, and the Democratic minority on the Thompson Committee contends that the evidence isn't conclusive.

Now we learn that President Clinton approved the transfer of missile guidance technology to China, despite a Pentagon finding that a similar transfer had damaged national security, and despite Justice's own ongoing probe. The approval for the sale by Loral Space and Communications came at the behest of its chairman Bernard L. Schwartz, the largest personal contributor to the Democratic Party in 1997.

Why in the world would an ambitious prosecutor such as Mr. La Bella walk away from this kind of probe? The most likely answer is frustration. When Mr. La Bella was appointed, Susan Schmidt and Roberto Suro of the Washington Post reported on the previous Justice probe. They reported that Justice investigators were precluded from investigating anyone covered by the Independent Counsel Act, so the probe "studiously avoided" seeking such information. One lawyer in the investigation told them, "You can't ask someone whether a covered person committed a crime."

The Justice Department says that quote "did not and does not accurately characterize the procedures followed by the Campaign Financing Task Force." Its spokesman adds that the Attorney General has said many times that both before and during Mr. La Bella's tenure the task force "had the authority to pursue all leads wherever they lead." Yet Mr. La Bella's probe is sputtering out like the one before it.

Faced with the kind of obstacles the Schmidt-Suro story described, getting out as gracefully as possible would be the second thing an energetic prosecutor would do. The first would be to recommend an independent counsel, as so many others before him have done. Asked whether Mr. La Bella has done this, a Justice spokesman says, "The Justice Department has not commented on its internal deliberations during the Task Force's ongoing criminal investigation."

Seems to us someone in Congress would have the power, and the obligation, to find out.

REVIEW & OUTLOOK

No Interest at Justice

Representative Dan Burton's campaign finance probe has a chance to redeem itself in hearings tomorrow. Last week Henry Waxman's Democrats found an opening against Chairman Burton to reduce the hearings to a farce, obscuring the 90-some potential witnesses who've taken the Fifth Amendment or fled the country, and also the Democrats' refusal to immunize even the smallest of small fry to continue the inquiry.

We wait to see what Mr. Waxman has in store for tomorrow's tale of political contributions and laxity at the Justice Department against a backdrop of banking crimes and serious drug suspicions. The story concerns 1992 contributions directed by one Charles Intriago, Florida Democratic fund-raiser and publisher of a newsletter, usually well-regarded in law enforcement circles, titled Money Laundering Alert. When Chairman Burton's investigators tried to interview Mr. Intriago, he joined the Fifth Amendment brigade and hopped the next plane back to Miami. Instead, the hearings tomorrow will feature Jorge Castro Barredo, scion of a Venezuelan banking family and recipient of Mr. Intriago's instructions.

Mr. Castro is now in jail, along with his uncle Orlando Castro Castro and his grandfather, Orlando Castro Llanes. They were convicted in 1997 of banking fraud by Manhattan District Attorney Robert Morgenthau, for luring Latin American depositors into a failing bank they controlled in Puerto Rico. Mr. Morgenthau's case did not concern money laundering, but he has said that his interest in Venezuelan banks arose from suspicions that they were linked to narcotics traffic in New York.

The Morgenthau investigation turned up a fax, pictured here, to Mr. Castro Barredo from Mr. Intriago directing political contributions by "you" and "Maria," a Castro in-law; both were U.S. citizens and eligible to make political contributions. But after agreeing to cooperate with prosecutors in return for a lighter sentence, Mr. Castro revealed that the contributions were reimbursed, as prosecutors put it at his sentencing hearing, "through a wire transfer from a company outside of the United States and controlled by a foreign citizen."

Such contributions would be patently illegal, and Mr. Morgenthau gave federal prosecutors the evidence, which included not only Mr. Castro's account, but supporting bank documents. It went first to the U.S. Attorney in Miami, and then

ALERT INTERNATIONAL, INC.

TELECOPY
1401 Brickell Avenue
Suite 570
P.O. Box 011390
Miami, FL 33101 U.S.A.
Fax: 305-530-9434
Phone: 305-530-0500

FAX #: 809-541-3138   Number of Pages 1
(including cover sheet)
DATE: 9-16-92
TO: Mr. Jorge Castro
AFFILIATION:
FROM: C. Intriago
COMMENT: Jorge
20 - DNC Victory Fund '92 - Fed. Acct. - (you)
20 - DNC Victory Fund '92 - Fed. Acct. - (Maria)
5 - OHIO Victory Fund '92 - Fed. Acct - (you)
5 - MARYLAND Victory Fund '92 - Fed. Acct. - (Maria)
Te ruego que me los mandes hoy por __

was assumed by the Public Integrity Section at Main Justice, which is to say the folks vigorously fighting the appointment of an independent counsel in the campaign contributions scandal. Justice officials came for an interview, and Mr. Morgenthau's office warned that the five-year statute of limitations on the 1992 contributions would soon expire.

When nothing further happened, Mr. Castro's lawyer kept pressing the issue to get his client credit for cooperation. With the final sentencing hearing approaching, Public Integrity head Lee Radek sent a letter saying that while Mr. Castro had cooperated in an interview, "there is at this time no further role for him to play in matters under investigation by the task force."

"[I]t appears as if a corroborated prosecution of political contributions that were illegal was provided to the United States Department of Justice and there's nothing to show for it," declared Judge Edward McLaughlin of the New York Supreme Court at Mr.

Castro's sentencing. "[I]t's not my responsibility nor is it the Justice Department's responsibility to explain any of their decisions; the decision for whatever reason simply stands, but I think in fairness Mr. Castro Barredo must get the benefit of what appears to be his extensive cooperation."

It appears a shame that Public Integrity didn't get on the case before the statute expired. As long ago as April 1996, the New York Times had reported that Mr. Intriago was an old friend of Orlando Castro Llanes, the family patriarch, that indeed Mr. Castro Llanes was a founding partner of Money Laundering Alert and that Mr. Intriago dismissed the conclusion of an investigator for his newsletter who found evidence that as much as $3 billion in mysterious funds had flowed through the Castro bank accounts in New York.

After the 1993 inauguration, Mr. Intriago managed to get Orlando Castro Llanes into the White House for a photo op with President Clinton, producing a photograph useful back in Venezuela. On the same trip, they also visited the State Department, where Mr. Castro Llanes presumably voiced longstanding complaints that he was the victim of rumors spread by Thor Halvorssen, a Venezuelan figure who'd aided Mr. Morgenthau's prosecution of cases involving the Bank of Credit and Commerce International. The flagship of the Castro empire, Banco Progreso, collapsed in the 1994 Venezuelan banking crisis; authorities there have charged that Mr. Castro Llanes looted the system of some $1 billion.

It seems to us this would have been an interesting case for Justice to take up, and that it's quite appropriate for a Congressional Committee to ask whether political contributions and influence may have played some role here. Mr. Waxman, no doubt, will go to the mat proclaiming there's nothing here but a right-wing plot to defame the Clinton Administration.

REVIEW & OUTLOOK

Sweeney and Trumka

The money-laundering scandal involving relationships between unions and the 1996 Clinton-Gore campaign is getting serious scrutiny on Capitol Hill this week. Today Rep. Pete Hoekstra's subcommittee will hear from John Sweeney, the AFL-CIO's president. Mr. Sweeney will be asked why his top deputy, Secretary-Treasurer Richard Trumka, has twice invoked the Fifth Amendment without getting kicked out of his job.

Mr. Trumka has refused to answer questions about his role in the illegal funneling of $200,000 to the 1996 campaign of Teamster President Ron Carey, whose fraudulent re-election has been annulled by federal monitors. There is a 40-year-old AFL-CIO rule expelling officers who take the Fifth to shield themselves from corruption charges. But Mr. Trumka remains in office.

Mr. Sweeney informed his executive council last November that Mr. Trumka would stay in his job because the federation's 1957 policy "calls for removal only when the union determines that the Fifth Amendment is being invoked to conceal discovery of corruption."

So what exactly does Mr. Sweeney think the Trumka invocation was all about, anyway? Last November, Teamster election monitor Kenneth Conboy, the former federal judge who ordered a re-run of the 1996 Teamsters election, issued a report that raises red flags about the role Mr. Trumka and the AFL-CIO played in Mr. Carey's re-election.

Martin Davis, a Carey consultant who has pleaded guilty to

embezzlement of union funds, claimed that Mr. Trumka agreed to launder $150,000 in Teamster-owned funds through the liberal group Citizen Action and then steer it to Mr. Carey's campaign. Furthermore, Mr. Conboy noted that Mr. Davis had asked Mr. Trumka to raise another $50,000 in cash, which was "funneled into

John Sweeney

the Carey campaign." Mr. Conboy also found that top leaders of two other unions, the Service Employees International Union and AFSCME, agreed to participate in similar illegal efforts to help Mr. Carey.

Rep. Hoekstra's inquiry has been stonewalled at every turn. Carey deputies at the Teamsters are refusing to comply with subpoenas for documents that would explain how taxpayers spent some $20 million in 1996 monitoring a worthless union election. The Clinton Administration has also tried to impede the probe. This month it sought to bar Stephen Silbiger, a Labor Department investigator, who had been detailed to work on Capitol Hill, from helping Mr. Hoekstra. Rep. Hoekstra accused Labor officials of not wanting Mr. Silbiger to work with him "because they know how knowledgeable he is." Last week, Labor reversed its decision and approved Mr. Silbiger's assignment to the Teamster probe.

Union leaders like John Sweeney are forever giving speeches in which they claim some sort of moral superiority to their employers' business practices. So now no matter how much union abuse in the 1996 elections surfaces, we're supposed to accept Mr. Sweeney blandly waving it all off the table. If that is indeed the kind of performance on view today when the Hoekstra committee examines the Trumka affair, then perhaps the House should vote the Teamsters in contempt for refusing to turn over relevant records.

Review & Outlook

On Breaking a Stonewall

The steady din coming out of the White House is beginning to sound like summer locusts high in the evening trees: unfair, unfair, unfair, unfair. No matter the subject, source or substance, it's all unfair. Here's Rahm Emanuel scratching over the weekend at House Oversight Committee Chairman Dan Burton: "Never before in history has a chairman done what he has done."

Well, never before in history has so much chutzpah carried so many so far. The weekend doesn't pass that Kenneth Starr, Dan Burton or some other critic of the Clinton compound isn't accused of violating Marquis of Queensbury rules for the manner in which they chip and chisel at the vast stonewall that now separates this White House from the rest of the country.

How else to break a stonewall built with the power of the executive branch and the complicity of Democrats in Congress?

We are reminded of the wonderful colloquy last December between FBI Director Louis Freeh and Rep. Burton.

Mr. Burton: "Over 65 people have invoked the Fifth Amendment or fled the country in the course of the committee's investigation. Have you ever experienced so many unavailable witnesses in any matter in which you have prosecuted or been involved?"

Mr. Freeh: "Actually, I have. . . . I spent about 16 years doing organized crime cases in New York City, and many people were frequently unavailable."

Since that exchange, the number of the unwilling has risen to more than 90 witnesses. Among those pleading the Fifth are key Clinton operatives John Huang and Mark Middleton, Democratic fund-raisers Nora and Gene Lum, Florida witness Charles Intriago, and a gaggle of low-level figures tied to the Al Gore/Hsi Lai Buddhist Temple fund-raiser, to the shakedown of the Arapaho Indian tribes, and to the Charlie Trie network. Mr. Trie's partner Antonio Pan has fled the country, as have key probe figures Ted Sioeng, Pauline Kanchanalak and others. Among those refusing to be interviewed overseas by U.S. investigators are such central figures as the Riadys of Indonesia and Mr. Trie's money source, Ng Lap Seng of Macau.

On April 23, Democrats on Mr. Burton's committee blocked grants of immunity to four witnesses, even as the Justice Department expressed no objection. The four were associates of Johnny Chung, the Lums and Ted Sioeng. Clearly, the committee's 19 Democratic votes against immunity were what caused an impatient Speaker Gingrich's criticisms last week. Still, what seemed to most preoccupy the Beltway through that cycle was whether Mr. Burton had violated community standards by calling the President a scumbag.

Washington's textual deconstructionists were similarly shocked at the release of the Hubbell prison tapes, obsessing over the manner in which they were *edited*, but showing less interest in the tapes' substance—"I guess I have to roll over again"—which more than hints at a coverup.

Janet Reno

All that activity is over in the House of Representatives. The Senate, meanwhile, has been in conversation with career U.S. Attorney Charles La Bella. The air has filled up the past 48 hours with attempts to delegitimize the weekend disclosure of Mr. La Bella's recommendation to Janet Reno in November that she appoint an independent counsel for campaign finance. Against these rationalizations, Senate Republicans should here follow the House's cue and play hardball. And with good reason.

Janet Reno is using the independent counsel law as a shield. In fact, the Attorney General has always had the power to make such an appointment; this is precisely what was done during Watergate and Teapot Dome. The law was created to further *enable* such a decision, not to erect Ms. Reno's casuistical barriers.

Kenneth Starr, for his part, exists as a court officer under that same law, appointed by a decision of the Attorney General and named by three federal judges. This office of independent counsel, in the course of its history, has met with Susan McDougal's contempt of a federal court (leading to a second indictment yesterday), with the White House's inability to disclose Rose Law Firm billing records that later just appeared, with former Associate Attorney General Webster Hubbell's welshing on promised cooperation after pleading guilty to two felonies, and with at least three separate White House claims of privilege.

Each of these is a large stone in the White House stronghold. The serial claims of privilege are especially egregious, given the context. To date, Judge Norma Holloway Johnson has kept Secret Service privilege and executive privilege litigation under seal. Defensible, perhaps, under normal circumstances, but set against the White House's record of suppression, we strongly think these proceedings should be open.

Norma Johnson

On this page recently, attorney Douglas Caddy, who represented E. Howard Hunt and other Watergate Plumbers, described how Judge John Sirica used outrageous sentences to compel cooperation, which is to say, compel the truth. We don't recall screams from civil libertarians then, recognizing we suspect that it takes a hardball to break a stonewall mounted by a President.

One more point about then and now. Eventually in the course of Watergate, GOP politicians who cared deeply about the integrity of public institutions stepped forward and helped justice take its course. Where are such Democrats today? When a Congressional committee has received permission from Justice to immunize four useful witnesses, why is Henry Waxman able to get 19 Democrats to stand solidly in opposition, like a stonewall?

MAY 6, 1998

REVIEW & OUTLOOK

The Teamsters Issue

The Teamsters, the nation's largest union, could yet turn out to be the Democratic Party's Titanic. The question of the moment is how many more icebergs the union and its Democratic friends are going to hit.

Last week it ran headlong into the U.S. Attorney in New York, Mary Jo White, who indicted the Teamsters' former political director, Bill Hamilton, on charges that he funneled money to the Democratic Party in an effort to get its donors to give money to Teamster President Ron Carey's campaign. In that indictment, Ms. White cites nine "DNC overt acts" relating to a "conspiracy" to launder the union's money into the Carey operation.

But even as this investigation proceeds, the Teamsters are somehow supposed to be rerunning that tainted election. Last week, a federal monitor gave the green light for another presidential run by James P. Hoffa, the man Mr. Carey narrowly defeated in the fraudulent 1996 election. But holding a clean election isn't going to be easy.

For starters, it's not clear who will pay for it. Congress has voted to bar taxpayer funding of the rerun, but a Second Circuit court has ruled the Teamsters can't be forced to pay for it. Beyond the funding problem, there's the fact that the Teamsters' central office remains firmly in the hands of Carey loyalists, whose direct involvement in the 1996 election was criticized by Michael Cherkasky, the Election Officer appointed by a federal court. Balloting by the 1.4 million-member union for their new president won't end until late

September, so what's to ensure that the central office won't subvert this election?

In a sensible world the Clinton Administration would install apolitical managers during this vulnerable period. Instead, the political and financial alliances forged during the 1996 campaign, the very ones federal attorney White is investigating, make it unlikely that the Administration will alter control of the Teamsters' central office.

That control could be worth millions in campaign money this fall. In 1996, the Teamsters' political action committee was the nation's largest, giving 97% of its $10 million in contributions to Democrats. The Teamsters contributed $3.4 million to candidates last year and already have some $1 million on hand for the 1998 election.

Even as all this political giving flowed in one direction, the Teamsters were under federal supervision by an Independent Review Board since 1989, when union officials signed a consent decree intended to root out corruption. It is probably not fair to say the consent decree hasn't worked. The Mafia, by comparison, soldiers onward but is no longer in control of New York City's cement deliveries. But it would be fair to say the Teamsters problem now is not so much mob corruption as *political* corruption.

Former federal Judge Kenneth Conboy, in his recent ruling that Mr. Carey couldn't run, said that his campaign involved "a species of labor racketeering." The problem has to do with misuse of the union's own funds. The diversion of funds out of the union and into politics helped cause the union's net worth to fall to only $702,000 last year from $157 million in 1991. The draining of the Teamsters' treasury raises the question of what else has been going on, even as the Independent Review Board watched.

In 1994 the board issued a report clearing Mr. Carey of all corruption charges related to a New York local he had run. A letter written by review board chairman Frederick Lacey a few months before release of that report suggests the board was partial to Mr. Carey. In a letter Mr. Lacey wrote to Thomas Puccio, the court-appointed trustee of a mob-connected Teamster local, Mr. Lacey wrote that he "ought to have in mind what would happen if you brought Carey down in that there were 'old guard' Teamsters throughout the country that were hoping that Carey would be eliminated as a candidate in 1996 so that the clock could be turned back to what it was when I first came on the scene as Independent Administrator."

The Teamsters clock, in fact, has been spinning wildly. We know that U.S. Attorney White has established that AFL-CIO Secretary-Treasurer Richard Trumka sent a letter requesting $150,000 from the Teamsters and that the AFL-CIO then donated an identical amount to Citizen Action, a left-wing group, which in turn paid $100,000 to the November Group, a Carey-connected consulting firm, to send out last-minute mailings trashing Mr. Hoffa. There is evidence that DNC officials attempted a similar money loop from the union's treasury to Democratic state parties to the November Group. Mr. Trumka has twice invoked the Fifth Amendment when asked about these charges.

So the potential criminal liability here includes Messrs. Carey and Trumka as well as officials of the DNC and two other Democratic campaign committees. The Hamilton indictment is a logical step going up the food chain. But it remains to be seen whether Ms. White will follow through.

There were assurances from every quarter that with Charles La Bella the Justice Department's campaign finance prosecution was in capable hands. Now comes the startling news of Mr. La Bella's departure with the job undone. This effectively means that Ms. White is now the most notable federal prosecutor looking at the campaign fund-raising scandals. As such she ends up carrying the burden of demonstrating that the Justice Department's professional prosecutors corps is capable of carrying to completion the investigation of the Teamsters union and its ties to the DNC and the Clinton-Gore campaign of 1996.

REVIEW & OUTLOOK

Democrats and Coverups

Even as the Clinton Presidency's seventh independent counsel was summoned forth yesterday, the Democrats were putting out a lot of energy to shovel coal at the little flame beneath the Dan Burton teapot. We keep wondering if everyone in the Democratic Party thinks this tempest is a good idea. The individuals one sees as party spokesmen seem to think so.

Take the chairman of the Democratic National Committee itself, Colorado Governor Roy Romer. Governor Romer announced Sunday that the GOP has become "the party of investigations." That may be

Dan Burton

because the Democrats have been working so hard to become the party of coverups.

Now, we don't doubt that it's possible to wave all this away as partisan tit for tat. Problem is, serious Democrats know that this scandal is about a lot more than tat.

But as of this weekend, House Minority Leader Dick Gephardt and veteran infighter Rep. Henry Waxman had decided it was somehow in their interest to demonize Dan Burton and Dave Bossie of the Burton staff, to threaten a quixotic

vote to oust Mr. Burton from his committee chairmanship and to vote again tomorrow to block immunity for four campaign-finance witnesses. (The four witnesses are associates of key figures in the fundraising story—Johnny Chung, Ted Sioeng and Nora and Gene Lum.)

Incidentally, it was reported yesterday that prior to the release of the one-hour outtake of current notoriety, at least a dozen reporters spent time in the Burton committee's offices, taking notes on the entire 150 hours of Hubbell jail house tapes. Our own reading of this incident is that the transcript prepared by Dave Bossie pulled out the same quotes that a knowledgeable reporter would have fixed on, that if the entire 150 hours were reviewed by any experienced prosecutor, the so-called "exculpatory" passages would be of de minimus significance to the issue of whether Mr. and Mrs. Hubbell were expecting a pardon if the former Associate Attorney General would "roll over again."

It's hard to see how anyone could be shocked by any of this. But this is the age of cable TV political talk shows, where guests are expected to feign shock at virtually everything. John Dingell, the House Democrats' master hang-'em-high committee chairman, used to arrange to have full, detailed news stories appear the same morning his victims were scheduled to testify. Senator Joe Biden stretched Ed Meese on the rack with such exquisite attention to thresholds of pain that Mr. Meese's wife sat nearby sobbing. Back then, the weekend commentators would run forward to kick the victims as they lay on the ground, rather than raise questions about the sanity of Messrs. Dingell or Biden.

But this is a local Beltway sport with its own arcane code of permissible brutality, not unlike Australian rules football. What concerns us (well, maybe "concern" isn't quite the right word) is that the Democrats may confuse the local cheers they're hearing for getting Dave Bossie disqualified with the larger reality of having to face the nation's voters in this fall's elections.

In so enthusiastically aligning themselves with the scandal strategists at the other end of Pennsylvania Avenue, the Democratic Party is skirting very close to becoming seen as institutionally complicit in whatever was being run out of the Clinton White House during the 1996 elections. Up to now there has never been a basis in fact for any such association. But as time passes, and as the details of these scandals accrete, and as a Henry Waxman tries to explain away preventing witness testimony as somehow Dan Burton's fault, the distinction blurs. How can it help that Attorney General Reno still passes her days judging whether this or that member of the Clinton Cabinet merits one more independent counsel, even as she insists that the 8,000-pound campaign-finance gorilla is no big deal?

It is worth noting, additionally, that while the Burton bonfire attracted the mobs, the week in fact began with news reports that District Judge Norma Holloway Johnson, a Democratic appointee, had ruled against President Clinton's executive privilege claims for his aides. Indeed, the Clinton team's record inside federal court-rooms has been mixed at best, nowhere near matching its vaunted skills at political public relations.

Even if the House Speaker decides to move jurisdiction for some of the Burton investigation to another committee, the substance—even the ultimate truth—of the underlying charges isn't going to change. Whether in Congress, in the press, with the Independent Counsel, or with the judgments of the federal judiciary, the drama of the Clinton Presidency is moving inexorably toward its denouement.

Much of the legal maneuvering and politicking now taking place in Washington around these scandals is intended to make certain that any such denouement unfolds *after* the fall's Congressional and state elections. But if the dam bursts before November, the electorate may reasonably ask why not a single member of the Democratic Party had the sense or courage to give them a warning.

Editorial Feature

Watergate Comparisons Are on the Mark

By HENRY RUTH

President Clinton is mulling whether to appeal Judge Norma Holloway Johnson's ruling against his claims of executive privilege. Such claims have inevitably given rise to comparisons with Watergate, comparisons Mr. Clinton brushed off at a news conference last week. Yet without passing judgment on the facts of the case—like anyone under criminal investigation, the president is entitled to the presumption of innocence—we can say that there are significant parallels between Watergate and Mr. Clinton's scandals.

A president's invocation of executive privilege during a grand jury investigation challenges three fundamental principles. First, that no one is above the law. Second, that the public has a right to every man's evidence. And third, as the Constitution proclaims in the wonderful thrift of Article II, that the president has a duty to "take Care that the Laws be faithfully executed."

The threat to these fundamental principles of federal criminal law is the first important similarity between Watergate and the allegations Kenneth Starr is investigating. The public can have faith in the integrity of the presidency only if it believes that the chief law-enforcement officer is faithfully executing the law. When he seeks to thwart a federal prosecution of himself, the public faith is necessarily challenged.

This inherent threat to basic principles increases when the law allows the chief law-enforcement officer to withhold evidence in order to protect another societal goal. After all, the law commands *all* executive-branch employees to report to the attorney general any evidence of criminal wrongdoing by any other federal employee. In President Nixon's executive privilege case, the Supreme Court faced a White House attempt to construct an absolute presidential privilege that would be unchallengeable for any reason in any judicial forum. The court resolved this clash between law enforcement and presidential leadership by recognizing a broad presidential privilege aimed at protecting the president's ability to secure unfettered advice, but allowing the invasion of that privilege when a prosecutor shows that it is necessary in order to gather evidence essential to a criminal trial.

A second similarity centers on the types of crimes being investigated: Both Watergate and the Starr investigation involve federal prosecutors' attempts to uncover a possible obstruction of justice by the president and others close to him. Nothing is more basic to the integrity of our justice system than that system's ability to prevent, and if necessary to discover, attempts to corruptly obstruct its normal workings. Some of Mr. Clinton's defenders argue that his alleged perjury and obstruction can be overlooked because they involve a civil case. But if a president obstructs justice, it threatens the justice system whether the case is civil or criminal. It is preposterous to argue that a president should be free to perjure himself and induce others to commit perjury in a civil case.

Mr. Clinton is also a subject of a criminal investigation as to hundreds of thousands of dollars in alleged "hush money" that Webster Hubbell received, in the form of both extensive payments from White House friends to Mr. Hubbell and a federal job given to his wife, who continues to work for the president despite her recent indictment for tax evasion. This matter has obvious surface similarities to Nixon's taped conversations with counsel John Dean on March 21, 1973, in which Nixon expressed to Mr. Dean the ready availability of $1 million to satisfy the Watergate burglars' family support needs.

Mr. Starr has stated that he also sees possible obstruction of justice in the White House's self-declared war on his office, his aides and his witnesses. This matter is similar to Charles Colson's guilty plea to obstruction of justice in Watergate: Mr. Colson admitted to leading the White House-orchestrated effort to discredit Daniel

Ellsberg and thereby influence potential jurors in Mr. Ellsberg's criminal trial for leaking the Pentagon Papers.

Mr. Clinton's invocation of executive privilege represents perhaps the most obvious parallel to Watergate, raising once again the appearance that the chief law-enforcement officer of the United States seeks to hide evidence from a federal prosecutor, from a federal grand jury and ultimately from the American people. It is no accident that millions of Americans, even a high percentage of those who approve of his job performance, no more trust Mr. Clinton to tell the truth than they trusted Nixon 25 years ago. The invocation of executive privilege can only feed public cynicism about politics and government.

Richard Nixon

We should hope that Mr. Clinton's exercise of executive privilege is limited to conversations that directly bear on national security. But as with Judge John Sirica in Watergate, Judge Johnson should be able to screen out from public disclosure any testimony of presidential conversations about Iraq or similar topics and yet allow Mr. Starr to investigate conversations that bear upon the grand jury's inquiry.

Beyond executive privilege, another imperative links Watergate and the Starr investigation. Possible obstruction of justice and perjury by a chief executive deserve full investigation. Whatever the final result, the public must believe that no man is above the law and that the grand jury was able fully to exercise its right to every man's evidence.

Mr. Ruth is a retired lawyer living in Tucson, Ariz. He served as Watergate special prosecutor and as deputy to his predecessors, Archibald Cox and Leon Jaworski.

Editorial Feature

Criticizing Clinton Got Me Audited

By JOSEPH FARAH

White House lawyers defending President Clinton's executive privilege claims go to great lengths to distinguish this scandal from a previous invocation of executive privilege, in Watergate. Unlike the Nixon White House, they say, Mr. Clinton's operatives don't use their power to get at critics. Well I'm a critic, and starting in December 1994, the White House counsel's office targeted me, the news organization I work for and one of my associates because of our investigation of administration corruption and coverups. Thanks to congressional investigators, I have the memos to prove it—and I plan to do so in a lawsuit filed last week against several Clinton administration officials.

The White House and the Democratic National Committee began building a secret dossier on me and the Western Journalism Center. In 1995, these files were used by Clinton aide Mark Fabiani to help prepare a 331-page report, "Communication Stream of Conspiracy Commerce," designed to discredit our investigations and the work of a few others researching Clinton administration scandals. The report, written and distributed at taxpayer expense, was leaked to selected reporters. To this day, the White House has refused Freedom of Information Act requests to provide us with a copy of the report and other files used to prepare it.

An Internal Revenue Service agent visited our accountant the next year to announce that the Western Journalism Center was the target of an audit and that our tax-exempt status as a 501(c)3 nonprofit was being challenged. The first document requests revealed the political nature of the intrusive audit. The IRS showed little concern with our bookkeeping procedures, our financial records or our fund-raising techniques. Instead, the tax collector questioned our journalistic standards and practices, our choice of investigative reporting projects and especially our continuing probes of the administration.

When our accountant questioned the direction of the audit, IRS field agent Thomas Cederquist responded: "Look, this is a political case and the decision will be made at the national level." The agent repeated this astonishing statement on a subsequent occasion.

Rather than take this un-American form of harassment lying down, I went public with my story in these pages. I demonstrated that our case was part of a broad pattern of political audits against those who had challenged the administration's ethics, policy and propriety.

The flurry of national publicity paid some immediate dividends. IRS Commissioner Margaret Milner Richardson, a close friend and political ally of the Clintons, unexpectedly resigned. Congress's Joint Committee on Taxation announced an investigation of the pattern of political audits. Other congressional committees focused attention on IRS abuses.

But the IRS escalated the pressure on us—expanding the audit into another tax year. Officials refused to allow me to exercise my legal right of tape-recording examinations. They demanded documents well beyond the purview of a financial audit—including all incoming and outgoing correspondence for a full year. They forced us to divert our limited staff time and resources to defending ourselves in a seemingly endless paper chase. Attorney and accountant fees spiraled.

Nine grueling months later, the IRS closed the case, extended our tax-exempt status and launched a face-saving internal investigation of its own agent—but not before the damage to our center had been done. The strain on our time and resources had nearly bankrupted the organization. As a result, half the staff had to be laid off and one of our two publications folded. Nearly two years after our ordeal began, Congress has yet to issue a report on political abuse of the IRS. The IRS has not granted our Freedom of Information Act requests to turn over the case file on the center.

President Nixon attempted to abuse the IRS and was shut down by his own bureaucracy; Mr. Clinton, however, has succeeded. Nixon compiled a media enemies list, but not one person on the list was ever audited or harassed; Mr. Clinton has managed to isolate or punish many of his press antagonists.

Such blatant political manipulation and media intimidation has a chilling effect on free speech and independent monitoring of the administration. That's why the Western Journalism Center filed a lawsuit last week against White House and IRS officials, asking for damages in excess of $10 million for interfering with our First Amendment rights. If the administration won't end its abuses, and Congress won't act, perhaps the courts will do the right thing.

Mr. Farah is editor of the Internet newspaper WorldNetDaily.com and executive director of the Western Journalism Center.

REVIEW & OUTLOOK

White House Losing Streak

Despite the system of government laid out in Philadelphia in 1789, the tension and crisis over Bill Clinton's conduct of the Presidency has for more than five years played out almost entirely under Beltway Rules. Under the modern revised system of American government, the three relevant government branches consist of pundits, pollsters and spinmeisters. Reconstituted as such, the U.S. system has been reaching conclusions such as: with Bill Clinton's approval rating at 63% and Kenneth Starr's at 23%, the President is winning, the Independent Counsel is losing and it is simply "all politics."

In pre-Beltway days the schoolchild's well-known fact was that the three branches are legislative, executive and judicial. It now turns out, as the latest White House maneuvers yesterday show, that the judiciary has decided to go its own way and render a series of rulings and decisions quite oblivious to the conclusions of the pundits, pollsters and spinmeisters.

For starters, last week the Supreme Court of the United States gave the Clinton White House a deadline of 4:30 p.m. yesterday to respond to Independent Counsel Starr's request for an expedited ruling on the District Court decision compelling grand jury testimony by Clinton aides Bruce Lindsey and Sidney Blumenthal on the Lewinsky affair. Just hours before that deadline, the White House let it be known that the President's legal team would drop any claim of executive privilege, consign Mr. Blumenthal to the grand jury and seek to claim attorney-client privilege for the more information-laden Mr. Lindsey, who happens to be a lawyer, and plead for further delay.

Now, the White House can be expected to present oral arguments over the next several evenings before Larry King, Geraldo and Charles Grodin. The White House strategy, it appears, is to argue that mere attorney-client privilege raises no constitutional issues of the "high moment" Mr. Starr described in his petition to the Supreme Court, and so there is no reason for the Court to expedite the Lindsey case.

The May 28 decision by Judge Norma Holloway Johnson, though, disposed of not only executive privilege but attorney-client privilege as well. "[T]he court holds that the governmental attorney-client privilege is qualified in the context of a Federal grand jury investigation and that, like the executive privilege, it can be overcome by a showing of need," she wrote. "The court finds that the O.I.C.'s showing of need has overcome Lindsey's assertions of the governmental attorney-client privilege. Accordingly, the court orders Lindsey to comply with the subpoena by answering the questions posed to him by the O.I.C. and the grand jurors."

Kenneth Starr

In plain language, the "executive" and the "client" here pertain to the same federal institution, the Presidency. If we know little else about Bill Clinton it is that he has subsumed all of his official functions and nonofficial forms inside one corpus—president, litigant, candidate, fund-raiser, hotelier. And so we find it hard to believe that the Justices will be swayed one way or another by the White House's attorney-client sophistry.

In its deadline filing with the High Court yesterday, the White House's legal battalion said that Mr. Starr's office had produced "no reason, other than its own opinion, why . . . the case is of such imperative public importance" to require expedited review. It seems to be Judge Johnson's opinion as well: "The O.I.C. has been authorized to investigate whether Monica Lewinsky 'or others,' including President Clinton, suborned perjury, obstructed justice, or tampered with witnesses." Nine days before this ruling, Judge Johnson ordered that Secret Service agents could be called to testify about Mr. Clinton's relationship with Ms. Lewinsky; yesterday Janet Reno announced that the Justice Department would appeal this ruling as well.

The courts have been active on other Clinton fronts. As Judge Johnson pointed out, the Eighth Circuit ruled against the White House to reject attorney-client privilege for government-paid lawyers (such as Mr. Lindsey). The Supreme Court refused to review. However, the High Court did accept an expedited review of the attorney-client privilege case involving lawyer William Hamilton, who is seeking to shield notes he took during a meeting with Vincent Foster just before his 1993 suicide; it will hear oral arguments next Monday.

Norma Johnson

To be sure, Mr. Clinton's spinmeisters have had some success portraying his many scandal controversies and Mr. Starr's investigation of them as mostly political noise unrelated to the serious matters of government. It is hardly surprising that the White House would prefer to make arguments to the Beltway system, where it often wins. Yesterday, however, this White House brushed up against the highest court in the land—and it blinked. In the arena of the federal courts, the Clinton team has repeatedly struck out.

Whose Privilege?

The Lewinsky affair suddenly shifted into high gear in the early summer of 1998 with a series of dramatic legal battles between Bill Clinton and Kenneth Starr. At issue was the right of a federal prosecutor to compel testimony in a criminal investigation, weighed against the right of a President to shelter his aides, guards and attorneys from giving evidence. The Clinton scandals had moved from making news to making law, most of it adverse to the President.

Following rulings by Chief U.S. District Court Judge Norma Holloway Johnson that White House aides and Secret Service employees had to testify in the Lewinsky affair, and facing the prospect of more delays from the White House, Mr. Starr sought to bypass the U.S. Court of Appeals and petitioned the Supreme Court for a fast-track decision in the matters. The High Court turned him down, but suggested that the appeals court "proceed expeditiously." It did. Within weeks, it rejected attorney-client privilege for White House lawyers and the proposed new "protective function" privilege for the Secret Service. The White House said it would take the attorney-client issue to the Supreme Court.

The Justice Department fought Mr. Starr to the high court on the protective function issue, seeking an emergency stay from Chief

Justice William Rehnquist. At high noon on July 17, in a day of Washington drama, Justice Rehnquist declined to issue the stay. Two hours later, the first Secret Service agents were testifying before the Starr grand jury.

But in a setback for the Independent Counsel, the Supreme Court ruled that the attorney-client privilege survived the death of the client, denying Mr. Starr access to notes taken by deputy White House counsel Vincent Foster's private lawyer concerning the Travel Office affair. Separately, U.S. District Judge James Robertson threw out Mr. Starr's indictment of former Associate Attorney General Webster Hubbell on tax-fraud charges, saying the Independent Counsel had strayed to far from his mandate. Mr. Starr announced plans to appeal.

Then in late July came two more bombshells: After holding out for six months, Monica Lewinsky agreed to testify before the Starr grand jury in return for full immunity. Within days, there was even bigger news: President Clinton had received a subpoena from the independent counsel, becoming the first chief executive in the country's history summoned to testify before a federal grand jury in a criminal inquiry.

After months of delay and turmoil, the Lewinsky affair was taking on a new sense of urgency. Meanwhile, in the campaign finance affair, pressure on Attorney General Reno continued to rise. The New York Times reported that Ms. Reno's own lead investigator, departing task force head Charles La Bella, had filed a memo recommending an independent counsel. Mr. La Bella, the Times reported, said in the memo that Ms. Reno had created an "artificially high barrier" to an appointment. In the Senate, the Judiciary Committee disclosed details about FBI Director Louis Freeh's memo saying an Independent Counsel was needed: "It is difficult to imagine a more compelling situation," Mr. Freeh had written.

In the House, the Government Reform and Oversight Committee issued a subpoena for the La Bella report, threatening Ms. Reno with a contempt of Congress sanction if she failed to comply.

Editorial Feature

Answer the Questions,
Mr. President

By PAUL J. CURRAN

Jimmy Carter and Bill Clinton are both Southerners, Democrats and former governors. Both are Baptists, and both ran for president as "moderates." But the similarities end there. Mr. Carter attended Annapolis and served with distinction in the Navy's Submarine Service. Mr. Clinton evaded military service by means that are, at best, suspect. Mr. Carter appears incapable of lying. "Malaise" and "lusting in my heart" are ready examples. Mr. Clinton seems to have problems with truth telling, and apparently has never confined his lust to his heart.

Most telling, however, are the two presidents' very different approaches when they became the subjects of criminal investigations.

In 1979, I investigated allegations of crime on the part of President Carter. These allegations involved loans by the National Bank of Georgia and the operations of the president's peanut warehouse business. From April to September, three colleagues and I presented the evidence to a federal grand jury in Atlanta. I found no basis to bring criminal charges, and I reported my findings in full to the attorney general and in as much detail as the law allowed to Congress and the public.

Subject: The President

My investigative powers were the same as those of Archibald Cox and Leon Jaworski of Watergate fame. Like them, I served as special counsel by appointment of the attorney general. Unlike Kenneth Starr, I was not governed by the independent counsel statute that mandates appointment by a three-judge panel.

Until Mr. Starr's appointment to investigate President Clinton, I was the last person charged with responsibility for an investigation whose specific subject from the outset was the president of the United States. The differences between the way Mr. Carter dealt with my investigation and the way Mr. Clinton is dealing with Mr. Starr's are striking. They tell a lot about the two men and their attitudes toward the rule of law. These differences also help explain why Mr. Starr's investigation is taking years and mine took just seven months. Here is what the record shows:

- In March 1979, at the outset of my investigation, Mr. Carter pledged publicly to cooperate fully, and that is precisely what he did.

Jimmy Carter

At the outset of Mr. Starr's investigation, Mr. Clinton also pledged publicly to cooperate fully, but he has not done so.

- Mr. Carter, members of his family and others associated with him responded fully to all subpoenas, made no motions to quash subpoenas, and raised no claims of privilege, spurious or legitimate. Mr. Clinton and his associates have litigated the validity of subpoenas and have invoked claims of executive privilege, attorney-client privilege and spousal privilege.

Claims of privilege, of course, can be valid, depending on the circumstances. But they can always be waived. (One factor that federal prosecutors regularly use to measure a subject's cooperation is his willingness to waive privilege claims in order to bring out all relevant facts.) Moreover, unlike Mr. Carter, Mr. Clinton has not directed or even asked others to cooperate. Susan McDougal is a prime example.

- Mr. Carter suffered the indignity of being investigated in silence. No leaks or spin emanated from him or his people, and there were none from my side either. Mr. Clinton and his people have leaked, spun and dissembled endlessly. Indeed, Mr. Clinton has mounted a full-scale media campaign for months, including vicious attacks on Mr. Starr and his staff, most of which, as Mr. Clinton knows, Mr. Starr cannot answer without breaking the law by breaching grand jury secrecy.

• Mr. Carter's lawyers and allies made no public statements about the merits of my investigation, nor did I. In fact, they said nothing about it and cooperated fully, in accordance with Mr. Carter's instructions. Mr. Clinton's lawyers and allies shoot their mouths off and constantly attack Mr. Starr and his staff's ability and integrity.

On this record, it is manifest that, despite the pledge of full cooperation that he made to the American people, President Clinton, unlike President Carter, has done the opposite. He has permitted, if not encouraged, his aides and supporters to assault the independent counsel and Mr. Starr's efforts to discharge his statutory responsibilities—responsibilities entrusted to him by three federal judges in accordance with an act of Congress that Mr. Clinton himself signed into law.

The record also shows that Mr. Clinton's approach to the independent counsel's investigation is the same one that Mafiosi and subjects of so-called white-collar crime investigations regularly take: litigate subpoenas, raise every possible claim of privilege, attack the prosecutor as unethical or worse. After all, this is the American way; it's what we've come to expect from lawyers and their moneyed clients. This is not, however, appropriate conduct for our president. Jimmy Carter understood this. Bill Clinton does not.

This unseemly record begs the fair question: Why is President Clinton not cooperating, as he told the American people he would? Why is he permitting his lawyers and allies to act as if they were defending John Gotti or a corporate executive or a labor leader with big problems that he doesn't want to see unearthed? A cynic would say because he's guilty. A skeptic would say because he may well have criminal law problems.

The president and his defenders, however, say that the independent counsel is out to get him, not fairly but foully. This is nonsense for at least two reasons. First, Mr. Starr, a former federal appeals judge and former solicitor general of the United States, has a deserved reputation for integrity, and there is no legitimate basis to conclude that he has failed to live up to it in his conduct of the investigation.

Second, Mr. Starr could not possibly frame Mr. Clinton even if he wanted to. There is simply no way to manufacture a case against the president and have it stand up. Once brought, charges don't disappear. Indictments either get dismissed, pleaded to or tried. Moreover, trumped-up charges could never survive the scrutiny of an impeachment process. A phony case would destroy the reputation and career of Mr. Starr and the lawyers on his staff as well.

If the president really believes, as his cronies claim, that Mr. Starr is corrupt, he has the duty to direct the attorney general to fire the independent counsel. That Mr. Clinton has not issued such a directive is itself compelling evidence that he doesn't really believe that Mr. Starr is corrupt or partisan. Another reason may be that, under the independent counsel statute, Mr. Starr would have the right to seek judicial review of his firing in the U.S. District Court for the District of Columbia. What a show that would be!

After all the stalling runs its course, the day will come when Mr. Starr must invite or subpoena Mr. Clinton to answer under oath all of the pertinent questions that have arisen during the course of all of the inquiries that the attorney general and the three-judge court have entrusted to Mr. Starr—Whitewater, Filegate, Travelgate, etc. Mr. Starr will seek to examine Mr. Clinton either before a grand jury or, by agreement with the president and the grand jurors, by deposition for later submission to the grand jury. I employed the latter course in 1979 when I questioned Mr. Carter under oath in the White House.

Mr. Starr cannot possibly finish his investigation without questioning, or at least trying to question, Mr. Clinton. When Mr. Starr issues his invitation or subpoena, the president has three options:

He can challenge on legal grounds Mr. Starr's right to question him at all. This is a loser, but it will delay the investigation even longer.

He can do the right thing and answer the questions under oath, as President Carter did with me back in 1979. As president this is his obligation to the country.

Taking the Fifth?

Or he can assert his privilege under the Fifth Amendment. He has this constitutional right, the same as every other citizen. The president, however, is not just another citizen. If Mr. Clinton goes this route, there can be little doubt that he will face impeachment. The vast majority of the American people believe that "taking the Fifth" may properly be viewed as evidence of guilt, a common-sense conclusion that courts apply routinely in civil cases. If the president takes the Fifth in response to hundreds of questions, Mr. Starr will report this fact to Congress and the three-judge panel that appoints independent counsels, Mr. Clinton will be finished as our leader, and probably finished as our president.

Mr. Clinton should answer all the questions under oath, just as President Carter did. His presidency rides on his decision and the nation's response to it.

Mr. Curran, a New York lawyer, is a former federal prosecutor.

Editorial Feature

Secret Service Privilege: A Matter of Life or Death

"One must indulge the wild assumption that the President will risk his life in order to engage in illegal or embarrassing conduct outside the perception of his protective detail."

—From Independent Counsel Kenneth Starr's brief to compel Secret Service agents to testify in the Monica Lewinsky case.

"Proximity is developed through trust and confidence and the feeling of the protectees that they have confidentiality in regard to their private lives . . . this ruling will expose the Secret Service protectees and others to a greater risk . . ."

—Former Secret Service agent Timothy McCarthy on NBC's "Meet the Press," commenting on a judge's ruling that the agents must testify.

Politics and People

By Albert R. Hunt

Mr. Starr's sole experience as a politician consists of briefly considering running for the Republican senatorial nomination in Virginia. Mr. McCarthy is the Secret Service agent who in 1981 took a bullet in an act that may well have saved Ronald Reagan's life. When it comes to the battle over Secret Service agents testifying, I'll go with Tim McCarthy.

To be sure, some of President Clinton's legal maneuvers in his battle with the independent counsel seem aimed at stonewalling; the initial sweeping claims of executive privilege—subsequently pared back—were reminiscent of Nixon's specious claims, even if the two presidents' situations aren't parallel.

But the catalyst for the so-called "protective function privilege" is the Secret Service. Lewis Merletti, the agency's director, has never discussed the case with the White House. But he is convinced that agents testifying—not about any crimes they may have witnessed but to provide potentially corroborating evidence in Mr. Starr's sex-related case against the president—would jeopardize the Secret Service's relationship with future presidents and even raise the risk of assassinations.

Walter Dellinger, the former Acting Solicitor General and an eminent law professor, says this is a compelling argument. "This is the strongest of the president's privilege assertions," he says.

Mr. Starr's supporters insist that the legal case, which the independent counsel this week asked the Supreme Court to consider expeditiously, is a sure winner. They charge this is an "outrageous" new privilege invented by a Clinton White House determined to put law enforcement officers above the law. Perhaps they're right on the legalities, but they are dead wrong on the substance.

No one argues that this privilege would change the obligation of the Secret Service agents to report any crimes they witness. If an agent sees a presidential relative snorting cocaine in the Oval Office or sees a vested interest giving cash to the vice president for a political favor, it's a violation of law not to report such criminal offenses immediately. In the Lewinsky matter, there is no serious suggestion that any agent saw any crime.

Mr. Starr isn't the first to try to get the Secret Service to break their code of confidentiality in matters not directly related to witnessing a crime. In 1992, for example, the Senate POW/MIA hearings tried to subpoena an agent to testify on a conversation he may have overheard involving George Bush. The then-Secret Service director, John Magaw, a Republican appointee, vehemently objected, noting that since 1901 "no Secret Service employee has ever been required to disclose information he or she may have overheard by virtue of a protective assignment." Committee Chairman John Kerry wisely backed down.

To appreciate the Service's position, it's essential to understand their philosophy of presidential protection, which is "cover and evacuate." In short, they seek to foil any attacks on a president by putting themselves in the line of fire. Obviously this involves constant and close proximity to the president.

Within a second after John Hinckley fired the first shot at Ronald Reagan in 1981, Agent Jerry Parr had pushed the president into a car and his partner, Agent McCarthy, stepped into the line of fire. If those agents had been kept at a further distance, Mr. Reagan probably would have been killed.

By contrast, the Israeli protective service, Shin Bet, relied on massive superior force. But after Prime Minister Rabin was assassinated in 1995—there wasn't a protective agent within seven feet of him— the Israelis almost immediately summoned the Secret Service to show them how to change their system.

But for cover-and-evacuate to work, agents say, they must have the complete confidence and trust of the president. A chief executive can order agents to keep their distance. Surely, as Mr. Starr argues, a president isn't going to intentionally court danger. But if there's a legitimate fear that agents can be compelled to testify about any conversations he held with a contributor, a political strategist or even a family member, then it only stands to reason that the trust and confidence so essential to proximity will weaken.

Mr. Starr says agents have testified on previous assassination attempts, on the Watergate taping system, and on the removal of files from former White House Counsel Vince Foster's office. But none of these affected presidential security—indeed testifying about assassination attempts might enhance future security—or could affect a future president's ability to trust the confidentiality of the agents.

Moreover, it is nonsense to argue that the testimony in this case would be very limited. "To pretend this is narrow is absurd," says Mr. Dellinger. "The limits are almost nonexistent on what a grand jury may ask. This would be an exception to the president's privacy and the confidentiality of his security arrangements."

The charge that the protective function privilege claim is another Clinton ploy breaks down when one considers it is supported by George Bush and by every living former director of the Secret Service. Mr. Merletti, a Secret Service employee for almost a quarter century who once headed a presidential protective detail, and before that was a Green Beret in Vietnam, is a man of deeply held convictions. The decision of the Justice Department to appeal the unfortunate ruling compelling agents to testify was demonstrably not politically motivated. It was made by the attorney general and Solicitor General Seth Waxman, both public figures of impeccable integrity and independence; already they've differed with the Clinton lawyers on the issue of executive privilege.

It may be that the courts will lack the political insight or the guts to appreciate the stakes involved here. If so, and the agents are forced to testify, Congress should then write a new privilege. The Secret Service is the very best protective agency in the world. But if Ken Starr gets his way, that distinction will be seriously jeopardized. Just ask Tim McCarthy or Jerry Parr.

REVIEW & OUTLOOK

Asides

New Defense for Monica

Washington is a small town. Plato Cacheris, one of Monica Lewinsky's new lawyers, is a close friend of Bob Bennett, President Clinton's lawyer. In fact, Mr. Bennett recommended Mr. Cacheris as an attorney for Kathleen Willey, when he talked with her lawyer. Mr. Cacheris is also the attorney for Mark Siegel, the Democratic consultant who last year accused Rep. Dan Burton of threatening to punish him if he didn't raise contributions for the Republican chairman. No doubt Mr. Cacheris will aggressively represent his client, and no doubt he is aware that several lawyers representing principals in the Lewinsky case are working together. The Journal's Glenn Simpson reports that several have formed joint-defense agreements to share information about the Starr grand jury.

REVIEW & OUTLOOK

Tabloid Criticism

Surely the media could use some intelligent criticism, and we actually had some hopes for Steve Brill's new media magazine, Brill's Content. But while Mr. Brill has a sure eye for promoting his latest property—having sold his interest in Court TV and the American Lawyer for Time Warner's $20 million—the deadly news from his first outing is that he thinks like a lawyer.

That is to say, in considering the investigation by Independent Counsel Kenneth Starr, whether it's true that the President of the United States is out suborning perjury and obstructing justice is not the important thing. To a lawyer's mind the important thing is whether the investigators have dotted all the "i"s and crossed all the "t"s and asked "mother may I" at all the right moments. So Mr. Brill never ventures an opinion about whether Bill Clinton had sex with Monica Lewinsky, but finds an ethical violation because Mr. Starr and his staff have talked to the press.

If Mr. Brill is going to be a journalistic critic, he's going to have to learn to think like a journalist. "Dog bites man, no story," the journalistic adage goes, "Man bites dog, that's a real story." In hyping his scoop on the Sunday TV rounds, Mr. Brill says "no other lawyer on the planet" has Mr. Starr's reading of the law. Hmmm, so no other prosecutor has ever talked to the press on background about pending cases. Now, that's surprising news to us, real man-bites-dog. We would have thought it would be equally surprising to someone who ran American Lawyer.

Never mind, it got Brill's Content on the front page of the New York Times. Apparently it was news to the weekend editors of the Times that reporters were being briefed by Mr. Starr. The Times story by the Times' Adam Clymer said "Michael Oreskes, the Washington bureau chief of The Times, said that the paper did not discuss its sources." The Washington Post put the story on page A10, and the Los Angeles Times ran a few paragraphs on A22, under the sensible headline, "Starr Goes on Record on Off-the-Record Talks During Probe."

The New York Times did follow up the next day by reporting—under a page A16 headline, "Exception to Rules May Not Apply to Starr on News Leaks"—that Justice Department guidelines do allow disclosures "about matters about which the community needs to be reassured that an appropriate law-enforcement agency is investigat-

Steve Brill

ing the incident." This exception would seem to us to cover a lot of ground, given that Mr. Starr is investigating the President of the United States, and has to defend himself from constant attacks by the White House. For their part, White House minions have taken their latest cue from Claude Rains in "Casablanca," saying they're "shocked" by Mr. Brill's disclosures.

How this battle has actually played in the press, it happens, is the subject of a new report by a more traditional press watchdog, the Center for Media and Public Affairs. The center did a sound-bite by sound-bite analysis of the 561 Clinton scandal stories the three major network evening news programs carried between January 1 and April 30 this year. Mr. Clinton counted 44% positive and 56% negative, while Mr. Starr came out at 26% positive and 74% negative. Paula Jones fared even worse, with 78% negative, "with most of the criticism originating from the Clinton camp."

That Mr. Starr "engaged in prosecutorial misconduct" was already a well-established theme, accounting for no less than 12% of all coverage. Excluding comments by Mr. Starr and his staff, some 89% of sources quoted were negative toward Mr. Starr. Again the White House attack team was widely quoted; the Center's Media Monitor newsletter notes, "Kenneth Starr lacked defenders but not critics."

"[N]o one should read or listen to any media outlet that consistently shows that it is the lapdog of big, official power rather than a respectful skeptic," Mr. Brill concludes. In case anyone is confused, he adds, "The big power here is Ken Starr. Prosecutors usually are in crime stories, and the independent counsel's power is unprecedented." Unprecedented precisely because the investigation concerns the most powerful man in the world, who had plenty of personal defenders even before Mr. Brill arrived to help out.

On careful reading, in fact, Mr. Brill's own account clearly shows that Mr. Starr and his aides were not "orchestrating" anything; they were responding to revelations by Linda Tripp, her publicist friend Lucianne Goldberg, Kathleen Willey and others not bound by any requirement of grand jury secrecy. But on the Brill's Content cover, this becomes reporters "Lapping up Ken Starr's leaks."

Headlines that don't deliver, charges thrown hither and yon, themes that make the commonplace a scandal, the appointment of villains, and in general a lot of screaming that adds up to "buy this rag"—we don't know what lawyers may call this, but we journalists have seen it before. Maybe we need some new press critics to give it its proper name, rank sensationalism.

Editorial Feature

Foreign Policy for Sale...

By CHAS. W. FREEMAN JR.

If you open an auction house, don't be shocked if all sorts of people show up to place bids. That's the lesson of the so-called Chinese influence-buying scandal, the charge that minions of the Chinese government made campaign contributions to affect the Clinton administration's foreign and trade policy.

Foreign interest in the outcome of American political contests is as old as the republic. But the alleged involvement of the Chinese government, a relative newcomer to Washington political scandals, with the legion of fund-raisers for President Clinton, no stranger to scandal, makes this a headline grabber.

Some of the foreign money that flowed into Democratic Party campaign coffers in 1996 came from influence peddlers with real or claimed connections to China. So, it appears, did questionable funds from mysteriously affluent Buddhist nuns, Indonesian fat cats, a Macao casino operator and a Thai lobbyist. Meanwhile, individual American friends of Armenia, Ireland, Israel, Taiwan, trans-Caspian pipelines and other places and projects continued ponying up to assure favorable U.S. policies.

Sales Skills

All this cash is testimony to the considerable sales skills of Washington's political operatives. They have convinced a growing number of donors, foreign and domestic, that policy decisions, like nights in the Lincoln bedroom, go to the highest bidder.

It wasn't always so. During the Cold War, when the survival of the United States was clearly at stake, Americans accepted that foreign policy was too serious to be made in the same way as domestic policy. With the end of the Soviet threat, however, members of Congress feel freer to pander to the foreign-policy obsessions of campaign-contributing interest groups, regardless of other considerations that bear on the broader national interest.

In the past, Americans looked to the president to ensure that the national interest, and not just special interests, shaped foreign policy. The implication of the current scandal, however, is that presidential decisions are now also on the auction block. If so, what part of our political process can we count on to make decisions by reference to the national interest?

Foreign policy has been franchised out to special interests. Whichever interest group cares most about an issue gets to shape the policy and to have a big say in the appointment of the officials who will carry it out. Some nations reap disproportionate amounts of taxpayer-funded aid from this system. Others get sanctions imposed on their foes. More than 100 foreign nations are now subject to or threatened with U.S. sanctions.

China is so big, and the issues it raises are so complex, that it is impossible to auction it to a single franchisee. So Congress has practiced time-sharing. One week U.S. China policy is given over to the nonproliferators. The next week it is the turn of the human-rights advocates, then the antiabortionists on the Christian right, the Taiwan lobby, partisans of the Dalai Lama, some section of the business community, and on and on.

Have elements of the Chinese government now decided to bid in the great American policy-franchise auction? Given the extent to which American politicians have succeeded in promoting the impression that money can buy access, influence and policy decisions in Washington, some in China must surely have been tempted to do so. The first allegation against China, after all, was that someone at the Chinese Embassy in Washington had phoned Beijing to advocate the allocation of $2 million to counter Taiwan's much larger efforts to influence U.S. politics.

More than a year of investigation has failed to turn up any evidence that the Chinese government took this suggestion. But suspicions persist, despite the laughably small amount of money the

Chinese were allegedly talking about. Did a Chinese Embassy official really believe anything serious could be done in an American general election with just $2 million? California politicians have just spent over $100 million on a *primary* election.

The Chinese government, which combines its "butchers of Beijing" image in the U.S. with the public relations instincts of Godzilla, is a uniquely credible miscreant. China's image problems may have something to do with the fact that up to now it has remained remarkably aloof from American politics. China is one of the few major foreign countries *not* to have hired a lobbyist in Washington or engaged a U.S. public relations firm. But the real reason the allegations won't go away has nothing to do with the Chinese: Americans now harbor a reasonable doubt about whether our government is for sale.

Hence the resonance of the allegation that campaign contributions persuaded the Clinton administration to turn a blind eye to efforts by Loral to improve the reliability of China's satellite launch vehicles, and, by extension, Chinese ICBMs. After all, Loral's president, Bernard Schwartz, reportedly contributed more than $1 million to the Democratic National Committee in 1996. Could such generosity have been truly disinterested?

And Johnny Chung gave the DNC $100,000 out of $300,000 he received from his well-connected Chinese military business partner, an official of the Chinese satellite launch company, which has close ties to the Chinese military's rocket forces. Mr. Chung now says that his partner confided to him that about $35,000 of the money she gave him came from Chinese military intelligence. If so, it is not clear what the Chinese military wanted for its money. At the time it allegedly gave the cash, it was resisting pressure from foreign insurance companies to let Loral have a look at its rockets to determine the cause of several launch failures.

Targeted at U.S. Cities

The U.S. intelligence community is divided about whether anything Loral may have done could have brought about more than marginal improvements in China's missiles, if that. Most outside experts are even more doubtful. Still, some of China's ballistic missiles are presumably targeted at U.S. cities. The possibility that any American might have connived in improvements in China's ability to strike the U.S. is a serious charge that must not remain unresolved.

The main problem, however, is not the Chinese or other foreigners and what they may or may not have done to exploit the electoral greed of American politicians or the interests of U.S. companies doing business abroad. The main problem is the open invitation our political system now appears to extend to influence buyers on every continent. Foreign governments think they can purchase the favor of American policy makers either directly, through illegal contributions, or indirectly, by teaming up with sympathetic domestic interest groups in the U.S.

As we investigate the Chinese, we should be taking a good, hard look at ourselves. How did we lose our political integrity? What can we do to get it back?

Mr. Freeman, chairman of Projects International Inc., was the principal American interpreter during President Nixon's 1972 visit to Beijing.

Editorial Feature

... As a Dishonest President Cheapens Our Ideals

By CLAUDIA ROSETT

The white Goddess of Liberty Statue in Tiananmen Square was gone by daybreak. No doubt when the Chinese government has finished dealing with its people, the tidy square will be presented again as a suitable site for tourists, visiting dignitaries and the Chinese people to come honor the heroes of China's glorious revolution. It will be important then to remember the heroes of 1989, the people who cried out so many times these past six weeks, "Tell the world what we want. Tell the truth about China."

—THE WALL STREET JOURNAL
JUNE 5, 1989

Tanks were still rolling through Beijing when I filed that report to this newspaper on June 4, 1989, a day that brought the Chinese government's repressive machinery out of the shadows and into full, televised view. The country's rulers had sent the army shooting its way into Tiananmen Square, the symbolic heart of civic life in China. Today, the great lie has long since been patched back into place: the lie that the same Communist Party that ordered the killings has the right to speak for the Chinese people. The square is home again to official ceremonies in which China's dictators welcome their guests—with pomp, without protest. And President Clinton's plans to become the first American president to visit China since the Tiananmen crackdown have sparked lots of talk over how to deal with the vast square in central Beijing that has become a symbol both of China's cry for freedom and of its repression.

It is debatable whether any U.S. president should dignify China's dictatorial regime, first by going there and second by following the official script through Tiananmen. But the question at hand is not whether *any* president should go. More to the point, the answer is that it is grossly inappropriate for this particular president to go. In a speech last Thursday, Mr. Clinton defended his planned visit to China, which begins next week, as a "principled, pragmatic approach." The pity is that even if there is some sound reason for the leader of the free world to visit China right now, and even if Mr. Clinton makes the correct call to speak out in memory of Tiananmen—husky voice, teary eyes and all—he is still the wrong man to lecture the Chinese.

The mismatch comes because the uprising we call Tiananmen Square was at its core about a simple thing: telling the truth. Sick of corruption, desperate for a more just society, the Chinese turned out by the millions in a mighty effort to roll back the vast, sleazy lies Beijing's communist dictatorship felt free to inflict on them. From the beginning it was close to hopeless that by peaceful rebellion the Chinese could overthrow one of the world's most ruthless regimes.

Nonetheless, many risked their livelihoods, and some risked their lives, in the hope of being heard. Part of what transfixed the world was the sudden outpouring of sweet sense and normal human yearning, from a nation where for years the folks who spoke up in public had mainly recited the mottoes of Chairman Mao or droned on about irrigation projects. For a brief season, the Tiananmen protests overturned all that. What the Chinese told the world, over and over; what I heard from them day after day on the streets, was that they too wanted freedom, wanted democracy—that this was the truth about China. They were desperate to unhitch politics from lies, to couple public life with truth.

Mr. Clinton, as it happens, is not a figure history is likely to associate with a strong streak of truth-telling. The flaw here goes beyond a dash of hypocrisy—though there's been plenty of that. Recall that during his 1992 campaign, Mr. Clinton denounced President Bush for a China policy that "continues to coddle aging rulers with undisguised contempt for democracy, for human rights and for the need to control the spread of dangerous weapons technologies." Since then, not much has changed in that part of the China equation—except that Beijing, possibly with the help of lax controls by Mr. Clinton's administration, has been perfecting missiles that by some reports are now capable of hitting Los Angeles or New York.

The larger problem is that Mr. Clinton travels in his own haze of lingering questions about the truth. He has in recent years looked the American public in the eye to say he did nothing untoward with Monica Lewinsky, or Gennifer Flowers, or investments in Arkansas, or whatever. More important, he has left unanswered a wealth of questions about Chinese government money helping to fund his 1996 re-election campaign, and the subsequent easing of rules effectively restricting the transfer of missile technology to China.

With so many questions yet to answer, Mr. Clinton is in no position to do any honor to the Chinese people—either to those who died in 1989 defending the hope of an honest society, or to the Chinese who may quietly preserve those dreams today. Mr. Clinton's tale is by now a far cry from such prized apocrypha of the American presidency as young George Washington confessing that he cut down the cherry tree—a legend long loved for its stress on truth in politics. The world might well expect that Mr. Clinton, faced with similar circumstances, would deny knowledge of the cherry tree's condition but promise to get to the bottom of it.

As the Chinese people could roundly explain today—were they free to speak up—lies at the top levels of politics are dangerous and deeply corrupting to any society. When Chinese protesters in 1989 quoted the Gettysburg Address and built their own Statue of Liberty, they were aspiring to the kind of open, honest society that Americans, too, have long treasured. To the extent that Mr. Clinton has devalued the importance of truth-telling in American politics, he also debases the dreams of the Chinese who died trying to send the message that they wanted freedom. For Bill Clinton to go to Tiananmen and keep silent would be terrible. For him to go there and speak up would be revolting for its hypocrisy. Bad choices all around, but then that's often the price of lies.

Ms. Rosett is a member of the Journal editorial board.

REVIEW & OUTLOOK

America Visits China

We hope that whoever is making the big decisions in China at the moment doesn't confuse the retinue arriving in Beijing today with the institution of the American presidency. Any such misapprehension on the part of the Chinese could lead to misjudgments about the political will of the nation that is paying them the honor of this visit, in the person of President Bill Clinton.

Whatever the real meaning of Mr. Clinton's high approval ratings, there is little question that his standing among political peers is diminished from the norm for American presidents, the consequence of his own misjudgments about the proper conduct of a presidency. But whatever the Chinese may have on Bill Clinton the foreign fundraiser, China's own policy had better reflect the prudence and nuance required to deal with all the formidable sources of institutional American authority. For reasons reaching back 200 years, the presidency is larger than any particular occupant.

However serious the momentary problems, the presidency is organically bound up with the other primary institutions of American life—the Congress, an independent judiciary, organized government petitioners or lobbies, the economy's many players, the military and the voters who elected him. When addressing President Clinton, China's leadership is dealing with the "United States," a nation whose superpower status is based on the strength and manifest success over a long period of time of its collective institutions, a great many of which today have a keen interest in what China does.

The interconnectedness of U.S. institutions may well have been a simple verity at one time, but the content of our politics has changed so much recently that it bears repeating, for our benefit and for Mr. Clinton's hosts. Here at home we've had to come to grips all at once with several unfamiliar phenomena—an unprecedentedly personal presidential style, a presidency soon seen to possess great personal flaws, and all this occurring with the simultaneous rise of unprecedented amounts of prime-time TV dedicated to deconstructing the self-perpetuated Clinton melodrama.

For the next week, of course, it will all be broadcast back across prime time from China as camera-ready pomp. It will be accompanied, as it was in the United States Senate yesterday, by constant reminders of Chinese political contributions, decisions on Loral satellites, questions of human rights. These are legitimate issues that deserve to be aired. China may well be a great and important power, but it is incredible to think that so great a power could still exist in the late 20th century that literally forbids access to great portions of its land mass. For the part of the world that has civilized itself and is rapidly integrating its economic activities, this automatically arouses legitimate interest in China's notions of individual rights.

We would submit to our conservative friends, though, that heaping blame on China lets Mr. Clinton off easily. The Chinese contributors came to his open invitation, after all, which in turn is part of a pattern of behavior reaching back to Arkansas and Oxford. And beyond fund raising, the President does have a responsibility to maintain the office he holds. A soap-operatic presidency in a world of instant telecommunication, as George Melloan noted on these pages Tuesday, does not translate well into a sturdy U.S. foreign policy. Mr. Clinton was most recently seen getting stiffed by the prime minister of pipsqueak Greece.

All of this plausibly puts Mr. Clinton at a big disadvantage dealing with the likes of China. Whatever he may do there—and we certainly don't expect much more than modest initiatives—and whatever the Chinese may attempt to do to Mr. Clinton, we think it is important for the Chinese and people like them to understand that behind President Clinton stands a universe of American institutions that will support him—which certainly does not mean blind assent to any conceivable deal. For example, China's insistence that open and democratic Taiwan does not deserve membership in this world's organizing institutions, such as the WTO, will meet resistance from important quarters inside the U.S. If Mr. Clinton suggests support for any such notion, he too will meet resistance.

While it has become fashionable for some American commentators to regard China as akin to the immutable adversaries of the Cold War, there is clearly little basis for so unsparing a view. China is changing, often for the better and in important ways. Its notions of human rights are retrograde, but amid the wider Asian economic turmoil, it has conducted its affairs admirably. In short, if the Chinese do not misjudge the nature of what is visiting them, there is a basis for achieving the kinds of incremental progress expected from such presidential sojourns, even from a presidency as excessively ripe as this one.

June 24, 1998

Editorial Feature

Clinton's Lessons From Watergate

By Monica Crowley

Twenty-six years ago last week, five men were arrested at the Watergate complex in Washington for breaking into the Democratic National Committee headquarters. The arrests started a series of events that led to the resignation of the 37th president. Today the 42nd president faces allegations of criminal wrongdoing, including the very charge that destroyed Richard Nixon's presidency: obstruction of justice.

Though Nixon died in 1994, long before Monica Lewinsky, Paula Jones and Johnny Chung became household names, he had seen enough of the Whitewater scandal and the Clintons' stonewalling that he was compelled to ask: "Didn't anyone learn anything from Watergate?"

It was inconceivable to Nixon that the same political mistakes and ethical lapses could be made by people who had self-righteously condemned those of Nixon and his administration—people like Hillary Rodham Clinton, who served as counsel to the House Watergate Committee. Nixon could not have predicted that the tactics that failed to protect his presidency seem to have worked, at least so far, for Bill Clinton. Buoyed by a powerhouse economy and peace at home and abroad, Mr. Clinton has refused to answer questions and invoked every imaginable privilege to delay the investigations, without suffering a precipitous drop in his approval ratings.

As the investigations move forward, however, there is no guarantee that this approach will continue to be effective. Like Nixon before him, Mr. Clinton believes that he does not owe the American people or the independent counsel an explanation—even though he, like Nixon, promised early on to cooperate fully with investigators. And, again like Nixon, Mr. Clinton is playing the odds that the evidence will be insufficient to prove the charges against him, at least while he is in office.

Mr. Clinton, however, has one advantage that Nixon did not: the lessons of one who has gone through the fire before him. In his final years and with perfect hindsight, Nixon examined the mistakes and consequences of the scandal that destroyed his presidency and told me what he would—and would not—have done differently. Mr. Clinton would be wise to consider these reflections.

First and above all, Nixon said that he should have gone directly to the American people immediately following the news of the break-in at the DNC. Since he had neither known about nor ordered the bur-

Richard Nixon

glary, he thought in retrospect that he should have addressed the American people before he got involved in the coverup, while the truth was still on his side.

For Mr. Clinton, it is too late for this option. During the early days of the Lewinsky scandal, it seemed as if he were weighing the possibility, saying that it was a legitimate issue, that the American people deserved answers, and that he wanted to divulge "more rather than less, sooner rather than later." Once his lawyers advised him to keep silent, however, he foreclosed the option of honesty.

Second, Nixon said that he would have briefed the American people regularly on the progress of the investigation and kept the process as open as possible.

Mr. Clinton would be well-advised to listen to Nixon on this point. Although we have not yet seen great public pressure for answers from the White House, the president should realize that stonewalling only makes him look as if he is concealing serious wrongdoing. Nixon once said that the American people were forgiving, "but only if you level with them from the beginning." Mr. Clinton has obfuscated, keeping every aspect of his side of the story shrouded in secrecy. As Nixon learned, this approach is not only stupid politically but a violation of the public's trust.

Third, Nixon regretted firing his loyal lieutenants—Chief of Staff Bob Haldeman and domestic policy adviser John Ehrlichman—for their roles in the coverup. Once he asked for their resignations, he was perceived as vulnerable and losing control of the situation; their departures marked the beginning of the end.

So far Mr. Clinton has not fired any of his close advisers. Indeed, he has used them to present a united front to the prosecutors. His confidant Bruce Lindsey, adviser Sidney Blumenthal and personal secretary Betty Currie still have their jobs, despite testimony before the grand jury and speculation over their roles in an alleged coverup. If Mr. Clinton wants to avoid spilling more blood into the water, he should be sure that they continue to work in his White House.

Fourth, Nixon said that he would have destroyed the tapes—even though that in itself would have constituted obstruction of justice. If the special prosecutor were going to press obstruction-of-justice charges, Nixon, in retrospect, would have done something to protect himself and force the investigators to build a largely circumstantial case—without his help. Nixon didn't destroy the tapes, because at the time he believed that there was enough exculpatory evidence on them to neutralize anything incriminating.

The question of whether Mr. Clinton has tampered with evidence remains under investigation, but by viewing the crisis as a high-stakes challenge, he is courting the same danger Nixon did: obscuring of his better judgment.

"Let me tell you something about crises," Nixon said to me in March 1992. "When you are president and in the middle of one, one that isn't international or even domestic because you can separate yourself from those and think rationally, but I mean personal crises that can blow up into political ones . . . you get so wound up that you can feel your better judgment go out the window."

This is not a comforting notion. These scandals consume Mr. Clinton's time and energy and damage his moral authority and the morale of those responsible for serving him. Such an environment breeds bad decisions, not just in areas related to the scandals but in those involving public policy. Mr. Clinton could restore some faith in his ability to do his job if he started waiving privileges and telling the truth.

Nixon's most personal regret related to Watergate was that as president, he failed to create an atmosphere in which events like the break-in were unthinkable. If Mr. Clinton did not establish a climate in which sex scandals, fund-raising abuses and scandals over illegal foreign money were unthinkable, then he also failed to set an appropriate standard of conduct and must be held accountable for the consequences.

Because Watergate ended badly for Nixon, there were only two main things that, upon reflection, he would not have done differently, both of which are instructive in Mr. Clinton's case. First, he did not regret invoking executive privilege; he felt that attempting to protect the confidentiality of his conversations was worth the unanimous 1974 Supreme Court decision against him in *U.S. v. Nixon*.

Mr. Clinton, however, has chosen not to press his luck on executive privilege, and will not appeal Judge Norma Holloway Johnson's decision to compel White House aides to testify. He is, however, taking a Nixonian stand by citing attorney-client privilege in his appeal of Judge Johnson's ruling that Mr. Lindsey must testify. If the Supreme Court rules against him, Mr. Clinton will join Nixon on the short list of presidents who have tried unsuccessfully to hide behind privilege.

The other action that Nixon did not regret taking was his last act as president: resigning. When it became clear that he did not have enough votes to survive impeachment in the House and a trial in the Senate, he decided to end the constitutional crisis.

Whether or not Mr. Clinton faces a similar decision, he is already damaged: marginalized, increasingly irrelevant, his tenure an intermission between the Reagan-Bush era and the next period of vigorous presidential leadership. Although Nixon will always be known for Watergate, he had some towering achievements as well, such as détente with the Soviet Union and rapprochement with China. Mr. Clinton's accomplishments—a balanced budget, a role in brokering peace in Ireland—are more modest than Nixon's and cannot possibly counterbalance the scandals. Unless Mr. Clinton is willing to listen to and learn from Nixon's regrets, he may have grave regrets of his own—not least of which that his failure to behave ethically diminished the presidency and robbed the American people of some of their faith in the system.

Ms. Crowley is author of "Nixon Off the Record" (1996) and "Nixon in Winter: His Final Revelations About Diplomacy, Watergate and Life out of the Arena" (1998), both published by Random House.

JUNE 29, 1998

Editorial Feature

Scalia Was Right
About the Independent Counsel Law

Ten years ago today, in *Morrison v. Olson*, the Supreme Court upheld the constitutionality of the independent counsel statute by a lopsided vote of 7-1, with Justice Antonin Scalia as the sole dissenter. It is most unusual that a lone dissenting justice in a major constitutional law case lives long enough to see his views thoroughly vindicated. But for Justice Scalia, vindication has come in his lifetime. Indeed, it came within merely a decade.

Much of Justice Scalia's constitutional analysis needed no subsequent experience to be vindicated: He argued that the independent counsel law violates both Article II of the Constitution, which does not permit the executive power of prosecution to be given to an official not controlled by the president, and the Appointments Clause, which requires principal officers of the U.S. to be nominated by the president and confirmed by the Senate. But Justice Scalia also predicted that the statute would cause no end of mischief and could do "great harm" to our system of government. The experience of the past 10 years has proven him prophetic.

Rule of Law
By Paul Cappuccio

First, as Justice Scalia noted, while it sounds good in theory that "every violation [of law] by those in high places" should be investigated and prosecuted, the reality is quite different. Experience shows that the independent counsel statute often traps targets and independent counsels alike into long, drawn-out probes of matters that professional prosecutors would not likely pursue.

The statute requires the attorney general to order the appointment of an independent counsel based on a very low threshold showing of possible wrongdoing. The independent counsel is under a statutory duty to get to the bottom of the charge, no matter how unimportant it may be or how expensive and prolonged the investigation. Once an independent counsel is appointed to investigate a matter, the answer "On balance, I don't care to pursue it because the country has more important things to worry about" is not acceptable. The statute effectively removes the critically important check of prosecutorial discretion.

Second, the statute has had a profoundly negative effect on the willingness of talented persons both to serve in the administration and, if serving, to exercise their legitimate constitutional powers vigorously. Every covered government official knows that he is always just one step away from significant, perhaps permanent, harm to his reputation and from having to spend a lifetime's savings on legal costs.

This chilling effect was established most vividly by *Morrison v. Olson* itself. In that case, which Justice Scalia most aptly described as the "wolf [that] comes as a wolf," a rather routine political dispute between the executive branch and Congress over the scope of executive privilege was transformed into a lengthy criminal investigation of the Justice Department officials who counseled the president to assert executive privilege. It matters little that after years of hounding, those individuals were cleared of wrongdoing.

Third, as Justice Scalia noted, the possibility that an overzealous or partisan independent counsel could abuse his broad and virtually unsupervised powers is both real and obvious. But at the same time that the mechanism of the independent counsel is too powerful, it has also proven too weak. It is unthinkable that an agent of the White House could get away with "declaring war" on a federal prosecutor under the control of an attorney general who was investigating the White House for wrongdoing or that White House officials and supporters could get away with going on television night after night to condemn and disrupt such an investigation by the Justice Department. The attorney general would not stand for such conduct and might well consider obstruction of justice charges.

But the Office of the Independent Counsel is virtually powerless to defend itself against assault. An independent counsel has two choices: He may either remain mute and allow the White House to distort the facts and undermine the progress of the investigation, or he may respond publicly, thereby provoking the inevitable countercharge that he should not be commenting to the press about a pending investigation. In short, there is no institutional force to back up and protect the independent counsel from attacks on his investigation. It is precisely the "independence" of the office that allows it to be isolated and attacked when the White House's back is up against the wall.

Finally, and perhaps most damning of all, consider the experience of the past decade in light of the solitary purported advantage of independent counsel statute—that the American people would have more faith in an investigation of high government officials conducted by an independent counsel. On this critical score, the statute has been an abject failure.

Many Republicans will believe forever that Larry Walsh was out to get Presidents Reagan and Bush and may have even timed announcements and indictments to affect the 1992 election. Similarly, notwithstanding an impressive record of convictions and guilty pleas, many Democrats believe the White House's spin that Kenneth Starr's investigation of the Clintons is politically motivated.

It doesn't matter that both groups of detractors are almost surely wrong. What matters is that experience has demonstrated that the American people apparently have less faith in an independent counsel investigation than they would have in an investigation conducted by career Justice Department officials or by a special prosecutor appointed and controlled by the attorney general.

That has little to do with the performance of independent counsels themselves. Rather, it can be attributed to the twin realities that investigations of high-ranking government officials necessarily bring political controversy and the independent counsel (unlike the Justice Department) is more easily isolated by a partisan political attack by the White House and its defenders. The statute has utterly failed to achieve its overriding goal—promoting greater faith by the American people in investigations of high-ranking government officials.

While the statute's failure should not be used as an excuse to abort the current investigation into whether President Clinton committed fraud, perjured himself, intimidated witnesses or otherwise obstructed justice, 10 years after the Supreme Court's decision in *Morrison*, we all owe it to Justice Scalia to admit just how right he was. And we owe it to ourselves to do away with this ill-advised experiment in "good" government.

Mr. Cappuccio is an attorney in Washington, D.C., where he is a partner of Mr. Starr. He was formerly a law clerk to Justice Scalia.

JULY 6, 1998

Editorial Feature

Why Clinton Wants To Be Impeached

Close advisers to President Clinton have been signaling a new strategy in dealing with the independent counsel's investigation: Trigger the impeachment process to force the allegations against the president into a political, rather than a legal, realm. Mr. Clinton now appears to prefer the impeachment process to an appearance before the grand jury. It is an extraordinary shift in strategy both legally and personally. It is also a strategy that may trigger a dangerous game of constitutional chicken with a presidency in the balance.

Rule of Law

By Jonathan Turley

On every television network, presidential advisers have been calling for Independent Counsel Kenneth Starr to take the charges against Mr. Clinton to Congress rather than wait for testimony from the president. White House Counsel Charles Ruff stressed that the president has already said everything he needs to say on the charges. Echoing other White House confidants giving virtually identical statements, former White House Counsel Jack Quinn stated: "I'm advising that Mr. Starr should send his report to the House, and, if [Congress] so chooses, to start those proceedings."

The president's silence in the face of serious allegations of criminal conduct has created a circumstance unanticipated by the drafters of the Constitution when they debated the impeachment clause. The drafters assumed that, faced with allegations of high crimes or misdemeanors, any president who wished to stay in office would rush to fully and publicly answer the allegations raised against him, not to leave them uncontradicted.

Consider the two prior presidents subjected to impeachment procedures. In 1868, President Andrew Johnson publicly admitted violating a federal law that he viewed as unconstitutional. (Congress had prohibited Johnson from replacing Secretary of War Edwin Stanton, an anti-Johnson cabinet member, without its approval.) He was impeached but not convicted. In 1974, President

Bill Clinton

Richard Nixon had a choice between answering the charges and resigning; he chose to resign. In contrast, Mr. Clinton has signaled for the start of impeachment proceedings. He has refused to answer the charges publicly and has declined several invitations by Mr. Starr to deny the allegations under oath before the grand jury.

In his new strategy, Mr. Clinton appears to be adopting the Susan McDougal defense: He will not testify because he does not approve of the prosecutor. In Ms. McDougal's case, she was rightfully held in contempt for her silence and sent to jail.

The same fate does not await the president. Rather, our system expects presidents to answer criminal charges. Upon taking office, the president takes an oath to uphold and enforce the laws of the United States. For this reason, any president must be prepared to answer serious allegations of crimes under oath as a minimal requirement of office. A president who is not willing to answer allegations under oath can, like Nixon, resign.

Mr. Starr could settle the issue by issuing a subpoena to compel the president's testimony. In the highly unlikely case that Mr. Clinton exercised his Fifth Amendment right against self-incrimination, Mr. Starr could compel his testimony by granting him immunity. This would be immunity from the use of the testimony in a prosecution, not a later impeachment proceeding. Thus, the testimony could be submitted to Congress to establish the president's sworn position on the specific allegations.

Mr. Starr would need the permission of Judge Norma Holloway Johnson to disclose grand jury information to the House, including testimony of the president. Such a request would not be unprecedented since grand jury transcripts have been used in the impeachment of at least one judge.

While Mr. Starr has discretion about whether to subpoena the president to testify, he has no choice about whether to report to the House. Under Section 595(c) of the Independent Counsel Act, Mr. Starr is required to "advise the House of Representatives of any substantial and credible information" of conduct that "may constitute grounds for impeachment." If Mr. Clinton remains silent, the allegations supported by witnesses in the grand jury will be uncontradicted by the president under oath. In such a case, Mr. Starr would be legally required to report charges such as perjury to the House as supported by "substantial and credible information."

It's important to note that the House doesn't sit in judgment on the merits in such disputes. Rather, under the Constitution the House is charged with determining whether there is sufficient basis for trial in the Senate. It is required to review the evidence much like a grand jury and vote to approve or reject the articles of impeachment. A simple majority is required.

The president's silence would make it extremely difficult for the House to avoid drafting articles of impeachment. House Judiciary Chairman Henry Hyde can be expected to invite the president to testify upon examination, but such an invitation would likely be declined. Without the president's sworn testimony refuting the charges, the House wouldn't have a legitimate basis on which to refuse to submit the matter to the Senate.

Henry Hyde

In the absence of the president's testimony before the grand jury or the House Judiciary Committee, the House's only basis for rejecting the articles of impeachment would be to formally exclude such crimes as perjury and obstruction of justice as grounds for impeachment. This would be as unprecedented as it would be dangerous for the country. Perjury may be the most threatening of potential crimes since it is the crime that shields all other crimes or misconduct from the public. Perjury and obstruction of justice clearly fall within "high crimes or misdemeanors." Since the House decides only whether the underlying crimes (if proven) would merit impeachment, the

Constitution requires that the question of guilt be given to the Senate.

If impeached, the president would be called to testify before the Senate with Chief Justice William Rehnquist sitting as the presiding judge. This would be the last opportunity for the president to testify. Even if he were not convicted by the required two-thirds of voting members, impeachment would be no small cost for a president hoping for a positive legacy. Rather than joining the ranks of Lincoln and Jefferson, Mr. Clinton now appears willing to join Johnson and Nixon in history simply to avoid testifying under oath. It is, of course, the president's choice to trigger these events. In taking such a course, however, the president stands on the wrong side of history.

Mr. Turley is a professor at George Washington University Law School in Washington, D.C.

Editorial Feature

Leak Charges Don't Hold Water

By BYRON YORK

Is there anyone who hasn't accused Kenneth Starr of improperly leaking evidence from the Monica Lewinsky investigation? After the publication of Steven Brill's lengthy attack on the independent counsel's ethics, suggestions that Mr. Starr has wrongly divulged secret information have been repeated so frequently that they have assumed an aura of certitude. But the accusations of leaking are at odds with the facts. A look at the evidence in the Lewinsky matter shows that far from being the leakiest independent counsel in history, Mr. Starr is perhaps the most secretive.

First, consider the tape of Ms. Lewinsky talking to Linda Tripp on Jan. 13 at the Ritz-Carlton Pentagon City, a recording made by Federal Bureau of Investigation agents working for Mr. Starr. Any report to Congress or other action by Mr. Starr likely would rely on that tape more than those recorded by Ms. Tripp herself, for the FBI recording was made under his supervision. On Jan. 15, Mr. Starr's deputies played portions of the tape for Justice Department officials as part of the independent counsel's request to expand his mandate to cover the Lewinsky matter. Snippets of the tape's contents have been reported by Newsweek's Michael Isikoff. But Mr. Isikoff has said his magazine got them without any help from the independent counsel's office. And most of the FBI tape remains secret, because Mr. Starr has kept it that way.

Second, grand jury testimony. Vernon Jordan, a key witness in the case, says that he has testified "truthfully, honestly and to the best of my ability" before one of Mr. Starr's grand juries. But no one knows what Mr. Jordan said inside the federal courthouse because Mr. Starr has kept it a secret. (Mr. Jordan has chosen not to detail his testimony.) Likewise, nothing has been published about the substance of the testimony of White House aides Sidney Blumenthal, Marsha Scott, John Podesta and many others, because Mr. Starr keeps it tightly under wraps.

Third, the ongoing negotiations between the independent counsel's office and the White House. It is known, for example, that Mr. Starr has written to President Clinton asking him to order Secret Service officers to testify before the grand jury. Mr. Clinton, who has publicly said he is cooperating with the investigation, refused, just as

Kenneth Starr

he had turned down Mr. Starr's several written requests that he encourage Whitewater witness Susan McDougal to testify. Both facts were made public by the court. Before that, the public did not know about them—because Mr. Starr kept them secret.

The most notorious leak that has occurred was that Mr. Clinton's secretary, Betty Currie, told investigators that her boss tried to get her to reconcile her version of events with his testimony in the Paula Jones lawsuit. (The alleged coaching session happened just after Mr. Clinton gave a deposition in that lawsuit.) Evidence of possible witness tampering would have been enormously valuable to members of the Jones legal team; the Currie story, like much else in the Jones case, was known by parties other than Mr. Starr by the time it made its way into the press. Which leads to an important point in the leaking debate: *There has not been a single leak of vital information since the Jones case was dismissed.*

Compare Mr. Starr's record of secrecy to other federal investigations. Look at the apparent leaks coming out of the Justice Department's campaign finance investigation. On May 15, the New York Times reported that Democratic fund-raiser Johnny Chung had told investigators that he funneled tens of thousands of dollars from a Chinese military officer to the Democrats during President Clinton's 1996 re-election campaign. The Times attributed the information to lawyers and officials with knowledge of the Justice Department's campaign finance probe. Last month, this newspaper ran a story headlined "Campaign-Finance Probe Finds Little Evidence of Criminal Wrongdoing at DNC, White House." The article reported that investigators haven't seen any proof that DNC officials knew that some donations to the Democratic Party were improper.

There has been no outcry from the White House about leaks flowing out of the Justice Department. After all, the department is simply following the guidelines articulated by Deputy Attorney General Eric Holder, who in 1995 wrote that the public has a right to be kept informed about the status of high-profile prosecutions. The value of prosecutors talking to the press, Mr. Holder wrote, "has become particularly pertinent in recent years because powerful figures increasingly seem to characterize criminal investigations of their alleged illegal conduct as 'political witch hunts.' "

For an example from the past, look at the Iran-Contra investigation. In January 1994, just before the release of Independent Counsel Lawrence Walsh's final report, lawyers representing several former Reagan and Bush administration officials asked the three-judge panel that oversees independent counsels to seal the document, arguing that it contained secret grand-jury information protected by Federal Rule of Criminal Procedure 6(e). The judges refused and ordered the report made public because, they said, it had all been leaked to the press anyway. "The purpose of Rule 6(e) is to preserve secrecy," the judges wrote. "Information widely known is not secret."

Such wholesale leaking simply has not happened in the Lewinsky case. If Mr. Starr had leaked like a sieve, as his critics contend, the logical inference is that by now all his evidence would be public knowledge. Yet clearly it is not. Despite what his enemies say, Mr. Starr is playing by the rules.

Mr. York is an investigative reporter for The American Spectator.

REVIEW & OUTLOOK

Victimhood

The Clinton spin machine has succeeded splendidly in turning Paula Jones, Linda Tripp and above all Kenneth Starr into villains. As an encore, it now presents Susan McDougal and Webster Hubbell as victims, not felons. And it's standing by pending the decision on which way to spin Monica Lewinsky.

Mrs. McDougal has been assiduously courting victimhood since parading in chains outside of one of her various courtrooms some

Susan McDougal

three years ago—her best publicity shot since riding a white stallion in hot pants to publicize Whitewater real estate. Her endless jailhouse interviews have complained of persecution (and at one point accused Jeff Gerth of the New York Times of bribing her late husband). Most recently she persuaded a judge to release her from jail for better treatment of a bad back—a decision widely billed as a setback for Independent Counsel Starr.

Next week Mrs. McDougal is slated for another trial before another prosecutor, the Los Angeles County bunco squad having nabbed her for allegedly bilking Zubin Mehta and his wife through a credit card scam. Earlier, of course, an Arkansas jury convicted her of fraud in the original Whitewater transactions, along with Jim McDougal and former Arkansas Governor Jim Guy Tucker. When asked whether the President's testimony at that trial was truthful, she refused to answer and went to jail to launch her victim-hood campaign.

In the improbable victim contest, Judge James Robertson has topped Susan with Webster Hubbell, former Sugar Bowl tackle, former Justice Department major domo and convicted embezzler from the Rose Law Firm. Poor Webb was double-crossed by Mr. Starr, the judge ruled, over immunity offered when he agreed to supply documents under subpoena. The immunity issues are obscure, but what's a subpoena for if a prosecutor has to give immunity to get documents? In any event, Mr. Hubbell's wife, his accountant and his lawyer were never promised immunity, so the case against them goes forward. A ruling limited to the technicalities of immunity would mean that the accomplices go to trial while the principal goes free, even though his own attorney specified he was in fact guilty of not paying taxes on the money he received from the Lippo Group and others after being run out of the Justice Department.

Webster Hubbell

To dismiss the case entirely, Judge Robertson ruled that the independent counsel didn't have jurisdiction to prosecute Mr. Hubbell's tax crimes, overruling an explicit mandate from the three-judge Special Division in charge of Independent Counsels. The appellate judges on the Special Division, the District Judge decided, did not have the power to expand Mr. Starr's mandate without a mother-may-I from Attorney General Janet Reno. Facing the same issue, two prominent members of the D.C. district bench, Royce Lamberth and Thomas Penfield Jackson, had already come to precisely the opposite conclusion. When Judge Henry Woods ruled that Mr. Starr did not have the authority to bring a tax case against Governor Tucker and two associates, the Eighth Circuit Court of Appeals not only overturned, but bounced Judge Woods right off the case. (Judge Woods was a long-time Clinton crony, while Judge Robertson is merely a Clinton appointee.)

Judge Robertson's ruling will be appealed to the D.C. Circuit, which is also the mother court of the Special Division. A panel of this same court just unanimously rejected the Administration's invention of a special privilege for Secret Service officers. It ruled that three

Secret Service officers will have to answer Mr. Starr's questions about whether the course of their duties led them to hold discussions of Monica Lewinsky and her presence around the Oval Office.

If they do offer embarrassing testimony, experience suggests, the Secret Service agents can expect to be slimed with anything available, including their own personnel files. No one at the Pentagon has been disciplined for the admittedly illegal release of material from Mrs. Tripp's files, but meanwhile she is being investigated by a Democratic prosecutor in ever-fastidious Maryland for taping her own phone calls. Similarly, a Democratic prosecutor in Arkansas has invoked seldom-used state insurance laws to bring charges against David Hale, despite his immunity agreement as a witness cooperating with Mr. Starr.

As for Ms. Lewinsky, even the departure of the unctuous William Ginsburg and the arrival of a seasoned plea-bargaining team does not seem to have ended the impasse. As we read the tea leaves, she

Monica Lewinsky

is willing to testify about Presidential sex but unwilling to say who was involved in helping her draw up the "talking points" she gave Mrs. Tripp instructing her to commit perjury in the Paula Jones case. Mr. Starr is of course far more interested in the latter. If, say, the President sent her to Bruce Lindsey for legal instruction, both would be involved in obstruction of justice; this in turn would cast serious shadows over the Administration's administration of justice in Whitewater, campaign finance, the FBI files and other matters far transcending sexual peccadilloes.

Pending Ms. Lewinsky's decision to cooperate or pull a Susan McDougal, the spin machine is warming up both the villain and victim ramps, ready alternatively to blacken Mr. Starr for picking on a young thing, or slime Ms. Lewinsky as a Vanity Fair exhibitionist. Our advice to the independent counsel would be that the White House can't drive his poll ratings much lower, and that he should indict the little tart and get the show on the road.

REVIEW & OUTLOOK

Whither Justice?

Attorney General Janet Reno deserves tough questioning when she appears today before the Senate Judiciary Committee. The biggest question is the same one people have always asked about her tenure: Is Janet Reno's Justice Department part of the problem or part of the solution?

The problem is not primarily culpability; it is *accountability*. Sufficient, serious questions have been raised about the manner in which this White House raised money for the last Presidential campaign that the public at least deserves some answers. It can use the voting booth this fall and in 2000 to vote thumbs up or down on those answers. But instead of providing a solution to a problem of public trust, Ms. Reno's Justice Department continues to perform in a manner which ensures that these questions will drift away like so many soap bubbles.

Yesterday, as an example, her department hoisted what surely appears to be another boulder onto the stonewall around the Starr investigation. Justice announced that it would appeal to the full U.S. Court of Appeals the recent order by a three-judge panel that Secret Service officials testify in the independent counsel's criminal probe of the Lewinsky affair.

The Justice Department's attempt to create an entirely novel "protective function" privilege on President Clinton's behalf has now been rejected twice by the courts. Though the appeals panel noted the idea was not entirely unreasonable, it concluded that the investigatory needs of this case outweighed any such privilege. Translation: There's enough here to merit getting to the bottom of it.

Relatedly, a federal appeals court ruling is imminent on yet another White House privilege claim—that of Clinton counselor Bruce Lindsey that his conversations with the President are protected by attorney-client privilege and therefore he may refuse to answer questions before the Starr grand jury. Translation: Because Bruce Lindsey has a law license, anything he and Bill Clinton ever talk about is "privileged." Ergo, the Clinton-Lindsey partnership is accountable to no authority under U.S. law.

As a consequence, these matters will most likely wander the long and winding road toward a final reckoning with the Supreme Court sometime around October. Talk show hosts will conclude that the American people are tired of it all. Translation: Stonewalling works.

It might be truer to say that people are not so much tired as they are discouraged. They become discouraged, for example, when they read a story on the New York Times front page yesterday that the Justice Department's campaign finance task force is on a slow boat to oblivion.

Janet Reno

Some 21 months after allegations of significant improprieties surfaced, Times reporters Don Van Natta and David Johnston write, "law enforcement officials concede they have no big cases to show for their effort and express doubts that they will obtain evidence to warrant prosecution of senior White House or Democratic Party officials." Justice officials doubt they will ever get answers to "the heart of the inquiry: whether there was a plot by the Chinese military behind contributions to the Democratic Party."

Earlier this year, Senator Fred Thompson's investigating committee voted out a report identifying six campaign finance figures—senior DNC operative John Huang, Indonesian tycoons James and Mochtar Riady, fund-raisers Charlie Trie and Maria Hsia, and businessman Ted Sioeng—as having ties to the Communist regime in China. The principals have denied the accusations, and Democrats on the Thompson Committee contended the evidence was inconclusive.

With the exception of the glad-handing former Little Rock restaurateur Charlie Trie, no one who could remotely be termed a central figure has been indicted. The others rounded up by the Justice task force are all small fry, as reflected in Monday's indictment of Thai businesswoman Pauline Kanchanalak for making more than $600,000 in illegal donations to Democratic Party entities from 1992 through 1996. Ms. Kanchanalak lit out for Thailand a long time ago, destroying records on the way out.

Ms. Reno's appearance before the Judiciary Committee should serve as a reminder that Monica Lewinsky is not Mr. Clinton's only problem. The heart of the campaign finance scandal, as we have noted before, rests in the Oval Office, not in Beijing. The President himself launched John Huang's career as a senior DNC fund-raising emissary at a September 13, 1995, meeting that included Mr. Huang, James Riady of Indonesia, Arkansas operator and Asia-traveling middleman Joseph Giroir, and Bruce Lindsey, who as we know is bound by attorney-client privilege.

Indeed, the unifying theme of all Mr. Clinton's problems—from the Whitewater investigation to the present day—is one of obstructive intent. Don't ask the Clinton team about anything because they don't have to tell—and never will. For the record, the Judiciary Committee should make this Administration's Attorney General explain one more time why her Justice Department is the solution to the needs of public accountability.

Editorial Feature

Election '98:
Bill Trades Places With Newt

They aren't advertising it, but Republicans think they may have a secret weapon this election year: President Clinton.

That's the ironic backdrop in a battle for Congress that is so far a pudding without a national theme. The biggest issue could yet be the president himself. That prospect helps explain why Democrats are now scrambling to change the subject, while Republicans are more confident than any time in months that they'll add to their majorities.

Potomac Watch
By Paul A. Gigot

This shouldn't be happening to a president with 60% approval ratings. But in a low-turnout election, intensity matters as much as sheer numbers. And right now the voters who loathe Mr. Clinton are more motivated than those who like him.

"I'm worried that all of the right-wing Republicans who hate the president are fired up to vote, and everybody else is happy," laments Democratic Rep. Jim Moran of Virginia.

That's what happened when the GOP won a recent special House election in New Mexico. And the trend is showing up in private Republican polling. Only 40% of voters who approve of the president say they're inclined to vote this fall, while 55% of those who disapprove plan to show up. Anger usually motivates better than contentment.

Maybe we should call it Monica's revenge. The more Mr. Clinton skirts accountability for scandal from Congress or the courts, the more some Americans may yearn to vent their frustration the only way they can—at the ballot box.

All the more so if Kenneth Starr sends up a report to Congress between now and Election Day. It'd be too late to begin politically tricky impeachment hearings, but early enough to invite voter retri-

Bill Clinton

bution. Says one GOP strategist whose view is gaining ground in Congress: "A Starr report works in our favor."

Especially among voters who say a "decline in moral values" will be their most important voting issue this fall. Six in 10 of those voters (comprising 12% of the electorate) say they're certain to cast a ballot, according to a recent GOP survey. Compare that with the mere four in 10 who care most about education or Social Security and say they'll show.

The ironies here would be richer than Bill Clinton's defense lawyers. Only three months ago these same social conservatives were supposed to be upset with the GOP. But their annoyance with the president may yet trump any frustration with Congress.

Meanwhile, the same Democrats in Congress who have stoutly defended Mr. Clinton would be the ones who suffer most for his, er, sins. The "perjury doesn't count if it's about sex" defense may work better for Geraldo than for swing-district Democrats.

Newt Gingrich

All of this would reinforce the typical midterm election theme that a GOP Congress is vital to check a Democratic president. "This is where Clinton's low personal ratings [30%] matter," says one ranking GOP strategist. "Voters don't want to give people they don't trust total power." Speeches like the one Senate Majority Leader Trent Lott delivered this week charging that China got vital U.S. space technology are designed to drive home that point.

House Republicans are confident enough now that they're raising their budget for competitive races by another $20 million or so. A realistic gain is still just five or 10 seats (added to their 11-seat majority). But if they do catch an anti-Clinton wave, members think they could gain 20.

No wonder Democrats have been hunting for something other than the Clinton scandals to talk about. They tried tobacco, but that went pfft. Campaign finance moves editorial writers but no one else. They finally have a political winner bashing HMOs, but Republicans are only too happy to say me-too and endorse regulations almost as intrusive as Ted Kennedy's.

Democrats may end up saving the day by killing any health-care bill in the Senate just so they have something to run on in November. "What we have is Democrats who believe in the issue but won't pass it, and Republicans who I thought didn't believe in it trying to pass it," says Deborah Steelman, a GOP health-care expert.

The other Democratic hope is for an October showdown with Congress. "You haven't seen this much disorganization in Congress since the 1995 government shutdown," says White House spinner Rahm Emanuel, in a hint of the vetoes over education and the environment to come.

Bracing for this, Republicans plan to pass a tax cut (and they'd better), giving them something positive to talk about. They'll also hold back as bargaining chips items that Mr. Clinton wants, such as $18 billion for the International Monetary Fund. At least autumn won't be dull.

In 1996, Mr. Clinton used Mr. Gingrich as a foil to win re-election. This time Republicans are counting on Mr. Clinton as their foil to re-elect Speaker Gingrich. What would these two Baby Boom political icons do without each other?

REVIEW & OUTLOOK

The Shot Clock Runs

The shot clock may be running out on the Clinton-Reno-Rubin stonewall squad. It's been awhile since the nation's capital saw court action involving a President as dramatic as what unfolded yesterday.

Independent Counsel Kenneth Starr forced the action by subpoenaing the head of Mr. Clinton's Secret Service detail to appear before a grand jury. At 9:22 a.m., Agent Larry Cockell complied by showing up at the district courthouse. Meanwhile the Justice Department had asked the full Court of Appeals to block the testimony. After losing before both the district court and a three-judge appellate panel, the lawyers were asking the full appeals panel to reconsider the government's claim of a "protective-function privilege" for the Secret Service, as asserted by President Clinton's front man, Treasury Secretary Robert Rubin.

About an hour later, urgent news came over the wires that the Appeals Court indeed had blocked the Cockell testimony. Press reports described this as "a major victory" for the Justice Department. The court's own statement read: "The purpose of this administrative stay is to give the court sufficient opportunity to consider the merits of the motion."

"Sufficient opportunity" turned out to be about three hours. At 2:06 p.m. a Bulletin announced that the appeals court had refused to reconsider the three-judge panel's decision ordering the Secret Service's testimony. Writing for the nine judges who heard the appeal, the court said: "This court has ruled that the privilege does not exist; no judge on the court has even requested a vote on the Justice Department's suggestion for rehearing." The department will now try to convince Chief Justice Rehnquist to buy the Administration's argument.

These dramatic events unfolded the day after the Senate Judiciary Committee revealed that FBI Director Louis Freeh's memorandum on Janet Reno's decision against an independent counsel for the Clinton-Gore campaign finance operation had stated: "It is difficult to imagine a more compelling situation for appointing an independent counsel."

Editorial Feature

Clinton Can Avoid The Starr Chamber

By JACK QUINN

In the past few weeks, a posse of official and unofficial spokesmen for Independent Counsel Kenneth Starr have argued that President Clinton has a legal obligation to testify before Mr. Starr's grand jury. The central point of this misguided theory is that the president's failure to testify before the grand jury would contravene his oath of office. Sen. Orrin Hatch (R., Utah), chairman of the Judiciary Committee, has even suggested that a presidential failure to testify in the face of a subpoena from Mr. Starr might be an impeachable offense.

But this argument, advanced on these pages by law Prof. Jonathan Turley, is grossly out of step with our history and Constitution. No American president has ever been subpoenaed by a prosecutor to testify before a grand jury—not in Watergate, Iran-Contra, Teapot Dome, the Andrew Johnson impeachment—not ever.

The president's oath is to uphold the Constitution and the presidency, which includes a duty, under the doctrine of separation of powers, to resist unreasonable encroachment by the other branches. That's why, during the trial of former Vice President Aaron Burr for treason in 1807, President Jefferson strenuously resisted the court's subpoena. Since Jefferson's time, presidents repeatedly have resisted actions of the other branches when they believed it would weaken the institution of the presidency.

If I were still the president's lawyer, I would advise him to challenge a subpoena from Mr. Starr on constitutional grounds. Given its effect on the Constitution and the presidency, the argument that the president must answer unproved allegations against him before a grand jury is scary. If Mr. Starr were deemed to possess such power, it would not be limited to independent counsels, because any state or local prosecutor could similarly haul a president before a grand jury. That is simply not what the Founders intended.

The Founders contemplated that a sitting president would be subject to impeachment proceedings and removal from office before any criminal proceedings could ensue. As Alexander Hamilton wrote in "The Federalist Papers": "The President of the United States would be liable to be impeached, tried, and, upon conviction of treason, bribery, or other high crimes and misdemeanors, removed from office; and would afterwards be liable to prosecution and punishment in the ordinary course of law."

There is a profoundly important reason for this: because the American people elect the president, the people will countenance his removal from office only through a process carried out by public officials elected to Congress—not by an unaccountable prosecutor determined to ensnare him. As Hamilton noted, the "awful discretion" of impeachment "forbids the commitment of the trust to a small number of persons."

This separation-of-powers argument is underscored by the nature of the unproved allegations against Mr. Clinton. In his Paula Jones deposition, the president already answered more than 90 questions about Monica Lewinsky under oath, denying the central allegations against him. Mr. Starr has access to this testimony, and a new subpoena would seek only to compel more testimony about Ms. Lewinsky from the president. Under the independent counsel statute, if Mr. Starr believes he has substantial and credible evidence that the president may have committed an impeachable offense, he must make his report to the House, not pursue the president on his own.

If Mr. Starr does not believe he has such evidence—and Mr. Starr's own spokesman recently acknowledged that he does not—then what would be Mr. Starr's basis for calling Mr. Clinton to testify? To satisfy his curiosity about the president's sex life? To set a perjury trap for the president? To question the president on a speculative whim about potential offenses? To build a potential perjury case against Ms. Lewinsky for lying about an arguably immaterial question in a civil affidavit in a lawsuit that has been dismissed? Are any of these goals worth ignoring Jefferson, Hamilton and 200 years of history?

There are, of course, other contexts in which one may argue that a president's testimony can properly be sought. But this is not the Nixon tapes case, in which the prosecutor wanted physical evidence, rather than testimony, from a president, and in which, more importantly, the tapes were subpoenaed as part of the prosecution of people other than the president. Nor is this the Paula Jones case, in which the president was held by the Supreme Court to be subject to civil suit while in office.

Kenneth Starr

Here the issue is whether the president must give a prosecutor testimony relating to allegations of crimes that might lead to impeachment proceedings. Whether the president can be removed from office is a question for the House, which can pass articles of impeachment, and the Senate, which would thereafter conduct a trial. This allows the legislative branch of government to act as a check on the prosecutors and to impart the public sense of what should be regarded as impeachable. In other words, the appropriate "grand jury" here is the House of Representatives. The House should not be able to duck its responsibility and let Mr. Starr do its work.

There well may be a political argument for Mr. Clinton to say more about his relationship with Ms. Lewinsky. And if the American people were to demand to know more, their elected representatives could take up that demand. That is the only process the Constitution contemplates with regard to a sitting president. And it is the only process that respects our democratic form of government.

This emphatically does not mean that impeachment proceedings should begin. Rather, it means that Congress finally should make the judgment that Mr. Starr and his cheerleaders have been unwilling to make—that the American people are right in feeling that this inquiry is grossly out of proportion and should soon come to an end.

Mr. Quinn, a former White House counsel, is an attorney in Washington.

Letters to the Editor

Clinton and Starr At the End of the Day

Arguing that Independent Counsel Kenneth Starr has no legal right to compel President Clinton to testify before a federal grand jury, former White House Counsel Jack Quinn ("Clinton Can Avoid the Starr Chamber," editorial page, July 17) asserts that President Clinton has "a duty, under the [Constitution's] doctrine of separation of powers, to resist unreasonable encroachment by the other branches [of government]." Mr. Quinn asserts that any such demand by Mr. Starr would be "grossly out of step with our history and Constitution," noting that Thomas Jefferson "strenuously resisted" a subpoena issued during the trial of Aaron Burr in 1807.

Tellingly, Mr. Quinn omits an interesting fact: President Jefferson lost. Chief Justice John Marshall not only ruled that Burr could subpoena the president in the same manner as any subpoena "directed to a private citizen," but noted that the court had the power to compel compliance with such a subpoena. Chief Justice Marshall recognized that the president's unique Constitutional Responsibilities (for example, as Commander in Chief) might provide compelling reasons why he should not have to comply. Nonetheless, Marshall ruled, the court would act as "the guard . . . to protect [the President] from being harassed by vexatious and unnecessary subpoenas"—not the person seeking the subpoena, and most emphatically not the president himself.

Chief Justice Marshall's central point, that the president "does not embody the nation's sovereignty" and "is not above the law's commands," formed the constitutional basis for the Supreme Court's rejection of another presidential subpoena, which Richard Nixon "strenuously resisted" in 1974. "But this is not the Nixon tapes case," Mr. Quinn insists, where the special prosecutor wanted "physical evidence, rather than testimony." Because President Nixon resigned shortly after the Supreme Court's decision, we will never know whether Special Prosecutor Leon Jaworski, after reviewing the tapes, might have called President Nixon to explain their contents in person to the grand jury. Even so, the Supreme Court has never suggested that such a distinction exists. Indeed, perhaps anticipating such an eventuality, the court stressed in the Nixon case that "the public . . . has a right to every man's evidence," and that any exceptions to that "ancient proposition of law" should not be "lightly created nor expansively construed, for they are in derogation of the search for the truth." Like any other citizen, the court noted the president could invoke his Fifth Amendment right against self-incrimination or, in some circumstances, refuse to disclose conversations protected by a recognized privilege.

President Clinton's continual invocations of executive, attorney-client and "Secret Service" privileges in response to the grand jury's investigation have been rejected by the federal courts in almost every instance as being insufficient to outweigh Mr. Starr's proffered reasons for seeking evidence. These judges have recognized that Mr. Starr's continuing efforts to get at the truth certainly do not require "ignoring Jefferson, Hamilton and 200 years of history." It is the president's scores of lawyers, aides and mouthpieces, continuing to vilify Kenneth Starr and devise spurious "privileges," who must ignore legal precedent and constitutional history. These smart lawyers know full well that at the end of the day, Bill Clinton will be entitled to only one legitimate privilege—the right to remain silent.

Eric H. Jaso

New York

Editorial Feature

Subpoenaing the President

The White House appears intent on producing a constitutional re-run of Watergate. In the latest episode of the Monica Lewinsky saga, Independent Counsel Kenneth Starr reportedly is near a decision on whether to subpoena President Clinton's testimony before a grand jury. Mr. Starr has invited Mr. Clinton to testify voluntarily at least six times, and each time he has refused; his advisers say he will refuse again if asked. A subpoena is a judicial order to a witness to appear and supply testimony or other evidence; failure to obey triggers contempt sanctions that can include jail time or fines.

Rule of Law

By John Yoo

Past and present White House advisers are suggesting that Mr. Clinton will refuse to obey a subpoena. According to them, the Constitution requires that criminal charges against a president must occur through the impeachment process, rather than via criminal indictment, or after an impeachment and the president's removal. Thus, they reason, if a sitting president cannot be indicted then he cannot be subpoenaed, because he would not be subject to the "compulsory processes of the court" such as sanctions. Sen. Orrin Hatch, chairman of the Senate Judiciary Committee, countered last week that presidential defiance of a subpoena by itself could serve as grounds for impeachment.

If he listens to his advisers, Mr. Clinton would be the first president to formally assert a complete freedom from the criminal justice system solely because he is president. He would not be hiding behind the Fifth Amendment right against self-incrimination or the privilege for executive branch communications. Although as a political matter the House might be unwilling to impeach a president for failure to obey a subpoena, such an action would stand on firm constitutional footing.

The Constitution does not explicitly grant the president the sweeping immunity from judicial process sought by his advisers, and precedent and tradition have rejected such an extreme claim. First, ever since *Marbury v. Madison* (1803) the Supreme Court has exercised the authority to determine whether presidential action is legal under the Constitution and federal laws. Second, as the Supreme Court declared last year in *Clinton v. Jones*: "Sitting Presidents have responded to court orders to provide testimony and other information with sufficient frequency that such interactions can scarcely be thought a novelty."

In the treason trial of Aaron Burr, for example, Chief Justice Marshall ruled that a subpoena could be issued to President Jefferson. Jefferson was leery of being dragged all over the country to testify and was personally opposed to obeying the court. Nevertheless, he cooperated and offered to be deposed. Presidents Monroe, Grant, Nixon, Carter and Ford all produced evidence for criminal proceedings. Mr. Clinton already has given videotaped testimony twice in such actions.

Ignoring this history, the White House could follow two strategies. The president could defy a subpoena and then essentially dare a federal court to impose contempt sanctions. Or, as suggested by former White House Counsel Jack Quinn in these pages on Friday, Mr. Clinton could challenge a subpoena all the way to the Supreme Court solely on the grounds that the president is immune from criminal investigation until after impeachment. Mr. Quinn is ambiguous on what happens if the president loses such a challenge, but his approach implies that the president could refuse to obey the Supreme Court.

If he were to pursue this confrontational course, Mr. Clinton would be going beyond even Richard Nixon in abusing the presidency. In the Watergate tapes case, the federal district court in Washington, D.C., at the request of the special prosecutor, issued a subpoena to

President Nixon to provide the tapes to a grand jury. Invoking a claim of executive privilege, the White House fought the subpoena all the way to the Supreme Court, which unanimously sided against the president.

After his loss, Nixon could have made the same arguments that White House lawyers are floating today, defied the subpoena and refused to release the tapes, thereby plunging the nation into the ordeal of an impeachment. Luckily for the nation, Nixon chose not to press claims of presidential power to such extremes.

Like Nixon before him, Mr. Clinton is not the only individual involved in this scandal. In the Nixon case, the Supreme Court found that the president had to turn over the Watergate tapes because they were necessary to provide indicted defendants with fair trials. Mr. Clinton's testimony might be just as necessary to guarantee fair trials to defendants in the Whitewater/Lewinsky investigation. In any event, if there were evidence of criminal wrongdoing by the president, the sensible course would be for Mr. Starr to name Mr. Clinton as an unindicted co-conspirator and then refer the case to the House for impeachment proceedings. One might even consider the independent counsel statute, in part, as a congressional delegation of authority to conduct a preliminary impeachment investigation.

As Mr. Quinn rightly points out, the subpoena in the Nixon case was for tapes, not personal testimony. Certainly no court or prosecutor wants to transform the Nixon precedent into a tool for harassing the president, thereby preventing him from executing his office. Yet, as the Supreme Court observed in *Clinton v. Jones*, a court can use its powers to schedule judicial proceedings to suit the convenience of the president. It also would be odd, to say the least, if the president had to testify in Paula Jones's civil suit yet could refuse to appear in a criminal proceeding (especially if the case involved actions he took outside of his official duties).

In his ultimate defense, Mr. Clinton could claim that his theory of the presidency and impeachment trumps the authority of the federal judiciary to interpret the Constitution. While some presidents, notably Jefferson and Lincoln, have suggested that they possess such power, they also understood the rule of law demands that it never be exercised except in dire emergency (such as civil war). Mr. Clinton, who promised to tell "more rather than less, sooner rather than later," would risk a constitutional crisis to conceal alleged sexual peccadilloes.

A president determined to fulfill his constitutional duty to faithfully execute the law, and conscious of the need for compromise and stability in our political system, should testify voluntarily rather than force a court to issue a subpoena against him. It would be unfortunate if Mr. Clinton were remembered by history for provoking such a breakdown of the rule of law.

Mr. Yoo, acting professor at Boalt Hall School of Law, the University of California at Berkeley, was general counsel to the Senate Judiciary Committee in 1995-96.

Review & Outlook

Bad Faith at Justice

Whether Republican or Democrat, the next Presidency's first years are going to be spent repairing the damage this Presidency has done to Washington's institutions. Next to the Oval Office, there is probably no more respected institution than the Justice Department in whose service generations of attorneys have served with earned honor and pride. Not now. That respect is eroding.

Yesterday morning the New York Times reported that Justice's departing campaign-finance prosecutor Charles La Bella had delivered a report to Attorney General Janet Reno arguing that her refusal to appoint an independent counsel for alleged Clinton fundraising abuses was wrong. This is the same conclusion reached earlier by Director of the FBI Louis J. Freeh.

As reported by the Times, "Mr. La Bella concluded that the Attorney General had misinterpreted the law, creating an artificially high standard to avoid invoking the independent counsel statute."

Virtually all who have followed these matters are at a point of exasperation. The most charitable have given Janet Reno the benefit and deference traditionally accorded an occupant of her office. There is no more left to give. In declining to make the independent counsel appointment she cites the advice of "my people." What people? What are their names?

On a matter of the highest moment—allegations that an incumbent President or his agents repeatedly violated federal laws—the American people have legal opinions from the director of the FBI and the individual brought into Justice to investigate those charges. What possible justification or explanation can remain for Ms. Reno's repeated appeals to anonymous opinions from some Oz inside Justice?

We will offer an explanation. This version of the Justice Department is not acting in good faith. It isn't an honest broker. An honest prosecutor, Charles La Bella, was brought in to serve as that broker, and he quit, leaving behind a withering judgment of Ms. Reno's "legal analysis."

The air around Justice is quite noxious now, and it is in such an atmosphere that a Senator such as Arlen Specter would talk of seeking a writ of mandamus to force Ms. Reno to do her legal duty. And there is talk in Washington, not unreasonably, of whether a Cabinet member can be impeached. Perhaps, but not easily.

Madison, addressing this point in the First Congress, believed that burden fell on the President: "I think it absolutely necessary that the President should have the power of removing from office; it will make him, in a peculiar manner, responsible for their conduct, and subject him to impeachment himself, if he suffers them to perpetrate with impunity high crimes or misdemeanors against the United States, or neglects to superintend their conduct, so as to check their excesses."

Fat chance of that. Janet Reno, by all accounts, desperately wanted reappointment, and she got it. Her behavior since toward this White House has reflected gratitude. And once this reality is squarely faced—that Justice is led by a grateful Attorney General whose reservoir of good faith is empty on matters touching this White House—other realities must also be faced.

If the department's pose on an independent fund-raising counsel is indefensible, one may reasonably wonder: What else?

To begin, it is hard to believe that this department could be trusted, in the matter of investigating alleged leaks from Mr. Starr's office, with rummaging through the independent counsel's most sensitive documents with no possibility of that material finding its way to the White House.

Has the department's investigation of the Teamsters been tanked? Has Ms. Reno impeded the work of Espy Independent Counsel Donald Smaltz, as he charged two months ago? What explanation is there for the Department's failure to comply with the Vacancies Act, drawing the wrath of even Democratic Sen. Robert

Byrd? Why have the Internal Revenue Service's two requests for an investigation of Illinois Senator Carol Moseley Braun's egregious fund-raising practices elicited no response at Justice?

For five years Washington has lived with constant charges—from critics, Congress, the press and from the courts—that this Presidency has pressured or abused the institutions of government. Whatever the eventual disposition of Janet Reno's reputation, at issue now is the future credibility and reputation of the institution, the Department of Justice, that she purports to speak for.

Letters to the Editor

Attorney General Is Impeachable

Your July 24 editorial "Bad Faith at Justice" suggests that there is some question as to the constitutionality of impeaching an attorney general. No doubt exists. The Constitution (Article 2, Section 4) declares that "The President, Vice President, and all civil Officers of the United States shall be removed from office on Impeachment..." The Attorney General is a civil officer.

During the course of American history, only one cabinet member has been impeached. That was William Belknap, secretary of war to President Grant. Belknap was acquitted by the Senate.

It is interesting to recall the words of Founding Father James Madison, in a speech during the First Congress. Madison said: "It is very possible that an officer who may not incur the displeasure of the President may be guilty of actions that ought to forfeit his place. The power of this House may reach him by means of an impeachment, and he may be removed even against the will of the President."

STEVE CHARNOVITZ

New Haven, Conn.

Editorial Feature

Reno Gets By
As Gates Gets Burned

What's Janet Reno got that Bill Gates doesn't?

Charm? Money? It must be something special, because the attorney general sure gets better treatment at the hands of Republican Senate Judiciary Chairman Orrin Hatch.

Ms. Reno still refuses to name an independent counsel for campaign finance, and barely deigns to answer Senate questions about it. Last week she treated Mr. Hatch as dismissively as a cub reporter at her Thursday press appearances.

Potomac Watch

By Paul A. Gigot

Don't "wave editorials at me," she rebuked Mr. Hatch. Yet Ms. Reno emerged with barely a political scratch.

Microsoft Chairman Gates, on the other hand, was foolish enough to cooperate with the Utah senator. He testified under oath in March, and for his trouble has become Mr. Hatch's favorite whipping boy. His aides have all but called Mr. Gates a liar, and he's held hearings that are merely showcases for Microsoft competitors.

This juxtaposition reveals a lot about the balance of power in Washington. Mr. Gates runs a wealth-creating business, but that only makes him a ripe political target here. Ms. Reno could be abusing her high office to protect the president, but she wields the levers of law enforcement and fights back.

Rather than tangle with Ms. Reno, Mr. Hatch prefers to pick on

Mr. Gates. Indeed, his attack on Mr. Gates gives Ms. Reno cover for her own antitrust jihad against Microsoft. And Republicans wonder why the Clinton administration gets away with so much?

On recent facts alone, Ms. Reno should be feeling more political heat than any attorney general since John Mitchell. Her own FBI director says "it is difficult to imagine a more compelling situation for appointing an independent counsel." He's now seconded by Ms. Reno's hand-picked campaign-finance prosecutor, Charles La Bella, who's walking away from the case. When Ed Meese's deputies resigned in protest over less momentous issues in the 1980s, a political firestorm erupted—and he later resigned.

Ms. Reno has also just been rebuked by a federal appeals judge for inappropriately "acting as the president's counsel" to blunt Ken Starr's probe. And her Teamster investigation, so threatening to labor's alliance with Democrats, seems stalled in the southern district of New York. Those of us who thought Clinton Justice deserved a chance to prove its independence have to admit we were wrong.

But Ms. Reno must figure she can get away with all of this because she always has before. Despite a year of GOP complaint,  she has paid no political price. Her judicial nominees slide through as they always have. Her budget is bigger than ever.

Even her civil rights deputy, Bill Lann Lee, wields power on an "acting" basis though he was rejected by Mr. Hatch's committee. According to his spokeswoman, Mr. Hatch's response to this effrontery has been to explore "amending the Vacancies Act." Ms. Reno must be impressed.

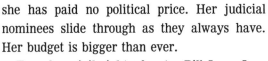
Orrin Hatch

In hearings, senators handle Mr. Clinton's most valuable player like delicate china, afraid to question her motives. They hail her "integrity" before they utter a word of criticism. But if their criticism is nothing but a difference of opinion, what's the big deal? None of them dares to suggest that Ms. Reno has named special counsels in minor cases (Henry Cisneros) precisely so she can avoid naming one when it most matters politically (against the president).

She also wields her gender like a shield, knowing the male Republicans on Judiciary lack the nerve to even consider impeaching her. Sure, they'll whine and stomp their feet. Pennsylvania's Arlen Specter now threatens a dubious lawsuit, but Ms. Reno knows that's also a dodge from the riskier politics of confrontation.

The same immunity doesn't apply to Mr. Gates, who faces lawsuits from Justice and 20 states. Far from scrutinizing this effort, Mr. Hatch has been urging them on. His one-sided hearing in March portrayed Mr. Gates as a robber baron, and he's kept the heat on since.

Mr. Hatch is a courtly man who likes to think he's fair. Yet he has unleashed his staff to show where Mr. Gates "could and should have been more forthright with the committee." Thus what looks to me like an honest disagreement over contracts is portrayed by Mr. Hatch as deception.

Mr. Hatch's pursuit of Microsoft is so tenacious that he's losing Republicans on his own committee. Few senators attended his latest anti-Microsoft show yesterday, while three have sent him a letter questioning Justice's support for foreign governments that want to sue Microsoft.

No one seems sure why Mr. Gates has become the senator's great white whale. Some cite Utah-based Novell Inc., whose software was crushed by Microsoft. Others think he wants to be president, or a Supreme Court justice, and so he craves the publicity a Republican gets when he attacks business.

Or maybe Orrin Hatch really believes that a software company spreading prosperity is a greater threat to our democracy than an attorney general who defies the Senate, spurns her advisers and avoids the clear meaning of the law.

Editorial Feature

A Corrupt Union Escapes Justice

By Rael Jean Isaac

When the Justice Department entered into an "operating agreement" with LIUNA, the mob-ridden Laborers International Union of North America, Attorney General Janet Reno hailed the agreement as a new model for racket-busting. Under the February 1995 agreement, the union would clean its own house over three years, and if the Justice Department was not satisfied with the union's progress, it would have authority to impose a previously agreed-upon consent decree and take over as it had the Teamsters. Laborers President Arthur A. Coia, described in a Justice Department memo as a "mob puppet," would remain in place, supervising the cleanup.

But although Justice professes itself satisfied with progress and has extended the arrangement until next January, there is evidence that there is less to the internal reform than meets the eye. Justice had best return to the drawing board while the threat of the consent decree still gives it clout over the union.

Raised Eyebrows

The agreement raised eyebrows at the outset, for it created the appearance that Mr. Coia's wooing of Bill and Hillary Clinton had paid off. LIUNA was one of the largest donors to the Democratic Party, and Mr. Coia contributed the maximum possible to Mr. Clinton's legal defense fund. What's more, Mr. Coia was an outspoken political ally, even breaking ranks with the entire labor movement to campaign for the North American Free Trade Agreement.

Financial and political support brought social access, from break-fasts at the White House with Mrs. Clinton to trips on Air Force One with the president. A House Judiciary subcommittee documented more than 120 such contacts.

The Justice Department's draft complaint under the Racketeer Influenced and Corrupt Organizations law demanded Mr. Coia's ouster and declared that LIUNA has been "continuously and system-atically controlled, exploited and dominated in the conduct of its affairs by the Cosa Nostra." The complaint arrived on Mr. Coia's desk the same day as the president's thank-you note for the gift of a specially made golf club.

When the Justice Department abruptly backed down on its demand for Mr. Coia's ouster, the appearance of White House inter-ference led to July 1996 House hearings. But those hearings backfired on the Republicans. Justice Department officials stoutly denied that any pressure had been brought to bear. Rather, they said, Justice had been given an attractive offer: Never before had a union offered to purge itself of mobsters at its own expense, backing this up by hiring a team of former federal pros-ecutors and FBI agents, with no one, Mr. Coia included, off limits for investigation.

Arthur Coia

Last Nov. 6 Robert D. Luskin, LIUNA's attor-ney who is acting as chief prosecutor of corruption within the union, announced that he was finally instituting corruption charges against Mr. Coia. But eight months later, union members do not know what the specific charges are or what has transpired in the secret internal proceedings. Kenneth Boehm of the watchdog National Legal and Policy Center says that although the team has at its command numerous former FBI field agents, there have been no in-depth investigations of Coia's activities in Rhode Island, his home base, or in Connecticut, where Mr. Coia had close ties to Local 230 and the District Council.

This shouldn't be surprising. The Justice Department had claimed that its decision to allow LIUNA to investigate itself was based not on Mr. Coia's high-profile friendship with Mr. Clinton but on the cre-dentials of the investigative team. LIUNA's general counsel, Michael Bearse, later assured Congress that the union, "by entrusting oversight and enforcement to independent officials of unquestioned integrity," had ensured that investigations would be conducted "free from all internal or external political considerations."

But Justice should have seen a glaring conflict of interest at the outset. For the man who sold Justice on the proposal that saved Mr. Coia's neck was LIUNA's lawyer, Mr. Luskin. True, earlier in his career he had served as special counsel to the Justice Department's organized crime section. But was it realistic to expect him to turn overnight from Mr. Coia's advocate into Mr. Coia's investigator, while he continued to be paid by the union? A telling early sign suggested that Mr. Luskin continued to think like a Coia-partisan. In April 1995, U.S. district Judge Emmett G. Sullivan asked why, given the Justice Department's 212-page draft complaint against Mr. Coia, he had not been removed. Mr. Luskin's response, according to the Providence Journal-Bulletin, was that the draft complaint was a government bargaining tool, not an accurate depiction of the union and Mr. Coia.

Equally troubling, it turns out that Mr. Luskin, at the very time he was working out the unprecedented agreement between Justice and Mr. Coia, was allegedly accepting "hot" money, to the tune of $700,000, from Stephen A. Saccoccia, a Patriarca crime family associate now in prison for money laundering. Mr. Luskin was representing Saccoccia on appeal from his 1993 sentence of 660 years. Saccoccia's assets were frozen under a court order, and the money had come to Mr. Luskin in the form of gold bars and Swiss wire transfers. Mr. Luskin settled a case brought by the U.S. attorney's office in Rhode Island, which accused him of "willful blindness" in accepting these "surreptitious and anonymous payments." Earlier, a federal judge had shot down Luskin's argument that his financial arrangements with Saccoccia were protected by attorney-client privilege. Mr. Luskin, claiming he had no idea the money was part of Saccoccia's ill-gotten gains and calling the government's action "despicable," nonetheless forfeited $245,000.

A second member of the four-man team in charge of LIUNA's anti-corruption campaign has political ties to Mr. Coia's pal the president. W. Neil Eggleston, who has the role of appeals officer, worked in the Clinton White House counsel's office when the Whitewater investigation began and now represents Mr. Clinton in his effort to assert attorney-client privilege in the Monica Lewinsky investigation. Mr.

Eggleston also represents Labor Secretary Alexis Herman, now the subject of an independent counsel probe into suspected corruption.

While the other two members of the investigative team do not carry political baggage, it is hard to imagine results embarrassing to the White House surviving the LIUNA internal appeals process under Mr. Eggleston's control. And given that the Clintons ignored repeated warnings from both Justice and the FBI to stay clear of Mr. Coia, his ouster would embarrass them.

The effect of the operating agreement so far has been to reinforce Mr. Coia's power in LIUNA. Overnight he became the champion of "reform," and he has taken credit for the trusteeships imposed on district councils in New York, Chicago and Buffalo—an unavoidable action, given the detail with which the Justice Department's draft complaint described the mob's robbery of Laborers' pension and welfare funds in these councils.

But elsewhere, Laborers rank-and-file reformers complain that the old pattern of corruption backed by intimidation and violence continues, with the Luskin team failing to take appropriate action. In July 1997, 53-year-old Steve Manos, vice president of Local 230 in Hartford, Conn., was threatened, cursed at and beaten when he probed union expenditures at an executive board meeting. Mr. Manos was wearing a wire; audible on tape are a string of unprintable curses, the sound of Mr. Manos being slammed against a concrete floor, and the ominous cry "We own you now!" as he is chased to his car. But although this local had a record of corruption (the previous business manager is in prison for taking a $500,000 bribe to invest $5 million of union pension funds in a worthless real estate scam), this incident resulted only in a mild reprimand from Mr. Luskin. On May 4, Mr. Manos testified in a congressional hearing that "Luskin's actions, in effect, have facilitated the racketeering activities directed at me."

Severe Head Injuries

Joe Portiss, a member of Local 1089 in Sarnia, Ontario, and his daughter, Laura, say they have compiled extensive documentation on violations of LIUNA's ethics code by the local's executive board. Ms. Portiss says the Luskin team has ignored their complaints. She describes a long pattern of intimidation and violence, of which the worst was a 1983 group assault on her father at a LIUNA meeting, in which he sustained severe, permanent head injuries. She says she now endures a steady stream of harassment and threats but is prepared to keep up the struggle "no matter how much they scare me— and they do, to be perfectly honest. I am afraid of them."

Few Laborers expect Mr. Coia will be gone when the government's chance to intervene lapses in January. Alex Corns, business manager of a small Hod Carriers local in San Francisco, has been struggling against corruption in his district council with scant help from Mr. Luskin's team. Says Mr. Corns: "This isn't a reform process. It's a retreat until the government is out of the way."

Ms. Isaac writes on public policy issues.

REVIEW & OUTLOOK

Sidney's Subpoenas

Congressional Democrats are just now pondering whether to jump
ship on the White House over resisting Kenneth Starr's subpoena of
President Clinton. As an indication of where this vessel is bound,
they might want to take a look at Sidney's subpoenas, that is, those
just issued by Sidney Blumenthal, hitman for the First Lady.

It has taken Mr. Blumenthal's fancy to start subpoenaing journalists, including our editorial board member John Fund. The subpoena
directs Mr. Fund to deliver "any and all documents relating to Sidney
Blumenthal" by Friday July 31 or Tuesday August 4—depending on
which document you read of the two Mr. Fund was served at home at
8:15 Saturday morning. Mr. Blumenthal's wife and something called
"The Blumenthal Project" are also included. Finally, there are any
and alls for Matt Drudge, the Drudge report, Michael Ledeen,
Barbara Ledeen, Richard Carlson, Tucker Carlson of The Weekly
Standard and David Brock, formerly of The American Spectator. If
you need a road map, this is Mr. Blumenthal's private enemies list,
except that one-time enemy David Brock has apparently switched
camp to become an ally.

From his White House ward, Mr. Blumenthal imagines he's
acquired the right to subpoena all this by virtue of his private libel
suit against Mr. Drudge. The Internet's Drudge Report once reported a rumor that Mr. Blumenthal had been accused of wife-beating,
an accusation Mr. Drudge quickly withdrew and apologized for. Mr.
Blumenthal nonetheless sued, and is now using his lawsuit on behalf

of Bill Clinton, setting out to harass and intimidate the President's critics, including this newspaper. Our attorney likely will have to file motions to quash this abuse of the subpoena power.

Mr. Blumenthal was of course wronged by publication of the unsubstantiated rumor, but this may be a $1 lawsuit. Mr. Drudge apologized, and Mr. Blumenthal is a public figure. Quick retraction both mitigates damages and serves as evidence against the personal animus public figures typically have to show to recover punitive damages. Presumably the subpoenas are trying to establish a source for Mr. Drudge's comments, but it's a curious exercise for a libel plaintiff to show the defendant had a source. Asked about this, Mr. Blumenthal's lawyer said he wants to question Mr. Fund so he can sue him next—then disavowed this burst of candor by denying the subpoena is a fishing expedition.

Sidney Blumenthal

To state the obvious, The Wall Street Journal did not print the Blumenthal rumor. Mr. Blumenthal now asks us to account for any reporting that led us not to print it. For the record, Mr. Fund did attend a Washington dinner four years ago with Mr. Brock at which the rumor was broached, but the two stopped talking after a falling-out over FBI agent Gary Aldrich's accusations of White House security breaches. Mr. Fund has never discussed Mr. Blumenthal with Mr. Drudge and has never heard of anything called "the Blumenthal Project."

But of course this is not a rational damage suit, but a political jihad on behalf of the President of the United States. Just what are all documents "relating to Sidney Blumenthal"? We would be glad to send the three volumes of our Whitewater collection, compiling the evidence it is Mr. Blumenthal's job to obscure. We also have a nice collection of articles on feminism by Barbara Ledeen, and on national defense issues by Michael. The impossible sweep of the subpoena is evidence of at best a fishing expedition, at worst an attempt to punish with logistical burdens.

Abuse of the legal process, not sexual acrobatics, is the Clinton Administration's most serious sin. We have the Attorney General spurning requests by the head of the FBI and her own handpicked investigator to name a campaign finance independent counsel. We have Craig Livingstone rummaging through FBI files, including, we belatedly learn, those of Mr. Aldrich and Linda Tripp. We have missing documents appearing in the White House family quarters. We have Janet Reno blessing an investigation of The American Spectator on just how it spent its money producing articles critical of the President. And now we have Mr. Blumenthal's speciously private effort to harass critical journalists.

This is a sign of desperation that all Democrats ought to ponder as they get sucked deeper and deeper into the Clinton vortex. Howard Kurtz of the Washington Post reports of an earlier White House report attacking Sue Schmidt of the Post, and chartered by Hillary Clinton at the suggestion of Mr. Blumenthal before he joined the White House. Press Secretary Mike McCurry sequestered all copies, telling a staff meeting, "This is the dumbest idea I've ever heard in my life." With his usual keen timing, Mr. McCurry announced his resignation last week, as Sidney's subpoenas were being drafted.

REVIEW & OUTLOOK

The President's Subpoena

Throughout the five years of his Presidency, Bill Clinton has received high marks from every precinct for one skill: spin. The reality of any objective event, a Filegate, is taken by the President or his agents and "spun" into a kind of post-reality consensus favorable or non-threatening to the Presidency. There is even now a book about it titled "Spin Cycle." But on every washing machine ever built there's one inexorable reality about the spin cycle: it stops.

Kenneth Starr's subpoena to a sitting President suggests that after five years, the spin cycle is starting to slow.

The first, strong sign came on Thursday a fortnight ago, when the full panel of the federal appeals court for the District of Columbia turned away the President's claim of a protective-privilege function for his Secret Service detail. The panel's decision pointedly said none of its members was interested in hearing the government's argument. Then on Friday an appeal to the Chief Justice also fell flat, with Justice Rehnquist saying he doubted the White House would prevail before the full Supreme Court. Yesterday, a D.C. Circuit Court panel ruled 3-0, including two Clinton appointees, that top aide Bruce Lindsey is not entitled to claim lawyer-client privilege on his conversations with the President. And yesterday Monica Lewinsky herself spent the day with Starr prosecutors.

The truth is, Bill Clinton has finally spun himself into a place where spin does not exist. Federal courts aren't perfect places; they can play politics and yes, they often "make" laws. But it is beginning to dawn on the political community that Mr. Starr's subpoena to the President—indeed the whole of his clash with the Presidency—has risen to a realm of unavoidably austere issues of constitutionality and the rule of law.

If you're a Democrat, the President's timing couldn't be worse. This is all happening within whistling distance of two events: a national election to form a new Congress and the presentation of Mr. Starr's full report to the current Congress. That is, the Democratic Party, already scratching to prevent slippage in its Congressional membership, must now face the prospect of loading the Clinton Presidency onto the donkey cart and hauling the whole legal morass forward to November. Will they bear this load?

Maybe—but maybe not.

The Starr subpoena is forcing Democrats toward the one choice they'd always hoped to avoid: They have to choose whether to go the distance with Bill Clinton, or get off before November. Insofar as getting off is difficult, the next-best choice is to make sure that if Mr. Clinton is along for the ride, he at least remains presentable in public. Comments from prominent Democrats this past weekend made it clear that the behavior of the nation's highest legal officer is much on their minds.

House minority leader and bellwether Dick Gephardt said: "I have always believed that Bill Clinton would do as he said he would do. He would get all the necessary information to the Independent Counsel." Senator Joe Lieberman suggested, "I think he's got to talk to the prosecutors and the grand jury, so it's not even a choice in the end."

Our reading of these events is that the Democratic Party elders have begun to see what the White House may never see—that what worked till now has become, all of a sudden, indefensible. Mr. Clinton himself signed the reauthorization of the Independent Counsel law, and it is the clear language of this law that the President is a *covered person*. In other words, whether or not a President can be summoned by the Podunk DA, Mr. Clinton's own pen gave a special position to subpoenas from Mr. Starr's office.

The President may choose again to order his lawyers to further fight, litigate and delay the Independent Counsel's subpoena. It is not so clear what he might order his spinners to do about resulting court rebuffs stretching from here to November. The arguments now are strictly about accountability, in the courts and at the polls. ˙

REVIEW & OUTLOOK

Asides

Correction

The appeals court decision Monday against the White House's claim of attorney-client privilege for counselor Bruce Lindsey was on a 2-1 vote. Initial press stories, quoted in yesterday's editorial, reported a 3-0 vote. Judge David Tatel dissented, arguing that "I think Presidents need their official attorney-client privilege to permit frank discussion not only of innocuous, routine issues, but also sensitive, embarrassing or even potentially criminal topics."

In the majority view of Judges A. Raymond Randolph and Judith W. Rogers, "Only a conceit among those admitted to the bar could explain why legal advice should be on a higher plane than advice about policy, or politics, or why a President's conversations with the most junior lawyer in the White House counsel's office is deserving of more protection from disclosure than a President's discussions with his vice president or a Cabinet secretary."

Beyond Monica

As the matters chronicled in these volumes sped through the summer of 1998, a decisive corner was turned between 10:00 and 10:05 p.m. EST on August 17. For five minutes, the American public saw the unvarnished Bill Clinton, trapped between his own lies and a former White House intern's offering of state's evidence and a semen-stained dress. The President was bitter, self-pitying, evasive, unconvincing and anything but contrite.

Earlier that day, Mr. Clinton had testified for at least four hours before Kenneth Starr's grand jury, appearing via video link from the White House. Over the same weekend, he was engaged in preparations for the anti-terrorist cruise missile attacks launched three days after his testimony. The President reportedly had refused six previous invitations to testify voluntarily both before and after Mr. Starr reached an agreement with the former intern, Monica Lewinsky, giving her and her mother blanket immunity in return for full and truthful testimony. Mr. Starr ultimately issued a subpoena—the first for a sitting President—but withdrew it when Mr. Clinton agreed to appear.

In the immediate wake of his speech and testimony, the President's poll ratings held up, but his political support started to erode. Press commentary was withering, even from liberal and Democratic sources. Facing a November election, party stalwarts moved to a neutral position. Only a praetorian guard continued to make the President's case, and Kenneth Starr pressed on. While the Lewinsky matter became clearer, Mr. Starr's charter also called for him to investigate any crimes relating to the Whitewater land transactions and loans, the Travel Office firings and the misappropriation of FBI files. Possible obstruction of justice in the Lewinsky episode was clearly related to possibilities of the same offense in the other matters—not only by a President subject to impeachment but by underlings subject to possible indictment. And as the Journal noted, the Presidential admission of sex with a subordinate strengthened the Paula Jones case as it headed for appeal.

The President's speech backfired, but perhaps it was inevitable—in his genes, as the Journal speculated. And what, after all, could he say? When the prospect of a Presidential apology was first floated, the Journal published what its editors consider their favorite editorial of all these volumes—"Mea Culpa" (August 4) by deputy editor and resident stylist Daniel Henninger:

"Yes, I lied about Monica. . . . And yes, I advised Monica to lie, pretty much the way I advised Gennifer Flowers to deny the same stuff years before. . . . Now's the time to admit I was in the middle of arranging hush money for my good friend Webb Hubbell . . . And yes, I had my good friend Vincent Foster sign a fraudulent tax return for 1992, omitting the gift I received from Jim McDougal when he assumed the Whitewater debts. I sincerely hope this didn't have anything to do with Vince's suicide . . .

"I want to apologize to Paula Jones for all the loose talk about trailer trash and $100 bills. . . . The money received from Asian interests, not to mention AFL-CIO contributions in violation of the Beck decision, were the key to my 1996 election, and for this I extend deepest apologies to Bob Dole. . . . Finally, I would like to take this opportunity to apologize for the lies I told to Col. Holmes concerning the ROTC, and I guess I should apologize to the guy who took my place in Vietnam."

In short, a summary of these four volumes in 800 words.

Review & Outlook

Beyond Monica

In the moments after the news flashed across wire services that Monica Lewinsky had received blanket immunity from the independent counsel, the White House replied that President Clinton was pleased that "things are working out" for her. The thought was more appropriate than the source; perhaps Ms. Lewinsky may now begin the familiar but much-needed process of assembling an adulthood.

The Republic, however, is left with a problem. President Clinton, his lawyer announced yesterday, will drop his opposition to the Starr subpoena and give videotaped testimony from the White House. He is already on record that he had no sexual relationship with "that woman" and asked no one to lie, points she is now ready to contradict, presumably supported by corroborating testimony from Secret Service agents and others. The point here is not sex, but lying and abuse of office.

We suspect, further, that when Mr. Starr's report is finally delivered, it will dwell on Ms. Lewinsky merely as the clearest case of a pattern of behavior Mr. Starr has been investigating for four years. It will likely dwell instead on the profusion of lies, abuse and obstruction suggested by the graphic we ran on this page February 12. Ms. Lewinsky might have profited from the advice in a Rolling Stones song, predating her birth but familiar to the adults she has been hanging around with, in which Mick Jagger sings languidly and ominously: "Don't play with me, 'cause you're playing with fire."

Playing with fire is Bill Clinton's life force, as is clear now to a great many older and more experienced people stretching back through the Whitewater land partnerships and forward through relationships with the Rose Law Firm, Tyson Foods, the Lippo Group, the Democratic National Committee, several Cabinet secretaries, the Teamsters Union and various former White House aides, financial backers and star-struck women.

All these entities (and boy, are there a lot of them) have as their own Clinton legacy a common experience: Each got into trouble, often of a seriousness sufficient to send them to jail, not merely because they associated with Mr. Clinton, but because the machinery of the law moved to establish *the truth* of what they did for him.

In each case, the principals either lied about what they did, only partially explained what they did or refused any explanation. That in turn over the past five years caused Congress, the courts and prosecutors to issue subpoenas, call grand juries, hand down indictments and obtain convictions to establish the truth.

Bill Clinton

Webster Hubbell, appointed to a high position in the Department of Justice, went to jail for corrupting his partnership with the Rose Law Firm. Top officials of Tyson Foods have been convicted of or pleaded guilty to charges of corrupting Mr. Clinton's Agriculture Department. The Democratic National Committee, acting as agents for Mr. Clinton's re-election campaign, debased the laws governing elections. An independent counsel was appointed by the court to investigate a Secretary of Commerce's role in that corruption. Teamster President Ron Carey has just been barred for life from the union.

Before that there was the Travel Office affair, Filegate and the Health Care Task Force's violations of federal laws. In each instance, the Clinton operatives didn't push the edge of the envelope; they burst it, violating the good faith that undergirds our laws and processes of government. When the press asked who fired the Travel Office employees, when Congress asked who misused hundreds of raw FBI files or when a federal judge asked for cooperation from Mrs. Clinton's health-care advisers, the relevant Clinton appointees in each instance, and repeatedly, gave replies that were laughably not the truth. I lied to my diary. Those White House documents just appeared.

And before all this there was news of Hillary's commodities coup, $1,000 transformed via cattle futures into $100,000. And before everything else happened, there was Whitewater.

On May 28, 1996, Independent Counsel Kenneth Starr, appointed to investigate allegations of lawbreaking in the Clinton's Whitewater land deals, obtained convictions in federal court against Jim McDougal, his wife Susan, and the then-governor of Arkansas Jim Guy Tucker. Later, Jim McDougal said the Clintons went through people's lives "like a tornado." One such life was Susan McDougal. Susan McDougal sat in a jail cell rather than simply say whether Bill Clinton's testimony in her trial was truthful. That is, whether he lied.

This has been a story about lying as a philosophy of life and a philosophy of government. Monica Lewinsky, the girl in the beret seen so often staring upward into the eyes of the President of the United States, is but one character in the cast attached to the personal and political tragedy of this Presidency, which may have arrived at its denouement.

Maybe reducing the whole thing to "Monica" makes it somehow comprehendible. It is important, though, to properly understand what is happening now in this one instance. Preceded by a great number of adults who in the orbit of the nation's highest office acted with less honor than she, this young woman, with her immunity and under oath, will presumably speak the truth. If so, she will speak for many.

Editorial Feature

Dems Stand by Their Man.
Good Luck!

Give Democrat Chaka Fattah credit. At least the Philadelphia congressman was willing to defend President Clinton in public this week. The rest of his party colleagues were taking the fifth, so to speak.

Mr. Fattah bravely went on CNBC's "Hardball" to argue that Monica Lewinsky's immunity deal with Ken Starr is no problem. This startled Chris Matthews, the show's host and former spinmeister to Democrat Tip O'Neill, who asked, "So this is *good* news for Bill Clinton? . . . That the woman's gonna bring state's evidence against the president, charging him with having a sexual relationship with a 21-year-old?"

Potomac Watch

By Paul A. Gigot

Mr. Fattah was left stammering that Ms. Lewinsky may be imagining a "fantasy relationship."

Other Democrats in Congress may soon have to reach similar depths of political improvisation. For seven months—or four years, if you take the entire Starr probe—they've loyally supported the president's strategy of stonewall and delay. Now they discover they've delayed long enough to face a Starr report or indictments just weeks before they run for re-election. Dr. Faust knew all about this kind of bargain.

For a while it looked like the Tammy Wynette strategy might pay off for Democrats. Mr. Clinton had raised a pile of cash for them, despite the scandal. He'd moved left on the issues, promising to veto GOP bills and fight for theirs. He gave them hope of retaking the House—which is the only reason such old bulls as John Dingell chose to stick around.

By hitching themselves to Bill's Starr-bursting, Democrats hoped to avoid the GOP's fate of 1974. In that Watergate year, Republicans thought Nixon's August resignation would absolve them in November. But their own voters were so demoralized they didn't turn out, and Democrats gained 48 House seats.

"The first person who stands up now and says something, the dam breaks, and who knows what happens then?" explains one Democrat. Better the devil they doubt (Bill Clinton) than the devil they know (Newt Gingrich).

But the price for slavish spinning is high and rising. Burdened by scandal, Mr. Clinton has lost his power to persuade. Republicans have shredded his agenda with no discernible downside. Mr. Clinton can't create public support for the issues—tobacco, campaign reform, education, HMOs—Democrats want to run on.

Instead Democrats now find to their horror that the president himself may become the issue this fall. "We're creating an unnecessary referendum on Clinton, which is exactly what the party was not planning to do," says Brian

Monica Lewinsky

Lunde, a rare Democratic consultant who'll speak on the record. "Now the election is getting nationalized around the scandal."

This makes GOP scandal calculations that much easier. Mr. Starr's report will now come too late for Congress to hold impeachment hearings before November. "There's just not enough time on the schedule," says House GOP campaign chief John Linder. But a report might come soon enough for the press to broadcast, and voters to absorb, damaging details about abuse of power.

Imagine an autumn with Linda Tripp's tapes made public, Monica Lewinsky's testimony on TV, and coverup facts uncovered. Republicans can take the high road, while reporters ask Democrats whether they favor a Clinton perjury loophole: It's OK for a president to lie under oath, as long as it's about sex and the Dow is above 9000.

Fear of this nightmare helps explain the clamor among honest liberals that Mr. Clinton now offer a Mea Monica Culpa. Everyone from Leon Panetta to Lanny Davis(!) is pushing the grand apology. The president could say he had to lie to protect Hillary, or more emotive yet, Chelsea. He wanted to spare them, and the country, embarrassment for his personal lapse. But he's been a good president and . . . you can write it yourself.

In our therapeutic culture, this might even work. It would sure make life easier for Democrats, who could attack Republicans for bloodlust, without having to defend the president's misbehavior.

But don't hold your breath. An apology would require Mr. Clinton to overcome a lifetime of political habit. He has lied his entire career and been rewarded for it. He has learned that if he can persevere long enough, and smash back hard enough, he can survive. He also knows that a confession on perjury still wouldn't answer the questions about obstructing justice.

So look for more of what White House aides privately call "thermonuclear war." Look for Monica to join Linda Tripp on the trash heap of Clinton history, and for the attacks on Ken Starr to resume.

Mr. Clinton will accommodate when he is forced to do so politically—as he has in answering Mr. Starr's subpoena. He knew Democrats couldn't support him if he resisted. But even here his spinners boast that they forced Mr. Starr to make concessions, especially on the scope of questions. This hardly sounds like a new desire to tell all.

We are watching the greatest barroom brawl of our age. The trouble for Democrats is that their reward for standing by their man may be to get a bottle smashed over their heads before Bill Clinton does.

Editorial Feature

Clinton's Nature and The Nature of Politics

When William Jefferson Clinton visited The Wall Street Journal after his 1982 political comeback in Arkansas, he left no lasting impression other than as a nice young Democrat with a useful talent for saying the right things in the right places. It seems safe to recall that none of us who met him thought of him as a future U.S. president. This was no Dwight David Eisenhower or Franklin Delano Roosevelt, but just an unprepossessing, innocent-looking lad from Arkansas.

Global View

By George Melloan

How wrong we were, of course. Bill Clinton was hardly an innocent. He employed his already evident political skills to propel himself to the very top, attaining the awesome powers of U.S. chief executive and commander-in-chief. Possessed of enormous self-confidence, he even proved to be reasonably competent on the job. No disasters have befallen the country on his watch. Some American voters suspected character flaws from the beginning and the numbers increased as the press and prosecutors delved more deeply into the man's conduct of offices past and present. But still he was a young, nice-looking, amazingly articulate politician and the country was prosperous. So he was able to deflect the frequent charges of misconduct even as associate after associate paid a price in jail terms and lost reputations for having been his friend.

Now he is in the most serious trouble of his career. If he should fall from his high perch because of his dalliances and disregard for legal norms there will be those who mourn his fate and vent their bitterness at the critics who laid him low. Others will blame the "system," which they will say makes it impossible for a poor boy to get ahead in politics without seeking out questionable ways to raise large amounts of money. And there will be those cynics who buy a poisonous little soufflé of relativism concocted by the subtle propagandists of the Clinton White House: "He is no worse than all other politicians." Many others have woman problems—it's an occupational hazard—and even more are beholden to the moneyed interests who have financed their campaigns.

A truly detached listener, if one exists, would have to admit that there is a grain of truth in that argument. Political campaigns in the U.S. are extremely expensive, which means that would-be officeholders must spend a great deal of time with begging bowl in hand. Some very capable persons who would make admirable public servants are turned off by this requirement. It is true as well that male celebrities, whether basketball players, movie actors or politicians, are vulnerable to the advances of women attracted by their glamour or power. Some politicians have both power and glamour and are thus twice cursed. They also are "people persons," which makes them especially susceptible to the urge for intimate liaisons. Finally, given the central role compromise plays in the give and take of politics, it is not unusual for politicians to compromise to the point of illegality.

But while all these explanations can be offered for a president's shortcomings and no human being is gifted with moral perfection, it is important to keep in mind what is really at stake when a person in high office trespasses the law. Law itself comes under threat. Laws, fashioned out of public debate and enacted by elected representatives of the people, are what bind democratic societies together. They are the only protection against degeneration into disorder, chaos and ultimately civil violence. The iron principle that no man can be above the law is vital to the preservation of a society where men and women can feel secure in both their persons and property against the threat of injustice and abuses of power.

Clearly, it is imperative that this key principle be applied to the national leader with the ultimate responsibility for preserving and enforcing a rule of law. If his own lawlessness is treated with nonchalance, law itself will be eroded and corroded. Winston Churchill once wrote that in the British system of governance it is the unwritten duty of the party stalwarts who surround a prime minister to chop him down and replace him if he fails. In short, politics is not a sentimental business. At times, as was the case with Churchill, the fate of nations can be at stake. The only protection for those who are subject to a miscreant or incompetent leader's powers is a set of laws and traditions that subject him to the judgment of his peers. In the American system, it is the duty of party leaders, legislators, prosecutors and the courts to jointly make the fateful decision whether a president must go.

There is great merit in a political system that provides the means for bringing down, with some dispatch, an errant leader. Indeed, it might be said that this is one of the hallmarks of a healthy civil order. Look at the benighted corners of the world—Cuba, Iraq, Libya, North Korea—and you see failed leaders who cannot be dislodged. Saddam has sent hundreds of thousands of young men to their deaths with his mad military adventures and still is in power. Castro has inflicted poverty on Cubans for 40 years.

Not that Americans should wish for revolving-door governments, a la postwar Italy. But Italy's ferment is far preferable to Cuba's "stability." The economy works, for one thing. Its problem for years was that the door revolved but the same people kept going in and out. In recent years, there have been real changes.

There is a lot to be said for the British system, where the leader must endure competition and challenges in the Commons almost every week. A leader surrounded by his peers cannot afford to become too monarchical lest those peers cut him down to size. Subjecting him to questions in the Commons is also an effective way to keep him aware of his public obligations and the demands of probity.

Cutting down an American president is a more complex process and no doubt should be. He, unlike a British prime minister, is directly elected by mass vote. It must be seen that he not only has lost the confidence of his peers but also the confidence of the people themselves. It may seem when this is happening that journalists behave like jackals, but jackals do have their uses in maintaining the balance of nature. Holding the presidency of a great nation is not an entitlement; it must be earned every day. It seems that a lot of people, and presidents themselves, need to be reminded of that from time to time.

Review & Outlook

'Mea Culpa'

Everyone from Dick Morris to Orrin Hatch suggests that all will be forgiven if President Clinton confesses and apologizes. Never wanting to disturb an emerging consensus, we've given some thought to what Mr. Clinton might say:

Yes, I lied about Monica, and now that the evidence is growing incontrovertible I have to admit it. I did that to protect my innocent wife and child, and am sure they will forgive me.

And yes, I advised Monica to lie, pretty much the way I advised Gennifer Flowers to deny the same stuff years before. And yes, I put into motion events in which Monica asked Linda Tripp to lie, and also threatened Ms. Tripp if she wouldn't do it. I apologize to the American people.

Now's the time to admit I was in the middle of arranging hush money for my good friend Webb Hubbell. And yes, I put Craig Livingstone up to ransacking the FBI files. And yes, I told my good friend Governor Jim Guy Tucker he was the target of a criminal probe on Whitewater. And yes, I had my good friend Vincent Foster sign a fraudulent tax return for 1992, omitting the gift I received from Jim McDougal when he assumed the Whitewater debts. I sincerely hope this didn't have anything to do with Vince's suicide. I apologize to the IRS, and will send a check for the taxes owed.

I want to apologize to Paula Jones for all the loose talk about trailer trash and $100 bills. That's not right. I guess Kathleen Willey's life is ruined too. Kathy, seriously, I do apologize.

I want to apologize to the staff workers that Hillary and I fired from the White House Travel Office. I shouldn't have let my good friend Harry Thomason talk me into that. And the IRS audit we ordered up for UltrAir, sorry about that. My lawyers said then, "Mrs. Clinton does not know the origin of the decision to remove White House Travel Office employees." That was a lie, and I'm sorry my good friend David Watkins had to take the fall for it. I guess that means I need to apologize to Travel Office director Billy Dale for getting the Justice Department to indict and put him through a trial; I felt good that a jury acquitted him in two hours.

And yes, I met in the Oval Office in 1995 with Bruce Lindsey, John Huang, James Riady and Joe Giroir to set up a conspiracy to violate the campaign finance laws. The money received from Asian interests, not to mention AFL-CIO contributions in violation of the Beck decision, were the key to my 1996 election, and for this I extend deepest apologies to Bob Dole. In fact, I'll even apologize to Al Gore for making him my bag man at the Buddhist temple fund-raiser; sorry, Al. And renting out the Lincoln Bedroom to so many people I never met before; I hope you'll forgive me for that, too. I'm sorry about the drug dealers who snuck in without my knowing it for White House photo-ops. And Charlie Trie fleeing to China? What more can I say?

Bill Clinton

For anyone out there who's had to deal with my private investigators, Terry Lenzner or Jack Palladino, you have my blanket apology.

On Whitewater, there's a whole host of people I'd like to apologize to but time permits only a couple. Jim, you were right about Hillary and me being a tornado in people's lives. I'm trying to fix that here tonight. I'm sorry Susan had to do so much hard time rather than say whether I told the truth at her trial. There were also a bunch of Administration folks who had to resign for giving me a "heads-up" on my Whitewater problems, and I'm real sorry for what happened to them. And I apologize to that Resolution Trust woman, Jean Lewis, for the smear campaign we waged against her; that was bad advice, and I shouldn't have taken it.

This goes back a ways but it's time for me to apologize to Dan Lasater about that Little Rock cocaine conviction; Roger's testimony against you Dan was really the only option; I hope my pardon helped.

Federal Judge Royce Lamberth deserves my apologies. My lawyers' reluctance to come clean with him over Hillary's Health Care Task Force drove him to say a government "should be held accountable when its officials run amok." And he was right about that. I shouldn't have told all those people who testified to the D'Amato committee to claim loss of memory; that kind of set a bad precedent.

And yes it's true that Hillary's $100,000 commodity coup was a well-disguised bribe from Jim Blair and Tyson Foods. I stiffed the Tyson folks in 1979 when they wanted to put larger trucks on Arkansas roads, but have made up for it, and Mr. Blair has owned us ever since.

Finally I want to take this opportunity to apologize for the lies I told to Col. Holmes concerning the ROTC, and I guess I should apologize to the guy who took my place in Vietnam.

So now I can say that I sit before you tonight with a clean conscience. I ask the American people who elected me to forgive me for misleading them for five years, and I promise never again to tell a lie, engage in illicit sex, obstruct justice or abuse the powers invested in my high office. I hope after the little time we've spent together here this evening that I have earned your trust. God bless the American people for their infinite understanding.

Review & Outlook

Asides

No Coverage?

It seems a chunk of Linda Tripp's grand jury testimony wasn't about Monica Lewinsky but instead about how Clinton allies tried to intimidate her. Ms. Tripp told Tony Snow of Fox News last Thursday that White House deputy counsel Bruce Lindsey had told her she would be "destroyed" if she went public. She also reported that Ms. Lewinsky conveyed such messages as, "You have two children to think about" and that talking to reporters "is a dangerous thing to do." Surprisingly, the Media Research Center reports no broadcast networks except Fox covered these explosive allegations. Why not?

Editorial Feature

Doesn't He Ever Get Dizzy?

By CHRISTOPHER MATTHEWS

Bill Clinton is the best. What Michael Jordan can do with a basketball, this man can do with words.

"No one wants to get this matter behind us more than I do," he told a group of White House reporters in the Rose Garden last Friday, "except maybe all the rest of the American people."

With that engaging, unexceptional statement, the president connected with the millions of Americans groggy with Monica, Linda, Lucianne and the soiled dress. What he said, moreover, was patently true. Who would not agree that the man standing amid the flowers wants this mess behind him?

The audience thus prepared, Mr. Clinton then delivered the message he and his people had crafted to get him through the weekend: "I am looking forward to the opportunity . . .of testifying. I am anxious to do it." This same fellow, who had dodged six prior requests to testify voluntarily, and who agreed to talk only after the independent counsel had served him with a subpoena, was now suddenly eager to clear the air. What made Friday's performance a real classic, however, was that most of the audience didn't even notice the dizzying spin Mr. Clinton had executed.

In my book "Hardball," I explained the art of spin as "a traditional two-step: first, admit you have a problem, thereby establishing credibility, then use the enhanced credibility to define the problem in a way that keeps the political damage to a minimum." In Friday's press conference, Mr. Clinton managed to disguise an obvious untruth—that he was eager to testify—by prefacing it with an obvious truth—that he wanted the scandal behind him.

Bill Clinton proved his deftness at spin in his national debut. The night of the 1992 New Hampshire primary, he went on TV at 10 p.m. to declare himself the day's big winner. The man who'd come in eight points behind Paul Tsongas was now the self-crowned "Comeback Kid."

Mr. Clinton didn't invent spin any more than Michael Jordan invented the fake. President Reagan and his aides were masters of the art, as their handling of the David Stockman mess demonstrated. Budget director Stockman had told reporter William Greider that the president's budget numbers "didn't quite mesh." Chief of staff James Baker let it be known that Mr. Stockman was going for a "trip to the woodshed" with the president. The "woodshed" line refocused public attention from the substance of Mr. Greider's story to the soap opera of a lieutenant's betrayal—a masterpiece of spin.

But Mr. Clinton has added several new dimensions to the game. For example, White House reporters are regularly rebuffed with the charge that an unwanted question deals with "old news." "We've been at this six months," presidential press secretary Michael McCurry said last Wednesday after Monica Lewinsky agreed to give state's evidence, "and it hasn't really changed." First the truth; then the untruth.

Another Clinton variation on the old two-step is simply to change the story without admitting it. He denied the authenticity of tapes produced by Gennifer Flowers, then apologized to New York's then-Gov. Mario Cuomo for something he'd said on them. He denied ever breaking the drug laws, then amended the record to say he may have broken the laws of Britain "a time or two." He denied having sex with Ms. Flowers in 1992, then remembered in 1998 that he may have done it once. In each case, he told a small truth, tucking away the large untruth that had preceded it.

We all await the Big Spin when Mr. Clinton gets grilled by the grand jury on Aug. 17. The lawyers in the White House, including Mr. Clinton himself, are wary of admitting he failed to tell the truth in his Jan. 17 sworn testimony. At the same time, many leaders in both parties are urging that he offer some further explanation of his relations with Ms. Lewinsky.

One way for Mr. Clinton to meet both goals is to spin. He could tell the country he "never claimed to be perfect," then proceed to deny the affair itself. The press would file their stories under the large headline: "PRESIDENT SAYS HE'S 'NOT PERFECT.'" Only the small headline would say, "Denies Lewinsky Affair." Of course, he would still face Monica and her dress, but the public would feel they'd really heard enough of this. The Clintonites would roar their approval of the president's "character." Mr. Starr would be left hanging, asking for a hair sample or some even cruder specimen from a man who'd already told the country he was no saint.

Bill Clinton, the politician and the man, will do what he will. But if he does try a spin, it's our job, as citizens and reporters, to catch him.

Mr. Matthews is the San Francisco Examiner's Washington bureau chief and host of CNBC's "Hardball."

REVIEW & OUTLOOK

Asides

Two Trains Running

Events of the past two days show the extent to which the Clinton saga is running in two directions—one legal, the other political. Alas, it appears the two directions are headed straight at each other. Possibly a drop of nearly 300 points in the Dow Jones Industrial Average yesterday suggests the markets see a train wreck coming.

Yesterday, for the second time in a month, Chief Justice William Rehnquist refused to stay a ruling by the U.S. Court of Appeals against a White House privilege claim. Last time it was the Secret Service. This time it's the President's lawyers, specifically Bruce Lindsey.

On Monday, the Administration's lawyers were turned down by the full appeals court with a speed many observers found startling. Legal scholar Jonathan Turley correctly noted that one consequence of using his lawyers this way is that Mr. Clinton "may ultimately be viewed as something of a constitutional spendthrift who easily frittered away the privileges of his office."

Meanwhile, there was a fairly astonishing development on the political front, where the principles of fair play are not so well established as in court. It appears that former Justice Department campaign-finance prosecutor Charles La Bella has just been paid back for not being a team player. Recall that Mr. La Bella was brought in from Southern California last year to put the bungled Justice Department campaign probe back on track. Then when he resigned, it was said that he would return to his federal attorney's job in San

Diego. Before departing Mr. La Bella recommended that Attorney General Reno appoint an independent counsel, as did FBI Director Louis Freeh.

Yesterday came news via the New York Times that Mr. La Bella had been passed over for the U.S. Attorney job in San Diego. Instead, California's Democratic Senator Barbara Boxer has nominated Gregory Vega, president of the Hispanic National Bar Association, for the post. Senator Boxer's daughter is married to Hillary Rodham's brother, and yesterday the Congressional Hispanic Caucus vowed to stand by Mr. Clinton "to the end."

REVIEW & OUTLOOK

The Veto Presidency

In between prepping for his Monica testimony, President Clinton has been out traveling and threatening Congress with a string of vetoes. The important thing to keep in mind is that these events are, well, intimately related.

Mr. Clinton has decided that his best chance of serving out his presidency is to achieve nothing with it the rest of this year. So he is promising in advance to veto everything Republicans send him, even bills that include much of what the President once said he wanted. Where, we wonder, are the protests from Beltway elites who claim to favor moderation and "compromise"?

This veto strategy only makes sense if Mr. Clinton's one goal is to please Congressional Democrats. In search of a November majority, Democrats need issues, and vetoes offer hope of creating some. The President gives Democrats an ideological incentive to stick with him, whatever their doubts about his ethics. And if the election breaks right, then John Conyers and Barney Frank replace Henry Hyde at House Judiciary.

But to satisfy Democrats, Mr. Clinton must invoke the illogic of vetoing bills because they give him half of what he wants. Because Congress won't pass a big cigarette tax increase, he now refuses to sign any additional restrictions on cigarette sales. Because Republicans won't subsidize International Planned Parenthood, Mr. Clinton won't accept an offer to pay American arrears to the U.N. And because Congress won't open up employers and insurers to medical lawsuits, Mr. Clinton says he won't sign any regulation of HMOs.

These are the threats of a self-indulgent, self-absorbed presidency. No one in a democracy gets everything at once, especially in America's system of separated powers. Republicans learned this lesson the hard way in 1995, when Newt Gingrich made the monumental error of promising to shut down the government over the budget. Though Republicans later passed bills to keep the government running, Mr. Clinton vetoed them and spun Newt's quotes against Congress.

This year, however, it is Mr. Clinton who says he will shut down the government if he doesn't get his way. Congress "may decide to send me a bare-bones budget that fails to expand the critical investments we need to make, from education to summer jobs to school modernization to child care," the President said Aug. 3 in Maryland. "I will not accept a budget that fails to do this."

Bill Clinton

Other Presidents have threatened vetoes because Congress spent too much, but Mr. Clinton may be the first to saber rattle because Congress is spending too little. With the memory of 1995 still in the public mind, Mr. Clinton may assume he can spin another shutdown against the Republicans. With a high-profile showdown just before the election, he might even figure he could mobilize enough base Democratic voters to win the House.

But this time Republicans should portray Mr. Clinton as the one who's unwilling to compromise. On HMO reform, House Republicans can fairly argue they've passed the regulations they think are needed, and which deserve time to see how they work. (The Senate is still debating its HMO bill.) Most health insurers oppose the GOP plan, too, so it's hardly fair to say Republicans are in the pocket of industry. Our own preference would be to see nothing pass. But if nothing passes, it will be because Mr. Clinton's veto saves the industry from Republicans.

It's unfortunate, but probably true, that Republicans can't depend on the media to report these facts. Instead the media will act as the Clinton echo chamber, much as they already have on his HMO horror stories. For weeks the press has been repeating the President's tear-jerking anecdotes about patients suffering at the hands of evil managed-care providers. But the Washington Post's Howard Kurtz, who performed the apparently obsolete feat of checking out these tales before transcribing them into the paper, reported Monday that many of them turn out to be simply untrue. The Clinton White House must be agog at how much unfiltered falsity it's able to transmit via the airwaves and print these days.

But if Republicans start early enough they can still win a fight over Mr. Clinton's vetoes. We even recommend they pass a continuing resolution in September funding the government for the entire year, to show their real intentions early. Voters deserve to know that one of the consequences of scandal is a veto-everything Presidency.

REVIEW & OUTLOOK

The Smash-Mouth Presidency

When Kenneth Starr examines President Clinton before the grand jury on Monday, the questioning will be about sex only in the sense that Watergate was about a "two-bit burglary." Watergate was about abuse of the powers of the Presidency to obstruct justice on an otherwise pedestrian crime. So, too, with Whitewater, from the time the Resolution Trust criminal referral was sidetracked in the first year of the Clinton Administration to the current preoccupation with Monica Lewinsky.

Mr. Clinton's spin team no doubt is searching for an angle to turn Monday's performance to his advantage. The President has been given the extraordinary privilege of having his lawyer at hand during his testimony, and we don't imagine David Kendall will be a potted plant; he will raise objections to some questions, and the legal hassle over privileges will start all over again. Meanwhile, the Clinton defense will return to business as usual— trying to blacken, threaten and intimidate critics, witnesses and anyone else who stands in their way.

Consider Linda Tripp: It may be that her seclusion in a safe house is an overreaction to death-threat phone calls common to controversial figures. And perhaps Monica Lewinsky's warnings about "team player" and "not a good career move" and "two children to think about" were not after all passed along from the President himself. Laying all that aside, we know that a Pentagon operative reached into her confidential personnel file and leaked ancient but derogatory information to a pro-Clinton reporter, and that for this illegal act no one has been disciplined. We know, too, that Ms. Tripp faces a Maryland prosecution for taping her phone conversations with Ms. Lewinsky; the prosecutor has admitted that precedents make his case dubious but 49 Democrats in the state legislature urged the prosecution.

Consider Kathleen Willey: It may be a coincidence that she had three car tires vandalized with nails and that her cat vanished as she was preparing to give a deposition about the President's sexual advances. But can we dismiss the report by ABC's Jackie Judd that Willey says a jogger approached her shortly before the deposition, asking about the car, the cat and her children by name, summing up, "Don't you get the message?"

Consider David Hale, lest you think that only women get hustled: Hale pleaded guilty to Whitewater felonies and became a pro-prosecution witness before the jury that convicted Mr. Clinton's former business partners, the McDougals. He then came under prosecution for insurance code violations from a local prosecutor and Clinton crony.

Arkansans have been especially affected. For example, Whitewater witness Don Denton lost his job after testifying. Whitewater witness Bill Watt lost his pension after testifying.

Consider Billy Dale, lest you think that innocents are exempt: For standing in the way of an Arkansas takeover, the former White House Travel Office head lost his job. The IRS launched an unexpected audit of UltrAir, the private charter service he'd hired. Janet Reno's Justice Department indicted and tried Mr. Dale on fraud charges that a District of Columbia jury dismissed in two hours.

Consider Kenneth Starr, lest you think that judicial officials are immune: Lay aside the constant public charges of partisanship against the former judge, solicitor general and GOP lawyer picked by Democrats as an impartial ethics adviser on which elements of then-Senator Bob Packwood's private diary should be made public. Some fed the rumor mills the false allegation that Mr. Starr had a sexual affair in Little Rock. Also, that one of his staff members was gay.

Consider Impeachment: The Internet magazine Salon, financed by some of the President's fast-track friends, has lately been full of talk about a "sexual scorched-earth plan," a "Doomsday machine" and a "Romesch strategy." As explained by former Clinton aide George Stephanopoulos on ABC when the Lewinsky matter first surfaced, Ellen Romesch was the East German spy who had an affair with President Kennedy. Congressional oversight was stilled then by the threat that "we're going to open up everybody's closets." Salon quotes its sources in the Clinton camp as saying those in Congress targeted for scrutiny include Speaker Newt Gingrich, Majority Leader Dick Armey, Oversight Chairman Dan Burton and even the venerable Henry Hyde, who would chair any impeachment hearings.

This is not the way we want the Presidency run. Despite Mr. Dooley's adage that politics ain't beanbag, there have to be conventions and limits somewhere. What Mr. Starr's inquiry is ultimately about is whether the Clinton Administration will set the standards by which our politics are conducted in the future. The Independent Counsel will be derelict in his duty if he fails to make this issue clear in Monday's questioning, and even more so in his eventual report to the Congress.

REVIEW & OUTLOOK

Sidney Strikes Out

Most American jurisdictions have a one-year statute of limitations on slander, in no small part to preclude the kind of mischief White House gunslinger Sidney Blumenthal has been trying to perpetuate via his libel suit against Matt Drudge. Mr. Drudge's quickly retracted rumor about Mr. Blumenthal beating his wife was published on August 10, 1997, so on Monday his professed hope of a slander suit against Mr. Drudge's source turned into a pumpkin.

Mr. Blumenthal's mouthpiece, William McDaniel, still has not taken Mr. Drudge's deposition to ask about his source. He did, however, manage to interrogate Michael Ledeen about various articles he'd written—e.g., "and you compare the Clinton White House to the Corleone family, don't you?" The deposition also covered a long-standing grievance Mr. Ledeen has had with Mr. Blumenthal from the latter's days as a journalist. In 1987 the Washington Post published a letter from Mr. Ledeen denying dirt Mr. Blumenthal had dug up from Italian sources, including a publication that ultimately agreed to a settlement in a libel suit brought by Mr. Ledeen.

Barbara Ledeen, also deposed, was asked about the funding of the Independent Women's Forum; both depositions are crowded with questions about conservative activists, a kind of shooting gallery for future harassment. As the statute expired, no Drudge sources have been discovered.

The subpoena to our John Fund, who has repeatedly denied any communication with Mr. Drudge, has been indefinitely postponed.

Our attorney offered an affidavit swearing to the lack of communication, adding "you have no further legitimate reason to pursue any discovery from Mr. Fund." The letter also pointed out that New Jersey, where the subpoena was served, has a shield law protecting journalistic sources.

Now, what has been going on here? While threatening slander suits in Vanity Fair and discussions with other attorneys, did Mr. McDaniel forget to look up the statute of limitations? He didn't mention it while crying on Larry King's shoulder the other night. More likely the supposed slander suits were never the point; Mr. Blumenthal was simply using his lawsuit to carry out his task of harassing Clinton foes.

Sidney Blumenthal

"I never imagined that in America I would be hauled before a federal grand jury to answer questions about my conversations with members of the media," Mr. Blumenthal pontificated on the courthouse steps after his grand jury appearance in February. "Ken Starr's prosecutors demanded to know what I told reporters and what reporters had told me about Ken Starr's prosecution." Mr. McDaniel added, "He was hauled down here today in a blatant attempt to intimidate him from searching out and speaking the truth about Mr. Starr's prosecutors."

Mr. Blumenthal is free to talk about what happened in the grand jury room while everyone else there is forbidden to offer a competing version, but many in the press uncritically accepted his spin. (Almost surely it will repeat this mistake when his boss faces the grand jury Monday.) Indeed, commentators held the subpoena a Starr mistake; it made Mr. Blumenthal a "1st Amendment martyr" (Stuart Taylor), or allowed him and other Clinton allies to posture as "the pitiable victims of his own abuse of power" (William Safire).

We have not noticed a similar First Amendment outcry about the White House unleashing Mr. Blumenthal to subpoena reporters, or for that matter about the Justice Department investigation of how The American Spectator spent money reporting stories hostile to Mr. Clinton. So let us take this opportunity to speak for ourselves: There is no reason to believe that Sidney Blumenthal is a wife beater. There is every reason to believe he is a raving hypocrite, a partisan with no scruple or principle, and a disgrace to his former profession.

Editorial Feature

It's Nobler to Quit, Mr. President

By PAUL F. CAMPOS

As the Lewinsky investigation degenerates into a series of ever more sordid revelations, one question gets too little attention: What course of action would be best for the country? The person in the best position to do something to avert a national nightmare is, of course, Bill Clinton. And it is becoming increasingly clear what he ought to do: resign from the presidency.

I say this as someone who twice voted for Mr. Clinton and who in the past few months has repeatedly defended him both on national television and in the national press. And I say it as someone who believes that Kenneth Starr's investigation marks a watershed in the annals of legalistic excess. Those who are tempted to revel in Mr. Starr's quest might ask themselves if their country is better off because Republicans and Democrats are willing to transform our legal system into a political weapon.

Nevertheless, the time has come to put the national interest ahead of any apportioning of the blame for this multifaceted disaster. Mr. Clinton's resignation would accomplish several things at once:

• It would spare us the national trauma of seeing our president either admit to having engaged in shameful conduct which he then denied in a series of degrading and illegal lies, or, alternatively, of watching him make under oath yet another batch of increasingly incredible denials that in the end will only add fuel to this scandal's destructive fires.

- It would free the political system from the paralysis that has gripped it in the months since this scandal became the obsessive focus of life in the nation's capital.

- It would allow us to begin to reconsider the insane practice of conducting national politics through strategic litigation and prosecutorial inquisition.

- By allowing Al Gore to become president, it would both re-energize a moribund Democratic administration and serve as the ultimate rejoinder to those among Mr. Clinton's opponents who for strategic reasons have exaggerated their horror at his various sins.

- It would secure Mr. Clinton's place in history as a man who, for all his flaws, revealed at a moment of true national crisis that he possessed the strength of character necessary to put the nation's best interests ahead of his own political survival.

If Mr. Clinton should choose to walk away from the White House on his own terms, comparisons will of course be made to the resignation of Richard Nixon. But unlike Nixon's surrender, Mr. Clinton's resignation, at least if it comes soon, will not be an acceptance of the inevitable—after all, he is still in little danger of being impeached. Under the present circumstances, such a decision will be understood by all but the bitterest cynics as the truly heroic act of a man who sacrificed himself for the good of the nation.

In practical terms, the Clinton presidency is already finished; Mr. Clinton is a mere figurehead. If he chooses to serve out the remaining 2½ years of his term under such circumstances, no one will be more pleased than those who unleashed the legal machinery of the federal government in an attempt to annul the results of our last presidential election.

Mr. Clinton still has it within his power to perform an act that will raise him far above the squalid controversies of the past few months, and which will prove beyond doubt that his love for his country is stronger than his personal ambition. Nothing would so honor his office as his decision to leave it.

Mr. Campos, a professor of law at the University of Colorado, is author of "Jurismania: The Madness of American Law" (Oxford University Press, 1998).

Editorial Feature

Woodward and Bernstein Lose Their Fastball

A big reason I got into journalism was Carl Bernstein and Bob Woodward.

As a college reporter, I cheered their zealous pursuit of Watergate in "All the President's Men." But it seems the years have given the pair second thoughts about holding politicians accountable under the law.

Potomac Watch

By Paul A. Gigot

Or so I conclude from their views about presidential scandal expressed Sunday on NBC's "Meet the Press." Mr. Bernstein, the legendary rebel, now sides with the White House establishment.

"It's as if you have a kind of Nuremberg prosecution for war crimes and you end up with a kind of jaywalking offense," he said of Kenneth Starr's probe. "That's not to minimize the spectacle of a president of the United States lying under oath," he added, having just done exactly that.

Mr. Woodward was more balanced, but he still embraced Mr. Bernstein's new "proportionality" standard, at least for President Clinton.

This all matters because it sums up Washington's emerging conventional wisdom on the eve of Mr. Clinton's Monica testimony. Once upon a scandal the standard in this city was truth. But as evidence mounts that Mr. Clinton hasn't told the truth, the goal posts are being moved. The new consensus says Mr. Clinton may have lied under oath but it's no big deal. The Beltway establishment wants a plea bargain even before Mr. Clinton has copped a plea.

It's hard to believe the young Woodstein, as the pair were once known, would have fallen for this line. Their Nixon book, which I reread this week, is a morality tale about doggedly exposing White House deceit. The movie based on their book ends in what is portrayed as triumphant justice, with "Nixon Resigns" flashed as a headline.

Mr. Bernstein now says the Clinton scandal is merely about a "private consensual sexual" matter that bears no resemblance to Watergate. But why must every political scandal measure up to Watergate to be serious? This is another example of the Baby Boom conceit that nothing in human experience ever matches its own moral crusades.

Mr. Bernstein argues that Mr. Clinton has merely committed perjury, and merely about sex. But perjury in civil suits is serious enough that Mr. Clinton's own Justice Department has brought or pursued on appeal at least 12 such cases since 1993. Only this year Clinton Justice tried psychiatrist Barbara Battalino for denying a sexual relationship in a civil suit. She was sentenced to a year's probation and $3,500 in costs.

Moreover, in the first article of impeachment against Nixon, plank one was making "false or misleading statements" to U.S. officials. Plank eight was "making false or misleading public statements for the purpose of deceiving the people of the United States into believing that a thorough and complete investigation had been conducted." Why is lying less offensive in the 1990s than it was in the 1970s?

Plea bargains also typically require the accused to admit to something. But Mr. Clinton has never taken responsibility for anything untoward in his entire presidency. For seven months he's reneged on his own promise to tell the country what happened between him and a 22-year-old intern who worked for him.

This alone has turned his tawdry private conduct into a public issue. He has forced the country to explain oral sex to children. He has pursued feckless privilege claims that have diminished the presidency for his successors. He has dragged the Secret Service and his own aides into his muck, suggesting that Monica Lewinsky was merely seeing his secretary Betty Currie on those 37 White House visits. Crimes or not, these are abuses of office.

And all of them are relevant for Congress to consider, even if

Mr. Starr's report to Congress involves *only* the Monica matter. Mr. Starr floated a trial balloon this week suggesting this approach, which would be a mistake. A judgment about what's impeachable is above all political, and best left to Congress. It should be Congress that judges, for example, if the more than $700,000 in job payments to Webster Hubbell were meant as hush money.

Once we know the facts, perhaps Congress will choose to impose a sanction short of impeachment. Perhaps the country would rather tolerate perjury than risk toppling the icon of our economic boom. But before Americans can decide how much to value the truth, they have a right to know it. The first step in political accountability is public knowledge, as Carl Bernstein and Bob Woodward once taught us.

Richard Nixon

But if those two reporters no longer recommend "All the President's Men" as a guide to political standards, let me suggest another film. In Robert Bolt's magnificent "A Man for All Seasons," Thomas More loses his head because he is the only man in England who won't lie about sex. (Not his own, but King Henry VIII's.)

At one point Sir Thomas hears his son-in-law assert that he'd cut down every law in England to beat the devil. To which Sir Thomas replies, "Oh, and when the last law was down and the devil turned 'round on you, where would you hide, Roper, the laws all being flat?"

Kenneth Starr's inquiry is about making sure our laws aren't made flat.

Editorial Feature

The Dangers Of Defending Clinton

By Daniel E. Troy

When President Clinton testifies before Kenneth Starr's grand jury on Monday, his lawyer, David Kendall, will be sitting next to him. This isn't the way it usually works. If you were testifying before a grand jury, you would face prosecutors and jurors alone, with your lawyer waiting outside the room in case you need to consult him.

By winning for his client the right to testify under these circumstances, Mr. Kendall may be endangering his own career as a lawyer. For if Mr. Clinton makes statements to the grand jury that contradict any fact, small or large, Mr. Kendall has learned about while representing the president, Mr. Kendall could risk disbarment unless he immediately withdrew from the case. If Mr. Clinton's testimony is less than entirely truthful, he could also jeopardize his own continued bar membership.

David Kendall

Mr. Kendall is a member of the bars of New York, Maryland and the District of Columbia; Mr. Clinton is admitted to practice law in Arkansas. Both men are governed by these states' codes of professional conduct. Most relevant to Monday's testimony is an ethical rule in the District of Columbia stating that a lawyer "shall not knowingly . . . counsel or assist a client to engage in conduct that the lawyer knows is criminal or fraudulent." Nor may a lawyer "offer evidence that the lawyer knows to be false."

The authoritative comment on this rule, on which courts rely in applying it, says that when "the lawyer may learn of the client's intention to present false evidence before the client has had a chance to do so," the lawyer is forbidden "to present the false evidence." Thus, before Mr. Clinton testifies, Mr. Kendall must assure himself that he does not "know" Mr. Clinton intends to commit perjury.

No one expects that Mr. Clinton has told Mr. Kendall he intends to lie to the grand jury. But if Mr. Clinton has told Mr. Kendall a fact, and Mr. Clinton contradicts that fact under oath with Mr. Kendall sitting next to him, Mr. Kendall could be deemed to have "knowingly" presented false evidence if Mr. Kendall knows that other evidence contradicts Mr. Clinton's testimony. Further, as one court has said, lawyers may not "turn a blind eye to the facts." Thus, for Mr. Kendall to be ethically safe, he needs to have heard from Mr. Clinton a credible explanation for the evidence of 37 visits from Monica Lewinsky, the allegedly stained dress and the return of Ms. Lewinsky's gifts to Betty Currie, among other things.

Even if Mr. Kendall is not duty-bound to withdraw before Clinton testifies, he would have certain ethical obligations if he were to "know" at a later time that Mr. Clinton had lied during his testimony. The District of Columbia rule requires that "a lawyer who receives information clearly establishing that a fraud has been perpetuated on the tribunal shall promptly reveal that fraud to the tribunal." There is one key qualification to this requirement. The comment states that "if the notification of the tribunal would require disclosure" of a client confidence, a lawyer may not "inform the tribunal of the fraud." In such a case, however, the lawyer is obligated to call upon his client to "rectify the fraud."

Most criminal lawyers avoid this entire dilemma because they do not accompany their clients into the grand jury. At trial, a lawyer can influence whether to put his client on the stand, and can control his questioning of that client. But by sitting next to Mr. Clinton on Monday, Mr. Kendall puts himself in a uniquely dangerous situation.

What happens on Monday? Assume that Mr. Kendall has counseled the president not to commit perjury, but that Mr. Clinton does so anyway, with Mr. Kendall by his side. At that point, Mr. Kendall seems ethically bound to stop the questioning and counsel his client to tell the truth. Moreover, if Mr. Clinton lies in response to one question, that might suggest that he would do so in answering subsequent questions on the same topic. At a certain point, Mr. Kendall could be charged with "knowing" that his client was going to commit perjury, which would again require him to interrupt matters, this time to withdraw from the case.

Few lawyers would want to be put in this position, which could require some very quick, on-the-spot judgments. At a minimum, Mr. Kendall is likely to be distracted by the ethical pitfalls he may be facing as a result of Mr. Clinton.

Mr. Clinton himself runs a considerable risk of disbarment if he commits perjury. Rule 8.4(c) of Arkansas's Code of Professional Conduct states that "it is professional misconduct for a lawyer to . . . engage in conduct involving dishonesty, fraud, deceit, or misrepresentation." The American Bar Association's authoritative comment on this rule makes clear that one of its purposes is to deter "moral turpitude," which may "be construed to include offenses concerning personal morality, such as adultery and comparable offenses, that have no specific connection to the practice of law."

Many lawyers have been disbarred for lying to a court, even without having been convicted of perjury. The New Hampshire Supreme Court, disbarring a lawyer for his failure to disclose material facts in one pleading, observed that the "privilege [of practicing law] does not come without the concomitant responsibilities of truth, candor, and honesty."

If Mr. Clinton fails to tell the truth on Monday, he risks not just his own bar membership, but also Mr. Kendall's continued ability to earn a living. I hope that David Kendall's name is not added to the list of lives ruined by the misfortune of having a relationship with President Clinton.

Mr. Troy, a Washington lawyer, is an associate scholar at the American Enterprise Institute.

Editorial Feature

Rule 6(e) and the Public's Right to Know

In response to a motion filed by President Clinton, Chief District Judge Norma Holloway Johnson has ordered that Independent Counsel Kenneth Starr appear at a hearing and "show cause" why he should not be held in contempt for violating the grand jury secrecy provision, Rule 6(e).

At first blush, that may seem extraordinary, but such orders are not uncommon in Washington grand jury investigations that attract intense media coverage; Washington Mayor Marion Barry and ex-congressman Dan Rostenkowski both obtained show cause orders

Rule of Law

By Theodore J. Boutrous Jr.

after alleging that the U.S. attorneys who prosecuted them engaged in grand jury leaks. As the D.C. Circuit Court of Appeals recognized in its Aug. 1 decision addressing the president's leak allegations against Mr. Starr, a grand jury target needs only to make a "minimal" *prima facie* showing—based solely on an assessment of news articles—of improper grand jury leaks, and then the burden shifts to the prosecutor to "show cause" by demonstrating that he did not violate Rule 6(e).

Resolution of the leaks dispute in the Lewinsky investigation could depend at least in part on the meaning of the formerly obscure, now frequently discussed, Rule 6(e). That provision precludes a narrowly identified group of people—basically prosecutors, grand jurors and court reporters—from disclosing publicly "matters occurring before the grand jury." The rule doesn't cover grand jury witnesses. In the words of the D.C. Circuit, witnesses can walk out of the grand jury room and "proclaim from the rooftops" their own testimony or anything they learn while inside the grand jury room or from discussions with prosecutors and investigators.

On its face, then, the rule's secrecy requirements are quite limited. The D.C. Circuit, in a 1987 opinion written by Judge (now Justice) Ruth Bader Ginsburg in *Senate of Puerto Rico*, emphasized this fact, explaining that Rule 6(e) is intended to prohibit prosecutors only from disclosing "what took place within the grand jury chambers." In that same opinion, the court declared that it had "never embraced a reading" of Rule 6(e) "so literal as to draw 'a veil of secrecy over all matters occurring in the world that happen to be investigated by a grand jury.'" Indeed, the court went on to say that "there is no per se rule against disclosure of any and all information which has reached the grand jury chambers." Rather, "the touchstone is whether disclosure would 'tend to reveal some secret aspect of the grand jury's investigation.'"

But Chief Judge Johnson so far has interpreted Rule 6(e) far more sweepingly, as shown by her June 19 show cause order. Relying on a brief passage in the D.C. Circuit's May 5 opinion in the case of *In re Motions of Dow Jones*—a case addressing the extent to which the press and public possess rights of access to the judicial records and proceedings relating to Mr. Starr's probe—the judge declared that Rule 6(e)'s secrecy restrictions cover "not only what has occurred and what is occurring, but also *what is likely to occur* [before the grand jury]," including evidence that the prosecutor collects on his own outside the grand jury room and the prosecutor's own views about the "strategy or direction of the investigation."

Rule 6(e), however, cannot be read so broadly. The rule's plain text covers only matters "occurring before the grand jury." Reading the phrase "likely to occur" into the rule violates the most fundamental principles of statutory construction.

Moreover, the D.C. Circuit itself already seems to be having second thoughts about the language from the *Dow Jones* case. In a little noticed footnote in its Aug. 1 decision on the president's leak allegations against Mr. Starr, the court of appeals, referring to its discussion of the scope of Rule 6(e) secrecy in *Dow Jones*, went out of its

way to "note the problematic nature of applying so broad a definition, especially as it relates to the 'strategy or direction of the investigation,' to the inquiry as to whether a government attorney made
unauthorized disclosures."

Establishing an overly broad, unduly vague definition of grand
jury secrecy under Rule 6(e) poses several risks, including discour-
aging prosecutors from disclosing important information that the
public has every right to obtain. To be sure, prosecutors—including
independent counsels—are required to abide scrupulously by Rule
6(e)'s admonition against disclosing what goes on inside the grand
jury room. They also must refrain absolutely from expressing their
opinions about the guilt or innocence of any citizen or otherwise
seeking to prejudice a judicial proceeding, as set forth in
Department of Justice policy guidelines and ethics rules. But those
same provisions recognize that there is a strong, legitimate need to
keep the public informed about criminal investigations.

In fact, the U.S. attorneys' manual states that, in deciding
whether to make public statements about ongoing criminal matters,
"careful weight must be given in each case to the constitutional
requirements of a free press and public trials as well as the right of
the people in a constitutional democracy to have access to information about the conduct of law enforcement officers, prosecutors and
courts, consistent with the individual rights of the accused."

Deputy Attorney General Eric Holder likewise has stated that the
public has "a right to be kept reasonably informed" of high-profile
investigations of powerful figures. And the Supreme Court has
observed that openness in government, including criminal justice
proceedings, is necessary to "protect the free discussion of government affairs" so that "the individual citizen can effectively participate in and contribute to our republican system of government."

In a case like the Lewinsky matter, where the investigation's
nature and subject matter, witnesses, targets and similar matters
are widely known to the press and public, the secrecy concerns of
Rule 6(e) are least compelling. The D.C. Circuit's *Dow Jones* opinion
acknowledged this point: "When information has become sufficiently widely known it has lost its character as 6(e) material."

At the same time, the need for public scrutiny is at its most compelling when an independent counsel is investigating a sitting president and is charged by statute with submitting any evidence of

potentially impeachable offenses to Congress. Such cases should be fought on a public stage in full public view to the greatest extent possible.

Mr. Boutrous is a Washington attorney representing Dow Jones and other news organizations in seeking public access to the records and proceedings arising from the Starr investigation.

REVIEW & OUTLOOK

Other Women, Other Lies

When Richard Nixon asked Leonard Garment whether to burn the Watergate tapes, the reply was: If they're exculpatory, as you say, don't burn them. If you decide to burn them, let me know because I'm leaving the government. Today's Len Garment is Presidential attorney David Kendall, whose resignation would shatter what remains of Mr. Clinton's Presidency.

Mr. Kendall's delicate position was elaborated on this page Friday by Daniel Troy; Mr. Kendall knows the truth, and his job is to massage it in the interests of his client. However, if a client flatly commits perjury legal ethics oblige the lawyer to resign. Ken Starr has finally succeeded in pushing the spinmeisters out of the loop; the President is now in the hands not of those who put personal loyalty above all, but someone who in the end owes a higher loyalty to the law, not to mention his partners at Williams & Connolly. So in today's testimony, the carefully orchestrated leaks tell us, we will get the truth, as best as Mr. Kendall can massage it.

What this looks like was suggested by the Journal story to which Paula Jones's lead attorney replied in our letters column, and detailed in a lengthier New York Times article Friday. To wit, Mr. Clinton did not commit perjury in denying a sexual affair with Monica Lewinsky, because he was not talking about sex as the world understands it; he was following a definition that resulted from the vagaries of the courtroom. Presidential attorney Robert Bennett objected to the plaintiff's expansive definition of sexual contact, and

Judge Susan Webber Wright abbreviated it in a way that can be construed as defining sex to mean the President manipulating a woman's erogenous zones, but not *her* manipulating *his*.

This wondrous position solves Mr. Kendall's problem, but whether it solves Mr. Clinton's is another matter. In political terms, the public has been remarkably forgiving, but there is a sense that the President has gone to the well too many times; somewhere on the tube we just caught the remarkable vignette of Pat Schroeder praising Henry Hyde. Even in strictly legal terms, the President's admissions with respect to Ms. Lewinsky may give him problems with two other women in court, Paula Jones and Susan McDougal.

Paula Jones

The floated defense, after all, is that in the Paula Jones case Mr. Clinton was toying with the court and making a dupe of Judge Wright. The Eighth Circuit Court of Appeals is currently considering Mrs. Jones's bid to reinstate the case dismissed by Judge Wright; oral arguments will probably be held in late fall with a decision next spring. The Court put a gag order on her brief, but her defense had already posted it on the Internet. It particularly challenges Judge Wright's ruling excluding the Lewinsky matter as irrelevant to Mrs. Jones's claims.

This decision is clearly nonsensical. Mrs. Jones alleges Mr. Clinton solicited oral sex; Ms. Lewinsky has now testified that in her case it was consummated. Surely this, as well as Kathleen Willey's reports of mashing, suggests a pattern of behavior. The exclusion was a public relations sop to the President, or at best a convenience for the judge, who was preparing to dismiss the case on other grounds.

One of these grounds has already been overturned by a subsequent Supreme Court decision. The Eighth Circuit, governing federal courts in Arkansas, had required tangible career harm to prove sexual harassment. The High Court reversed in a case involving repeated sexual advances; the opinion added, "we express no opinion as to whether a single unfulfilled threat is sufficient."

Judge Wright held that the single episode, while surely offensive, did not rise to the required level of "outrage." But it is hard to imagine a judge ruling a jury should not even hear an allegation of a similar offense if it were against, say, a corporate CEO. In setting the bar for outrage, in excluding Lewinsky evidence, in defining sexual contact, Judge Wright has been remarkably solicitous of the President. Hillary Clinton's charges of prejudice against Arkansas sound daft to most, but still resonate in parts of the Little Rock elite, who no doubt populate the clubs and drawing rooms in which the judge must live. The Eighth Circuit is another place—while hesitant about sexual harassment also suspicious of Clinton legal conceits.

Meanwhile, Susan McDougal is on trial again, this time on embezzlement charges in California. After that, she is scheduled to go back to Arkansas to face further contempt and obstruction charges for refusing to answer Mr. Starr's questions. The questions in her case, as in the Lewinsky case, revolve around Presidential perjury. To wit, she refused to say whether the President knew of the Master Marketing loan at the heart of her Whitewater conviction, and whether he testified truthfully at her trial.

Susan McDougal

If he testified truthfully, there was little reason for her to go to jail for contempt or now to face further charges. In all likelihood, she was having an affair with Governor Clinton at the time, as her husband reported, and told him about the fraudulent loan from David Hale's government-backed small business investment company. Of the $300,000, some $50,000 ended up in Whitewater accounts in which Governor and Mrs. Clinton were partners. If he knew, he was complicit in a conspiracy to defraud the taxpayer. If he lied under oath, this time it was not about sex but about money.

While it's hard to read Mrs. McDougal's mind, the new revelations ought to instruct her. In telling the truth, Ms. Lewinsky took the first step toward putting her life into some kind of order. And certainly the President's current predicament means a pardon to someone refusing to testify against him would be a ticket to impeachment. Mrs. McDougal may yet see that her future lies in cooperation with Mr. Starr, giving him testimony about Presidential perjury. Even if she does not, Mr. Starr owes Congress a chance to weigh what we already know here. Proof of a specific crime beyond a reasonable doubt pertains to sending someone to jail; the issues to be balanced here are pattern of perjury and trust in the nation's highest office.

In short, no spin of the President's testimony today is likely to end his troubles; both politically and legally, it is more likely to ensnare him further. The lesson was well drawn long ago by Sir Walter Scott: "O, what a tangled web we weave, When first we practise to deceive!"

REVIEW & OUTLOOK

Lying to Ourselves

Told that his standards are out of date, a character in an Alan Bennett play replies: Of course, that's why they're called standards. The quip occurs to us because from now on the arc of Bill Clinton's presidency is not so much about his standards as about the nation's. By now the important question is whether we as a nation are going to keep lying to ourselves about Bill Clinton.

For many years the American public has suspended disbelief about this President. To oust a befuddled George Bush, a plurality of voters wished away Gennifer Flowers and lying about the draft as the mistakes of youth. The public chose to overlook Whitewater, especially after it was consigned to a special counsel to investigate. It has given him a pass on election abuses involving foreigners and the Teamsters. And for the last seven months, Americans have withheld judgment regarding an intern less than half his age.

In a practical sense, this is understandable. We disagree with those conservatives who attribute this non-rush to judgment to national moral decay. In good economic times, Americans are naturally wary of upsetting the political status quo. Regarding the Lewinsky case in particular, moreover, there is a natural revulsion against the attendant tawdriness. Some polls suggest that many older Americans don't believe a President would even be capable of such behavior. These aren't signs of decay but of residual public modesty.

Even more important, the public is entitled to give a twice-elected

President the benefit of the doubt. Impeachment is a high sanction, not without costs, and Americans are understandably hesitant to invoke it. Especially when their political and opinion leaders haven't been helpful in sorting out the issues. The Barney Frank Democrats have dismissed all criticism of Mr. Clinton as partisan, while the Orrin Hatch Republicans are afraid to act like a genuine opposition. The watchdogs of the press have poked up a frenzy from time to time, but if we may say so, we've been nearly alone in understanding from the first that the Clinton character was a huge news story waiting to erupt in one form or another.

The event of Mr. Clinton's testimony brings us to a watershed from which the public can no longer avert its eyes. Faced with the prospect of nothing less than a dress soiled with his own semen, the President last night confessed that his relationship with Monica Lewinsky was "wrong." He professed to accept "complete responsibility," then went on the attack. For seven months he had rubbed the nation's nose in the muck, but he and the lawyer who advised him complained of the length and cost of the Starr investigation. White House spinmeisters—read it all on the internet in Salon -- asked us to believe his wife had no clue until his wrenching confession last weekend. The President asked us to feel his pain; let the healing begin, his supporters chanted; put this behind us, he pleaded.

We've come too far for such cheap redemption. At a minimum, the price of public absolution must be complete public accountability. In the matter of Monica, this is much more than sex. It includes, for example, the Presidential truth about such questions as what his state of mind was when he talked to Betty Currie prior to her testimony on those visits from Ms. Lewinsky. There is also the matter of Paula Jones, whose increasingly plausible account surely rates an apology even if it does not legally constitute sexual harassment. Susan McDougal and Webb Hubbell, who can no longer realistically expect pardons, should be released to tell the truth.

More broadly, an accounting should include a complete Starr report to Congress not merely on the Lewinsky case but covering all of the subjects under the independent counsel's mandate. Legal technicalities aside, the public needs to know how its government has been conducting itself. What acts may be impeachable and what standards of evidence apply are questions the Congress must decide, not ones for Mr. Starr to predetermine. On the other hand, if Mr.

Starr can exonerate Mr. Clinton on Filegate or Travelgate, Americans deserve to know that, too—not merely have it asserted by the same White House spinners who assured us Mr. Clinton never had sex with Monica Lewinsky.

Perhaps the evidence in the end will warrant some lesser sanction than impeachment. But to shrink now from truth and judgment in the name of "healing" is to make all of us complicit with Mr. Clinton's behavior. If we as a nation want to define political deviancy back up, the first step is to admit to ourselves how much we've been willing to look the other way.

Editorial Feature

Why He Must Go...

By WILLIAM J. BENNETT

Bill Clinton's five-minute address to the American people Monday night was the most deceptive, shameless and self-pitying speech ever delivered by an American president. Almost every sentence was dishonest:

- *"[Kenneth Starr's investigation] has gone on too long, cost too much and hurt too many innocent people."*

This is deceit of a high order. Since January, Mr. Clinton has invoked and invented every privilege imaginable to slow Mr. Starr's investigation. The president refused to appear before the grand jury a half-dozen times, until he was finally forced to do so by the threat of subpoena. His acolytes declared an unprecedented "war" on an officer of the court and employed brutal tactics against him. It is Mr. Clinton who, for the past seven months, has lied to his wife, his daughter, his cabinet and his supporters. He lied under oath, and he publicly, emphatically and repeatedly lied to the American people. He encouraged his supporters and aides to defend, and become complicit in, his lies.

Starr Made Him Do It

Instead of telling the truth in January and putting an end to this squalid matter, he allowed his friends and colleagues to become enmeshed in it and in legal problems of his own making. They were forced to testify before the grand jury and incur large legal bills. Now, at the very moment when Mr. Starr's investigation has been vindicated and Mr. Clinton has been revealed as a liar, the president blames others. In his own brazen way, the president justifies his lies. "I had real and serious concerns about an independent counsel investigation," he now complains. Ken Starr made him do it.

- *"I was also very concerned about protecting my family. . . . I intend to reclaim my family life for my family."*

Let's be blunt. If Mr. Clinton genuinely cared about "the two people I love most—my wife and our daughter," he would not be chronically unfaithful to them. He would not have had oral sex with an intern barely older than his daughter a few hundred feet from where his family slept. He would not betray his family's trust time after time. He would not have sent forth his wife to defend him with preposterous claims of a "vast right-wing conspiracy." Mr. Clinton's real message is: *I will betray my wife and daughter when it's convenient—and I will hide behind them when it's necessary. And then I will do it all over again.*

- *"I must take complete responsibility for all my actions, both public and private. . . . I am solely and completely responsible."*

This is the archetype of the modern confession: The president bravely takes "complete responsibility" for his "wrong" and "mislead[ing]" actions and then demands that he suffer no consequences. "Our country has been distracted by this matter for too long, and I take my responsibility for my part in all of this," the president said. "That is all I can do." Note carefully the last four words: *all I can do*. In fact, the president can do much more. He can do the right thing and resign. But instead, by his actions he now directs us thus: *I lied, misled and shamefully used people—both aides and citizens—to cover for me. Forget about it. Get over it.*

- *"While my answers were legally accurate, I did not volunteer information."*

We can add this sentence to other famous Clinton evasions, next to what he said about marijuana ("I didn't inhale"), the draft ("it was simply a fluke I wasn't called") and his affair with Gennifer Flowers ("The story is just not true.") Only Bill Clinton could answer "no" when asked if he had an extramarital sexual affair, then reluctantly admit (because of overwhelming evidence) that he had oral sex—and still contend that his first answer is true. He is a chronic, incorrigible liar. As Sen. Bob Kerrey (D., Neb.) put it: "Clinton's an unusually good liar. Unusually good."

- *"But [the Lewinsky scandal] is private . . . It's nobody's business but ours. Even presidents have private lives."*

The Lewinsky scandal cannot be "private" when Mr. Starr's investigation was expanded because of Attorney General Janet Reno's finding that there existed credible evidence of criminal wrongdoing by the president. Nor can it be "private" when the president made an emphatic public denial, sent out waves of White House aides to defend him, used government employees to try to destroy the independent counsel, used his allies to destroy the reputation of women, used his White House lawyers to delay the investigation, invoked executive privilege, and tacitly encouraged millions of unwitting Americans to defend him. Nor can the Lewinsky matter be "private" when the matter involves a squalid sexual relationship between the president and a young intern in the Oval Office. The Oval Office is always open for business, the president always under oath, always on duty.

- *"I ask you to turn away from the spectacle of the past seven months, to repair the fabric of our national discourse, and to return our attention to all the challenges and all the promise of the next American century."*

Mr. Clinton has done more than Jerry Springer, Howard Stern or anyone else to coarsen and debase our national discourse. Thanks to him, parents of young children must now hit the mute button when the national news is on television. He has made words like "semen" and "oral sex" part of our political lexicon. On sexual matters he has done the impossible: given Hollywood the moral high ground. At the Academy Awards, host Billy Crystal joked that a lot has changed: "A year ago, the White House was complaining there was too much sex in Hollywood."

Years ago, Hollywood made a fine movie, "The Last Picture Show," in which the character Sam the Lion scolds a group of boys for their mean and gross sexual conduct by calling it "just plain trashy behavior. I've seen a lifetime of it and I'm tired of putting up with it." A good summary, that—and a good lesson from Hollywood to Washington.

This corrupt and corrupting president is responsible for all of this and much more. Now that he has been forced by the evidence to make an angry, grudging, evasive admission of an "inappropriate" relationship with Ms. Lewinsky—still having refused to answer any of the important questions—he simply tells us it's over and time to move on.

Demoralizing Lessons

But there is only one way we can move on, and that is if Mr. Clinton is removed from office. He will probably never resign, so that leaves only impeachment. And he will only be impeached if American citizens become outraged. Until now, much of the public has decided to suspend judgment, avert its gaze, minimize what is happening and hope the Clinton scandals will soon pass, having wrought minimal damage. That has been a flight from reality and responsibility.

Every American president is an heir of George Washington, father of our country. President Clinton is a father, too, and his actions, if allowed to go unpunished, will teach demoralizing lessons to children. In the future, perjurers will invoke Bill Clinton as their legal father and adulterers will invoke him as their moral father. It will happen many times. This cannot be so.

He is a reproach. He must be repudiated.

Mr. Bennett is author of "The Death of Outrage: Bill Clinton and the Assault on American Ideals," just out from Free Press.

Editorial Feature

... And Why His Legal Jeopardy Will Only Grow

By Bradford A. Berenson

President Clinton told the nation on Monday night that it is time to "move on" and put an end to the investigation of his affair with Monica Lewinsky. Unfortunately for Mr. Clinton, the investigation cannot be ended. Independent Counsel Kenneth Starr is legally obligated to continue the inquiry until he either issues a report to Congress or concludes that he does not have, in the words of the statute that controls his investigation, "substantial and credible information . . . that may constitute grounds for an impeachment."

In that regard, the president's grand jury testimony may have made matters worse, rather than better. Impeachment is a political process once it begins, but the decision about whether to begin the process will depend in large measure on matters of law. In the wake of his testimony, Mr. Clinton may be more vulnerable than ever to potentially serious allegations of criminal misconduct in the Paula Jones case. Depending on Mr. Starr's evidence, the president may also have paved the way for Mr. Starr to include in a report to Congress the most damaging allegation of all: that Mr. Clinton committed perjury before the grand jury.

On the question of perjury in the Jones case, the president appears to have tried to thread the needle, admitting a sexual relationship with Ms. Lewinsky but contending that his denial of that relationship in the deposition was, as he said Monday night, "legally accurate." The problem is that the needle has no eye. Recent spin-talk has suggested that the Jones definition of sexual relations is open to an interpretation that would not cover receiving oral sex. But this is nonsense.

Under that definition, "a person engages in 'sexual relations' when the person knowingly engages in or causes contact with the genitalia . . . of any person with an intent to arouse or gratify the sexual desire of any person." "Any person" obviously includes the president, and the definition makes no distinction based on specific sex acts or an individual's active or passive role in them. If Ms. Lewinsky had sexual relations with Mr. Clinton, he—need we really say it?—had sexual relations with her.

Thus, the president cannot plausibly claim that his lie under oath in the Jones suit was unintentional or made in good faith. His only available defense would be to argue that the lie was immaterial. But this argument does not exonerate him of *moral* culpability for lying under oath. What's more, the law on this point is unsettled; the most compelling view is that the materiality of a false statement under oath is judged as of the time the statement is made, rather than in light of subsequent events (such as Judge Susan Webber Wright's decision to exclude Lewinsky evidence from the Jones suit or her later dismissal of the suit).

Mr. Clinton made other questionable statements under oath in the Jones case, and Mr. Starr's prosecutors may have substantial evidence that these statements were false. Mr. Clinton's admission of an "inappropriate" relationship with Ms. Lewinsky makes it almost certain that his claimed failure to remember ever being alone with her, except perhaps on one or two occasions when she brought him a pizza or papers to sign, was a lie. And the president gave answers under oath concerning his discussions with Ms. Lewinsky about her subpoena, the nature of his meeting with her around Christmas 1997, and his encounter with Kathleen Willey, all of which we now know have been contradicted by the testimony of those women.

The safest bet in this entire matter is that Mr. Starr has considerably more evidence than any of us are yet aware of. But even if he had no other evidence, these conflicts in testimony alone, particularly in light of the president's now-admitted lie on a closely related subject, would likely be sufficient to merit inclusion in an impeachment report. In such a report, Mr. Starr must include any and all allegations of criminality that are supported by "substantial and credible information"; he does not need to prove beyond a reasonable doubt that Mr. Clinton committed a crime.

Then there is the question of obstruction of justice and subornation of perjury in the Jones suit. When Mrs. Jones's lawyers first began questioning the president about Monica Lewinsky, Mr. Clinton's lawyer Robert Bennett vigorously objected, treating Judge Wright to an extended discussion of how Ms. Lewinsky's affidavit denying any sexual relationship with the president ought to preclude an inquiry into this subject. Mr. Clinton sat mute during this exchange and deliberately allowed his lawyer to urge upon the court evidence the president knew to be false and fraudulent. Mr. Clinton's evident lack of surprise, coupled with his parallel denials under oath, tend to support the inference that he and Ms. Lewinsky were indeed operating in tandem.

In addition, now that Mr. Clinton has in effect admitted lying under oath, he is going to have a difficult time convincing Mr. Starr that there was an innocent explanation for seeking the return of the gifts he gave Ms. Lewinsky or for the assistance his powerful friends gave her in her job search. What could have motivated these contemporaneous actions other than an effort to conceal the relationship? Friendship might explain job help, but it certainly would not explain taking back gifts. And whatever explanation of the gifts the president offers is going to have to square with the accounts of both Ms. Lewinsky and of his private secretary, Betty Currie. Otherwise, the contradiction in testimony would surely qualify as "substantial and credible information" that would have to be included in an impeachment report.

Mr. Starr also has testimony from Ms. Lewinsky and Ms. Currie about conversations they had with the president in which he reportedly coached them, albeit indirectly, about what he wanted them to say if they were questioned. This, too, could form the basis for a finding in the report of witness tampering or obstruction of justice, even in the absence of other evidence. The president might deny these conversations occurred or he might explain them differently, but it is unlikely he would win any credibility contests.

This highlights the single most important respect in which the president's testimony may have exacerbated his legal and political problems. A strategy of full confession and apology might have made his conduct in the Jones case even harder to defend than it now is, but at least it would have confined his problems to whatever occurred before this week. The strategy Mr. Clinton followed instead—admitting as little as possible, to the point of refusing even to admit that his sexual relationship with Ms. Lewinsky rendered his testimony in the Jones suit false—means that the prosecutors may have ample basis to make a case that the president committed perjury or obstruction of justice in the grand jury proceeding. The president's reported refusal to answer certain questions without adequate legal justification could also represent an effort to impede the due administration of justice.

Mr. Starr may, therefore, end up issuing a report to the House alleging not only that the president personally committed perjury, witness tampering and obstruction of justice in the Jones suit, but also that coverup efforts by the president himself continued through the grand jury investigation, even after he was fully aware of the consequences.

Such a report, if backed up by persuasive evidence, would be politically devastating. And no matter what happens as a result of the president's political jeopardy, he will remain in legal jeopardy even after he leaves office. For the statute of limitations will not have expired by Jan. 20, 2001. Far from putting the Lewinsky affair behind him, the president's testimony may simply have aided its transition into a new and even more damaging phase.

Mr. Berenson is a Washington lawyer.

REVIEW & OUTLOOK

I, Clinton

A lot of good Americans have a lot of thinking to do in the wake of President Clinton's remarkably revealing speech Monday night. There is a government that needs to be run the next two-plus years, and two centuries of political institutions that need to be protected and nurtured. Mr. Clinton made it plain that he is not going to be much help.

Bill Clinton

The extraordinary features of the five-minute address are by now widely remarked. Even while confessing a relationship he could no longer plausibly deny, the president did not utter the word "apologize." He confessed to "misleading," not to lying. He contended his previous testimony was "legally accurate," meaning that he was hiding behind a convoluted definition of "sexual contact," while at the same time hotly asserting the details of his sexual contact were "private." While pretending to take responsibility for his actions, he proceeded to blame his problems on everyone else in general and Independent Counsel Kenneth Starr in particular. In total, it was not an expression of contrition but an outburst of anger.

For better or worse, this was not the politically astute ploy. For weeks Judiciary Chairman Orrin Hatch was reaching for the President's hand; apologize and we can move on. From another point on the political spectrum, Leon Panetta, the President's former chief of staff, was writing the same script. Each ended up with a thumb in his eye. Headed for a head-on collision with Mr. Starr, Mr. Clinton mashed the accelerator in a constitutional game of chicken.

This is anything but the way to "move on" or get the matter "behind us." Now of course, we've been expressing severe doubt that any such thing would be possible in any event, at least without a mea culpa for matters reaching far beyond Monica Lewinsky and into the realm of criminal intent. And perhaps Mr. Clinton's defiance reflects the same calculation, that if he gives an inch his defenses will collapse, that his best bet is to make clear that any final assault would be painful for his critics, for innocent bystanders and for the Republic.

Perhaps, but our bet is that instead what the nation heard Monday night was the real Bill Clinton. He did not apologize or truly accept responsibility because he cannot; it is not in his genes. He does not admit to lying because he lies without remorse, without even recognizing it. He blames others because he deeply believes he is the wronged party. And despite the insistence of advisers he does not recognize his own peril.

Throughout the world and throughout history, as we've written before, national leaders have typically not had normal, well-adjusted personalities. Completely adjusted personalities seldom go into politics, and even more seldom show the drive and willingness to sacrifice needed to climb to the top. We've sparked debate among psychiatrists in our letters column before by mentioning that the traits described in the paragraph above (along with sexual problems and a charming air) are the classical symptoms of a condition called antisocial personality disorder. Of course, one expects to find sociopaths in jail rather than at Oxford or in the White House, and we would not pretend to a clinical diagnosis. Even so, an understanding of this collection of human traits seems to us a great help in making sense of the Clinton Presidency, as it was again Monday night.

Now the President is digging himself even more deeply into the bunker, and flitting off to celebrity fixes in the Hamptons and Martha's Vineyard. Happily the Cold War is over, and while foreign policy problems may linger no true crisis is imminent. Madeleine Albright is a steadying influence. There are clouds on the economic horizon, despite prosperity and yeasty markets, but Alan Greenspan is on watch and Robert Rubin no lightweight. The Republic functioned for 18 months with President Wilson incapacitated by a stroke.

The truly serious problem lies at the Justice Department, deeply compromised by the President's stonewall defense. Perhaps Janet Reno will yet make an honest woman of herself with appointment of a new independent counsel on campaign finance abuses; surely the Congress is mounting appropriate pressure to that end. At the FBI, Louis Freeh has recognized a higher responsibility. At great sacrifice to his own career and reputation, Kenneth Starr has been upholding the rule of law. The saving grace of Monday afternoon's circus was that in the end the President had to answer to the law. Whatever the President's anger at the intrusions, he did not prove to be an emperor.

For the longer term, the important thing is that the nation digests the lessons it is so painfully learning. This means that the process must grind forward. Mr. Starr must report to the Congress; what Congress needs from him is much more than a "gotcha" on sexual perjury, but a broader collection of evidence that the President may have set a climate of disrespect for law that has permeated our institutions. We hope that Congress, perhaps with new leaders rising, would face up more squarely than it has to airing the essential issues. Whether or not impeachment is necessary or appropriate could be decided in due course, but clearly the worst outcome would be for responsible Americans to blink before Mr. Clinton's anger, making him an emperor after all.

Editorial Feature

Hillary's Advice:
Impeachment Has Its Uses

The second most instructive document in Washington these days involves not President Clinton but his wife.

No, not the Whitewater billing records. It's a 1974 report by the Democratic staff—of which Hillary Rodham was a member—of the Judiciary Committee contemplating Richard Nixon's impeachment.

That superb historical survey concludes that the Framers viewed impeachment as "one of the central elements of executive responsibility in the framework of the new government as they conceived it."

Potomac Watch

By Paul A. Gigot

It quotes approvingly Alexander Hamilton, in Federalist 65, that impeachment should apply to "those offences which proceed from the misconduct of public men, or, in other words, from the abuse or violation of some public trust. They are of a nature which may with peculiar propriety be denominated POLITICAL, as they relate chiefly to injuries done immediately to the society itself."

We have arrived where Hamilton and Hillary both foresaw we would. This is the big picture to keep in mind as Clinton defenders moan about the "trauma" of impeachment, the "damage to the country," or the "need to get this behind us."

Impeachment isn't fun, but the Founders understood--and our current first lady once agreed--that it could also be cleansing. Consider the benefits of impeachment today:

1. *It's educational like nothing else is.* For both angry Republicans and scared Democrats, resignation will be the politically easy escape. But if a twice-elected president is going to leave early, most Americans must first be persuaded it's necessary and just. Impeachment hearings are the only way to bring the country along to such a judgment, preventing later resignation remorse.

That's why Democrat John Dingell, the senior member of the House, deserves credit for urging the public release of Kenneth Starr's report. After disclosing the main report today, Congress should release the 2,000 pages of backup testimony too. Better everything come out on the record than have it become sludge for Drudge and Geraldo.

2. *It reasserts the primacy of fact and law.* The Clinton years have seen the apogee of spin and political artifice. Now we will relearn that the truth does have consequences.

Mr. Starr focused his report on the Monica Lewinsky matter, I am told, because its evidence is overwhelming and multi-sourced. This leaves the White House with the rebuttal that it's "just a sex case." But that defense may not work with voters who read evidence of law-breaking, witness tampering, and even the abuse of the Secret Service to protect illicit sex.

"These are serious offenses that go to the heart of our justice system," says Ronald Rotunda, who helped write the report as a consultant to Mr. Starr and was a member of the Senate Democratic staff during Watergate.

Mr. Starr is unloved because the independent counsel law made him the one to break up our national contentment. But his persistence despite the polls proves again that in America the law holds even presidents accountable.

3. *It may rehabilitate our political institutions.* Congress has hardly distinguished itself during the Clinton years, and many assume impeachment will be another food fight. Certainly Barney Frank and Bob Barr may end up wrestling in the mud.

But my guess is that most members on both sides of the aisle will rise to the occasion. It happened with Peter Rodino, the New Jersey

Democrat, who until Nixon's impeachment was derided unfairly as a hack with unsavory friends. But he kept a cool demeanor and a somber tone, and helped make Nixon's departure inevitable.

Grown-ups are asserting themselves now, too. Pat Moynihan, a Democrat with gravitas, says the country can survive impeachment and Congress should "get on with it." Look for younger voices to emerge on Judiciary, too, perhaps California Republican and former judge Jim Rogan or Democrat Zoe Lofgren.

The most important Republican grown-up is Judiciary Chairman Henry Hyde, who is feared by the White House precisely because he

Henry Hyde

can't be morphed into Al D'Amato. His political savvy is already apparent in his choice of staff.

His impeachment counsel, David Schippers, is a Chicago Democrat unhip to partisan Washington but steeped in the history of impeachment. In 1974, New York Times columnist (and now Clinton defender) Anthony Lewis quoted Mr. Schippers in 1974 as concluding that Nixon had committed impeachable offenses. Don't expect Mr. Lewis to quote him this time.

4. *It helps Democrats.* Really. Democrats are fated to suffer some guilt-by-association in November no matter what happens, but they can limit the damage by reasserting their independence on impeachment. Like Joe Lieberman last week, they have a chance to rise above their morally embarrassing "everybody does it" defense of the last two years.

Impeachment hearings will force the country to have a much-needed debate about standards, both political and moral. An argument over Bill Clinton's misconduct won't be elegant, but it will set parameters for acceptable future behavior by all politicians. Lying well will no longer be considered a civic virtue.

No president since Nixon has done more than Bill Clinton to define political deviancy down. So it's only right that the country use his now likely impeachment hearings to begin redefining it back up.

Review & Outlook

The Other Clinton

In *l'affaire Lewinsky*, Hillary Clinton is obviously a woman wronged, all the more so if you watch soap opera news. Andrea Mitchell of NBC reports that Mrs. Clinton copes well with her husband's behavior because she is "deeply religious" and "incredibly angry" at Kenneth Starr. CBS's Eric Engberg rhapsodizes that this is "not just a political thunderclap, but a family tragedy."

Hillary Clinton

Mrs. Clinton in fact is the leading symbol of the problem of a bill of impeachment focusing on sexual behavior and the ensuing coverup, no matter how carefully documented. This emphasis on the personal obscures the *systemic* nature of the Clinton coverups, indeed, the Clinton mode of governance. It is probably too much to expect that the soaps would recall that she, not he, turned the $100,000 commodities strike back in 1978 under the tutelage of Jim Blair of Tyson Foods. The statute of limitations had expired by the time this bribe was disclosed, but it also happens that Mrs. Clinton is smack in the middle of some other, unfulfilled items of Mr. Starr's mandate.

The mandate started with the original Whitewater-Madison Guaranty land deals, over which Mr. Starr has already convicted Jim and Susan McDougal and former Arkansas Governor Jim Guy Tucker. Mrs. Clinton's work at the Rose Law Firm covered a deal called Castle Grande; the Resolution Trust Corp. concluded that the Castle Grande deal was a "sham transaction" designed to conceal Madison's ownership. The Rose billing records from the firm were under subpoena for two years before they miraculously appeared on a coffee table in a room at the White House. Fed up, Mr. Starr summoned Mrs. Clinton in January 1996 to a Washington grand jury for an explanation. It also happens that in September 1996, the Federal Deposit Insurance Corp. concluded that a document drafted by Mrs. Clinton had been used by McDougal's Madison S&L "to deceive federal bank examiners."

Mr. Starr has determined that Deputy White House Counsel Vincent Foster died by his own hand at Fort Marcy Park in July 1993, but the probe into the aftermath of the death remains open. Mrs. Clinton played a key role in limiting access by federal investigators to Mr. Foster's office, and her chief of staff, Maggie Williams, was seen leaving the area with an armful of folders. A year later, in the face of media and Congressional pressure, the White House revealed that Whitewater files removed from Mr. Foster's office had been kept at the personal residence for five days before being turned over to the Clintons' personal attorneys.

Mr. Starr's mandate also includes the misuse of FBI files, a subject covered in the sixth deposition of Mrs. Clinton by Mr. Starr's investigators last April. And finally, Mr. Starr is supposed to report on the Travel Office firings. A 1993 memo by then-White House director of administration David Watkins directly contradicting Mrs. Clinton surfaced during a House investigation. Vincent Foster "regularly informed me that the First Lady was concerned and desired action--the action desired was the firing of the Travel Office staff." The Watkins memo was discovered after White House lawyers had submitted an April 1994 statement on behalf of Mrs. Clinton saying she "does not know the origin of the decision to remove the White House Travel Office employees."

Mr. Starr's grand juries, where the matters above have been vetted, were meeting yesterday, indicating that investigation of the balance of his mandate goes forward. It is of course asking a lot for Mr. Starr to get some clear deposition of the issues concerning not only the President but the First Lady. But if he fails to do so, we doubt that justice will have been served or the public adequately informed about how its government has been run.

REVIEW & OUTLOOK

Starr's Hour

Who better to bring Bill Clinton to justice than a hymn-singing son of a fundamentalist minister? Kenneth Starr's investigation of the Clinton White House, culminating in the report just sent to Congress, has played out amid a constant chorus of opinion from all those quarters that have recently set the terms and tone of American culture.

Kenneth Starr

Until this moment, the chorus has been that whatever Mr. Clinton's moral and political transgressions, there was something about Kenneth Starr that was equally off-putting and reprehensible.

This is curious and instructive, given Mr. Starr's impeccable pedigree: Clerk to Chief Justice Warren Burger. Justice Department chief of staff. A judgeship on the D.C. Circuit Court, the nation's second most important. Solicitor General. A figure of integrity so imposing that Democrats helped choose him as Independent Counsel for the Packwood case. And now Clinton Independent Counsel, a position in which he has already convicted 14 criminals, including an Associate Attorney General and the Governor of Arkansas.

Something off-putting? What something? We would go so far as to suggest that the "something" about Ken Starr that so rubbed many opinion-makers the wrong way was the clear understanding that he was not just prosecuting Bill Clinton; he was prosecuting the entire culture that gave birth to what Bill Clinton represents.

Everyone does it. It's only sex. Whatever the crimes of the Whitewater land deal, it was all so long ago. No one cares.

The carriers of these opinions--in newspapers, on the airwaves--were the voices of an American and European culture that since the 1960s has been undergoing a relentless moral transformation, a transformation that before certain recent economic difficulties was engendering talk of an "Asian Century."

Under this new rubric, the verities that guided the generation that fought World War II were deemed inappropriate for the social forces that got up and running during the 1960s. In place of earlier ideas about right and wrong behavior came the strong belief that the particularities of any one person's circumstances left any moral judgment troublesome. And so eventually most people, including the churches, simply stopped judging. Anything goes, so everything went.

This is precisely what Senator Joseph Lieberman was talking about when he took to the floor of the Senate last Thursday to denounce not merely Bill Clinton's behavior, but Mr. Clinton's own barely audible assessment of that behavior as "not appropriate." This is precisely the warning issued on the floor of the Senate Monday by Senator Robert Byrd, who excoriated the slovenly culture that serves as context to the Clinton scandals.

But no such clear-eyed view of the nation's moral lodestar has been evident during the time of the Starr investigation. Instead the sophisticates of that culture, deploying the same tangled chains of logic that allowed so much else through the doors the past 30 years, managed to write venomously about both Bill Clinton and Ken Starr. By these lights, Mr. Starr was somehow equally at fault for violating the newer mores.

He wasn't "fair," they said, dragging before the grand jury that poor girl's mother, who hid her daughter's evidence, and now demands $10 million to tell her daughter's story. Mr. Starr wasn't very "nice." In short, he isn't one of us.

That's for sure. Quick case in point: He never aspired to be dean of, say, Yale Law School; instead, he desired, and was vilified for, preferring Pepperdine--wherever that is. What the Pepperdine episode showed was that Mr. Starr really was not at all part of the world his critics lived in and dominated.

These, of course, are the same two worlds that now compete for primacy in American politics. One pleads for re-establishing commonly held rules of the road. The other insists that social and moral diversity has rendered such commonality impossible—and, as they like to add, get used to it.

We guess that Ken Starr, and indeed the prosecutors from both parties who have worked with him, never could get used to the world that the evidence of their investigation of the Clintons laid before them. Indeed, it's possible that they were, as Senator Hollings said a few days ago, "fed up."

Yet against the vilification of the Clinton spinsters and the mockery of the pundits, Mr. Starr persisted to the point at which we have now arrived--the brink of an impeachment. Explaining this peculiar behavior, we now have journalistic exegeses of what shaped Ken Starr. What drives him, we are inclined to say, is nothing more complicated than a sense of political and legal duty. We doubt that before the 1960s anyone would have asked twice.

In the world Mr. Starr represents the law does not "spin"; it stands still, at its best defending civilized behavior against moral chaos. Throughout the Clinton investigations, Mr. Starr was, in effect, asked repeatedly to let it go, to accept the chaos of one President's turbulent life. He said no.

Now the nation is about to read through the hundreds and hundreds of pages specifying just what it was that Ken Starr would not accept as lawful or appropriate in a Presidency. It will be an instructive exercise, above all for the sophisticates ridiculing the notion that some standards are not passing fashion but eternal.

Editorial Feature

Mr. Clinton Has
No Presidency to Defend

By ROBERT REICH

We had all assumed that 1996 was the last big campaign of Bill Clinton's political life, but we were wrong. The last one is beginning now. The apparent choice: either believe Ken Starr's allegations of presidential lawbreaking and conclude that no one who has broken the law can remain president; or accept the president's apologies, view the allegations as disputable at best and conclude that, regardless, they stem from private acts that do not justify removal of a duly elected president.

Most of us—even including those of us who have campaigned for him in the past, known him for years and served with him in Washington—are angry and confused, not yet willing to choose, searching for another option, wishing that the whole thing would go away. No chance. This will drag on.

How can we get beyond this, over this, through this? By recognizing that Kenneth Starr's allegations are much beside the point. I doubt the public wants a president impeached for lying about sex, or even for encouraging others to do so. But there are two deeper offenses that grow out of what the president has already admitted to, that pose far greater threats to his presidency, and that make it especially difficult for the nation to move on. Even if he survives a congressional impeachment, Bill Clinton will be "virtually" impeached unless he addresses them.

The first is of these offenses is what is understood as a "character flaw" (for those who wish to blame Mr. Clinton) or a "compulsion" (for those who wish to blame demons in his psyche). Mr. Clinton took a wild, bizarre risk when he carried on an "inappropriate" relationship with then 21-year-old Monica Lewinsky. It occurred just months before the 1996 presidential election, four years after he almost lost the Democratic nomination over charges of sexual recklessness, and six months after Paula Jones charged in a civil lawsuit that then-Gov. Clinton had asked her to perform oral sex in a hotel room—charges against which he knew he might have to defend himself in court.

It was also a time when corporate America, universities and the U.S. military were under heightened scrutiny for permitting men in positions of power to exploit female subordinates sexually, and Ms. Lewinsky herself was the most subordinate of subordinates—a mere intern in the White House, barely out of college.

Consider, too, that the liaison went on for many months, and that there was a high probability that Ms. Lewinsky would talk about it with friends, family or others, that it occurred in and around the Oval Office, where security guards and gatekeepers would see her come and go, and that it included gifts and telephone calls which would constitute further evidence of a relationship. Consider all of this, and you are likely to be baffled by Mr. Clinton's behavior. You might conclude that something is not quite right with the president. What happens to presidential power when he shows such lack of judgment? Power inevitably subsides.

The second offense is the public lie—not simply the fact of it (presidents aren't always honest), but its passionate intensity. Better than any president of the television age, Bill Clinton has mastered television—looking directly into the camera; speaking firmly but softy; pausing for reflection; lower lip sometimes protruding in defiance, or folded under upper teeth in a show of determination; sometimes smiling gently, eyes twinkling; sometimes brows furrowed and jaw clenched in a display of conviction; sometimes eyes moist and brows tilted slightly upward, showing empathy or contrition. Like the great method actors of a previous generation, Mr. Clinton feels the emotions he expresses; his performances could not be so convincing were they anything but sincere. And yet they are still performances.

In January the president told America with stunning conviction that he had not had a sexual relationship with Ms. Lewinsky. On

Aug. 17, he looked into the eyes of America and said his January statement had been "misleading." Many who witnessed both performances thought the January one the more convincing. Hence, Mr. Clinton's second problem: If he can so convincingly fake a lie, how can the public believe anything else he says—including his current stream of apologies? Despite protestations that the Lewinsky affair was his private business, the betrayal was indubitably public because the denials were so passionately public. He spoke to America with the same emotional intensity he has brought to countless public issues. What happens to presidential power when credibility is so blatantly forfeited? It inevitably subsides.

More apologies won't restore this president's power, nor will a formidable White House campaign to defend this presidency against impeachment. What Mr. Clinton must do is explain why he risked everything and then lied so baldly about it, and assure us that he has changed his ways. Most Americans want to forgive him, yet presidential power depends less on absolution than on an affirmative commitment of public trust. Without trust, Mr. Clinton has only the public's approval of how he is doing his job, which rests largely on the continued strength of the economy—a perilous foundation. Absent trust, America will remain mired in this controversy, unable to focus on large issues which need our attention. Lacking trust, Mr. Clinton has no presidency to defend, and we have no president to lead us.

Mr. Reich, President Clinton's first secretary of labor, is a professor of economic and social policy at Brandeis University.

Editorial Feature

American Caligula

By PEGGY NOONAN

For seven months I have kept on my desk a picture from a tabloid. It is of two close friends of President Clinton, Linda Bloodworth-Thomason and the actress Markie Post. They are laughing and holding hands in joyous union as they jump up and down at where fate has put them down. It had put them in the Lincoln bedroom. They were jumping up and down on Lincoln's bed.

It seemed to me emblematic of the Clinton White House, a place where opponents' FBI files were read aloud over pizza and foreign contributors with cash invited in the back door. I thought: Something's wrong with these people, they lack thought and dignity. But most of all they seemed to lack respect, a sense of awe—not the awe that can cripple you with a false sense of your smallness but the awe that makes you bigger, that makes you reach higher as if in tribute to some unseen greatness around you.

That, it seemed to me last week, as the president spoke each day and the Starr report was published—that was Mr. Clinton's problem, his real sin—a fundamental lack of respect for his country, for its citizens, for his colleagues, for all of us. The pollsters have it wrong when, seeking to determine whether he can continue to govern, they ask, "Do you respect the president?" The real question is, "Do you think he has any respect for us?"

'We Must Win'

I think he showed with a chilling finality last week that he does not. I believe he demonstrated that people and principles are, to him, objects to be manipulated. You can tell preachers you cherish scripture, tell Monica you cherish her, it doesn't matter. The object, as Dick Morris says the president told him, is to "win."

Never, in all of last week, did he explain why he put the country through eight terrible months of dissension and distraction, when he easily could have spared it the trauma (and spared his career too). Never did he explain why he sent his media generals out every day to lie for him with conviction, and to slime his opponents. It was telling that when he spoke to the evangelicals he said some people needed apologizing to, and that first, and "most important," was his family. What followed was a litany of his friends and his staff. His country came in dead last in the litany, as it has in his actions.

In the report and in his comments it was clear that the most important thing to Bill Clinton is, now and always, Bill Clinton. But what was amazing is that he seemed last week to think that we feel that way too.

And so he spoke of the scandal as his "journey." He said it has helped him grow. He said it may make him stronger. He said it has been an exhausting week for him. He said this has been the most difficult time of his life. But then, as if to comfort us in our concern, he offered context: It may turn out to be the most valuable, too.

He noted that his drama may make American families stronger. He said it provides an opportunity for healing. He spoke moistly, glisteningly of the early days of his first presidential run "when nobody but my mother . . . thought I had a chance of being elected." He talked of a little boy who told him "he wanted to be a president just like me." The boy was "husky, like I was," the president said moistly, glisteningly.

He compared himself to Mark McGwire. Would you want Mr. McGwire to give up now, he asked? But Mr. McGwire is a champion because he has shown himself the past 10 days to be what is now an amazing thing, a celebrity who is a good man. This is the exact opposite of what Mr. Clinton has shown. The weird solipsism, the over-the-top self-dramatizing continued in the Starr report. There Mr.

Clinton was not Mark McGwire but, as he told Sidney Blumenthal, a "character in a novel," a victim of a sinister force weaving a web of lies about Monica Lewinsky and him. He compared himself to the hero of "Darkness at Noon."

He told evangelical ministers at a prayer breakfast that he had reached "the rock bottom truth of where I am." He said he has "sinned." He bit his lip, lowered his moist eyes, and said his "spirit is broken." He then went on to a raucous awards dinner where he laughed gaily, waved and announced, "Hillary and I have been . . . just lapping this up!"

For all he seemed to be, in Flannery O'Connor's phrase, a pious conniver. As he spoke to the evangelicals, I was reminded of his great learning experience in 1980, after he lost his re-election race for the governorship. Knowing the people of Arkansas had come to see him as different, as too liberal and too Yale, he immediately went out and joined the only local church choir that sang on TV every Sunday morning. People liked it. He manipulated them for gain, to win. And in 1982 he won.

The problem is not that he is an actor. As an actor he puts not only Ronald Reagan to shame, but Laurence Olivier. The problem is that he thinks people will believe anything, that if he says a thing it is true. He absorbs his lies, and becomes them. The country suffers for this.

Mr. Clinton seems—and this is an amazing thing to say about a president—to lack a sense of patriotism, a love of country, a protectiveness toward her. He dupes the secretary of state, who must be America's credible voice in the world, into lying for him to the public and press. He fears his phone is being tapped by foreign agents, opening him to international blackmail. But he does not discontinue phone sex. Instead he comes up with a cover story. He tells Ms. Lewinsky they can say they knew they were being bugged, and it was just a "put on." He sends the first lady to go on television, where she denies the Lewinsky charges and says, "This is a battle. . . some folk are going to have a lot to answer for."

It is similarly amazing to say of an American president that he is decadent—an Ozarks Caligula, as a placard he passed last week put it. While being sexually serviced he keeps the door ajar so his secretary can alert him to calls; while taking one from a congressman he unzips his pants and exposes himself so he can receive oral sex. He masturbates in front of his young lover in the bathroom near his study, and in a staff member's office. When Ms. Lewinsky asks him about rumors that he'd attempted to molest Kathleen Willey, he is indignant: He would never approach a woman with small breasts. When the Lewinsky story breaks, he asks a pollster, a man newly famous for letting a prostitute listen in while he advised the president on strategy, if he should tell the truth. The pollster tells him no. The president responds, "Well, we just have to win then."

It is interesting, by the way, that of the self-described hundreds and hundreds of women Bill Clinton has been involved with, it is Ms. Lewinsky who has done the most damage. The reason I think is that in picking her he made a crucial mistake: He chose someone much like himself. She describes herself as insecure as she makes demands. She learned to manipulate in this manner through the culture of therapy. Her wants are justified because she is, after all, burdened with fears, and can be comforted only by the meeting of her demands. He picked someone with as grand a sense of entitlement as his own. At the end of the affair she demands that he feel contrition; she also demands a job with these words: "I don't want to have to work for this position. . . . I just want it to be given to me."

And he picked someone who is, like himself, an exhibitionist. It never occurred to Ms. Lewinsky to be discreet about their affair, not to tell a dozen friends and family about the cigar, the nicknames. But then discretion has never really occurred to him, either. That's how we know about so many of his affairs. He always leaves a trail, an open door. He wants us to know.

I once saw the president in one of those big Washington hotel dinners a few years ago shortly after he talked about his underwear on TV. He was in full self-deprecating mode, teasing himself for his mistake. But he went on a little too long; he talked too much about it, and the crowd seemed to be thinking what I was: Doesn't he know that as he stands up there going on and on about his shorts we are starting to imagine him in his shorts? The poor man doesn't know. And then I thought: Yes he does! He wants us to imagine him like that. And he has lived out his presidency so we can.

Caligula made his horse a senator; Mr. Clinton made his whoring a centerpiece. Both did so because they lacked respect and concern for anything but themselves. Ancient times could tolerate its Caligula, but Mr. Clinton is, quaint phrase, the most powerful man in the world, the leader of the free world, the chief executive of the United States, commander of our armed forces, the man who one day may be forced by history to unleash a nuclear missile. It is not tolerable that such a person be in such a position, and have such power.

Not Good Enough

Jesse Jackson once said, "God isn't finished with me yet," and it was beautiful because it was true. God isn't finished with any of us. Maybe he will raise up Bill Clinton and make him a saint, a great one. Maybe he will make Bill Clinton's life an example of stunning redemption. But for now, and now is what we have, Bill Clinton is not wise enough, mature enough, stable enough—he is not good enough—to be the American president.

In the therapeutic language he favors, an intervention would seem to be in order. That would be impeachment, for the high crime and misdemeanor of having no respect for his office, for his country, and for its people.

Ms. Noonan is the author of, most recently, "Simply Speaking ReganBooks, 1998).

REVIEW & OUTLOOK

A Call to Duty

The Starr report calls for the Congress to embark on the solemn duty before it and, barring some miracle as the evidence develops, bring this scandal-ridden Presidency to its sorry conclusion.

Mr. Clinton's supporters are now reduced to arguing "it's only sex," and oral sex is not sex and he never touched her erotically while depositing semen on her dress. This comes not only from his paid lawyers, but from a surprising number of commentators and Democratic Congressmen so far willing to debase themselves defending such preposterous positions. They will gather their wits and their dignity, we predict, as the process unfolds.

Bill Clinton

We are quite prepared to argue that "only sex," as detailed in the Starr report as opposed to some truly private matter, is quite sufficient grounds for removing a President. Turning a star-struck intern into a workplace sexual toy, no matter how willingly she consented, would after all be grounds for dismissal from any other position of high responsibility in American life. Why should the President be judged by different standards; is he above the laws that apply to the rest of us?

The President has admitted the affair, his rebuttal brief argues, but it does not rise to the level of an impeachable offense because the Constitutional phrase high crimes and misdemeanors "denoted political offenses, the critical element of which was injury to the state." But of course the state is deeply injured when the personal behavior of its head turns him into a world laughingstock; he has destroyed his capacity to lead either at home or abroad. Beyond that, the Starr narrative describes, among other things, the blackmail of the President of the United States by a 24-year-old. Someone so bereft of discretion as to put himself in that position is not capable of discharging the duties of his office.

High political judgment and the capacity to serve, the debate will establish, is what impeachment has historically been about. The first person removed from office by a Senate impeachment vote, for example, was Judge John Pickering in 1803. The articles of impeachment stated that he appeared on the bench "in a state of total intoxication, produced by free and intemperate use of intoxicating liquors; and did then and there frequently, in a most profane and indecent manner, invoke the name of the Supreme Being, to the evil example of all the good citizens of the United States; and was then and there guilty of other high misdemeanors, disgraceful to his own character as a judge and degrading to the honor of the United States."

Despite the White House spin, of course, it is not "only sex." The President has perjured himself, tampered with witnesses, obstructed justice and abused the powers of his office to conceal his own personal misconduct. Yes, he and his lawyers offer convoluted semantic arguments to deny these obvious truths, then complain that Mr. Starr's attempts to refute them even on their own terms are a "smear campaign." Other defenders argue that while his testimony under oath may be "technical" perjury, it doesn't count because it was about sex, only in a civil suit, etc. etc.

The denial that the President committed perjury is "nonsensical," former Clinton aide George Stephanopoulos said on ABC yesterday, but argued that impeachment would be a punishment that doesn't fit the crime. Outlining a possible White House fallback position, he went on to suggest something along the lines of the political settlement of the Gingrich ethics charges: An admission of perjury, a censure and a payment from Mr. Clinton to reimburse the government for the expense of delaying of the investigation. Some such course is likely to appeal on a political level to both Democrats and Republicans.

There is, however, a new-found sense of seriousness on Capitol Hill. Congress may be prepared to see some easy way out correctly, as granting permission for perjury and undermining the rule of law generally. As the debate proceeds, indeed, we expect that the President's offenses will be widely seen as what they are: an ongoing assault on the laws he is supposed to "faithfully execute." This assault continues today in the nonsensical White House justifications, with the President digging himself in deeper and deeper. Faithful execution of the laws has from the first been the Clinton issue; as hearings proceed, as surely they must, it will be here that the debate on impeachment ultimately turns.

The process, moreover, is likely to include further revelations. The pattern of behavior the Starr report describes almost certainly extends to other items under Mr. Starr's mandate—witnesses Webster Hubbell and Susan McDougal, for example. But in the others, the President has been protected by layers of aides, including the First Lady with spousal immunity; it has been hard to connect the dots directly into the Oval Office. The current charges revolve around sex because this was the one cover-up the President had to conduct personally. The Watergate crimes would probably never have been traced to the President except for the White House tapes; the semen-stained dress is this scandal's functional equivalent. But the Starr reports notes that investigations of other matters are nearing completion, and he had grand juries meeting last week. We can no doubt expect indictments of other parties, certainly in the sexual cover-up and quite likely in other matters as well. This will disclose new evidence and fuel the impeachment drive.

The Starr narrative shows again and again how Mr. Clinton has used those around him, debasing not only Ms. Lewinsky but his aides, his friends, his cabinet. In now offering the defense that he does, he invites all of us to join his own corruption. We hope that the Congress, and the public, have the good sense to say no, instead let justice be done. The process must begin, clearly will, and will have its own logic and momentum.

A Whitewater Chronology

Editor's note: *This comprehensive chronology includes the Monica Lewinsky affair, the campaign-finance scandal, and other events shaping Bill Clinton's journey from Little Rock to the Oval Office. It supersedes the chronologies in earlier volumes of* **A Journal Briefing: Whitewater.**

1976

Bill Clinton is elected Arkansas Attorney General.

Little Rock investment banker Jackson Stephens forms Stephens Finance with Indonesian banker Mochtar Riady to do business in Asia.

1977

Hillary Rodham Clinton joins the Rose Law Firm.

Jackson Stephens joins with former Carter administration budget director Bert Lance and a group of Mideast investors—later identified as key figures in the corrupt Bank of Credit & Commerce International—in an unsuccessful attempt to acquire Financial General

Bankshares in Washington, D.C. Amid the legal maneuvers surrounding the takeover attempt, a brief is submitted by the Stephens-controlled bank data processing firm Systematics; two of the lawyers signing the brief are Hillary Rodham and Webster Hubbell.

1978

August: The Clintons purchase a 230-acre land tract along Arkansas's White River, in partnership with Jim and Susan McDougal.

October: Mrs. Clinton, now a partner at the Rose Firm, begins a series of commodities trades under the guidance of Tyson Foods executive Jim Blair, earning nearly $100,000. The trades are not revealed until March 1994.

November: Bill Clinton is elected Governor of Arkansas. He makes Jim McDougal a top economic adviser.

1979

Feb. 16: The Federal Reserve rejects the bid by BCCI frontmen to take over Financial General Bankshares

June: The Clintons and McDougals form Whitewater Development Co. to engage in real estate transactions.

1980

November: Gov. Clinton is defeated by Republican Frank White. He joins his trusted friend Bruce Lindsey at the Little Rock law firm of Wright, Lindsey and Jennings.

1981

Jim McDougal purchases Madison Bank and Trust.

Aug. 25: The Federal Reserve approves a new bid—by largely the same group of BCCI frontmen—to acquire Financial General Bankshares.

1982

Financial General changes its name to First American and Democratic Party icon Clark Clifford is appointed chairman. BCCI fronts begin acquiring controlling interest in banks and other American financial institutions.

In Arkansas, Jim McDougal purchases Madison Guaranty Savings & Loan. It begins a period of rapid expansion.

November: Bill Clinton defeats Frank White, winning back the governor's seat.

1983

Capital Management Services, a federally insured small business investment company owned by Judge David Hale, begins making loans to the Arkansas political elite.

Jackson Stephens forms United Pacific Trading with Mochtar Riady to do business in the U.S. and Asia.

1984

Stephens and Riady join forces to buy First Arkansas Bankstock Corp., changing its name to Worthen Bank and installing 28-year-old James Riady as president.

Jan. 20: The Federal Home Loan Bank Board issues a report on Madison Guaranty questioning its lending practices and financial stability. The Arkansas Securities Department begins to take steps to close it down.

August: According to Jim McDougal, Gov. Clinton drops by his office during a morning jog and asks that Madison steer some business to Mrs. Clinton at the Rose Law Firm.

November: Gov. Clinton wins re-election with 64% of the vote.

1985

January: Roger Clinton pleads guilty to cocaine distribution charges and is given immunity from further prosecution in exchange for cooperation. He testifies before a federal grand jury and serves a brief prison sentence.

Jan. 16: Gov. Clinton appoints Beverly Bassett Schaffer, a long-time associate, to serve as Arkansas State Securities Commissioner.

March: Mrs. Clinton receives from Madison Guaranty the first payment of a $2,000-per-month retainer. Madison's accounting firm, Frost & Co., issues a report declaring the savings and loan solvent.

April 4: Jim McDougal hosts a fund-raiser to help Gov. Clinton repay campaign debts. Contributions at the fund-raiser later draw the scrutiny of Whitewater investigators.

April 7: The New Jersey securities firm Bevill, Bresler & Schulman files for bankruptcy amid fraud charges and an estimated $240 million in losses; one of the biggest apparent losers is Stephens-dominated Worthen Bank, which holds with Bevill $52 million of Arkansas state funds in uncollateralized repurchase agreements.

April 30: Hillary Clinton sends a recapitalization offer for the foundering Madison Guaranty to the Arkansas Securities Commission. Two weeks later, Ms. Schaffer informs Mrs. Clinton the plan is approved, but it is never implemented.

October: Governor and Mrs. Clinton lead a trade delegation to Taiwan and Japan.

Jim McDougal launches the Castle Grande land deal.

1986

Jan. 17: The U. S. Attorney for the Western District of Arkansas drops a money laundering and narcotics-conspiracy case against Arkansas associates of international drug smuggler Barry Seal. Arkansas State Police Investigator Russell Welch and Internal Revenue Service Investigator Bill Duncan, the lead agents on the case, protest; later, both are driven from their jobs.

Feb. 19: Barry Seal is gunned down by Colombian hitmen in Baton Rouge, La. He becomes the touchstone in murky allegations of covert operations, cocaine trafficking and gun running swirling around his base at Mena airfield in western Arkansas.

March 4: The Federal Home Loan Bank Board issues a second, sharply critical report of Madison, accusing Jim McDougal of diverting funds to insiders.

April: Roger Clinton is paroled from prison.

James Riady steps down as president of Worthen Bank.

April 3: David Hale's Capital Management Services makes a $300,000 loan to Susan McDougal in the name of a front, Master Marketing. Some of the funds wind up in a Whitewater Development Co. account. Indicted for fraud on an unrelated transaction in 1993, Mr. Hale claims that then-Gov. Clinton and Jim McDougal pressured him into making the loan.

August: Federal regulators remove Mr. McDougal from Madison's board of directors.

Oct. 5: Deceased Mena drug smuggler Barry Seal's C-123K is shot down over Nicaragua with an Arkansas pilot at the controls and a load of weapons and Contra-supporter Eugene Hasenfus in the cargo bay.

Oct. 24: Clinton friend and "bond daddy" Dan Lasater and nine others, most from the Little Rock bond trading community, are indicted on cocaine charges. Roger Clinton, who has cooperated with the prosecution, is named an unindicted co-conspirator.

November: Gov. Clinton wins re-election. Gubernatorial terms are extended from two years to four.

1987

According to Susan McDougal, Whitewater records are taken to the Governor's Mansion and turned over to Mrs. Clinton sometime during the year.

Officials at investment giant Stephens Inc., including longtime Clinton friend David Edwards, take steps to rescue Harken Energy, a struggling Texas oil company with George W. Bush on its board. Over the next three years, Mr. Edwards brings BCCI-linked investors and advisers into Harken deals. One of them, Abdullah Bakhsh, purchases $10 million in shares of Stephens-dominated Worthen Bank.

Jan. 15: Dan Lasater begins serving a 30-month sentence for cocaine distribution. In July, he is paroled to a Little Rock halfway house.

Aug. 23: In a mysterious case later ruled a murder and linked to drug corruption, teenagers Kevin Ives and Don Henry are run over by a train in a remote locale a few miles southwest of Little Rock.

1988

October: A Florida grand jury indicts BCCI figures on charges of laundering drug money. It is the first sign of serious trouble at the international bank.

1989

Manhattan District Attorney Robert Morgenthau begins a wide-ranging probe of BCCI.

March: Federal regulators shut down Madison Guaranty Savings & Loan, at a taxpayer loss of about $60 million. Jim McDougal is indicted for bank fraud.

June 16: Mena investigator Bill Duncan resigns from the Internal Revenue Service following clashes with

Washington supervisors over the probe.

1990

May: Jim McDougal goes to trial on bank fraud and is acquitted.

November: Gov. Clinton is elected to a second four-year term, promising to serve it out and not seek the presidency in 1992.

Dec. 3: The Federal Deposit Insurance Corp. cites the Riady family's Lippo Bank in Los Angeles for poor loans and inadequate capital.

1991

Yah Lin "Charlie" Trie, Clinton friend and Little Rock restaurateur, opens Daihatsu International Trading Co., with offices in Arkansas, Washington and Beijing. He later emerges as a central figure in the Clinton-Gore campaign scandal.

January: The Federal Reserve orders an investigation of BCCI's alleged control of First American Bank.

July 5: Regulators world-wide shut down BCCI amid widespread charges of bank fraud and allegations of links to laundered drug money, terrorists and intelligence agencies.

Aug. 13: Chairman Clark Clifford and top aide Robert Altman resign from First American.

Oct. 3: Bill Clinton announces his candidacy for president, denouncing "S&L crooks and self-serving CEOs."

1992

March 8: New York Times reporter Jeff Gerth discloses the Clintons' dealings with Madison and Whitewater.

March 20: Washington Times reporter Jerry Seper discloses Hillary Clinton's $2,000-per-month retainer from Madison.

March 23: In a hasty report arranged by the Clinton campaign, Denver lawyer James Lyons states the Clintons lost $68,000 on the Whitewater investment and clears them of improprieties. The issue fades from the campaign.

July 16: Bill Clinton accepts the Democratic Party's presidential nomination in New York.

July 22: A Manhattan grand jury hands up sealed indictments against BCCI principals, including Clark Clifford and Robert Altman. A week later, a grand jury in Washington and the Federal Reserve issue separate actions against Clifford and Altman.

August: Clinton friend David Edwards arranges a $3.5 million lead gift from Saudi Arabian benefactors to the University of Arkansas for a Middle East studies center.

Aug. 31: Resolution Trust Corporation field officers complete criminal referral #C0004 on Madison Guaranty and forward it to Charles Banks, U.S. Attorney for the Eastern District of Arkansas. The referral alleges an elaborate check kiting scheme by Madison owners Jim and Susan McDougal and names the Clintons and Jim Guy Tucker as possible beneficiaries. Later, Mr. Banks forwards the referral to Washington. In the heat of the campaign, the issue is sidelined.

Nov. 3: Bill Clinton is elected President of the United States.

December: Vincent Foster, representing the Clintons, meets with James McDougal and arranges for him to buy the Clintons' remaining shares in Whitewater Development Co. for $1,000. Mr. McDougal is loaned the money for the purchase by Tyson Foods counsel Jim Blair, a long-time Clinton friend and commodities adviser. The loan is never repaid.

1993

Jan. 20: Bill Clinton is sworn in as 42nd President of the United States.

February: Arkansas Gov. Jim Guy Tucker announces a $20 million Saudi gift to the University of Arkansas for a Middle East studies center.

March 23: At her first news conference as Attorney General, Janet Reno announces the firing of all U.S. Attorneys, the 93 top federal prosecutors in the nation, saying the administration wants to put in its own people.

March 24: Year-old press clips about Whitewater are faxed from Deputy Treasury Secretary Roger Altman to White House Counsel Bernard Nussbaum. Mr. Altman also is serving as acting head of the Resolution Trust Corporation, an independent federal agency.

April 20: Arkansas businessman Joseph Giroir, former chairman of the Rose Law Firm, incorporates the Arkansas International Development Corp. to bring Indonesia's Lippo Group together with American companies seeking to do business in Indonesia and China; Mr. Giroir later emerges as a player in the campaign-finance scandal.

May 19: The White House fires seven employees of its Travel Office, following a review by Associate Counsel William Kennedy III, a former member of the Rose Law Firm. Mr. Kennedy's actions, which included attempts to involve the FBI and the Internal Revenue Service in a criminal investigation of the Travel Office, are sharply criticized. Deputy White House Counsel Vincent Foster also is rebuked.

June 21: Whitewater corporate tax returns for 1989 through 1991, prepared by Mr. Foster, are delivered to Jim McDougal's attorney.

July 17: According to a White House chronology, Mr. Foster completes work on a blind trust for the Clintons. In Little Rock for a weekend visit, President Clinton has a four-hour dinner alone with old friend David Edwards, an investment adviser and currency trader.

July 20:   The Little Rock FBI obtains a warrant to search the office of David Hale as part of its investigation into Capital Management Services. In Washington, Deputy White House Counsel Vincent Foster drives to Ft. Marcy Park and commits suicide. That evening, White House Counsel Bernard Nussbaum, Clinton aide Patsy Thomasson, and Mrs. Clinton's chief of staff Maggie Williams visit Mr. Foster's office. According to testimony by a uniformed Secret Service officer, Ms. Williams exits the counsel's suite with an armful of folders.

July 21:   Early-morning calls are exchanged between Mrs. Clinton in Little Rock and White House operatives, including Maggie Williams and Susan Thomases. According to later Congressional testimony, Mrs. Clinton's concerns about investigators having "unfettered access" to the Foster office are conveyed to Mr. Nussbaum. A figure of later controversy, White House personnel security chief Craig Livingstone, is spotted in the Foster office area.

July 22:   Mr. Nussbaum again searches Mr. Foster's office, but denies access to Park Police and Justice Department investigators. In an angry phone call, Deputy Attorney General Philip Heymann asks, "Bernie, are you hiding something?" Documents, including Whitewater files, are removed. Details on the removal of Whitewater files do not emerge for months.

July 26:   A torn-up note is found in Mr. Foster's briefcase.

Aug. 14:   In New York, Robert Altman is acquitted of bank fraud in the BCCI case; Clark Clifford's trial is indefinitely postponed due to ill health.

Aug. 16:   Paula Casey, a longtime associate of the Clintons, takes office in Little Rock as U.S. attorney.

September: Ms. Casey turns down plea bargain attempts from David Hale's lawyer, who had offered to share information on the "banking and borrowing practices of some individuals in the elite political circles of the State of Arkansas."

Sept. 23: Mr. Hale is indicted for fraud.

Sept. 29: Treasury Department General Counsel Jean Hanson warns Mr. Nussbaum that the RTC plans to issue criminal referrals asking the Justice Department to investigate Madison. The referrals are said to name the Clintons as witnesses to, and possible beneficiaries of, illegal actions. The current Governor of Arkansas, Jim Guy Tucker, also is said to be a target of the investigation. Mr. Nussbaum passes the information to Bruce Lindsey, a top Clinton aide.

Oct. 4 or 5: Mr. Lindsey informs President Clinton about the confidential referrals. Mr. Lindsey later tells Congress he did not mention any specific target of the referrals.

Oct. 6: President Clinton meets with Arkansas Gov. Jim Guy Tucker at the White House.

Oct. 8: Nine new criminal referrals on Madison Guaranty are forwarded to U.S. Attorney Paula Casey in Little Rock.

Oct. 14: A meeting is held in Mr. Nussbaum's office with senior White House and Treasury personnel to discuss the RTC and Madison. Participants at the meeting later tell Congress that they discussed only how to handle press inquiries.

Oct. 27: The RTC's first criminal referral is rejected in Little Rock by U.S. Attorney Casey.

Nov. 3: Associate Attorney General Webster Hubbell recuses himself from the Whitewater case.

Nov. 9: In Little Rock, U.S. Attorney Casey recuses herself from the Madison case; in Kansas City, RTC investigator Jean Lewis is taken off the probe.

Nov. 18: President Clinton meets with Gov. Tucker in Seattle.

Dec. 19: Allegations by Arkansas state troopers of the president's sexual infidelities while governor surface in The American Spectator magazine and the Los Angeles Times.

Dec. 20:	Washington Times correspondent Jerry Seper reports that Whitewater files were removed from Mr. Foster's office.
Dec. 30:	At a New Year's retreat, President Clinton asks Comptroller of the Currency Eugene Ludwig, an old friend, for "advice" about how to handle the growing Whitewater storm.

1994

Jan. 20:	Amid mounting political pressure, Attorney General Janet Reno appoints Robert Fiske as special counsel to investigate Whitewater.
Jan. 27:	Deputy Attorney General Philip Heymann resigns.
Feb. 2:	Roger Altman meets with Mr. Nussbaum and other senior White House staff to give them a "heads-up" about the Madison probe. Washington RTC attorney April Breslaw flies to Kansas City and meets with investigator Jean Lewis; in a secretly taped conversation, Ms. Breslaw states that top RTC officials "would like to be able to say that Whitewater did not cause a loss to Madison."
Feb. 24:	Mr. Altman gives incomplete testimony to the Senate Banking Committee about discussions between the White House and Treasury on the Madison referrals.
Feb. 25:	Mr. Altman recuses himself from the Madison investigation and announces he will step down as acting head of the RTC.
March:	Top Clinton aides Thomas McLarty, Erskine Bowles, Mickey Kantor and others begin a series of meetings and calls to arrange financial aid for Webster Hubbell, then facing charges of bilking his former Rose Law Firm partners and under growing pressure to cooperate with the Whitewater probe; the meetings are not revealed until April 1997.
March 5:	White House Counsel Bernard Nussbaum resigns.
March 8:	Lloyd Cutler is named White House Counsel.

March 14: Associate Attorney General Webster Hubbell resigns.

March 18: The New York Times reports Mrs. Clinton's spectacular 1978 $100,000 commodity trades.

March 23: The Association of American Physicians and Surgeons files suit against Mrs. Clinton's health reform task force for violating the Federal Advisory Committee Act by holding secret meetings.

May 3: President Clinton meets with top advisers, including deputy chief of staff Harold Ickes, to discuss raising millions of dollars for the 1996 campaign.

May 6: Former Little Rock resident Paula Corbin Jones files suit against President Clinton, charging he sexually harassed her while Governor.

June: Indonesia's Lippo Group pays Webster Hubbell about $100,000 for undisclosed services as pressure grows for Mr. Hubbell to cooperate with the Whitewater probe; also in June, Lippo scion James Riady and associates meet at least five times with President Clinton and aides; reports of the payments and meetings emerge in 1996 and 1997.

June 30: Special Counsel Robert Fiske concludes that Mr. Foster's death was a suicide and clears the White House and Treasury Department of obstruction of justice on the RTC contacts, opening the way for Congressional hearings limited to the two subjects.

July: John Huang, president of U.S. operations for Indonesia's Lippo Group, joins the Commerce Department as a senior official with a top-secret clearance to oversee international trade.

July 26: Whitewater hearings open in Congress.

Aug. 1: The White House reveals that the Whitewater files removed from Mr. Foster's office were kept for five days in the Clintons' residence before being turned over to their personal lawyer.

Aug. 5 A three-judge panel removes Mr. Fiske and appoints Kenneth Starr as independent counsel. Mr. Starr continues to investigate all aspects of Whitewater, including Mr. Foster's death.

Aug. 12: The RTC informs Madison investigator Jean Lewis and two colleagues that they will be placed on "administrative leave" for two weeks.

Aug. 17: Deputy Treasury Secretary Roger Altman resigns.

Aug. 18: Treasury Department General Counsel Jean Hanson resigns.

Sept. 12: Donald Smaltz is named independent counsel to investigate Agriculture Secretary Mike Espy.

Oct. 1: Abner Mikva replaces Lloyd Cutler as White House Counsel.

Oct. 3: Agriculture Secretary Mike Espy resigns.

Nov. 8: In a political earthquake, Republicans gain control of the House and the Senate.

Dec. 5: In Little Rock, Madison Guaranty real-estate appraiser Robert Palmer pleads guilty to one felony count of conspiracy and agrees to cooperate with the Starr probe.

Dec. 6: Former Associate Attorney General Webster Hubbell pleads guilty to two felonies in a scheme to defraud his former Rose Law Firm partners and says he will cooperate with the independent counsel.

Dec. 7: Former Travel Office director Billy Dale is indicted on charges of embezzling office funds.

Dec. 19: The FDIC sanctions the Riady family's Lippo Bank in Los Angeles for failing to adhere to money-laundering regulations governing large cash transactions.

1995

Jan. 3: Republicans on the Senate Banking Committee, poised to move into the majority and renew the Whitewater hearings, issue a sharply critical report based on the summer hearings. It accuses Clinton administration officials of "serious misconduct and malfeasance" in the matters of the RTC criminal referrals and later congressional testimony.

Feb. 28: Arkansas banker Neal Ainley is indicted on five felony counts relating to Bill Clinton's 1990 gubernatorial campaign. He later pleads guilty to reduced charges and agrees to cooperate with the independent counsel.

March 21: Whitewater real-estate broker Chris Wade pleads guilty to two felonies.

March 27: Legal Times reports that Independent Counsel Donald Smaltz's probe has been "significantly curtailed by the Justice Department." In recent months, Mr. Smaltz had been exploring Arkansas poultry giant Tyson Foods.

May 5: Mena investigator Russell Welch fights off an attempt by the Arkansas State Police to discredit him, but is forced into early retirement.

May 24: David Barrett is appointed independent counsel to probe charges that Housing Secretary Henry Cisneros made false statements to the FBI.

June: Monica Lewinsky begins work at the White House as an unpaid intern in the office of Chief of Staff Leon Panetta.

June 7: An Arkansas grand jury hands up indictments against Gov. Jim Guy Tucker and two business associates in a complex scheme to buy and sell cable television systems.

June 23: A report for the RTC by the law firm Pillsbury, Madison & Sutro says that funds flowed to the Whitewater account from other Madison accounts, but adds that the Clintons "had little direct involvement" in the investment before 1988.

July 6: Daniel Pearson is named independent counsel to probe business dealings of Commerce Secretary Ron Brown.

July 18: The special Senate Whitewater Committee opens a new round of hearings in Washington; they quickly become mired in partisan disputes.

Aug. 8: In testimony before the House Banking Committee, RTC investigator Jean Lewis says there was a "concerted effort to obstruct, hamper and manipulate" the Madison investigation.

Aug. 17: Independent Counsel Kenneth Starr indicts Arkansas

Gov. Jim Guy Tucker and former Madison Guaranty owners Jim and Susan McDougal for bank fraud and conspiracy.

Sept. 5: Federal District Judge Henry Woods dismisses the cable TV fraud case against Gov. Tucker and two associates, saying Mr. Starr has exceeded his jurisdiction; the independent counsel appeals the decision to the Eighth Circuit court in St. Louis; the separate indictment against Gov. Tucker and the McDougals stands.

Sept. 13: At a White House meeting among President Clinton, Commerce official John Huang, Lippo Group scion James Riady, senior Clinton aide Bruce Lindsey and Arkansas businessman Joseph Giroir, a decision is reached to dispatch Mr. Huang to the Democratic National Comittee as a senior fund-raiser.

Sept. 20: White House Counsel Abner Mikva announces his resignation. The President names Jack Quinn, Vice President Al Gore's chief of staff, as his fourth White House counsel.

November: House Banking Committee Chairman Jim Leach informs colleagues that he will investigate allegations of drug smuggling and money laundering at Mena airport.

Nov. 16: After deliberating less than two hours, a Washington jury acquits former White House Travel Office head Billy Dale of embezzlement charges.

Dec. 13: Drug suspect Jorge Cabrera attends a White House Christmas party after donating $20,000 to Democrats; three weeks later, he is arrested in Florida with 6, 000 pounds of cocaine.

Dec. 29: A memo from former White House aide David Watkins, placing responsibility for the Travel Office firings on Mrs. Clinton, is discovered at the White House.

1996

January: John Huang leaves the Commerce Department to join the Democratic National Committee as a senior fund-raiser.

Jan. 5:	The White House announces that Mrs. Clinton's Rose Law Firm billing records, sought by the Independent Counsel and Congress for two years, have been discovered on a table in the "book room" of the personal residence.
Jan. 11:	At a news conference, President Clinton says he is nearly broke and owes about $1.6 million in legal fees stemming from Whitewater and the Paula Jones sexual harassment suit.
Jan. 22:	The White House announces that Mrs. Clinton has been subpoenaed to testify before a Whitewater grand jury about the missing billing records.
Feb. 5:	Federal District Judge George Howard Jr. rules that President Clinton must appear as a defense witness in the bank fraud case against Jim Guy Tucker and the McDougals.
Feb. 6:	Charlie Trie escorts Chinese arms merchant Wang Jun to a White House reception for donors.
Feb. 8:	The Wall Street Journal discloses that two of President Clinton's insurance policies have paid $900,000 into his legal defense fund.
Feb. 20:	Arkansas bankers Herby Branscum Jr. and Robert Hill are indicted on bank fraud and conspiracy charges relating to Bill Clinton's 1990 gubernatorial campaign.
Feb. 29:	The Whitewater Committee's mandate expires and Senate Democrats launch a filibuster to block an extension of the probe.
March 4:	Gov. Tucker and the McDougals go on trial for bank fraud and conspiracy in Little Rock.
March 15:	A three-judge panel of the Eighth Circuit Court of Appeals reinstates Independent Counsel Starr's indictment of Gov. Tucker and two associates in the cable television fraud scheme, and directs that Federal District Judge Henry Woods be removed from the case "to preserve the appearance of impartiality."
March 22:	Independent Counsel Starr's jurisdiction is expanded to cover the Travel Office affair.

March 25:	Arkansas insider David Hale is sentenced to 28 months in prison for defrauding the federal government.
April:	Monica Lewinsky is transferred from the White House to the Pentagon for "immature behavior." She meets former White House aide Linda Tripp, who later tapes their telephone conversations.
April 3:	Commerce Secretary Ron Brown and 32 others are killed in a plane crash in Croatia.
April 28:	President Clinton gives four hours of videotaped testimony in the White House as a defense witness in the Arkansas trial of Gov. Tucker and the McDougals.
April 29:	Vice President Al Gore attends a fund-raiser at the Hsi Lai Buddhist Temple in California, raising at least $140,000. The donations, some of them from monks who had taken a vow of poverty, later come under scrutiny.
May 28:	An Arkansas jury convicts Gov. Tucker and the McDougals on 24 counts of bank fraud and conspiracy.
June 5:	Documents obtained after a long struggle by the House Government Reform and Oversight Committee reveal that the White House has improperly obtained confidential FBI background files. "Filegate" mushrooms into another scandal.
June 17:	The trial of Arkansas bankers Branscum and Hill on charges of bank fraud relating to the 1990 Clinton gubernatorial campaign begins in Little Rock.
June 18:	The Senate Whitewater Committee releases a 650-page final report detailing a "pattern of obstruction" by Clinton Administration officials.
June 21:	Independent Counsel Starr's jurisdiction is broadened to cover "Filegate."
June 25:	The Supreme Court agrees to hear President Clinton's procedural appeal in the Paula Jones harassment suit, effectively delaying trial until after the November election.
June 26:	In an appearance before a House oversight committee investigating the Filegate affair, White House person-

nel security chief Craig Livingstone announces his resignation.

July 7: President Clinton gives videotaped testimony in the White House as a defense witness in the trial of Arkansas bankers Branscum and Hill.

July 15: After a tumultuous day of political drama, Jim Guy Tucker steps down and Republican Mike Huckabee takes over as Governor of Arkansas.

Aug. 1: A federal jury in Little Rock acquits Arkansas bankers Branscum and Hill on four bank fraud charges relating to the 1990 Clinton gubernatorial campaign; a mistrial is declared on seven other counts on which the jury deadlocks.

Aug. 15: After months of stonewalling, the White House releases 2,000 pages of documents to the House Government Reform and Oversight Committee; included is a long "task list" for dealing with the sprawling Whitewater probe.

Aug. 19: Awaiting a liver transplant, former Arkansas Gov. Jim Guy Tucker is given a four-year suspended sentence in the Madison Guaranty bank fraud case.

Aug. 21: Susan McDougal is sentenced to two years in prison for her part in the Master Marketing fraud scheme.

Sept. 4: Susan McDougal refuses to answer questions about Bill Clinton before a Whitewater grand jury and is ordered jailed for contempt.

Sept. 23: In a PBS interview, President Clinton says he has not ruled out pardons for Whitewater figures, touching off a campaign controversy.

Sept. 24: In the probe by Independent Counsel Smaltz, a federal jury convicts agribusiness giant Sun-Diamond of giving illegal gifts to Agriculture Secretary Mike Espy.

Oct. 8: Following disclosures by The Wall Street Journal of large illegal foreign donations, the campaign-finance story emerges as a major national issue one month before the presidential election.

Oct. 18:	Democratic National Committee finance vice chairman John Huang is suspended after growing reports of improper campaign solicitations.
Nov. 5:	Bill Clinton is re-elected President of the United States.
Nov. 8:	In a declassified summary of a report to Rep. Jim Leach, the CIA for the first time admits it was present at remote Mena, Ark., but denies any association with drug trafficking or other illegal activities.
Nov. 29:	Attorney General Janet Reno declines to name an independent counsel in the campaign-finance affair, retaining the matter as a Justice Department probe.
Dec. 13:	Jack Quinn, President Clinton's fourth White House counsel, announces his resignation.
Dec. 14:	Susan McDougal is transferred to California to stand trial on charges of embezzling $150,000 from conductor Zubin Mehta and his wife; she remains jailed on civil contempt charges stemming from her refusal to testify before a Whitewater grand jury.
Dec. 16:	President Clinton's legal defense fund announces it has returned $640,000 in suspect donations from Clinton friend Charlie Trie.

1997

Jan 7:	Charles Ruff is named President Clinton's fifth White House counsel.
Jan. 13:	The Supreme Court hears oral arguments as to whether the Paula Jones sexual harassment case should be delayed until after Bill Clinton leaves office.
Jan. 20:	Bill Clinton is sworn in for a second term as President of the United States.
Feb. 13:	Webster Hubbell is released from federal custody after serving 15 months for mail fraud and tax evasion.
Feb. 17:	Kenneth Starr unexpectedly announces he will step down as independent counsel to become dean of Pepperdine University Law School in California.
Feb. 21:	After a storm of criticism, Mr. Starr reverses his decision to leave the Whitewater probe, saying he will stay

on until investigations and prosecutions are "substantially completed."

March 3: Drawn deep into the campaign-finance scandal, Vice President Al Gore defends himself at a press conference, declaring that "no controlling legal authority" indicates his actions were illegal.

March 31: For the third time in seven years, the FDIC sanctions Lippo Bank, imposing a stiff cease-and-desist order due to bad loans and financial losses.

April 1: Facing imminent news reports, the White House discloses that in early 1994 top Clinton aides set out to funnel money to Arkansas insider Webster Hubbell, then under pressure to cooperate with the Whitewater probe.

April 14: Following a sentencing recommendation by Independent Counsel Starr about significant cooperation, Jim McDougal is given a sharply reduced three-year prison term for his role in the Madison Guaranty bank fraud case.

April 15: In a new public-corruption drive in Arkansas, former county prosecutor Dan Harmon is indicted on multiple drug and racketeering counts.

April 30: For a second time, Attorney General Reno turns down requests for an independent counsel in the campaign finance affair.

May 2: The White House announces it will appeal to the Supreme Court a previously sealed Eighth Circuit ruling that government lawyers must turn over to Independent Counsel Starr notes taken during conversations with Hillary Clinton.

May 27: The Supreme Court issues a unanimous decision ruling that Paula Jones's sexual harassment suit may proceed against President Clinton while he is in office.

June 11: An Arkansas jury convicts former county prosecutor Dan Harmon of running a drug-related criminal enterprise.

June 23: The Supreme Court declines to grant certiorari on Mrs.

	Clinton's notes, effectively compelling the White House to turn them over to Mr. Starr.
July 8:	Hearings into the campaign finance affair open before Senator Fred Thompson's Governmental Affairs Committee.
Aug. 27:	A Federal grand jury hands up a 39-count indictment accusing former Agriculture Secretary Mike Espy of illegally soliciting more than $35,000 in gifts from companies regulated by his department and attempting to conceal his actions.
Sept. 16:	Under fire and with the Justice Department probe in disarray, Attorney Reno names a new prosecutor, Washington outsider Charles La Bella, to head her campaign finance investigation.
Sept. 19:	News reports disclose that three associates of Teamsters union president Ron Carey have recently pleaded guilty to fraud charges in a fund-raising conspiracy involving labor movement figures and Democratic Party activists.
Oct. 10:	Confirming the findings of earlier investigations, Independent Counsel Starr issues an exhaustive report concluding that deputy White House counsel Vincent Foster committed suicide in Ft. Marcy Park, Va.
Oct. 31:	Senator Fred Thompson suspends hearings into the campaign finance affair after nearly four months of bitter partisan warfare.
Dec. 1:	Former Agriculture Secretary Mike Espy's chief of staff, Ronald Blackley, is convicted of lying to investigators about receiving $22,000 from associates who had dealings with the agency.
Dec. 2:	Attorney General Reno rejects appointment of an independent counsel to investigate campaign fund-raising calls made by President Clinton and Vice President Al Gore, saying she acted on "the facts and the law—not pressure, politics or any other factor." It is her third rejection of a special prosecutor for the campaign finance affair.

Dec. 17:	Monica Lewinsky and Linda Tripp are subpoenaed by the Paula Jones legal team seeking evidence of sexual misconduct by the President.
Dec. 28:	Monica Lewinsky reportedly visits Bill Clinton at the White House for the last time. News reports cite 36 previous visits.
Dec. 29:	Tyson Foods Inc. pleads guilty to providing former Agriculture Secretary Espy with $12,000 in illegal gratuities and agrees to pay $6 million in fines.

1998

Jan. 7:	In an affidavit filed in the Jones sexual harassment case, Monica Lewinsky denies a sexual relationship with Bill Clinton. According to later news reports, Ms. Lewinsky tells Ms. Tripp that she too must make false statements in the Jones case.
Jan. 12:	Linda Tripp reportedly turns over to Starr prosecutors 20 hours of surreptitiously taped telephone conversations with Ms. Lewinsky, including descriptions of efforts by the President to direct false testimony and obstruct justice, and graphic accounts of Oval Office sex.
Jan. 16:	Attorney General Reno secretly petitions the Special Division of the U.S. Court of Appeals for an expansion of Mr. Starr's jurisdiction into the Lewinsky affair, citing possible witness tampering and obstruction of justice.
Jan. 17:	In a six-hour deposition for the Jones case, President Clinton denies that he had an affair with Monica Lewinsky.
Jan. 21:	In a bombshell story, the Washington Post discloses the Lewinsky affair and the Starr investigation, touching off a media frenzy and the biggest crisis of the Clinton Presidency.
Jan. 26:	In a forceful televised denial following a White House

event, President Clinton says that he "never had sexual relations with that woman, Ms. Lewinsky," and that he "never told anyone to lie."

Jan. 27: Hillary Clinton appears on the "Today" show and blames her husband's problems on a "vast right-wing conspiracy."

Jan. 29: U.S. District Judge Susan Webber Wright, ruling in the Paula Jones sexual harassment case, excludes all evidence relating to Monica Lewinsky, saying it is not "essential to the core issues" in the lawsuit.

Feb. 3: Wanted Democratic fund-raiser Charlie Trie returns to the U.S. from China and Macau and surrenders to the FBI.

Feb. 11: Attorney General Reno asks for an independent counsel to probe Interior Secretary Bruce Babbitt's role in his department's decision to reject a casino application opposed by major Democratic Party contributors.

Feb. 18: Democratic Party fund-raiser Maria Hsia is indicted by a federal grand jury on charges of arranging to disguise illegal campaign contributions growing out of a fund-raising trip by Vice President Gore to the Hsi Lai Buddhist Temple in California.

March 5: Senator Thompson's Governmental Affairs Committee votes out a 1,100-page report chronicling massive campaign finance abuses furing the 1996 presidential race. At a Washington grand jury, in a plea bargain with federal prosecutors, Democratic fund-raiser Johnny Chung is charged with funneling illegal contributions to the Clinton-Gore campaign.

March 8: Jim McDougal, 57, dies after a heart attack in a Texas prison, where he was serving a three-year Whitewater fraud sentence.

March 15: Former White House volunteer Kathleen Willey appears on "60 Minutes" and says that President Clinton made a crude sexual advance and groped her at the White House, and that his associates later sought to assure her silence.

March 20:	President Clinton's lawyers invoke executive privilege for senior aides before the Starr grand jury in the Lewinsky obstruction probe.
April 1:	Federal Judge Susan Webber Wright of Arkansas dismisses the Paula Jones sexual harassment suit against Bill Clinton, ruling that Mrs. Jones had failed to demonstrate emotional or career harm. The President's spokesman declares "vindication."
April 13:	Jeff Gerth of the New York Times reports that the Clinton White House approved the transfer of missile technology to China at the behest of a major Democratic party donor, sparking a new campaign-finance controversy.
April 21:	The Clinton Administration invokes a new "protective function" privilege to prevent Secret Service officers from testifying before the Starr grand jury in the Lewinsky matter.
April 24:	Attorney General Reno confirms that Charles La Bella, installed only seven months earlier to inject credibility into the Justice Department's listless campaign-finance investigation, is departing to become interim U.S. Attorney in San Diego.
May 5:	U.S. District Judge Norma Holloway Johnson rejects President Clinton's effort to use executive privilege and attorney-client privilege to block testimony by senior aides in the Monica Lewinsky investigation.
May 22:	Judge Johnson rejects the administration's claim of a protective function privilege for the Secret Service. The Justice Department readies an appeal.
June 2:	Monica Lewinsky fires loquacious California malpractice lawyer William Ginsburg and hires veteran Washington attorneys Jacob Stein and Plato Cacheris. Negotiations on immunity for Ms. Lewinsky, stalled for five months, resume.
June 4:	The Supreme Court rejects Independent Counsel Starr's request for fast-track hearings on attorney-client and protective function privilege, remanding the

Index

matters to the U.S. Court of Appeals.

June 25: Four months into a two-year Whitewater fraud sentence, and after serving 18 months in prison for refusing to talk to an Arkansas grand jury about Bill Clinton, Susan McDougal is released from jail by a federal judge due to medical problems. She faces embezzlement charges in California unrelated to Whitewater, and an obstruction prosecution by Mr. Starr in Arkansas.

July 1: U.S. District Court Judge James Robertson throws out Mr. Starr's tax evasion case against Webster Hubbell, saying the Independent Counsel strayed too far from his mandate. Mr. Starr says he will appeal.

July 7: A three-judge panel of the U.S. Court of Appeals for the D.C. Circuit rejects a Justice Department appeal on protective function privilege.

July 16: In a day of high legal drama, the full U.S. Court of Appeals for the D.C. Circuit refuses to reconsider the decision by its three-judge panel ordering the Secret Service to testify in the Lewinsky matter. The White House rushes an emergency petition to Chief Justice William Rehnquist, asking him to issue a stay and block testimony.

July 17: Chief Justice Rehnquist declines to intervene in the protective function matter. Within hours, Secret Service officers are testifying before the Starr grand jury.

July 23: The New York Times discloses that departing Justice Department task force head, Charles La Bella, has delivered a report to Attorney General Reno strongly advising her to seek an independent counsel in the campaign finance affair.

July 25: The White House reveals that Independent Counsel Starr, in a dramatic and unprecedented maneuver, has subpoenaed President Clinton to testify before the grand jury in the Lewinsky matter. Mr. Clinton had rebuffed earlier requests for voluntary testimony. The historic subpoena is later withdrawn after the President agrees to testify.

July 27: The U.S. Court of Appeals for the D.C. Circuit rejects administration arguments that President Clinton's conversations with White House lawyers are shielded by attorney-client privilege, clearing the way for Mr. Starr to question deputy counsel Bruce Lindsey, a key Clinton confidant.

July 28: Monica Lewinsky is granted blanket immunity in exchange for full and truthful testimony before the Starr grand jury.

July 31: Paula Jones asks a U.S. appeals panel in St. Louis to reinstate her sexual harassment case against Mr. Clinton.

August 6: Monica Lewinsky testifies before the Starr grand jury. According to news accounts, she details numerous sexual liaisons with the President, recants her sworn testimony in the Paula Jones lawsuit denying an affair, and contradicts sworn and televised statements by Mr. Clinton. On Capitol Hill, the House Government Reform and Oversight Committee votes to hold Attorney General Reno in contempt of Congress for failing to turn over memos by FBI Director Louis Freeh and Justice task force head Charles La Bella concerning the campaign-finance probe. The sanction awaits a vote by the full House.

August 17: President Clinton testifies, via closed-circuit television from the White House, for four hours before the Starr grand jury. In an angry speech to the nation that night, he admits to an "inappropriate relationship" with Ms. Lewinsky, denies criminal wrongdoing, and attacks Independent Counsel Starr. Political support begins to erode.

August 20: Interrupting his vacation in Martha's Vineyard, Mass., President Clinton announces missile strikes against "terrorist-related facilities" in Afghanistan and Sudan.

Sept. 9: Independent Counsel Starr sends Congress a rep containing, in the words of his mandate, "substant and credible information" that "may constitu grounds for impeachment" of President Clinton.

Ansara, Michael, 37–39, 57–58

Archer, William (Rep.), 155

Arlington National Cemetery dispute, 117–121

Arlook, Ira, 57

Armey, Richard (Rep.), 498

Armstrong, C. Michael, 347–349

Arnold, Truman, 357

B

Babbitt, Bruce (Secretary), 66, 79–82, 91, 174–176, 242–244, 249–250, 323

Baile, Jack, 73

Barbour, Haley, 3–4, 13

Baron, Alan I., 18

Barr, Bob (Rep.), 92, 103–104, 155, 188–190, 532

Barr, William P., 286, 302

Barrett, David, 112

Barry, Marion (Mayor), 509

Battalino, Barbara, 504

Bearse, Michael, 463–464

Beck, Harry, 31–32, 41–42, 58, 96

Begala, Paul
  attacks on Starr by, 246, 277
  Lewinsky affair, 206

"Behind the Oval Office," 68–70

Bell, Griffin, 286, 295, 302

Bennett, Alan, 517

Bennett, Robert, 49, 136, 158–160, 162–163, 230, 296, 322–324, 406, 513–516

Bennett, Robert (Sen.), 20

Bennett, William J., 287–290, 350–355, 520–523

Berenson, Bradford, 331, 524–527

Berger, Raoul, 293–294

Berman, Alan, 106

Biden, Joseph (Sen.), 384

Black, Norton N., 72

C

D

E

F

G

H

I

J

leaks alleged in suit of, 433

Lewinsky affair and, 195–200, 206, 230, 258–259, 322, 350, 513–516, 524–525

sexual harassment suit, 2, 247, 309

Supreme Court denial of executive privilege, 110

Jordan, Vernon

Lewinsky affair and, 205–207, 231, 287, 327, 351, 432–433

post-Lewinsky support for Clinton, 280–282

Judicial Watch, 156–157, 316, 329

Judis, John, 24

Justice Department

appeals order for Secret Service officers' testimony, 438–440, 444–445

China technology transfer and, 348–349

Clinton Administration and, 111–113, 530

Coia investigation and, 84–85, 89–90, 462–466

Gore phone call investigation and, 22–24

independent counsel compared with, 76–78

La Bella and Freeh memorandums, 455–457

Litt nomination, 219–221

Public Integrity Section, 9–10, 45–50, 103–104, 132–133, 137–139, 373–374

Smaltz rebuke, 112, 147–150

K

Kanchanalak, Pauline, 27, 378, 440

Kantor, Mickey, 206

Kashoggi, Adnan, 45

Kasich, John (Rep.), 217

Katzenberg, Jeffrey, 280–282

Kefauver hearings, 4

Kemp, Jack (Rep.), 132

Kendall, David, 136, 159–160, 296

Clinton's testimony to Starr, 496–498, 506–508, 513–516

Filegate scandal, 156–157

leaks from Starr's office alleged by, 245–248, 257–259

M

N

O

Ovitz, Michael, 280-281

P

Palladino, Jack, 258-259, 296

Pan, Antonio, 378

Panetta, Leon, 250, 528-529

Parr, Jerry, 404

Paycheck Protection Act, 41-42

Peck, Mary Hulbert, 208-210

Peña, Federico (Secretary), 359-360

Pepperdine University, 246-247

Perelman, Ron, 281-282, 351, 355

Phillips, Carrie, 209

Pickering, John (Judge), 548

Podesta, John, 433

Polls supporting Clinton, 234-238, 252-255

Pomerantz, Mark, 192, 220

Portiss, Joe, 465

Portiss, Laura, 465-466

Presidential election campaign of 1996, 67-74, 177-182

Prins, Robert, 163-167

Project Vote, 39

Promise Keepers, 41

Puccio, Thomas, 381

Q

Quindel, Barbara Zack, 56-58

Quindel, Roger, 56-58

Quinn, Jack, 428, 446-450, 452-454

R

Rabin, Yitzak (Prime Minister), 404

Rabinowitz, Dorothy, 55

Radek, Lee, 46, 109-110, 137-139, 373

Raines, Ashley, 258

Randolph, A. Raymond (Judge), 472

Reagan, Ronald (President), 10, 12, 154–155, 404

Red Pagoda Mountain cigarette company, 163–167

Rehnquist, William (Justice), 321, 396, 431, 445, 470, 491

Reich, Robert (Secretary), 539-541

Reneau, Brenda, 31–32

Reno, Janet

  appointment of La Bella, 29

  campaign finance investigation and, 1-2, 9-12, 15, 140–141, 215–216, 283–285, 530

  China technology transfer and, 349

  Chippewa Indian casino investigation, 242–244, 249–251, 323

  Coia investigation and, 462–466

  Congressional testimony of, 122–124

  Freeh memorandum, 91–93, 103–104, 111–113, 455–457

  grants expansion of Starr investigation, 232–233, 354

  Hale investigation, 356–358

  Hatch and, 459–461

  Herman investigated, 307, 323, 328

  Hyde letter, 40-50, 103

  impeachment of discussed, 458

  independent counsel law, 189–190, 378–379, 396

  La Bella departure announced, 369

  record as Attorney General, 53–55

  review of Gore phone calls, 22–24

  Senate Judiciary Committee appearance, 438–440

Revlon Corporation, 351

Riady, James, 1, 7–8

  Huang investigation, 1, 7, 23, 26, 30, 42–43, 283–285, 348, 439

  Hubbell and, 355

  Indonesian bailout proposal, 52

  Trie and, 240, 261, 370

Riady, Mochtar

  campaign finance investigation, 283–285, 348, 370, 439–440

  Huang and, 261

  Lippo Group and, 7, 268, 271

Richard, Mark, 46

S

T

U.S. v. Nixon, 321

V

Vacancies Act, 132-133, 219-221

Van Natta, Don, 439

Vega, Gregory, 492

Venters, Chip, 73

Vlasto, Chris, 362-364

Volokh, Eugene, 336-339

W

Wald, Patricia (Judge), 46, 316

Walsh, Lawrence, 249-250, 426-427

Wang Jun, 4-5, 348-349

Washington, George (President), 210

Washington Post, 277, 323, 408, 469, 499

Washington Times, 258

Watergate, 201-203, 325-327, 386-388, 420-423, 549

Waters, Mary (Judge), 313

Watkins, David, 535

Watt, Bill, 497

Waxman, Henry (Rep.), 372, 374, 383-384

Waxman, Seth, 405

Weinstein, David, 96

West, Togo (Army Secretary), 119

Western Journalism Center, 389-391

White, Mary Jo, 138-139, 192-193, 380-382

Whitewater Development Co., 136, 158-160, 355, 357, 534

Wiczek, Jeanne, 314

Willey, Kathleen, 206, 247, 307, 309-310, 312-314, 317-320, 352, 366, 409, 497, 525, 545

Williams, Jack, 48

Williams, Maggie, 535

Wilson, James Q., 252-255

Wilson, Pete (Gov.), 97

Wilson, Rick, 298

Y

Z